# Journals of the Catechesis of the Good Shepherd

## 1984-1997

Catechesis of
the Good Shepherd
Publications

ACKNOWLEDGMENTS

Text © 1998, Catechesis of the Good Shepherd.
All rights reserved.

JOURNALS OF THE CATECHESIS OF THE GOOD SHEPHERD
© 1998 Archdiocese of Chicago: Liturgy Training Publications,
1800 North Hermitage Avenue, Chicago IL 60622-1101;
1-800-933-1800; orders@ltp.org; fax 1-800-933-7094.
All rights reserved.

www.ltp.org

This book was edited by Victoria M. Tufano. Audrey Novak
Riley and Bryan Cones were the production editors. The book
was designed by Joseph Conlon and Pete Pona. Karen Mitchell
was the production artist. The cover art is by Steve Erspamer.
It was printed in the United States of America.

Library of Congress Catalog Card Number: 98-87177

06 05 04 03 02   6 5 4 3 2

ISBN 1-56854-254-2

CGS1

Catechesis of the Good Shepherd Publications is an imprint
of Liturgy Training Publications (LTP). Further information
about these publications is available from LTP or from
Catechesis of the Good Shepherd, PO Box 1084, Oak Park IL
60304; phone 708-524-1210; fax 708-386-8032. Requests
for information about other aspects of the Catechesis should
be directed to this address.

Other Catechesis of the Good Shepherd publications:

Living Liturgy
*Sofia Cavalletti*

The Religious Potential of the Child
*Sofia Cavalletti*

El Potencial Religioso del Niño
*Sofia Cavalletti*

The Good Shepherd and the Child: A Joyful Journey
*Sofia Cavalletti, Patricia Coulter, Gianna Gobbi* and
*Silvana Q. Montanaro*

El Buen Pastor y el Niño: Un Camino de Gozo
*Sofia Cavalletti, Patricia Coulter, Gianna Gobbi* and
*Silvana Q. Montanaro*

History's Golden Thread: The History of Salvation
*Sofia Cavalletti*

The Catechesis of the Good Shepherd in a Parish Setting
*Tina Lillig*

Discovering the Real Spiritual Life of Children (video)
*Sofia Cavalletti, Gianna Gobbi, Tina Lillig* and *Maria Christlieb Robles*

# CONTENTS

**WINTER 1984**     1–22
   Religious Formation and Later Childhood, *Sofia Cavelletti*     4
   Preface to Italian Edition of The Religious Potential of the Child, *P. Dalmazio Mongillo, OP*     17

**WINTER 1985**     23–56
   Characteristics of the Good Shepherd Catechesis, *Sofia Cavelletti*     25
   When to Start Religious Education, *Silvana Quattrocci Montanaro*     31
   The Water and the Wine of the Eucharist, *Sofia Cavalletti*     34
   The Anointings at Baptism, *Catherine Maresca*     41

**SPRING 1986**     57–92
   The Characteristics of Catechists of the Good Shepherd, *Sofia Cavalletti*     60
   The Richness of Early Religious Experience, *Sofia Cavalletti*     66

**SPRING 1987**     93–126
   Social Justice: A Question of Relationships, *Sofia Cavalletti*     97
   Ten Years of the Catechesis of the Good Shepherd (Chad, Africa), *Lucia Cremona*     100
   Development of the Catechesis in a Lay School, *Sofia Cavalletti*     110
   Angelina and the Good Shepherd, *Catherine Wolf Maresca*     112

**FALL 1988**     127–146
   Twenty Years of an Atrium at Our Lady of Lourdes, *Tilde Camosso Cocchini*     131
   On Moral Formation, *Sofia Cavalletti*     132
   The Material (Chad, Africa cont.), *Lucia Cremona*     134
   Reflections on Social Justice, *Emilia Gonzales de Sandoval*     138
   Ten Years of the Catechesis in Rome (Santa Lucia), *Sandra Pollastri*     142

**WINTER 1989**     147–162
   On Moral Formation, *Sofia Cavalletti*     150
   Two Visions of Education, *Gianna Gobbi*     152

**WINTER 1990**     163–190
   "and a little child shall lead them": [formation of the catechist], *Sofia Cavalletti* and *Gianna Gobbi*     167
   The Development of the Catechist: Notes from Lecture by Silvana Montanaro and
      Maria Christlieb, *Millie Dosh*     171
   Maria Montessori and the Religious Education of the Child, *Silvana Montanaro*     177
   History of the Research on the Mass, *Sofia Cavalletti*     183

## Contents

SUMMER 1991 — 191–206
    The Bible in the Prayer Corner, *Nora Bonilla* — 194
    Communal Prayer, *Sofia Cavalletti* — 195
    Reflections on Prayer, *Sofia Cavalletti* — 196
    Catechesis with Adults (a letter to Sofia), *Eva Elesa Quiroz* — 200
    The Children Show Us How to Pray, *Carol Dittberner* — 202

WINTER 1992–93 — 207–230
    The Mustard Seed Is Planted in Japan, *Patricia Coulter* — 210
    The Montessori Cosmic Vision and the Bible, *Sofia Cavalletti* — 213
    A Visit with Sofia and Jerome [Berryman], *Carol Dittberner* — 218
    Sofia Reviews Berryman's *Godly Play* — 221
    Does God Have a Sense of Humor, *Mark Searle* — 222
    First Catechesis Course Given (Tanzania), *Claudia Schmitt* — 224

SPRING 1994 — 231–252
    O Taste and See, *Sofia Cavalletti* — 234
    The White Garment Worn for Eucharist, *Tina Lillig* — 238
    The Story of Bread for ages 9–12, *Sofia Cavalletti* — 240
    Enjoying the Gift: The Communion Retreat in the Episcopal Church, *Carol Nyberg* — 242
    Reconciliation for the Older Children, *Francesca Cocchini* — 246
    The Child's Spiritual Life: Another Perspective (Book review of *Vision and Character* by Craig Dykstra), *Nancy Wood* — 249

FALL 1995 — 253–278
    Letters from Rome [after the 1993 International Conference] — 256
    The Religious Experience with the Child 3–6, *Gianna Gobbi* — 258
    The Cosmic Character of the Mass, *Sofia Cavalletti* — 264
    Mystery of Faith and Prayers of Intercession — 265

WINTER 1996–97 — 279–298
    Letters from Sofia and Gianna (on material making) — 282
    The Essentials of Material Making, *Linda Kaiel* — 284
    On Materials and Meaning, *Alice M. Renton* — 285
    Why We should Make our Own Materials, *Claudia Schmitt* — 287
    How Do I Make An Album Page?, *Betty Hissong* — 288
    The Care of the Atrium, *Tina Lillig* — 290
    Consiglio Report, *Linda Kaiel, Rebekah Rojcewicz, Judy Schmidt* — 294
    Life of the Catechist: Healthy Priorities, *Kathy Van Duser* — 296

# INTRODUCTION

"Follow the child." These words of Maria Montessori have guided many Montessori teachers and catechists to observe the real needs of the child. This is the focus of our work in the Catechesis of the Good Shepherd, and the aim of our newsletters, now known as journals: to keep the child always before us. The child has been revealed to us through children's work and prayer and play.

The formal name for our work, the Catechesis of the Good Shepherd, was chosen because the Good Shepherd is the center of the Catechesis, and the theme for the child of three to six years. The Good Shepherd "calls his own sheep by name . . . and the sheep follow him because they know his voice" (John 10:3 – 4). We parents and catechists also hear the Good Shepherd calling us to this work around the child.

In August of 1983, a group of catechists gathered in Washington, D.C., with Dr. Sofia Cavalletti, one of the founders of the Catechesis. In those days, all of us who were doing this work in the United States knew one another, but we were scattered across the country. We decided that we needed a newsletter to help us keep in touch. It was a cold day in January of 1984 when I drove to the printer with the first issue of the newsletter. In my personal journal I wrote, "This is a most auspicious day; this morning I took the newsletter for the Catechesis of the Good Shepherd to the printer. It is the first issue in this cause."

We had chosen January 6, the Feast of Epiphany, for our publication date because it was on that same date in 1907 that Maria Montessori opened her first program for children, which would later give birth to the Montessori Method and also to the religious work which we celebrate in these newsletters. As I drove to the printer's office, I knew it was a historic moment in the history of Montessori in the world, and a very new moment for the Catechesis of the Good Shepherd. What none of our small group realized was how beautiful the blossom would be that would grow from the seed of our work.

Since that summer day in 1983 when we gathered, we have seen a slow but steady increase in the creation of atrium environments — our name for the place where the catechesis occurs — for children. One of the early issues of the journal notes that membership in the Catechesis of

# Introduction

the Good Shepherd Association numbered 73 people; now it is more than 500. As we have grown in numbers, we have also grown in scope: By 1986 we were collaborating with a group in Mexico who began producing the newsletter in Spanish. We watched in awe and gratitude as the work became ecumenical, and atria were created not only in Roman Catholic parishes but also in Byzantine Rite, Episcopal, Lutheran, United Methodist and other Christian churches. The flexibility of the Catechesis materials on the liturgy made it possible to adapt them to the needs of each denomination.

## About the Journals

When we decided to begin a journal for those involved in the Catechesis, we also decided that it should reflect what we do and how we understand what we do. We chose to place a quotation from scripture on the front page of most issues to emphasize our belief in the passage, "Your word is a lamp to my feet, and a light to my path" (Psalm 119:105). When we work with the children, we always read scripture passages as they appear; we do not paraphrase the words of scripture. The children have shown us how much they love the Word, and many times we hear them reciting the scripture or prayers of the liturgy from memory.

It was also important for us to include the children's work, their prayers and their artwork in the journals. Each issue placed before us the child, as observed in the atrium, an environment prepared just for children, an environment that has a retreat-like atmosphere. These pages are filled with the child's response in prayer and art to the presentations given in the atrium.

One of the greatest experiences we have in the atrium is to pray with the children. The youngest ones (three to six years) pray with spontaneity, with praise and thanksgiving. They thank God equally for mom and dad and trees and toys and dinosaurs. The older ones (six to twelve years) choose their own scripture texts and their own prayers; they select the music, and sometimes even accompany their songs with instruments. They pray with thanks and also in petition for the needs of their families, community and the world. The children are very liturgical people, responding to ritual and the special atmosphere of the atrium. We wanted this to be reflected in the journals as well.

I hope these pages will convey to you three things.

First, the atmosphere of the atrium, our work with the children and their great capacity for prayer. Also, see how the child leads us and how important it is to observe and "follow the child." You will also find how the child synthesizes the scripture and the liturgy. Seeing

## Journals of the Catechesis of the Good Shepherd

a connection between the parable of the Pharisee and the tax collector, and the gesture of the Preparation of the chalice, a child remarked: "The Pharisee thought he was the wine when he was only the water."

Second, the journals, which record our continued studies, represented by the theory papers written by Dr. Cavalletti and others, such as the papers entitled "Moral Development" and "The Characteristics of the Good Shepherd Catechesis." You will also find lists of our many formation courses, which have grown too numerous to include in the current journals.

Third, I hope you will gather from us a sense of our community, which is very far-reaching — now an international community — and also a very particular community that forms around the child. Like a school faculty that focuses on its community of children, the catechists of this community come together for formation, for building community and for sharing our observations of and experiences with the children. There are accounts of visits to different atria, such as a trip to Mexico, a new atrium in Africa and the work that has begun in Australia.

The language of the early newsletters may seem a bit dated because the movement toward inclusive language was not as widespread then as it is today. But we invite you to enjoy in these issues something of the history of the Catechesis of the Good Shepherd since its arrival in the United States. We often use a comparison to the mustard seed parable because our work has enjoyed a mysterious growth. It has always been slow, and mostly traveled by "word of mouth," with one parent saying to another, "Come, see the atrium, this special place for children."

In these pages may you see the child's love for God, and our love for the child.

Carol Cannon Dittberner
*First editor*

St. Paul, Minnesota
February 1998

# Catechesis of the Good Shepherd

### January 6th, 1984

*Rise up in splendor, Jerusalem! Your light has come, the glory of the Lord shines upon you. See, darkness covers the earth, and thick clouds cover the peoples; but upon you the Lord shines, and over you appears his glory. Nations shall walk by your light, and kings by your shining radiance.*

*Raise your eyes and look about; they all gather and come to you; your sons come from far, and your daughters in the arms of their nurses. Then you shall be radiant at what you see, your heart shall throb and overflow, for the riches of the sea shall be emptied out before you, the wealth of nations shall be brought to you. Caravans of camels shall fill you, dromedaries from Midian and Ephah; all from Sheba shall come bearing gold and frankincense, and proclaiming the praises of the Lord.*

Isaiah 60:1-6

Today we celebrate the Epiphany, the manifestation of the Light to the Nations, the coming of the three Kings, their gifts to the Baby Jesus. We celebrate gifting among our families and friends during the holidays, and some of us reserve some special gift for the Epiphany. But what is the true gift we see? It is not the one we give or the ones the Magi give - it is the gift which God gives to us: God becomes incarnate, becomes Jesus, becomes Emmanuel.

The scripture passage on the cover is taken from the Readings of the Day for January 6th from the Roman lectionary. On this day 77 years ago a great work began when Maria Montessori opened her first house of children. In her words:

> "The words of Scripture which on that day, the Epiphany, were read in the churches seemed to me an omen and a prophecy: 'For behold darkness shall cover the earth ... but the Lord shall arise upon thee, and the Gentiles shall walk in thy light....'
>
> "I set to work feeling like a peasant woman who, having set aside a good store of seed corn, has found fertile field in which she may freely sow it. But I was wrong. I had hardly turned over the clods of my field, when I found gold instead of wheat; the clods concealed a precious treasure....
>
> "One day in great emotion I took my heart in my two hands...and I stood respectfully before the children, saying to myself: 'Who are you then? Have I perhaps met with the children who were held in Christ's arms and to whom divine words were spoken? ....I will follow you, to enter with you into the Kingdom of Heaven.'"

Maria Montessori, <u>The Secret of Childhood</u>,<br>Orient Longman, India, pp. 127-130.

We feel, perhaps, some of the same emotion of birth and beginning; knowing a seed is sown, knowing a child will lead us, knowing the Light shines.

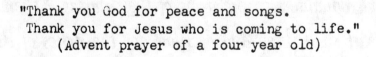

"Thank you God for peace and songs.
Thank you for Jesus who is coming to life."
(Advent prayer of a four year old)

We pray with great hope for the growth of this work, the Catechesis of the Good Shepherd, which calls us forth, into the Light.

January 6th, 1984<br>St. Paul, Minnesota

Pope John Paul II visits the atrium at Nostra Signoza di Lourdes. Each week he makes a pastoral visit to one of the parishes in Rome. This center was opened by Tilde Cocchini and now is conducted by Mirella Cassano.

*God came and brought peace to the world.*
*God came and brought love to the world.*
*God came and brought life to the world.*

 peace

 love

 life

By Jessica Nelson

Jessica Nelson, age 9

# Religious Formation and Later Childhood

by Dr. Sofia Cavalletti
translated by Patricia Coulter

It is known that the child after the age of six shows himself/herself to be very different from the pre-school child. Maria Montessori, in speaking of the planes of development, regarded the closure of the first to occur around six years of age, and that, therefore, this age signals the beginning of the second developmental stage.

It may be said -- even if such a simplification is perhaps exaggerated, but which may be considered indicative nevertheless -- that the young child is intent on probing the Mystery of the universe in its vertical dimension, that is, in its depths and heights, in a metaphysical relationship with God; whereas the older child fixes his gaze on the reflection of this Mystery, in the dimension of its vastness.

The world expands before the older child, displaying new horizons and new elements. From this comes that great thirst for knowledge found in later childhood. It is not a question of knowledge which is academic in character, but of an existential need to know the world which opens up for the child, in order to become capable of orienting oneself in it. The thirst for knowledge is such that it is not limited to the immediate environment in which the child lives; rather it extends so far that a new instrument is given to the child which enables him to know reality in its farthest reaches: the imagination. The imagination is not new, but there are new dimensions in this capacity, so as to be able to reach the universe.

The vital need to know has also a moral aspect, which is the reflection of the former. The older child wants to know what his/her place is in the world that he or she is in the process of discovering, and what his/her task is in it. Thus a new incentive is born to establish social relationships, and a new interest on the level of behaviour, of things to do. Work is the means by which the child comes to explore the world, and, at the same time, the means with which the child takes possession of it.

At this point we ask ourselves: Is the religious reality capable of satisfying the older child's deep needs, as it satisfies those of the younger child?

Experience has demonstrated that an affirmative answer can be given to such a question, because the older children, no less than the younger children, although in a different form, have received with naturalness and a profound and meditative joy the new elements of the Christian message which are presented to them. They showed that they knew these with a knowledge that is not scholastic but vital, in such a way that these elements become a part of their very person.

The Christian doctrinal deposit opens the older child to the boundless horizons of that "history" we call "sacred"; it is "sacred" because it is the realization of a plan which God is in the process of unfolding, and it is "history" because it is accomplished with mankind throughout time. It is a history that goes back to the beginning of time at creation, reaches its culmination at the Incarnation, and stretches forward, waiting for that moment in which "God will be all in all," and which we call the parousia, comprising therefore the past, present and future. It is a history which is not only exceedingly vast, but also extremely complex, and as such it may be presented from various points of view. It may be regarded as the history of many gifts which God is giving to His creatures: the good things of nature and the world, which man discovers, works with, and in doing so, makes his own; the persons with whom to create relationships of mutual enrichment; and finally, the gift of Himself in the person of the Son, who died and rose for us, the gift of a life stronger than death because it is the life of God Himself. From the resurrection to parousia, this gift is continually given sacramentally in the Eucharist in particular, which we can view as the "sacrament of the gift," for in it are found all the gifts of God as if concentrated and carried to their greatest level. At the parousia the gift of God's life will have reached all persons and filled all things. Gift, precisely because it is such, is not a unilateral action, but, by its very gratuitousness, elicits a response, in such a way as to become a bilateral act, which aspires above all to establish a relationship. It is the theme of covenant, fundamental in the Judaeo-Christian tradition.

In the immensity of history we can perceive a plan for communion: from the time when man began to work, he has left the results of his labour to others, and we, today, still enjoy the products of the work of persons so far distant from us in time. Who thinks, getting into a car, that we owe the discovery of the wheel to an unknown someone who, centuries and milennia ago, had in some manner worked for us? And yet a certain bond exists between that person and us, and among the many people who, before us, have taken the goods God prepared for us in the world, and worked with them. Thus we can imagine a whole system of relationships established between person and person, almost as if invisible bridges were constructed and linked together those of ages past and we who are living today. This occurs as well between one people and another: how many nations seem to us to have disappeared from history, and yet their inheritance has passed on to others, and in some manner it lives on even now. Invisible "bridges" also exist between one people and another.

But if we scrutinize history more attentively we become aware that the project for communion, which we can discover between person and person and people and people, does not have solely a horizontal dimension; it has a much vaster range, because it tends to unite Heaven and Earth. When God came among men in the person of the Son, we may say that the tension towards communion goes beyond the barriers of the human world, and unites together the world of God with the human world. The impetus towards communion acquires another dimension and hence becomes truly cosmic. It is the completion of a communion such as this that we, in the conflict and in the fragmentation of our present time, are awaiting in the future, at the parousia.

The cosmic communion which is being established has a vital character; it is not a matter of a common sharing of goods and values, but it is really a fusion of life. In what sense? It is in this context that the great Christological parable of the true Vine finds its place, which is aligned with that parable fundamental to early childhood: the good Shepherd. The parable of the true Vine lets us penetrate the mystery of the communion of life, which unites man and God together, through the mediation of Christ, and person with person, in Christ. The text speaks of Christ, who is the Vine, about people who are the branches, and of the Father who is the vinegrower. Just as the same sap runs through every part of the plant, so too in the true Vine is there one, vital principle, which is the same in Christ and in each branch of the Vine: the life of the risen Christ, the fullness of the life of God.

With this background, another aspect of the Eucharist can be put into focus: that of the sacrament of unity, of the sacramental action in which communion is created and expressed. That unique "sap" which gives life to each branch of the true Vine is nourished by the one eucharistic Bread, which comes to be broken and offered as food to each person. In the Eucharist, the tending of history towards communion finds its highest expression.

The unfolding of events, viewed from a perspective of profound meaning, allows us to see, sustained throughout the whole arc of history, a movement which is directed towards reuniting people among themselves, in an exchange of material, cultural and spiritual goods, and attains, in the communion with God, cosmic dimensions. If such a movement is visible in history's deep currents up to the day in which we are living, we can believe that it will continue to come about in the future on an increasingly vaster scale until it fills the entire universe. It is in this sense that we encourage ourselves to hope in the words of the prophets, thereby educating ourselves in hope.

It is the theology of history, that theology which is the basis of hope, and which permits us to hold ourselves immersed in the flow of history which transcends us and of which we are, however, a part.

The Christian proclamation offered in later childhood thus is built around the fundamental theme of communion, seen in the general framework of the unfolding of history. In early childhood we tell the child: "Listen, there is someone who is calling you by your name and is giving you his light, his life without end." To the older child we say: "Look around you and see, there is someone who is directing the history in which we live, and is guiding it towards communion."

Looking at history from a closer range, we also perceive ambiguity and conflict which makes us aware that this marvellous plan for communion is not accomplished without difficulty and opposition. Actually, we are dealing with a project in process of becoming, and it is not without, in attaining its fulfillment, contradiction and opposition.

At this point the *kerygma* becomes moral exhortation (*parenesis*).

It is the nature of gift to elicit a response; whereas a commercial transaction is terminated upon payment since it involves the exchange of *things*, gift, which involves *persons* instead, tends to establish a relationship between persons, one which is, wherever possible, lasting. In such a relationship, the person receives and gives: creation is a gift given to man, yet it is a gift which needs man in order to reach its fulfillment, so that the force of communion which drives history may grow stronger and spread. The true Vine needs people in order to bear those fruits which give glory to the Father. The broken Bread is offered to each person, but each must be ready to extend one's hand to everyone, without distinction, in the gesture of peace. In this manner the action of man is inserted into the vast design of history, which is in the process of being built, and if history involves persons and things in a plan for communion, then the resonance of man's action is cosmic as well.

There is an immediate continuity between *kerygma* and *parenesis*: there is no break in continuity between them because it is the proclamation itself which, by its very nature, becomes moral exhortation.

In relation to the greatness of the proclamation, the insufficiency, incapacity and resistance within each of us become apparent. And it also becomes evident that help from above is needed so that we can gradually manage to fill the gaps, to strengthen weaknesses, to overcome obstacles.

The invitation addressed to the older child to look around at the surrounding world so as to discern there the signs of communion, that God is creating with us and within us in our relationships with one another, is completed with the exhortation not to overlook the negative signs of separation and division between nations, between one person and another, and in the heart of each individual person.

We must teach older children to open their eyes to the reality of the negative aspects of history, but not before helping them to grasp its positive aspects. Never talk about the darkness before speaking about the light. The Christian message is a message of resurrection, and as such it proclaims to us that life is stronger than death and light is stronger than darkness. Only when our eyes are captivated by the beauty of light can we then look, without excessive disquietude, at the negativity of darkness. Only if our eyes have contemplated the beauty of the light will we be able to turn, from the struggle of the existence of darkness within us and around us, again towards the light with a call of entreaty full of trust. This call is the sacrament of Reconciliation.

This sacrament is the instrument of the victory of good over evil, and as well as focusing upon God's power in this struggle, it highlights another aspect of His love: that of the fidelity of a love which does not cease in the face of any opposition nor any refusal whatsoever, precisely because it is a love which is gratuitous to its very depths. In the context of the Christian message, the aspect of God's faithfulness in love has the same importance for older children as the protectiveness of His love holds for little children. It is this aspect -- in our estimation -- which corresponds to the new exigencies of later childhood, in which the older child finds that same serene peace, that enchantment which the younger child finds in the loving protection of the good Shepherd. In this way the face of God is gradually revealed in all its richness for the older child in his/her process of growing.

Departing from the kerygma we arrived at the parenesis, in order to return again to the kerygma. The religious attitude of life is response to an overwhelming proclamation and religious formation should consist above all in this proclamation. The religious attitude of life is relationship with God, and, in God, with one's brothers and sisters, and inasmuch as it is relationship, it is moral life constitutive of the person in a certain mode of being. The level of being affects the level of actions. But religious formation is intended to serve life at the deepest level of being, before the level of doing. In no sense different from early childhood, the individual's moral life relative to behaviour in later childhood does not spring forth except from that "being in love" which takes place at the most profound level of the person, and which can not be brought to life from moral exhortation but rather by the proclamation of a love without limits.

Obviously, this does not mean to exclude a certain quality of teaching which is explicity moral in character, as for instance with some parables and maxims of this nature. However, we should not treat such subjects by themselves, nor should they predominate; they should fall, as it were, on a field previously prepared, and the instrument which will have enabled the earth to receive and make them fruitful is the proclamation -- which leads to being in love: the proclamation given in early childhood, which forms the foundation for the structuring of the person, and the proclamation offered in later childhood.

The altered existential situation of the older child as regards the younger child calls for new content and also a didactic method that corresponds to the new capacities arising within the older child. We have mentioned the imagination, which allows the child to soar beyond the limited world which appears to the senses. If the adult knows how to offer the imagination an adequate stimulus, the older child will be able to initiate a process of knowing which will carry him a great distance, drawing him to ever broadening horizons, towards which the child will walk filled with wonder, and into which he will plunge himself with the whole of his being.

The material for children six years of age and over should be prepared in a way that takes all this into consideration, and it should therefore aim at striking the imagination. This is how to satisfy that vital need for totality, which is proper to all true knowledge. The moment of reflective, objective thought follows the moment when reality is taken as a whole; Paul Ricoeur says: "If the development of thought ... never consists in going from the simple to the complex, but always moves within the totality itself, this can only be a development in the philosophical elucidation of the global view."[1] In capturing the imagination we help the older child to catch hold of the "global vision", which is the departure point for all knowledge, we help the child to establish a relationship with what is being presented, so that it can be grasped with the whole of one's being.

We should not forget however that the older child is also beginning to think in a reflective and objective manner, that type of thinking which in a certain sense stands at a distance from the object known, creating "a fundamental cleavage between the object and the subject."[2]

In teaching, it is generally this second way of knowing that is favoured, with serious harm to the process of learning, which in this way looses its anchorage in the depths of the person and becomes a purely intellectual fact. "Philosophy", says Ricoeur again, "does not start anything independently: supported by the non-philosophical, it derives its existence from the substance of what has already been understood prior to reflection."[3] It is obvious how fundamentally important the non-philosophical -- that is, non-reflective -- moment is for religious formation. Nonetheless, the other moment has its importance as well, and requires attention. To strike the child's imagination without aiding him in the subsequent "elucidation" of what has been received would mean helping to give rise to a magma in the child, without contributing to bring it to order. It is clear however that the elucidation cannot be the point of departure, because it needs material to elucidate.

The adult, in helping the child, should keep the two moments of learning in mind: the child needs to be helped to discover the vastness of reality, receiving it by means of the imagination and intuitively abandoning oneself to it; and also the child needs to reflect on it through a form of thinking which tends rather to objectify it and in some manner to dominate it. It is unnecessary to underline the damage which can result from a religious formation in which the second moment of knowing is privileged; this latter moment on its own, due to its objective character, can distort the religious reality and can make God an object to be known from afar, and not a Person with whom to enter into relationship.

~ ~ ~ ~ ~

NOTES

[1] Paul Ricoeur, Fallible Man, trans. Charles Kelbley (Chicago: Henry Regnery Company, 1967), p. 8.
[2] Ibid., p. 129.
[3] Ibid., pp. 8-9.

This article appeared 5th February 1979 in "Vita Dell' Infanzia," Rome, Italy and is reprinted with permission.

# The Catechesis of The Good Shepherd in Chihuahua, Northern Mexico

June 1976: Sofia Cavalletti gave her first seminar in Mexico City, announcing the peaceful and unique joy of the child when encountering God.

In September a group of twelve children (3 to 4 years old), one catechist, and one assistant began an "Atrium." We had chairs and some tables placed around the altar from 3 to 6:30 on Saturday afternoon. Each child brought a chair; the tables were given to the Parish. The catechist began the work out of faith, saying to herself, "If Sofia said so, let's see...." Little by little the presentations began: the children, the catechist and the assistant were involved in the serene and unique joy experienced by many other children in different parts and environments of the world. After a few sessions the children said, "Why don't we come here every day? We could go to school in the morning and come to the 'Atrium' every afternoon."

The next year, 1977, another "Atrium" was opened with children from the Montessori school. This time the catechist came with me to meditate before going to the children. She was not at all convinced, especially with some presentations such as "The Epiclesis." I simply said to her, "Do it, and see what happens with the children." The children were thrilled more and more each week. They themselves educated the catechist to wonder and simplicity.

Today, 1983, Chihuahua has "Atria" in two Montessori schools and in four parishes. Visiting them this summer we experienced in these rooms an atmosphere of prayer. They are filled with the presence of God and of the children. The material is beautiful, refined and very, very simple. You can see love in every object of the "Atrium;" they have put together a great fidelity to the spirit and the material of Rome, and a creativity in using the things of the environment. We saw candlesticks made out of the tops of bottles of water with a nail in the center.

A marvelous thing to observe is how the "Atria" are a real community of children and catechists meeting God together. It is wonderful to listen to the catechists talking about the children with almost a "religious respect" and learning from them the Mystery of God. The catechists have had very little in the line of doctrinal formation and I think that the children themselves have taught them who God is. The parents and the priests are also knowing God through the children:

- One boy (8 years old) said to his mother, "Mom, I'm going to ask Jesus for a big present for my first communion." "What is it?" she asked. "The Holy Spirit," answered the boy. "And how is He going to give you the Holy Spirit?" asked the mother. "I don't know how He is going to do it, but I know I'm going to be very happy," said Jorge.

- A boy (3 or 4 years old) was meditating with the material of the Good Shepherd. At a certain moment he placed the Good Shepherd, the sheep, the hired man and the wolf inside the sheepfold. He explained, "They are all inside because with the Good Shepherd all become good."

- A very poor abandoned boy went to the "Atrium" when he was about five years old. Then he disappeared. Some years later he was thrown forever out of school one afternoon. He came to the door of the "Atrium" and said to the catechist, "I was expelled from school. I don't have a place to go and I thought I could come here where I was told about a Good Shepherd who loves me and cares for me." He came by himself without his mother bringing him. One day he made the collage of the Good Shepherd 17 times. He remained there for a while and then went into the neighborhood.

- A boy (8 years old), after listening to the Parable of the Prodigal Son, said to the catechist, "Don't tell me anything else. It is enough for me to know that God is that way. I don't need to hear more."

- There is a group of blind children in the Catechesis of the Good Shepherd. Two priests who helped them in confession said, "I wish I could see God the way these blind children do it." Another one told us how impressed he was listening to the blind children speaking joyfully about the Light of the Risen Christ.

- Andres (16 years old) has attended the "Atrium" since he was ten. This fall, with three of his friends, he is becoming a catechist. They are going to a very poor parish with the materials. Andres was asked to teach the children some prayers and he said, "No, these children will probably have only what we give them this year. I want to give them the most important things. I'm going to bring them what I had." He asked his mother for help to prepare every week.

Another interesting thing happening in Chihuahua is the "indirect way" of using the Catechesis of the Good Shepherd, what Sofia calls "Una diffussione capilare." Since 1976 the catechists working in the "Atria" have been involved in the Diocesan Department of Evangelization. The content and the spirit of this catechesis have entered into the other methods. For instance there is a model for evangelization in the families before First Communion. We inserted the presentations of "The Good Shepherd" and "The Eucharistic Presence" and also some other liturgical presentations. The Easter preparation in a very poor neighborhood in 1979 was made with the materials of "The Good Shepherd," "The Lost Sheep," "The Eucharistic Presence" and Baptism. This summer, 1983, Sofia and some members of the Diocese discussed this. Together we saw the "Atria" as "incubators" to prepare some people in a real experience of faith with children. These adults will, later on, announce the joy, the essentiality, and the wonder of the God-child relationship. Another catechist spoke of the "Atria" as a real need for some "particular children" who have "a special search and relationship with God." In her experience some children prefer to work with just the "Albúm."

Sofia's visit to Chihuahua this summer filled her and all of us with awe before the work of the Lord. The little "mustard seed" is growing and we can only burst forth in a BERAKAH (praise) for what God is and for His work in the vine.

by Maria de los Angeles Christlieb

NOTE: There are many, many atria in Mexico. Some are located in the f    cities: Chihuahua, Ciudad Juarez, Merida, Mexico City, Morelia, Torreon, and, on the Mexican border, El Paso. For a more complete listing contact Maria Christlieb, Cerrada San Jeronimo 16-3, San Jeronimo Lidice, Mexico D.F.

# The Washington Experience

Sept. 20, 1983

When I returned from Washington this summer my enthusiasm prompted me to write some immediate impressions. I'm sending this personal journal-like account to all of you who were part of the Washington experience and to those who were not able to attend, but wished to be there. I hope this gives the latter group and (future participants) some idea of the continuation and a share in the experience.

Sincerely,
Barbara Kahn


Like pilgrims to Canterbury, we found ourselves in Washington D. C. again, co-seekers with Sofia Cavalletti and visionaries of a world where the religious life of the child was paramount. Some people had begun their quest in 1975 when Sofia presented a five week course for the child from 3-6 in St. Paul, Minnesota. Others were first introduced to Sofia in Houston in 1978 and some had only begun the summer before in Washington. Of that last group of 27 people who had first met in '82, sixteen had returned in '83. Many of them bringing new disciples. The reunion of these people whose lives had crossed only briefly and with great time gaps was tearful and joyous.

We all came to this work perhaps with some of the same idealism that brings people into Montessori -- but with an added dimension. We had all experienced a lack at the very heart of the most normalized Montessori classes -- the spiritual dimension, and we knew Sofia Cavalletti had directed the last 30 years of her life to those needs.

The catechesis of the "Good Shepherd" is universal in its Christianity and not limited to Montessori settings. A little over half of the 30 were Montessorians. Eight were religious. Several were Directors of Religious Education in parishes, and many others were working in or establishing atriums in their churches.

An atrium is the foyer or entrance to the church where the early Christians gathered to be instructed in the truths of the church before they were fully initiated into the sacraments. Maria Montessori used the word atrium to describe a sacred place containing child-size models of what we would find in church. Sofia Cavalletti describes the atrium as a "place for celebrating the Word of God, for listening, praying and reflecting together, for meditation and work." (The Religious Potential of the Child) Such an atrium would contain the materials for conveying liturgy and scripture but more importantly would express the mood, beauty and sanctity necessary to the cultivation of prayer and openness in the child.

Yet no one had this ideal set up. One atrium was in the church basement, also doubling as a shelter for the homeless in the winter, leaving few minutes to air the room and set up before the children arrived. Another more established community arranged for families to donate part of their home, a basement or third floor, and this one atrium was used for all the classes of 96 children after school and on Saturday mornings. Many of the Montessorians had set aside a part of their classrooms with screens or dividers as a place where the child could meet God, but many more were frustrated because the schools where they taught were areligious. Several were interested in taking the catechesis of the Good Shepherd into hospital settings to be present to children and their families facing death.

The group was extremely diverse. Initially some personalities were potentially abrasive and incompatible. But the gentleness and patience of others, especially of Sofia, was such a visible sign of Christ's presence among us that we began to perceive others as more luminous and to recognize the shadows in ourselves. Perhaps since we met and shared on a spiritual level, the sense of belonging and mutual trust allowed us to be ourselves and to share our weaknesses openly and honestly. As we listened to Sofia present materials and background for the child we could look around the room and recapture the eight year old in the faces of the listeners. Originally we had all come for the sake of the "child", maybe for our own children, but as we kept coming again, we realized we were the children and the transformation was happening in us. Jean Vanier describes the qualities of our gathering in Community and Growth, Our Pilgrimage Together.

> This atmosphere of joy comes from the fact that we all feel free to
> be ourselves in the deepest sense. We have no need to play a role,
> to pretend to be better than the others, to demonstrate prowess in
> order to be loved. We have discovered that we are loved for our-
> selves, not for our intellectual or manual skills. When we begin
> to drop the barriers and fears which prevent us from being ourselves,
> we become more simple. Simplicity is no more and no less than

ourselves. It is knowing that we are accepted with our qualities, our flaws and as we most deeply are.

This meeting was different from those in St. Paul, Houston or Washington in '82. The distances that separated us and the support we offered one another needed a form. The catechesis of the Good Shepherd in North America had grown from a tiny mustard seed so small that you could blow it away, to a seed that was putting forth roots. As a group Sofia called us to address that need in our first session by preparing answers to four questions. Do we need an association? If so, what are the aims? What are the needs? How do we implement the needs?

Everyone's input was equally requested, valued and respected in dealing with these questions. For once the usual hierarchies between AMI and AMS were blurred and unimportant. Those who had been to Rome for either the two or three year course with Sofia made no distinction between themselves and others who had attended only summer courses in the states, and generously shared their album pages and materials in a spirit of trust.

We looked to the existing models in Rome and in Mexico which offered a traditional structure of President, Vice-President, Secretary and Treasurer for officers. The work there is much more centralized and concentrated geographically whereas our work in the United States and Canada is dispersed and scattered throughout the country. People here feel isolated in a world where religious education is limited to Sunday schools, church basements and workbooks and so need affirmation and support. Unity was our key aim.

Throughout these meetings and the course of the two weeks a spirit of prayer prevailed that was palpable. Personal desire for recognition, titles, power or authority was absent. Sofia has a chapter in her book, The Religious Potential of the Child, speaking of the role of the adult with the child as "merely servants." The thrust was not to elect officers but to discern through prayer and shared discussion our mutual gifts to be offered for the good of the whole.

The first stated aim of the association was "to involve adults and children in a religious experience in which the religious values of the child are predominant, keeping in mind that the contemplative nature of the child indicates to the adult a certain way of drawing near to God." The needs were numerous, but three were isolated as of immediate urgency: (1) The need for a center. (2) The need for continuing courses. (3) A newsletter. A center would give us an address, a credibility, an authorization and availability. At the least we needed a name. The courses need to continue with Sofia as the trainer and those who had been trained in Rome or Mexico as supporting trainers. A newsletter would provide articles, research findings, experiences and a question/answer exchange.

We proceeded cautiously, aware that we were charting a course for the next year, not the next ten years. Yet as the time was running out for more meetings we suggested in writing, names of people whose gifts would match the three most urgent needs. The almost unanimous consensus on matching people with tasks seemed to be proof that we were being guided by a power beyond ourselves. The elements which Vanier describes as essential to a community were part of the process: a life of silent prayer, a life of service and a community life in which all its members can grow in their own gift.

We left Washington the next day with the assurance that, yes, like the mustard seed, we were very small. But there was a power and force inside that seed transforming and creating something quite disproportionate to the seed. The growth was in us, our families, in the children we serve and in the larger sphere of our newly formed association. A community then "is not simply a group of people who love together and love each other. It is a current of life, a heart, a soul, a spirit. It is people who love each other a great deal and who are all reaching towards the same hope." (Vanier)

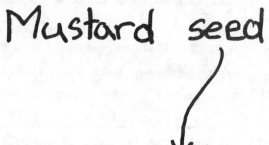

Kate Schmid, age 8

# Remembering...
# And I was there!

AND I WAS THERE!

A beautiful Roman lady....Sofia by name....was at Catholic University last summer (....and I was there!) To be greeted warmly by a joy-filled Sofia; to be privileged to listen to and to watch this very special teacher in a class room setting ....made my five days in Washington the highlight of my year.

The people sitting at the feet of Sofia: from north, east, south and west (Minnesota to Mexico....Toronto to Pennsylvania to Houston) made me believe that something special was happening there.

To be the invited guest at the formation of an "association" ....to be privileged to know first hand the calibre of minds and talents and charisms assembled around Sofia....made my visit a cause for celebration!

I will long remember the late night prayer meetings....I will re-live the shared meals and gabfests....I will never forget the wonderful celebrations of my 38th anniversary of ordination.

National Shrine....Oblate House....Feast of Mary's Assumption ....beautiful memories of beautiful people in our nation's capitol...........God Bless you, Sofia! and God Bless your very special friends who gave me this second experience of "the Catechesis of the Good Shepherd" in August of '83!!

Sincerely and gratefully,

Father Cecil G. Roufs

# Food for Thought...

I took a little child's hand in mine. We were to walk together for awhile. I was to lead him to the Father. It was a task that overcame me, so awful was the responsibility. And so I talked to the child only of the Father. I pointed to the sternness of His face were the child to displease Him. I spoke of the child's goodness as something that would appease the Father's wrath. We walked under the tall trees. I said the Father had the power to bring them crashing down with His thunderbolts. We walked in the sunshine. I told him of the greatness of the Father who made the burning, blazing sun. And one twilight we met the Father. The child hid behind me. He was afraid. He would not take the Father's hand. I was between the child and the Father. I wondered. I had been so conscientious, so serious.

I took a little child's hand in mine. I was to lead him to the Father. I felt burdened with a multiplicity of the things I had to teach him. We did not ramble. We hastened from spot to spot. At one moment we compared the leaves of different trees. In the next moment we were examining a bird's nest. While the child questioned me about it, I hurried him away to chase a butterfly. Did he chance to fall asleep, I wakened him, lest he miss something I wished him to see. We spoke of the Father. Oh yes, often and rapidly, I poured into his ears all the stories I thought he ought to know. But we were often interrupted by the wind blowing, of which we must trace its source. And then in the twilight we met the Father. The child merely glanced at Him and then his gaze wandered in a dozen directions. The Father stretched out His hand. The child was not interested enough to take it. Feverish spots burned in his cheeks. He dropped exhausted to the ground and fell asleep. Again I was between the child and the Father. I wondered. I had taught him so many things.

I took a little child's hand to lead him to the Father. My heart was full of gratitude for the glad privilege. We walked slowly. I suited my steps to the short ones of the child. We spoke of many things the child noticed. Sometimes we picked the Father's flowers and stroked their soft petals and loved their bright colors.....Sometimes we watched one of the Father's birds. We watched it build its nest and lay its eggs. We wondered, elated, at the care it gave its young.....Often we told stories of the Father. I told them to the child and the child told them again to me. We told them, the child and I, over and over again. Sometimes we stopped to rest, leaning against one of the Father's trees and letting His cool breeze cool our brows, never speaking. And then in the twilight we met the Father. The child's eyes shone. He looked lovingly, trustingly into the Father's face. He put his hand into the Father's hand. I was for the moment forgotten. I was content.

Source unknown

# preface to the Italian Edition of
# The Religious Potential of the Child

by P. Dalmazio Mongillo, O.P.

One who lives in communion with Jesus Christ rebuilds his or her own life and begins to listen to and taste the word which speaks of Jesus and was spoken by Him. One feels summoned and engaged in a personal way to assume responsibility with others, to leave the narrow shell of preoccupation with self, to expand the horizons of solidarity, and to create initiatives so that all may become "new," so that all may discover the joy of growing as the family of God (cf. Ephesians 2:20).

The love between persons, in Jesus Christ, when it is supported and not suffocated (cf. Matthew 25:25), enlarges the horizons of the spirit. It stimulates us, makes us conscious, responsible, and committed; it leads us to "lose" (cf. Luke 9:24; 17:33; Matthew 10:39), and so, to give and to transmit the life in which we discover ourselves to be transformed. It is in contrast to habits of control and alienation; it empties us of ambitions to power; it leads to the growth of the family and the good of all.

In Jesus Christ one comes to see that not every way of existing is life. Life becomes authentic when creatures begin to love as He loved (cf. John 13:34); life grows when it becomes gift; it develops when it is shared. There is only one _way_ to penetrate it, and that is to live in Christ the mystery of His existence; to live _as_ He lived, without resisting what He feeds us as branches of His vine (cf. John 15:1ff) and sheep of His flock (cf. John 10:1ff). We know life in living it and we live life in sharing it. Those who do not thwart this stimulus come to discern the way to support it, and collaborate in leading others to live together their own joyful experience (cf. 1 John 1:1-5).

To become, to be a Christian, means to live God's life in Jesus Christ, and to live it together, sharing it with all God's children. To live as a Christian and to live in "koinonia" are synonymous. We cannot become Christians by ourselves, apart from Jesus Christ and the family of those who live in Him and of Him. The Christian life is a journey in communion with others in Jesus Christ. It is born in communion with other believers; it grows and develops with the growth of communion among believers. It enters into crisis when it languishes and becomes asphyxiated; it cannot be obtained by "spontaneous generation;" nor is it cultivated _in vitro_.

Meditating on this, there comes to mind the link between the elements with which Jesus identified Himself: "I am the way, and the truth, and the life" (John 14:6): He is the way to "life," the truth about life and the way; He is the life that sustains our journey towards the fulness of truth (cf. John 16:13). Jesus not only gives life, He makes us become a source of life (cf John 7:38). He leads us to recognize and consolidate the bonds of communion with those who live in Him. He strengthens us to overcome the conflicts which hold back or compromise the growth of life, the knowledge of the truth, the discernment of the way. Those who share the hope in which they are saved, journey together; they recognize that they are vivified in the same wellspring, called to share the same happiness.

This is the perspective in which I reflect on catechesis: catechesis is to learn to live in the family of God, to grow together in sharing the same life, in the living awareness of the Love in which we are loved. Catechesis is letting ourselves be loved and saved. It is to nourish our desire for the Shepherd, to remain in His love, to rediscover the conditions and needs of life in communion, and to support each other in our search for the way to actualize it. Catechesis develops in continuity with the experience described in 1 John 1:1-5. I would qualify catechesis as the <u>concelebration</u> in which a portion of God's people, in Jesus Christ, acknowledges the Father, discovers itself to be loved and part of the journey of life that leads each person, together with others, to become the subject of initiative, capable of receiving and giving, and aware of one's own responsibilities. In catechesis the person becomes one who is known, called, accepted; king, prophet, priest (cr. 1 Peter 2:5ff): one who listens, speaks and co-operates in the building up of the family in an osmosis of life with the Father. The "celebration of catechesis" is growth in faith operative in charity (cf. Galations 5:6). We participate in it when we accept and live it in the listening and union which grafts us into the vital circuit of the communication of Agape.

The experience described by Sofia Cavalletti confirms, without any possibility of doubt, that simultaneity of giving and receiving, of listening and proclaiming, which is lived in the community that is united in the Shepherd. Her most surprising facts refer to the child who, when feeling welcomed by those who are living in Agape, really opens and expands in freedom, allows self to become involved, lets go of resistances and defenses, and spontaneously supports the Master's work. It is the child's original state which is to be nurtured and in which he or she will be found in order to be received as a child in the Kingdom (cf. Matthew 18:3).

Catechesis becomes more authentic the more that those who live and participate in it, each in their own condition, experience the joy of recognizing themselves to be united in the same life, journeying in the loving knowledge of the same truth. On this journey each person, with a different task, praises the Father, listens to and contemplates His mystery, manifests and shares what is experienced within, and welcomes the call to transform life so that it becomes worthy of humans. In catechesis the most loved concelebrant is surely the child. Contrary to what is generally thought, the child is endowed with unsuspected capacities for "koinonia;" the child has a specific "receptivity," a simple, clear, connaturality with God's love in Jesus Christ.

The catechist should recognize this attraction the Father exerts over the child (cf. John 6:44). The catechist should cultivate the seeds within the child, and in this delicate attention the catechist will also grow in redeemed humanity. The recognition of the Father in Jesus will be more intense to the degree that the communion in which the little family lives is alive, with respect for each person's path, in its acceptance, awareness and building of Church. The family lives gathered together in the Lord's name (cf. Matthew 18:20), and opens itself in concern for the reality of which it is a part. In the family of God, persons grow when they do not offer resistance to the Father's work; they learn to know Him, to discern His voice, to support His work, to contribute to the good of all, to respect the times of growth of each person, and to safeguard the prerogatives of each individual.

The Christian proclamation does not happen only where truths are announced verbally, but where the proclamation is lived by those who are united in the same communion (cf. 1 John 1:1-5). The validity of the experience Sofia Cavalletti presents seems to me to be based on this vital osmosis that unites and transforms the small community where the proclamation takes place, where it is received, lived, and communicated. This experience evidences how the conditions of the Christian proclamation, corresponding to the child's structure, satisfy the child's need for spontaneity, naturalness, and sharing.

We are not dealing with a new methodology as a substitute for others. Its "newness" is in the inspiration from which it originates; it is in the light of this inspiration that the forms into which it has been translated and expressed should be read. Should one attempt to ascribe its effectiveness to having hit upon just the "right" parable, we should recall the truth so often reiterated by Augustine and Thomas: even the letter of the Gospel would kill if the Spirit did not speak to the heart. Should one be led to maintain that it is centered in that space reserved for the child's "creativity," we should point out that the best fruit of this "journey" is not a more intense inventiveness, but rather the peace, the profound joy of the encounter with Jesus, the opening of the child to listening, the delicacy of the relationship established with the Father, and the capacity to love.

I neither underrate nor minimize the methodological elements. However I am convinced that the source of it all comes from the searching within that profound harmony and atmosphere of mystery, which spring forth from the communion among the children living in the Father's attraction and the person who recognizes and fosters it, so that the adult also lets self be taken into it and lives it together with the children. The Church builds itself and grows in accepting the Father's attraction, Who elicits the docile, spontaneous receptivity of the child and the discreet, delicate intervention of the adult.

So as not to misrepresent God's masterpiece and create another delusion, it is necessary to emphasize that catechesis with children is the "joyful contemplation" of the Spirit's work in the hearts of the little children He loves; as such, it is the respectful attention to the ways that favour its growth so that the dialogue between the Spirit and the Bride not be disturbed. It is not a matter of standing there watching, but of participating and sharing: the proclamation, listening, prayer, and stimulus to personalize it are all without substitute. It is respectful attention that leads us to step aside at the opportune moment in order to leave space for the dialogue with the interior Master, and not divert its development.


Catechesis is not a matter of accustoming children to making gestures or saying words. Catechesis is to help children have a "tactile," living experience of the relationship with the Shepherd, themselves, the other sheep, and the sheepfold. It is to sustain children when they become conscious of the existence of lost sheep and hirelings, and, therefore, of conflict and weakness. To "touch" the Shepherd, sheep, sheepfold is the experience of the <u>sacramentality of faith</u>. It is born and grows when one in the believing community enters into relationship with the Shepherd who saves. One experiences the delicacy of the Shepherd's hand that touches and caresses. One receives His urging to transmit this gift of love. Even in faith one knows the reality touched, with which one is familiar.

With the Shepherd who feeds us in the Eucharist, who speaks to us in the Scriptures, who upholds us along the journey of justice and communion, fears are lessened, responsibilities are clarified, and one realizes the truth in full light. And the Shepherd is not an object of study or research. The Shepherd is love to love, food to eat, blood to receive into the circulation of one's very existence. He is beauty to contemplate, word to hear, life to share, and body to give growth (cf. 1 John 1:1-5). In the signs through which the Shepherd comes into contact with us, He transforms us, makes us become "sacrament," Church, capable of nourishing and encouraging the mysterious "koinonia" which makes a creature into a child in the Father's house. Faith is life, and life is generated and transmitted in the family that lives in faith.

The proclamation makes us become listeners; it gives us ears to hear and eyes to see. The proclamation is born and grows in Jesus Christ, "pioneer and perfector of our faith" (Hebrews 12:2), who, through the community of the Apostles ("For I became your father in Christ Jesus through the Gospel." cf. 1 Corinthians 4:15), lives in families gathered in His name, in the little portions of His Church.

The proclamation that nourishes faith is not a verbal fact; it is the continuity of the work of the Lord Who willed all things, spoke their names, called them forth; and they came into being, existed (cf. Genesis 1:1-31). The proclamation is the fruit of love which generates life when it is offered as gift, when it is spoken, when it is given over in words and gestures that communicate it, that pour forth from a heart which gives itself in the initiative of letting itself become involved.

An indefinite range of alibis distracts us from going forward on this "journey." They imprison us in the shifting sands of intellectualism, and hold us back from entrusting ourselves to Love. To help one another unveil and dispel these is the responsibility of us all. The experience of Sofia Cavalletti, cultivated in her deep inspiration and actuated in the forms in which it is expressed, will advance the maturation of a style of catechesis that helps us to go forth along the "way of God."

~ ~ ~ ~ ~

From The Religious Potential of the Child by Sofia Cavalletti, translated by Patricia M. Coulter and Julie M. Coulter. Copyright 1983 by The Missionary Society of St. Paul the Apostle in the state of New York. First published in Italy by Citta Nuova Editrice. Used by permission of Paulist Press, 545 Island Road, Ramsey, New Jersey 07446.

# the Seed Grows...

hat follows is a description of some of the atria presently in existence in the United States and Canada. It is not complete. We invite those of you reading this newsletter who have an atrium to describe your atrium and send your description to us. We hope to focus on additional atria in future issues.

Chicago, Illinois. St. Giles Church Community sponsors atria for 86 children ages 6-11. Reverend Gregory Heille, O.P. and Tina Lillig work with approximately 20 other catechists, coordinated by Kathie Nash. Two environments serve 6 to 7 years olds; one serves 8 to 11 year olds. Space is donated by families in the community. One environment is in the basement of a private home, another is the entire second floor of a private home. The families allow the space to remain set up during the week. The catechists are free to work on materials anytime. The third space, for the older children, is a very large basement in a two-flat building. It includes a carpeted main room, kitchen for bread baking and enough space to create a sacred place and separate areas for materials. A family bought this building and donated it, choosing to support the work of Catechesis in this manner.
Contact: Tina Lillig, 918 Wisconsin, Oak Park, Il. 60304.

Cleveland, Ohio  Betty Hissong directs her own Montessori preschool. She includes an atrium in her classroom, enabling her children to have religious experiences within their school day. Also she meets weekly with a group of children, 4 to 5 years old, from the Ruffing Montessori School. These children come to Betty's atrium.
Betty Hissong, 2441 Fenwick Road, Cleveland, OH 44118.

Atriums (continued)

Cleveland, Ohio  The Montessori Center for Family Christian Education is a private religious education program with classes for 75 children ages four to twelve. The Center was formed five years ago from the desire of Catholic parents of the Ruffing Montessori School to have a uniquely Montessori religious experience for their children. Classes meet for an hour each Tuesday after school at the Catholic girls' high school adjacent to Ruffing. Barb Kahn and three other catechists work with these children, grades one through seven. They are exploring possible places for an atrium, but obstacles present themselves related to not being connected to a religious community and lack of a permanent facility.
Contact: Barb Kahn, 2859 Scarborough Rd., Cleveland Hts. OH 44118

Minneapolis, Minnesota  Carol Dittberner conducts two atria in St. Frances Cabrini Parish. Preschoolers meet at the Church on Sunday morning. This atrium is in its second year. Materials are kept in a specially designed cabinet in a room used for other purposes during the week. An elementary class meets also on Sunday morning in a private home donated by one of the families in the program. This class began in the Fall of 1983 with 16 children. The preschool has 22 children.
Carol Dittberner, 1429 Portland Avenue, St. Paul, MN 55104.

New Ulm, Minnesota  Mary Polta, with the support of Fr. Cecil Roufs, the pastor of St. Mary's Parish in New Ulm, conducts an atrium in the parish school for 2½ to 5 year olds. The class meets Tuesday mornings for two hours and is in its fourth year.
Mary Polta, 503 West Lyon, Marshall, MN 56258.

St. Paul, Minnesota  Rose Marie Paul, through her church community Christ the Redeemer located at the Catholic Youth Center in St. Paul, is working with four catechists and a group of 25 children from 2½ to 9 years old.
Rose Marie Paul, 4901 West 114th Street, Bloomington, MN 55437.

Toronto, Canada.  At the Centre there are three small groups of children: one group of little children who are coming for the first time this year; another group of older children have been here since the start; and a third group of handicapped children from the adjoining school for special catechesis relating to the preparation for and celebration of First Communion.
    There is growth also in the adult community surrounding the Centre. As well as the two catechists already active in the atrium there are also some parents who want to be with the little children as catechists. Through the ministry of the Capuchin community, there have also been a number of liturgical celebrations involving families and friends linked to the Centre, the most recent of which was a retreat day of prayer in celebration of the Holy Year.
Contact: Good Shepherd Centre, 97 Willingdon Blvd., Toronto, Canada M8X2H8.

Washington, D.C.  Christian Family Montessori School near Washington, D.C. has two primary classes that share an atrium. The teachers, Rebekah Francisco Rojcewicz and Sister Sheila Sentiff, have studied in Rome with Sofia. Rebekah offers in addition two atria programs for children from other schools, one for three to five year olds and another for five to seven year olds. Each group comes once a week for two hours on a weekday afternoon. The school is in its third year. The school has offered summer courses and workshops for catechists since October 1981. It is a parent cooperative school committed to providing quality Christian education with low tuition and scholarships to enable families of all incomes to participate.
Contact: Cathy Maresca, 3109-24th St., N.E., Washington, D.C.

# The Catechesis of The Good Shepherd in North America

This is the first Newsletter published in the United States of America dedicated to the work of the Catechesis of the Good Shepherd. It is our hope, together with Dr. Sofia Cavalletti, to form an Association in North America to further the work of the religious development of the child. The group of catechists who met last summer in Washington isolated three goals: 1) the selection of a center, 2) sponsoring of a workshop in the summer of 1984, and 3) the publication of a newsletter. These three goals are interim goals for one year only and they will be reassessed when we meet this summer.

The Center for the association and its administration is with the Christian Family Montessori School in Washington, D.C., Cathy Maresca serving as our coordinator. At this time there is no formal membership or membership fee.

Dr. Cavalletti will give a workshop this summer which will focus on the six to eight year old child and which will include the preparation for the first reception of the Sacraments of Eucharist and Reconciliation. The location of this conference will be either Houston, Texas or St. Paul, Minnesota; further information will be announced.

This Newsletter is the fruit of many peoples' hands; we thank all who have contributed both directly and indirectly. We encourage your response and comments to our first issue and welcome suggestions for future issues. It is our hope to publish a newsletter annually or semi-annually. Contributions to cover the cost of publication and mailing of this issue will be greatly appreciated. Please let us know if you would like to receive the next issue.

Please direct your inquiries, suggestions or contributions in care of:

    Cathy Maresca, Coordinator
    3109-24th Street, N.E.
    Washington, D.C. 20019

    (202) 832-2477

This Newsletter was compiled by:

Carol Dittberner, Rose Marie Paul, and Mary Polta in collaboration with Dr. Sofia Cavalletti

Published in St. Paul, Minnesota      Copyright (c) January 6th, 1984

# Catechesis of the Good Shepherd

### Winter, 1985

And in the region there were shepherds out in the field, keeping watch over their flock by night. And an angel of the Lord appeared to them, and the glory of the Lord shone around them, and they were filled with fear. And the angel said to them, "Be not afraid; for behold, I bring you good news of a great joy which will come to all the people; for to you is born this day in the city of David a Savior, who is Christ the Lord.

And this will be a sign for you: you will find a child wrapped in swaddling cloths and lying in a manger." And suddenly there was with the angel a multitude of the heavenly host praising God and saying,

"Glory to God in the highest, and on earth peace to those with whom he is pleased!"

Luke 2: 8-14

# A Letter of Love from a Catechist

From Francesca Cocchini

Even if I do not know all of you personally, there are so many great realities that unite us that I feel very close to you and your work.

I started working in the catechesis of the Good Shepherd 16 years ago, after having been at the center of Via degli Orsini as a child for many years. I met Sofia when I was 9 and since then I was linked to her through the Good Shepherd. When I reached the right age, I took the course and started working in the suburb of Rome, in a parish, where my mother had settled an atrium. I worked there six years. When the catechists of the area began to be able to work by themselves I moved to the atrium of Via degli Orsini, where I helped Sofia in the course for catechists. This is not my "official" work. I am a researcher in the department of Religious-Historical Studies of the University of Rome and my particular job is in the field of Christianity of the First Centuries. But catechesis is the work that is "incarnated" in myself - a work that is a part of my real being. I feel it to be mine as my name is mine.

In 1981 I went to Chihuahua, Mexico where I gave a course with Maria Christlieb. It was a wonderful experience.

I should know better your language in order to be capable to come to meet you. I really wish it so much. Sofia always comes back full of enthusiasm. I am looking forward to it. I send you my love. Be assured of my constant remembrance ... at least every Tuesday, that is the day of the catechesis in Via degli Orsini, when we always speak of you and of your work.

Francesca

# Characteristics of the Good Shepherd Catechesis

by Dr. Sofia Cavalletti

translated from the Italian
by Patricia Coulter

What are the principal points which distinguish our catechesis and because of which it is called the "catechesis of the Good Shepherd?"

I think the principal point to emphasize is the experimental character of our work. In what does this "experimental" character, which our work has always had and must continue to have, consist? What we have sought to discover during these thirty years is: What aspect of God corresponds most to the vital needs of the child throughout the diverse stages of development? And we insist on "vital needs" and not simply interests.

What we have been researching is precisely this-- that aspect, out of the infinite richness of God, which appeases and satisfies that religious hunger in children. That is to say, on one hand there is God with the infinite richness of His person; on the other hand there is the human person with vital needs, essential to one's being and for the formation of one's very life, needs which change according to age. For instance, there is the spousal aspect of God's love, which obviously does not relate to the young child's needs. There is a phase in childhood called the "delirium of omnipotence" during which the child attributes extraordinary powers to any person whatsoever. Therefore the "omnipotent" God becomes just one more person who is all-powerful, but it would not reveal the particularity of the person of God.

When we manage to focus on that aspect of God which is actually in harmony with the special need of that age, then we see that the child takes possession of the message with what I would call a special avidity, and that this message calls forth profound enjoyment in the child, that unique quality of joy which we have spoken of so often, which the child experiences when encountering the religious reality. It is a joy that resounds very deeply and places the child in a state of profound peace. It is really like seeing someone who is thirsty running to water, or the sight of someone who has met and found one's own vital environment, who enjoys it with his/her whole person, and not solely with the mind, and does not want to leave it.

A second characteristic is the deschooling of catechesis-- to free catechesis from anything of a scholastic nature. Catechesis is not just one more among many academic subjects which the child learns: Catechesis is listening together to and communal celebration of the Word in which there is only one Teacher, and certainly it is not we who are the teacher. If we have twenty children before us then there are twenty-one persons who are listeners.

There is a very special richness in listening together with children. In these days great emphasis is attributed to listening in community and this is assuredly right. However, when we are all adults there is a commonality among us by the simple fact that we are adults. When we listen with children they bring to the listening and the response to that listening a particular way of living religious experience, a special manner of being with God. And so if we let ourselves become involved in the Word of God with children we too can discover or rediscover a way of drawing close to God which is different from the adult community; we can discover or rediscover some fundamental values of the religious life which I would synthesize primarily as essentiality and enjoyment-- the presence of God in our life as the source of deep enjoyment.

Deschooling also signifies renouncing every form of control in the scholastic sense. This may be a difficult point for a catechist because it is a complete relinquishment of certain means which can give us a sense of security, a security which is, however, false. For it is the greatest realities-- those things which we most want to hand on to children and which they are most capable of grasping-- which are the very realities we cannot measure in any way. To what degree do we know or live the reality that God is love? To what degree do we know or live the reality of the death and resurrection of Christ? These are realities which even we are unable to measure to what degree we live them in our own life. Imagine trying to do that for others? Obviously we can check things of secondary importance, such as names associated with geography and the altar articles, but we will never be capable of knowing the intensity with which the child can live his/her religious experience nor how deeply or fully the message has entered into them. It is only the superficial elements we can control; these elements also happen to be those that interest us only to a certain point and are of no great concern whether the child knows them or not.

In this perspective of "controls," to question the child may be most misleading, because many times if we ask a child something, the child responds quickly. The reply that is so fast in coming is often of little value; it means that what the child answers is something rather superficial in his/her life, it is just in the mind, so that the answer can be given with rapidity. Deep responses are those requiring time to be formulated, because they come forth from the depth of the person. Persons without sufficient experience with children, seeing them hesitate before responding to certain questions, often think the child does not know anything.

Nonetheless there are certain things that can give us an indication as to the quality of our work, discovered through observing children: if the child manifests an attitude of concentration, displaying the behavior of one who has found his/her own vital milieu. The children's prayer may be in some way another indicator for understanding our work. If their prayer is rich and comes forth as an expression of enjoyment in and awareness of what has been received, the message has probably been conveyed in an adequate, living form.

But when we approach the area of prayer, it is evident just how inadequate the scholastic term "control" is. It is also evident how respectful we must be in front of the mystery of the relationship between God and the child. We must learn to wait, not to pretend anything, and maybe sometimes God will let us know something about this mysterious relationship.


Before speaking of the next aspect, i.e. the method we adopt, we should first emphasize the fact that the method must correspond to the content. It is not a matter of indifference which method we use, because the method is not a neutral thing, like an empty box into which we can put anything whatsoever. The method has a spirit, a spirit which interacts with the content, either aiding the exposition or actually distorting the content's nature.

In order for catechesis to have a truly living character it is necessary to present it to children not as a "ready-made" product, already complete and fully elaborated, but rather to offer children sources or suggestions for their reflection and meditation. We can contrast two methods, the method of definitions and the parable method. Definition, and the word itself says what it does, attempts to define and hence to limit that which is by its very nature illimitable, because what we are trying to communicate to children is that the Mystery is infinite. Therefore there is, I would say, a counterposition, an incompatability of nature between the definition and the message transmitted, namely, the knowledge of the mystery. Father Alonso-Schoekel of the Biblical Institute states that we need not search for the best definition but that the definition itself is mistaken as it is defining, delimiting.

In place of definition we put parable, which may be compared to a window opening onto ever expanding horizons. The "story" of the parables guides us towards an endless research. The parable's two elements, one from everyday life and the other transcendent, act as tracks or rails along which our reflection advances always farther and aid us to meditate always more deeply. That is not to say that with the parable we are meant to grab whatever thoughts pass through our minds; instead we need to follow this guide, provided by the two elements of the parable.

In contrasting definition and parable, a different image comes to mind: in dealing with definitions we think of a large, somewhat intimidating adult who has written something of little importance in a small book, which is held in front of a very small child who must receive what the adult has written there. The child, then, is receiving a "second-hand" experience, for though it is likely that it was an experience for the adult to write the book, it is still only his/her own experience. We need not transmit our own experience to children, we must try to help the child meet the mystery of God.

In dealing with parables, we think about a great Book through which the children and adults together are trying to know who God is. The parable is a great poverty enclosing an infinite wealth, a limitless richness. Just think of the scant, poor elements of some parables: a woman making bread is not an extraordinary event, yet it is from this poverty that we can reach the transcendent reality. The parable, which does not limit, which knows its own poverty-- though containing richness, is connatural with the Mystery. With the parable method there is not the danger of distorting the nature of the Christian message. It is clear that for the parable to remain parable, to conserve the wealth of its content, it should not be explained; once explained, we reduce the parable to the level of definition-- we limit, fix, and destroy its richness.

Our method has been termed a "spiral" method, in the sense that it evolves from a central nucleus-- the curriculum for children three to six years of age, which then opens toward more vast horizons. The program for the child under six may be considered the bud of a flower which then unfolds; but the flower is already there in the bud. Therefore the catechesis for very young children, which is elaborated by following their reactions and responses, contains the essential of the Christian message: God is love; Christ is risen.


Another important element in our catechesis is the attitude of the adult, which depends to a large extent upon the way in which we look at the child. If children are seen as having great religious capacities, which are of a special quality, different from the adult's. this will be reflected in the attitude the adult assumes toward them. If children are viewed as empty beings who have and know nothing, then the adult tends to shape them according to one's own experience, and to hand over to them one's experience.

If children have their own special religious richness, what we need to do is help them care for and nurture this inner wealth. In this case the more peripheral our assistance is the better it will be. In the realm of the spirit I do not think any person can give another direct help; to do so would be an undue, unjust interference. Our task is to assist the establishing of the relationship between God and the child, with all the limits any service includes. It is an act of service that we seek to render the child; it is one which trys to enable communication to occur between two poles of the relationship, God and the child, and to allow their relationship to unfold, with the adult standing aside.


In her book <u>Education and Peace</u>, Maria Montessori asks what education really is, and offers this response: Education is the preservation of the obedience to life. In this vision, the adult is in a position of standing vigilant, of guarding and protecting, watching for what is taking place. This view presupposes that the child has a natural "obedience to life," that the child naturally goes towards particular achievements. The adult therefore is in a stance of defending this capacity for obedience to life which is within the child.

How do we offer children this peripheral assistance? It is given with the materials and the prepared environment. What is the purpose of the material? To answer this we should keep in mind that there are different moments in catechesis: the first moment is the time for listening to and receiving the message; the second is the time when the listener reconsiders in one's self what has been heard and, as St. Augustine says, recognizes its truth. This is the moment when we truly learn, through an interior conversation with the Master "who teaches inside." As for the teacher, St. Augustine, in the fourteenth chapter of De Magistro, states that ego numquam possum docere, "I can never teach." A person cannot teach another the Mystery of God, we can only help the other to seek. To "teach" is translated into Italian as "insegnare," which means to show a way, to indicate a point, to help the person turn one's gaze toward a certain place. But as for reaching that point, everyone must go it by one's self. We cannot make any person really meet God; this each must do for one's self, listening and responding to the interior Teacher. The task of the material is precisely to aid children during this second moment of learning, to help them meditate on what has been announced and to do so at their own rhythm, without adult interference, with the inner Master; this is a mystery between God, who speaks to His creatures, and the child.

Certainly, there is a presence of the adult in the material, insofar as it has been prepared by adults and checked and refined by their observation of the children's reactions to it. Nevertheless, the help the adult offers the child is indirect in form, as it permits the adult to step apart at a particular moment and leave the child for his/her own one-on-one experience of the Word received.

For the material to be of real service to the child's meditation and prayer it should be extremely simple, adhering closely to the proposed theme, and without the adult's own improvisations. If the material merely issues forth as an adult invention, it is ineffective, as we have seen so many times. The more material is our own adult conceived invention, though it may give us greater satisfaction as it reflects our own ingenuity, the more ineffectual it is for children.

The prepared environment is called the "atrium," a term used by Maria Montessori in reference to that intermediate space in the ancient Christian basilica between the street and the actual place of prayer. The atrium should also be an intermediate environment, between the school and church. We could represent it as a place of spiritual retreat; it is also, without doubt, a place for work yet one in which work easily becomes prayer. As well, the atrium is a place of worship where children and adults celebrate the Word together, for catechesis is the communal celebration of the Word.

The interrelationship between the atrium and the community merits some clarification. The atrium is the place for children and their catechists; the community is wider, inclusive of all adults. Their functions are complementary I believe; the atrium without the community may lack the invigorating "oxygen" necessary for a full life. As a result the atrium may become a place for cultivating hot-house plants which would lack resistance required to live in the external world. The community without the atrium, unfortunately a common occurrence, contains a risk as well. The risk is that children may come close to very great realities and pass them by without notice; they may go along their own path unmoved by wonder at the world surrounding them, and untouched by the enchantment which the Word of God revealing Himself should create in us.

The next consideration, in speaking of the catechesis of the Good Shepherd, is whether or not it can be called anthropological. Nowadays there is great significance attached to the experiences of those we catechize. In contrast to this we propose the approach which takes into account not so much the experience as the exigency, or vital needs, of the person. Let us distinguish: an experience is something individual, which comes from the outside and impresses itself on the person, whereas an exigency is rooted in the very depth of the person, like a hunger impelling one towards determinate realities and acheivements of which the person has vital need for one's very existence. An exigency is not peculiar only to a single individual but it is within each human person and changes and develops according to the various age levels.

This may become clearer if we mention how we came to this awareness. We began to realize that there were some themes which all children, regardless of their environment, country or diverse cultural background, responded to in the same way. The reactions we observed in the children were above all: the desire to continue working at length on specific subjects; a sense of profound, serene peace which enabled us to see how these themes were grasped by the children to the depths of their beings; and a non-scholastic quality of knowing, a knowledge which showed itself to be deeply rooted within the child.

As this happened with all children, we were unable to say it depended on this or that child, on the fact that the presentation went better with one group than another, or on the special sensibility of some children as opposed to others. It was a general fact that could be perceived in all the children we worked with. We were not, therefore, dealing with this or that child who reacted this way; or was "the" child who responded in this manner because in these fundamental themes could be found the satisfaction and fulfillment of exigencies proper to that age.

The two principal themes which drew our attention to such needs are the great Christological image of the Good Shepherd and the light, to which children from exceedingly diverse and distant milieux reacted to in exactly the same way. We also saw how the children's responses to these images alter with age. For example, in little children the Good Shepherd image gives rise to the sense of protection and serene peace, "we are comfortable with the Good Shepherd;" gradually as children grow it is the faithfulness of God's love, highlighted especially in the parable of the found sheep, that is most striking to them. There is an obvious change in the fundamental needs of children, according to the different age levels.

In conclusion, I think it is possible to say that the catechesis of the Good Shepherd may be described as anthropological inasmuch as it most definitely affords attention to the importance of the person; yet it does so not with regard to individual, personal experiences but rather in relation to the foundational structure of the human person.

Finally, a characteristic of our catechesis is its fidelity to Catholic tradition. What do I mean when I say faithfulness to tradition? The themes we give to children are all points of the Christian message which have remained living in the Church's life up to today. Think, for example, of the importance that the Good Shepherd image has had in the tradition of the Roman catacombs, it is fundamental. This is true for other points as well: baptism as "illumination" is a fundamental theme in St. Paul's catechesis, as it is with the Church Fathers.

This is also the case with the exercise of the preparation of the chalice with wine and a few drops of water. This theme is found in the catechesis of the Fathers, in which it is given particular attention as a sign of the Incarnation, of the union of the divine with the human.

This is an important fact because the themes which have remained alive throughout such a long tradition, at least two thousand years old if we do not include the themes and symbols that go back to the Jewish tradition, are evidently themes which are essential to the life of the community.

Basically, it is no surprise that it is the child who has guided us to the choice of these themes. We did not choose them ourselves, they came forth from observing children and their responses.

It does not surprise me that it is the child, whose religious life is characterized most especially by its essentiality and whose very being is so "essential," who has led us to a selection of themes which have always been essential to the life of the community.

Anders Woodfill-Hanson, age 4.

# When to Start Religious Education

by Dr. Silvana Montanaro Quattrocchi

Dr. Silvana Montanaro Quattrocchi was born in Rome in 1927. She received her degree in Medicine and Surgery from the University of Rome.

In 1955 Adele Costa Gnocchi called her to join the Staff of the Montessori School for Assistants to Infancy (a Training School for specialists of the newborn and children of the first three years of life) teaching Mental Hygiene, Child Neuropsychiatry, Nutrition and Obstetrics.

Co-founder of the Instituto Medico Italiano per lo Studio dei Fenomeni di Rilassamento e Stati di Coscienza she serves as a Trainer in Respiratory Autogenic Training (R.A.T.). In Clinics and Hospitals she prepares couples to nurture children under 3.

A psychotherapist and a scholar of the problems of the evolutive age, she conducts workshops for parents and teachers (in different countries of Europe, U.S.A. and Mexico) to make them aware of the importance of the first years of life in the building of the human personality.

She currently directs the AMI Assistants to Infancy Training Courses both in Rome, Italy and Houston, Texas.

 

The mystery of the human being is really great - a body made a "living spirit" (Genesis 2,7). This puts us in a very special position towards our Creator and the rest of creation. The necessity of a relationship with God will always be present in the human being in every moment of his life.

Studies of the fetal psyche have clearly demonstrated the participation of the embryo and of the fetus to the life going on around him/her which arrives through the mother. The Bible illustrates this phenomenon very well when it talks of John the Baptist, a fetus of six months, who answers the salutation of Mary to Elisabeth (Luke 1,41).

In the last decade the interest and the studies of the human sciences has helped us to discover a little bit more who we are. The time of infancy is now known to be the fundamental time of development of our personality. To reach the complete development of the human person it is necessary to fulfill all his/her needs which include the wish to meet God because this person has, since the very beginning, biological, psychological and spiritual necessities. All of them have the same importance for a harmonious development of the person. The integration of the various components is the result of the experiences the new being will have in his/her environment so it is essential that all the potentialities receive the right "education" as a help to come out. The talents, the personal richness of the child, must find the possibility of being used to produce their fruits. The favorable soil for this development is the human community where each of us must be accepted and through its mediation the personality components can grow and form into a whole.

These components are at least six:

      religious activity          play activity
      cognitive development   freedom to choose what to do
      work with hands            unity with all human beings

The development of each human being is therefore strictly connected with the development which remains necessary all through life to be able to continue to progress towards perfection. But we are here interested only in the beginning of life - to underline the importance of a religious education in this period.

The pregnancy is a long time of 280 days during which the child is in a very special relationship with the mother but this relationship can be complete and reach the three levels (biological, psychological and spiritual) only if there is an immediate "answer" to the presence of the child. This answer must be not only the acceptance of his/her presence but must be united with the wonder for the miracle of the life: from the very small to the bigger, from one cell to the complexity of the human being who is the most extraordinary creature because in him/her it is reflected the image and likeness of God (Genesis 1, 26-27).

As we have a memory since the moment of conception it is good to offer to the child the sounds of simple prayers said with slow and clear voice or sung. These moments of "prayer with the child" can become repeated encounters with him/her during the day. In the morning and the evening the two parents can pray and sing together (the child is able to recognize the two voices very well) and we can have even during the pregnancy the praise and thanks to the Lord from the new family. We pray with the child because he/she is able to participate and these moments of religious life can become "points of reference" during the intrauterine life and can continue after the birth and contribute in reassuring the new born that not everything has changed in the new life. Why could not the parents sing one of their hymns of praise when the newborn is laying on the mother's chest before cutting the umbilical cord? The well known voices and music are really appropriate to receive the child into the new environment and to convey the continuity of the relationship. This experience of continuity is fundamental in avoiding the birth trauma: the child must feel still attached even if in a different way. It is to be understood that all the developmental phases should be only new ways of the same relationship with life.

A short but joyful hymn of thanksgiving can be introduced every time before the meal and another hymn can close it; we can use part of the prayers of the community in which we live or we can take phrases from the Psalms. The hymn must be a short one but can be repeated while we are going to the easy chair on which the milk is given and when the child is still in our arms before putting him/her back to bed.

Every time the child must be changed and we are in front of him/her, face to face, we can say: "I thank the Lord (or the Father, the Son and the Holy Spirit) for the gift of a child like you" and, of course, we will add all the loving and sweet things that are usually said on this occasion. The continuous acknowledgment of God's gift, represented by the presence of the child in our house, can have very important consequences for the baby and for the adults. The words of thanksgiving will bring to the child the meaning of having value which is so important in building self-esteem. The consciousness of our importance as human beings can be received only from our image reflected in the mirrors (the significant adults) that surround the child: for this reason the parents are the most significant ones. The same words can remind the adults that, in reality, the life comes from God and it belongs to Him and all this can make easier the "service to the life" which is the correct attitude of educators. The tendency to consider the child our possession with the subsequent block of his/her development can be avoided.

During the pre and post-natal life we can use Gregorian chant and symphonic religious music in accordance with the liturgical times. This special concert can be for all the family a very useful moment of relaxation and meditation.

The gesture language too is very important and can be understood early by the child; a Cross sign can be done slowly on ourselves or on the baby at the beginning and at the end of the day or entering and going out of the Church. The head can be bent in a gesture of salutation and we can smile to an icon of Christ or the Virgin every time we pass in front of them. The hands and arms can be elevated in a gesture of invocation when praying the "Our Father" or other special prayers. All these experiences, repeated in the everyday life, can start a religious education which will continue for ever, in different ways, according to the age.

A last suggestion in order to start well our relationship with the child: the newborn must be called, from the first day, with his/her real name. The name with which the child has been christened; the name used by the Good Shepherd to call him/her. For no reason must the name become shorter, or be preceeded by "little" or transformed into a nickname. In doing so we will demonstrate a religious respect for the greatness of the child. The fact that this greatness is hidden in a small body will transform the child into a living parable in front of our eyes and will help us to discontinue the mistake of giving importance in proportion to the size.

Dr. Montanaro writes: "I met Sofia and her work a long time ago when my first daughter (now 31) was 3 and started the Good Shepherd Catechesis. The way she and my other children were talking about God and the kind of works they were bringing back pushed me to do the entire Course with Sofia and Gianna until I got the Diploma in 1964. During the Course I developed a great interest for the Bible and its original texts so I decided to study at the Biblical Institute of Rome where, in five years, I then graduated.

"My collaboration with Sofia is in lecturing at her course on Child Psychology and Montessori Pedagogy. In the last years I took responsibility for the group of children preparing themselves for Confirmation. The presence of the Good Shepherd changed my life and I feel that is has even enhanced my understanding of psychology with a better insight into the relationship between the different parts of our personality." (October 9th, 1984)

by Elizabeth Mullin

Jesus is hearts.

Elizabeth Mullin, age 8.

# The Water and the Wine of the Eucharist

by Dr. Sofia Cavalletti

translated from the Italian
by Claudia Riordan

After Vatican II there was a tendency to eliminate the ever so many symbolisms that had been developing without sufficient base and, in the atrium of Via degli Orsini, some elements (e.g. the symbology of the priest's vestments) were dropped. There was also a discussion as to whether or not it was opportune to continue to present to the children the "mingling" of the few drops of water with the Eucharistic wine. We observed the children and we realized that they repeated the gesture with such a great concentration that it couldn't be something devoid of meaning.

We observed, moreover, that the older ones refer constantly to the mingling in order to express our participation in the Mass, particularly when it speaks of the fact that Jesus is not alone in offering Himself to the Father. Very often the children clarify our presence in the offering saying, "We are also in the chalice, in the drops of water."

It's one of those cases in which an element of the highest theology and an essential aspect of Christian life are seemingly connatural to the child, so much does he/she possess it in a deep and, at the same time, spontaneous manner. The meaning of the "mingling" is one of those things that the child has learned without knowing why: one of those things that is his/her own, which has penetrated into the deepest part of himself/herself, not so much through the words of the catechist but through the child's own personal meditation, helped by the work of the hands.

The "mingling" is also a document of that essentiality of the child which has guided us to lay aside some elements of the catechesis while preserving those which have remained alive in the tradition of the Church, even when we'd somewhat lost the meaning of them. Indeed, the "mingling" has a place in tradition which goes back to the first centuries, and the richness of its significance is made evident by the Fathers of the Church. From among the many citations that could be made, I select only a few.

Hear how St. Cyprian, Bishop of Carthage, expresses himself around 250 A.D.:

> Divine Scripture declared in the Apocalypse (1:15; 14:2; 19:6)*
> that the waters represent the people. And this we obviously see
> also in the sacrament of the chalice. In fact, as Christ carried
> all of us and carried our sins, so we see that in the water the
> people are signified, and that in the wine the blood of Christ is
> signified. Therefore, when the water is mixed with the wine in
> the chalice, it is the people that unite with Christ, it is the
> throng of the faithful that conjoin and unite with Him whom they
> believe in. This union, this mingling of the water and the wine
> in the chalice of the Lord is something that is inseparable.
> Thus nothing could ever separate the Chruch from Christ; nothing
> could separate from Him the people who are in the Church, and
> who faithfully and firmly persevere in the faith, so as to be
> always united with Him by a love which, of the two of them, will
> make one, unique whole. When the chalice of the Lord is conse-
> crated, water alone cannot be offered, just as wine alone cannot
> be offered. Indeed, if wine alone is offered, the blood of
> Christ is present without us; and if there is only water, the
> people are present without Christ.[1]

---

*English translator's note: St. Cyprian refers to Revelation 1:15. Revelation 14:2 and 19:6 are related references of great importance.

[1] St. Cyprian, *Letters*, Number 63.

Even before Cyprian, Irenaeus, Bishop of Lyons between 130 and 200 A.D., knew that there were some heretics, the Ebionites, who didn't admit to the union of God with the people and "for this reason they condemn the mixing of the celestial wine and want only earthly water."[2]

In the Middle Ages, St. Thomas Aquinas comes back to the subject in an explicit and precise manner; thus he writes in the Summa Theologiae:

> The wine which is offered in the Eucharist must be mixed with water. First of all, on account of its institution: for it is believed that probably the Lord instituted this sacrament in wine mixed with water according to the custom of that country (Prov. 9:5).
>
> Secondly, because it harmonizes with the representation of Our Lord's Passion....(John 19:34).
>
> Thirdly, because it serves to signify the effect of the sacrament, which is the union of the Christian people with Christ.
>
> Fourthly, because this is appropriate to the ultimate effect of this sacrament which is the entering (eschatological) into everlasting life. St. Ambrose says, in fact: 'The water overflows in the chalice and springs forth into life everlasting.'[3]

How many of the faithful have there been throughout the world and down through the centuries, who have followed the hands of the priest and of the deacon carefully pouring a few drops of water into the chalice?

It has been beautiful to rediscover the richness of this gesture with the children. It has been beautiful to see once again how the children have been our teachers in remaining faithful to all that is essential which has been preserved in the tradition of the Church.

Matthew Brown, Atrium of the Church of St. Frances Cabrini, Minneapolis, Minnesota.

In Matthew's words, the wine is "Jesus" and in the water are "Jesus' friends."

---

[2] Irenaeus, Bishop of Lyons, Against the Heretics, V, 1, 3.

[3] St. Thomas Acquinas, Summa Theologiae, III, qu. 74, art. 6.

# *Let us pray with the children*

Prayers of children 3 through 7

### Age 3

This spontaneous prayer took place at the children's liturgy when prayers of the faithful had begun. The children had all gathered in front of the altar after the priest had told the Nativity Story. The priest invited the children and adults to offer their Prayers of the Faithful. This child responded immediately and said into the microphone....

"This is a very special prayer." (long pause)
"This is a really good prayer." (another long pause)
"Dear God, our father and mother, thank you for our food."

Later we discovered this was the child's mealtime prayer.

### Age 4

"Thank you God for the light because we need to see."

"God bless God. God bless the sun. God bless everything. Bless even the dragons. God bless space. Bless us."

### Age 5

"Thank you father God for making the universe out of nothing; thank you father God for making me out of nothing. Thank you for light."

### Age 7

"The Good Shepherd is in front of us and beside us and behind us and He holds our hand so we don't fall or get into trouble or other stuff. He is in our heart, in our hearts is God. Alleluia. God bless us. We all know what God is (pause) Amen. Alleluia."

"My friend, name is God. When I ask him something he answers me."

"The Kingdom of God is the food and the water and Mom and Dad and John and Sopana and home and Bear (the family dog)."

### Age 6 and 7

"I will never look for things more beautiful, more good, more full of love than life in the sheepfold. Alleluia."
It is tiring, I know, to open the door open to the sap, but it is worth while, because there is no greater and more important thing in our life. Alleluia. Without the sap, we cannot live, because it is the life of Jesus in me. Alleluia."

"Thank you for the bread that makes us the same as you; and the same as others."

"Lord, I do not know how many thanks are necessary to fill you to the brim. And I have nothing to ask, because you give me everything and my praises are infinite."

"Peace is with us. Love is with us, because God is with us. God is peace, God is love, God is light. God is our salvation. Hurrah to the peace! Hurrah to the love! God died to save us, but then he was risen."

"Jesus, you put in our heart a light more beautiful and bigger than the light of the sun. I like the sun. I love you because you are good and you are more beautiful than the sun."

"Let me do, Lord, something like a bath in your light."

"God"-drawn by Michael Anderson on his 5th birthday, January 6th, 1985.

# Children in Front of the Mystery of Death

Let us begin collecting some of the reactions of children facing the mystery of death. We earnestly implore catechists to observe the children in this regard, also studying those elements of catechesis which help them the most in facing this reality. It is clear that each time that we announce resurrection we touch the subject "death," and we give the greatest help for accepting the mystery of it. It would be interesting for us, however, to know which themes are coming up most frequently in the expressions of the children when they find themselves faced directly with death because of their own illness or through the illness or death of dear ones.

Following are those accounts thus far recorded.

Sofia Cavalletti

Chihuahua, Mexico, 1980

Jorge is six years old; his mother died six months ago. During the last Mass at the catechetical center before vacation, he seemed distracted. But then all of a sudden, during the homily he gets up and says to the priest: "My mom has been dead six months and I want you to know that now she has more light." Then he sits down tranquilly.

From a letter of Emilia Sandoval, Chihuahua, Mexico, December 10th, 1983

In an air crash in Chihuahua, ten people from the same family die. Enrique, ten years old, the only survivor, loses his parents, three brothers, his grandparents, two uncles and a cousin. What could be done to help him?

The catechist of Enrique's group had presented the "Prayers of Intercession" from the Mass; the presentation had greatly impressed most of the children, but Enrique had remained skeptical and said, "Certain times I believe in this and in parousia; but certain times I don't succeed in believing." After giving it alot of thought, the catechist, Claudia, decides to go see the child at home. She asks, "Will you be coming back to catechism?"

"Yes, tomorrow I am coming."

"What will you do?"

"I will work with the prayers of the dead, starting from where I left off."

Then the catechist asks if he would like to do something special with his group in connection with what has happened. "What?" asks the child.

"We could do the Mass in the atrium with just your group and so remember your parents, your brothers, and pray hard to the Good Shepherd for you in this very difficult time that you're going through."

He brightened up his eyes, which before had looked lost, and he said, "I like the idea."

Note to reader: the next parts of the narrative are written in the first person.

So the Mass was done in the atrium. The children behaved with an impressive seriousness, understanding, and affection; they decided that the Gospel reading most fitting was The True Vine, explaining their own reasons with an impressive simplicity and depth: "We are all united in the Vine, those who are here and those who are no longer here. We are one in Jesus...." There were many comments, but through the emotion of the moment I have forgotten them. Enrique, at a certain moment, said, "Yes, we are all united; but the branches here on earth need one another," as if he wanted to say: "Don't leave me alone...."

We continued the preparation and the catechist asked him if he wanted us to light the Paschal candle and a candle for each one of the people who had died. There were ten candles ready for the members of the family. The child responded "yes," but that two candles were missing for the pilots. Then he asked Father Padilla if the children could read their "Prayers of Intercession." Father said yes and that then he would repeat them (because they are part of the Eucharistic Prayer).

We finished the preparation and began the Mass; before the Gospel the child lit the Paschal candle and the twelve smaller candles saying the name of each one of the dead. The True Vine was read and there were again more comments, then the Prayer of the Faithful which the children had prepared. And so the Mass continued until the "Prayers of Intercession" which the children read; Enrique wanted to read the prayer for the dead. Everyone did it with seriousness and they were very much involved with what they were doing. When it was finished, Father Padilla looked at me, took the Bread and the Wine, and continued the Mass. He did not repeat what the children had already said; it wasn't necessary. Everyone received communion and we felt the peace that the presence of Jesus had left there in all of us. The Mass ended, the priest left, and the children kept on singing for awhile.

Sofia Cavalletti, Rome, Italy, May 17, 1982

For the first time I present the new material on the "Prayers of Intercession." I present them to Silvia (ten years old, who had lost her father a few days ago) in such a way as to be able to talk to her about the presence of the dead during the Eucharist. I had never really been able to "talk" with Silvia; for the first time I see her conversing with animation and ease; in her eyes I catch flashes of light.

Betty Hissong, Cleveland, Ohio, June 18, 1984

Betty's atrium is part of her Montessori environment where the children meet daily.

Michael was 3½ when he entered my class last fall. He is a perfectly beautiful child, a deep thinking child, and delightful. His family is great too. Several weeks, however, after school started, Michael began to have real problems. At first I thought it was merely a delayed separation problem, but the usual remedies for this were not working. Rarely would a day go by without his crying, without his being fearful and anxious about really little things. I was convinced that he was basically a stable child emotionally, but that there was something extraordinary occurring that was causing him difficulties.

I was, of course, keeping in daily contact with his mother. Seems that a very close aunt of theirs was dying from cancer. The family was very involved in her care, in getting nursing help for her when she came home, and in trying to get her into a home for victims of cancer. There was a lot of stress in the family because of this and because of some business difficulties the father was also encountering. We tried everything- sympathizing with Michael, ignoring him, being firm with him. Nothing seemed to be working. Even the children were getting impatient with his fears and cries.

We had just made up our mind that Michael should undergo some special exam by a child psychiatrist. I'd find myself thinking about what to do with Michael all the time-night and day. And then one night, in the middle of the night, I remembered Patricia's (Coulter) telling about the little girl in the hospital who would not communicate with anyone until after the presentation of the Good Shepherd. The next day I took Michael aside for a private presentation of the Good Shepherd. I'm sure it was grace working. Michael became so involved. Even though he had never had the presentation before he seemed to realize almost immediately that he was one of the sheep. He was very peaceful and happy. I was afraid almost to believe what was happening; I was even telling myself that what I was experiencing was merely the result of Michael getting special attention from me. That day, however, Michael did not cry even once.

When his mother picked him up after school he immediately told her that he had not cried. She was almost afraid to ask any question and merely said, "Well, that's great, Michael." Then he said, "Well, aren't you going to ask me why?" She hesitated and said, "Well, if you want to tell me..." Michael then went on to tell her that he didn't have to be afraid anymore because the Good Shepherd was with him always. He told her all about the Good Shepherd. From that day on we started to see progress for Michael. We did get him to the psychiatrist who said, as I had suspected, that Michael was emotionally stable, but that the experience of the dying aunt was something that he was not yet able to handle well with his sensitive nature.

Today, Michael is great. His aunt did die in Jaunary, but Michael is O.K. Thanks to the Good Shepherd.

Prayer to God

If a bomb goes off, I want to stay alive.
I hope my gramma and grampa are back for my
birthday. I hope my great gramma stays alive
until she's 100. I hope no more of my friends
move away from me. I hope we have a happy life.
"Oh, the Lord is good to me, and so I thank
the Lord for giving me the things I need,
the sun, and the rain, and the apple seed.
The Lord is good to me."* Amen.+

---

*From the song, "Johnny Appleseed."

+"Prayer to God" by Joel Rice, age 6.

# The Anointings at Baptism

by Catherine Maresca

There have been many discussions among catechists about the difference between and the meaning of the two anointings of Baptism: The anointing with the oil of catechumens before Baptism, and the anointing with chrism after baptism. Careful reading of the following blessings will help to clarify this. The first two are the blessings of the oil and chrism by the Bishops at the chrism Mass, ordinarily held on Holy Thursday morning. The final two blessings are used for the anointings during the rite of Baptism itself.

BLESSING OF THE OIL OF CATECHUMENS

Lord God, protector of all who believe in you,
bless this oil
and give wisdom and strength
to all who are anointed with it
in preparation for their baptism.
Bring them to a deeper understanding of the gospel,
help them to accept the challenge of Christian living,
and lead them to the joy of new birth
in the family of your Church.
We ask this through Christ our Lord.

R.: Amen.


CONSECRATION OF THE CHRISM

God our maker,
source of all growth in holiness,
accept the joyful thanks and praise
we offer in the name of your Church.

In the beginning, at your command,
the earth produced fruit-bearing trees.
From the fruit of the olive tree
you have provided us with oil for holy chrism.
The prophet David sang of the life and joy
that the oil would bring us in the sacraments of your love.

After the avenging flood,
the dove returning to Noah with an olive branch
announced your gift of peace.
This was a sign of a greater gift to come.
Now the waters of baptism wash away the sins of men,
and by the anointing with olive oil
you make us radiant with your joy.

CONSECRATION OF THE CHRISM (continued)

At your command,
Aaron was washed with water,
and your servant Moses, his brother,
anointed him priest.
This too foreshadowed greater things to come.
After your Son, Jesus Christ our Lord,
asked John for baptism in the waters of Jordan,
you sent the Spirit upon him
in the form of a dove
and by the witness of your own voice
you declared him to be your only, well-beloved Son.
In this you clearly fulfilled the prophecy of David,
that Christ would be anointed with the oil of gladness
beyond his fellow men.

And so, Father, we ask you to bless this oil you have created.
Fill it with the power of your Holy Spirit
through Christ your Son.
It is from him that chrism takes its name
and with chrism you have anointed
for yourself priests and kings,
prophets and martyrs.

Make this chrism a sign of life and salvation
for those who are to be born again in the waters of baptism.
Wash away the evil they have inherited from sinful Adam,
and when they are anointed with this holy oil
make them temples of your glory,
radiant with the goodness of life
that has its source in you.

Through this sign of chrism
grant them royal, priestly, and prophetic honor,
and clothe them with incorruption.
Let this be indeed the chrism of salvation
for those who will be born again of water and the Holy Spirit.
May they come to share eternal life
in the glory of your kingdom.
We ask this through Christ our Lord.

R.: Amen.


ANOINTING WITH THE OIL OF CATECHUMENS

We anoint you with the oil of salvation
in the name of Christ our Savior.
May he strengthen you with his power,
who lives and reigns for ever and ever.

R. Amen

ANOINTING AFTER BAPTISM (with Chrism)

God the Father of our Lord Jesus Christ,
has freed you from sin,
given you a new birth by water and the Holy Spirit,
and welcomed you into his holy people.

He now anoints you with the chrism of salvation.
As Christ was anointed Priest, Prophet, and King,
so may you live always as a member of his body,
sharing everlasting life.

R.: Amen


Another difference between the two anointings is the difference between the oil and the chrism. The oil is olive oil and the chrism is a mixture of oil and perfumes or other sweet smelling matter. Also the anointing of oil takes place on the breast and both hands, while the anointing of chrism is on the crown of the head.

From all this information the catechist of 3-6 year old children must choose a few words which will introduce the essential meaning of each anointing. One way to go about this is to look for repeated themes, such as "strength" in the first anointing, or "joy" in the second. I am sure this will continue to be a point of discussion among us.

# Our Association takes birth

Dear Members and Friends of the Catechesis of the Good Shepherd,

During the weekend of November 2nd-4th the five board members of our newly-formed association met in Washington, D.C. We thank all of you who were supporting us in prayer. None of us felt "equal to the task," but we did feel the presence of the Holy Spirit and were blessed by a sense of unity among us. In our discussions and decisions, we tried to keep in mind the opinions and suggestions which were expressed by each of you who participated in the association-formation meetings in St. Paul this past summer.

The main agenda items we dealt with were:

1. <u>The Role of the Center</u>

    -After much prayer and discussion, the board reaffirmed the original definition of "the center" (as stated in the meetings in Washington, D.C. in 1983) as being both an office where the main work of coordination and administration is done and an atrium (or atriums) so that the religious experience of children is kept visible and at the heart of all the business we conduct.

    -For now, Washington, D.C. is the center and Christian Family Montessori School's atrium is the atrium of the center. The Association and CFMS are thus also financially linked in that ten hours per month of the association coordinator's time are spent in observing in the center's atrium and consulting with the atrium staff in order to insure that the work being done there is truly representative of the work of the Catechists of the Good Shepherd.

    -The board restated that the location of the center may change in the future. They also discussed the likelihood of including other atriums in the Washington area as part of the center and so to offer visitors a wider "sampling" of what the work is like.

    -The current work at the center includes a "membership drive," correspondence with catechists and others seeking information and advice, establishing a more solid relationship with the Church via the Archdiocese of Washington, printing a directory of members, compiling data on children's responses in various atriums, coordinating training plans, etc.

2. <u>Finances and Budget</u>

    -Although our financial needs at this point are fairly low and, so far, are being met, we anticipate greater expenses than income in the near future. Thus, we encourage you to send in your membership dues and to encourage others to join. Also, we ask that you pray with us for the right money sources to be made available.

    -An annual financial report will be made available at the annual "General Membership Meeting" to be scheduled during the summer courses.

3. <u>Regional Centers</u>

    -With the printing of the directory, you can learn who is in your area.

    -The board will offer help in other ways so that community can be built in the different regions (e.g. suggestions and guidelines for workshops and retreats) with the goal of eventually establishing more formal "regional centers."

4. **By-Laws**

    -We are in the process of incorporating as a non-profit organization and applying for a charter in the state of Maryland (since that is the actual address of the office and atrium).

5. **Newsletter and Directory Publication**

6. **Training**

    -The board, with Sofia's approval, has drawn up a tentative outline of training courses. They are:

    Course 1 - The 3-6 Cycle
    Course 2 - Conclusion of the 3-6 and Beginning of 6-8
    Course 3 - Conclusion of the 6-8 Cycle
    Course 4 - Sacramental Part of the 9-12 Cycle
    Course 5 - Typology (History of Salvation for 9-12)

    The above courses would continue to be three to four week summer courses. Included in the course work will be album making and checking, and an examination of some kind if the participant is seeking "certification."

    -The board reaffirmed our eventual goal of also offering "year-round" training as soon as such a program can be established.

    -The 1985 summer courses will be in St. Paul again, July 15th through August 2nd. Please see the course announcement on page 26 of this newsletter.

7. **Trainers and Assistants**

    -The board recognizes the great need we have for a larger pool of persons who are prepared to teach or assist in teaching of courses. We are working with Sofia on establishing requirements and training opportunities for trainers and assistants.

8. **Materials**

    -The board restated the importance of material-making as part of the catechist's spiritual formation and the building of community around the atrium (discovering and utilizing the skills of persons in the community). They also recognized the need for clearer guidelines for association members regarding the reproduction and selling of materials and are presently working on such guidelines. For now, we simply ask that you not reproduce or sell any materials in the name of the Catechesis of the Good Shepherd without first consulting with the Center.

    -The board is continuing to work with Sister Sheila Sentiff on the printing of a catechist's "manual" - a listing and detailed description of the materials.

    -We are also working with Sister Sheila and others in the making up of a "travel set" of materials which can be used at the summer courses.

Finally, the board made plans for a General Membership Meeting to be held in St. Paul just prior to the opening of the courses. The meeting will take place at 9:00 A.M. on Saturday, July 13th. Please refer to the Summer Announcement page for details. We hope to see many of you there. Also, we encourage you to write to the center:

- to ask for any needed assitance with your work
- to give input on the agenda items discussed above
- and, especially, to share your reflections on your work with the children and their specific responses in the atrium.

With prayers for you, your work, and the building of our community,

*Rebekah*

November 30, 1984

Rebekah Rojcewicz
Association Coordinator

# INNAMORAMENTO

"Innamoramento" is the name the members have chosen for our association. It is an Italian word which means "to fall in love, to be enamoured," and what we are about is "falling in love" with God.

Dr. Cavalletti says, "I think that innamoramento is the basis of religious life, and also of moral life because moral life and religious life are not two different things. If we help the child to establish a relationship with God in enjoyment, in innamoramento, then we have also done the best moral formation of the child. You all know how much psychology now stresses the importance of love in every field of human life. I think that a global innamoramento is possible for everybody before six. It may happen, of course, for anyone at any moment of our lives but before six it's possible and it's easy for everybody. It comes out quite naturally from the depths of their soul. They really fall in love quite naturally.....There are many things to be done after six but there is one thing to be done before six - and it is to help the children to fall in love." This quote is from a lecture, "Catechetics for the Child Under Six," presented at the North American College in Rome, Italy, in 1977.

The calligraphy for our stationary was done by Rebekah Rojcewicz; an example is above.

This past summer 48 catechists met in St. Paul, Minnesota to study with Dr. Cavalletti and Maria Christlieb. We met at the College of St. Thomas for three weeks: 20 participants studied the sacraments for children ages 6-8 with Sofia and 28 people were introduced to the Catechesis of the Good Shepherd for 3-6 year olds with Maria.

During the courses, meetings were held twice to solidify the actual beginnings of an association. We discussed legal proceedings of incorporation, by-laws, goals for the coming year and, most importantly, how the formation of this association would help in serving the children we work with. The first Board of Directors was elected by those present and they are: Rebekah Rojcewicz, Association Coordinator, Hyattsville, Maryland; Cathy Maresca, Administrator, Washington, D.C.; Carol Dittberner, Secretary, St. Paul, Minnesota; Barbara Kahn, Treasurer, Cleveland, Ohio; Sandi Yonikus, Consultant, Houston, Texas.

It was a busy and fruitful three weeks for all who attended. Our community grows in faith and love for each other as it grows and works "around the child."

Participants in Course I came from Canada, Mexico, and many parts of the United States. Photo courtesy of Bert O'Bryan.

Dr. Sofia Cavalletti and Maria Christlieb, St. Paul, Minnesota, August, 1984. Photo courtesy of Carol Dittberner.

Joan Miller, St. Paul, visits with Maria Reed from Phoenix, Arizona. Photo courtesy of Bert O'Bryan.

# Summer Course Announcements

We are pleased to announce the following courses for summer study sponsored by the Association for the Catechesis of the Good Shepherd. There will also be a Retreat and a General Membership meeting preceeding the courses. We are happy to welcome particpants to St. Paul, Minnesota again this summer, especially as it will be a time to celebrate the Tenth Anniversary of Dr. Cavalletti's first course in the United States, in St. Paul in 1975. The seed she planted then has taken root...

COURSE I: A CATECHIST'S TRAINING COURSE FOR THE 3-6 YEAR OLD CHILD-AN INTRODUCTION

    TRAINER: Maria Christlieb
    Maria studied with Dr. Cavalletti in Rome from 1979-81 and worked as Sofia's assistant in 1982. She has trained catechists in Mexico and the United States; she also holds the AMI Primary Diploma from Perugia, Italy. Maria spent last year studying in Jerusalem.
    DATES: July 15th-August 2nd, 1985
    LOCATION: College of St. Thomas, St. Paul, Minnesota
    DESCRIPTION: A course designed to attune the participants to the religious life of the young child. It will include lectures, demonstrations of materials, making a teacher's album, and practicing with the materials. Some of the subjects covered include: the religious capacities of the child, role of the environment, the parable method, Christ as the Light, Christ as the Good Shepherd, and the role of the adult.
    PREREQUISITES: None. Montessori teachers, religious educators, chaplains and parents are welcome to participate.

COURSE II: A CATECHIST'S TRAINING COURSE-EXTENSIONS FOR THE 3-6 YEAR OLD CHILD AND AN INTRODUCTION TO THE 6-8 YEAR OLD CHILD

    TRAINER: Sofia Cavalletti
    Dr. Cavalletti is a noted Hebrew and biblical scholar and Director of the Maria Montessori School of Religion in Rome. During the past 30 years she, and her co-worker Gianna Gobi, have developed the Catechesis of the Good Shepherd based on the philosophy of Dr. Maria Montessori. Her work in Rome includes a program for children ages 2½-12 years. Her most recent book, THE RELIGIOUS POTENTIAL OF THE CHILD, documents her years of experience with the children.
    DATES: July 15th-August 2nd, 1985
    LOCATION: College of St. Thomas, St. Paul, Minnesota
    DESCRIPTION: Completion of the materials and themes used with the 3-6 year old child including the Prophecies, Infancy Narratives and Liturgical Calendar. Introduction of materials for the 6-8 year olds, including the History of the Kingdom, the gifts, and discussion of the religious capacities of this age group.
    PREREQUISITES: Course I.

COURSE FEES: $400 for each course. The courses have limited space so early application is advised. To apply write to:
    Cathy Maresca
    3628 Rhode Island Avenue
    Mt. Rainier, Maryland 20712

A RETREAT FOR CATECHISTS

This Retreat will be led by Sofia Cavalletti and Brother Ignatius. Brother Ignatius has been in close contact with the Catechesis of the Good Shepherd through the work done in Toronto, Canada.

DATES: July 9th-12th, 1985
    (arrival on July 8th in the afternoon or evening)
LOCATION: Franciscan Retreat Center
    16385 Saint Francis Lane, Prior Lake, Minnesota 55372
FEES: $195
    This cost covers the fee for the Retreat and lodging with meals at the Retreat Center from Monday, July 8th through Sunday, July 14th.

This Retreat is open to any catechist who has completed Course I or to any persons having an equivalent initiation into the Catechesis.

For further details or registration please write:
    Cathy Maresca
    3628 Rhode Island Avenue
    Mt. Rainier, Maryland 20712

GENERAL MEMBERSHIP MEETING

Our Annual General Membership meeting will be held on Saturday, July 13th beginning at 9:00 A.M. It will take place at the Francsican Retreat Center in Prior Lake, Minnesota. Please note above as it follows the Retreat. Those members who would like to attend the meeting and the courses but who may not be attending the Retreat are encouraged to come. We will try to arrange lodging for you at the Retreat Center <u>if space is available</u> at the cost of $20 a day (meals and room) for Friday and Saturday nights.

Please write Cathy Maresca at the above address if you will be attending the meeting.

SUMMER SCHEDULE

Monday, July 8th-Arrival for those attending Retreat
Tuesday, July 9th-Retreat begins and continues until
Friday, July 12th-Retreat ends with noon meal
Saturday, July 13th-9:00 A.M. General Membership Meeting
Sunday, July 14th-Evening-Arrival of course participants
Monday, July 15th-Training Courses open and continue through August 1st
Friday, August 2nd-Closing and departure in the morning

ANNOUNCEMENT

Bert and Marty O'Bryan of Phoenix, Arizona are working on the film "Mustard Seed" which is planned for completion by this summer's course. A recent trip to Mexico to visit Maria Christlieb has produced several more hours of video-taped observations of the work in Mexico City and Chihuahua. This will be edited and included in the film to give an example of how this work has grown in a country where is has been supported by the local bishop and clergy, as well as many volunteer catechists. We were pleased to see how the work has flourished.

More information about the video will be made available after it is completed.

# A Report from Rome

by Mary Polta

I began thinking seriously of going to Rome to study at Sofia's Center for Catechesis in the fall of 1983. I had known about the Center since the early 1970's when, while studying at the Montessori Teacher Training Center in St. Paul, I had asked Mr. Joosten, the director, about Montessori Religious Education. "Learn Italian and go to Rome to Sofia Cavalletti's Center," he told me. At the time it seemed to be an impossible answer.

Sofia's coming to St. Paul in 1975 to present a course in English, on the other hand, seemed like a dream come true. For the five weeks of the course my mornings, afternoons and evenings were spent immersed in the catechesis of the child from 3-6 years. I made drawings of almost all materials presently in use in my Atrium today during that course. Participants from the course started almost immediately to go to Rome. Patricia Coulter went first, in the fall of 1975, to study for two years. Anna Guida went a year or so later. Sr. Sheila Sentiff went for one year. Since then more people have gone. In September of 1984 I went for $3\frac{1}{2}$ months.

Seeing the places and the people I had heard about felt unreal. The language was all in Italian. Two things helped: 1) the curriculum was the 3-6 year old child, and the liturgy, both of which were familiar; 2) the materials were present: seeing as well as hearing was possible. Also Sofia met with those of us who were non-Italian weekly to discuss the lectures in English. When Gianna Gobbi, Sofia's collaborator who is at the Atrium in Rome, presented materials to her group of five year olds and younger, my language was strong enough to understand most of it: Gianna's words are simple and few and she has the materials to show what she is talking about. Sofia's presentations to the middle group of 6-10 year olds, on the other hand, were more difficult to follow because of the extra amount of words needed.

The language is a difficulty. I attended Language classes daily for three hours for $2\frac{1}{2}$ months. These helped immensely. I am presently working to improve my language by reading simple Italian lesson books, listening to tapes, and reading Italian novels with the help of a dictionary.

I've begun working on an album. The album is arranged according to the Church year. It is looseleaf and there is just one album for all ages, $2\frac{1}{2}$ - 12 years. I put in lessons that have been presented to me. Those that I don't know about will be added as I learn about them.

The course in Rome is two years long. This year is on the child from 3-6 and the liturgy. It is material I have had many times; it is still new. I am not bored. I am beginning to see a little into what is cultural about the presentations and what is essential. (My Montessori training was Indian, the Atrium is Italian, and I have seen American presentations.) Watching Gianna welcome her children for the first time and Sofia presenting materials to her group of 6-10 aged children brought new understandings. I would like to see presentations to children added to our courses: a new dimension is added.

Seeing the children week after week being drawn into the mystery and wonder of life that is made visible through the materials increased my faith. I wish that it were the beginning of the liturgical year now so that those presentations given in Rome could be handed on immediately to the children in my Atrium! I hope I can bring some of the Spirit from Rome to Minnesota.

# The Children's Center in Houston, Texas

Introduction

The Children's Center is a research and development center for the study of the moral and spiritual development of children and their use of religious language in this process. The primary research tool is a worship-education center in which the children work with materials designed to incarnate images embodied in sacred stories, parables, and liturgy. These materials are placed on shelves which surround the child in the Center with the whole language system of the Christian Tradition. The children are presented materials and they respond in play and art which is photographed and video-taped for study.

The research population is a group of children from about 2½ to 12 years of age. About 40 families are involved in the Project. The children from 2½-7 years meet on Saturday mornings from 10:00-12:00. The children from 7-12 years of age meet from 1:00-3:00. The terms of involvement of the children are 12 weeks before Christmas and 12 weeks before Easter.

The Children's Center depends on the generous gifts of its supporters to make up the difference between its expenses and the fees charged for its services on Saturday morning. Scholarships are available to families and the cost of the research, service, and teaching exceed the income from the fees. The Children's Center has always been dependent on the gracious generosity of its host institutions over the years which continues with its new site at Christ Church Cathedral in Houston.

The Center's Director and Staff

The Center's Staff serves without pay. The primary teachers are Dr. Jerome W. Berryman, the Director, and Thea Berryman, his wife and a master teacher in the areas of music and dance at School of the Woods in Houston. The research staff which works under Dr. Berryman's direction is made up of a volunteer corps of professionals and aids devoted to this Project.

The Children's Center is based on a solid theological and research base in child development. Dr. Berryman is a professor of Theology and Ministry at the Institute of Religion in the Texas Medical Center. In addition he is an Adjunct Assistant Professor of Pastoral Counseling in the Department of Psychiatry at Baylor College of Medicine. His clinical work is carried on at Texas Children's Hospital in the Department of Pediatric Psychiatry and at the Houston Child Guidance Center on the Crisis Team there. His primary appointment is to the staff of Christ Church Cathedral.

Dr. Berryman's Montessori background includes certification from the International Center for Advanced Montessori Studies in Bergamo, Italy, and experience as a teacher, headmaster, and lecturer in training programs. The Montessori method and approach to religious education has been selected from the whole range of educational options as the most appropriate for this Project. Dr. Sofia Cavalletti's development of this method, her inspiration and vast experience, have had a major influence on this work.

Dr. Berryman and Dr. Cavalletti have been collaborators for several years, beginning in 1972 in Bergamo, Italy, through summer courses given in Houston and Mexico City, Dr. Berryman's presentation of a paper on "How to Observe the (Religious) Language in the Experience of the Child" in Rome, and his "Preface to the English Edition" for Dr. Cavalletti's recent book, THE RELIGIOUS POTENTIAL OF THE CHILD.

The Center's History

The concept for the Center was developed by Dr. Berryman during his work as Director of Christian Education at two Presbyterian churches in Houston. It began in 1975 and has used different formats, including integrating the children's experience in the Center with Sunday school and the worship of the congregation on

Sundays. The program on Saturdays began in 1979 and continues at the present time in the new location at Christ Church Cathedral.

Selected Publications

Following are some articles by Dr. Berryman relating to the Center's work and based on the pedagogical approaches of Cavalletti and Montessori. Further information and a more extensive bibliography may be obtained by writing to the Center:

> The Children's Center
> The Institute of Religion
> Texas Medical Center
> P.O. Box 20569
> Houston, Texas 77025
> Phone: (713) 797-0600

The Theory and Practice of the Center:

"Sofia Cavalletti: A Brief Introduction and Bibliography", The Constructive Triangle, Vol. V, No. 1 (Spring 1978)

"Being in Parables with Children", Religious Education, Vol. 74, No. 3, (May-June 1979)

"Religion and Montessori", Religious Education, Vol. 75, No. 3, (May-June 1980)

"Religious Images, Sick Children and Health Care", Children in Health Care: Ethical Perspectives, Association for the Care of Children's Health Special Edition, (Spring 1981). Note: This article is a major theoretical statement of "theological play" concepts and is relevant to the theory and practice of the Center as well as pastoral care of children in the hospital.

"Preface to the English Edition", The Religious Potential of the Child, Sofia Cavalletti, (New York/Ramsey: Paulist Press, 1983) Translated from the Italian, Il Potenziale Religioso del Bambino.

Children and Parents:

"Religious Development and the Role of the Parents", New Catholic World, Vol. 227, No. 1361, (September-October 1984)

General Developmental Aspects of Religion:

Life Maps: Conversations on the Journey of Faith, James W. Fowler and Sam Keen, ed. Jerome W. Berryman, second edition (Waco, Texas: Word Books, Inc., 1985). The second edition has a new concluding chapter by the editor. First edition, 4 printings, 1978.

Editor's Note: Dr. Berryman has also written several articles on the pastoral care of sick children and a list of these publications may be obtained by writing to the Center. In our next issue we would like to focus, in part, on the care of sick children and invite those of you who have used the Catechesis in a hospital setting, or a similar situation, to write to us. Please send the stories to: Carol Dittberner, 1429 Portland Avenue, St. Paul, Minnesota 55104.

# *the Seed Grows...*

## *Phoenix, Arizona*

Hello from Phoenix! We are still working toward the opening of Holy Family Catechetical Center and hope to begin in February, God willing. It has taken longer than we had expected; however, we continually praise God for His guidance and abundant blessings of our work and for helping us to remain faithful, above all!

It wasn't until December that we were finally able to begin renovating the space that had been donated by the Reed family. The "delay" was caused by fire in an adjacent building that resulted in the temporary storage of furniture in the Atrium-to-be. However, the Holy Spirit was simply increasing our time after the course for personal formation, giving us more time to review our notes and tapes of the lectures and to pray together. (We meet every Thursday evening for prayer and planning.)

After knocking out a few walls, waxing the floors, and a new coat of paint for the entire space, we were ready for our first parent meeting, the first in a series for parents on the Catechesis. A few days before the meeting, Maria Reed had an "untimely" fall cracking her kneecap which prevented her from attending the meeting. But as there is nothing "untimely" in the work of the Holy Spirit this only freed her to devote that evening to praying for a successful meeting.

And successful it was! The parents shared their observations with us of their children wanting more from what is currently offered through parish C.C.D. classes. We discussed the relationship between God and the child, using examples from Sofia's book and the course (including Paige Holloway's experience with her daughter asking that searing question, "Mom, does God talk to you???"). This led into the topic of the resulting role of the adult in the face of this relationship, and the need for a place and a way--the atrium and the materials, where and through which the child may actually experience the Word and the Liturgy. We finished with the presentation of the Good Shepherd which truly moved them. (And guess what? I didn't cry this time!)

Although our numbers were small, we are sure the mustard seed began to take root that evening in the Valley of the Sun. And, although this is the desert, we are confident that the Holy Spirit will see to it that the seed receives the water and care that it needs to grow and to produce wonderful fruit.

We pray for you all and for the work throughout the world, and we ask for your prayers for us in this wonder-full endeavor.

Peace to you all,
Bert and Marty O'Bryan, Maria Reed, 1338 Culver St. West, Phoenix, Arizona 85007

## *Lambertville, New Jersey*

The Jesus School of St. John the Evangelist Parish is a preschool for children from three to five years of age, conducted by the Trinitarian Sisters of Redemptor Hominis. The school is located on one floor of a relatively new building which formerly was the parish school. One room has been entirely devoted to the Atrium. Currently, there are twenty-three children enrolled in the program, one-half of whom attend school full time (27.5 hours per week), and the remainder for varying periods on a part time basis. Work in the Atrium is part of the child's experience every day he/she is in school. Indeed, the Atrium represents the focal point of the program. As of this date, Sisters Mary Badger, Marie Conaughton and Angela Gargano make up the teaching staff.

For more information please contact: Sister Marie Conaughton, TRH, P.O. Box 306, Lambertville, New Jersey, 08530. (609) 397-0593.

## Iowa City, Iowa

We separated about one third of the space in our Preschool for the Atrium materials. First, there is a prayer corner which has the candle and a beautiful edition of the Bible. Going around the room, the next area is a table with all the books for the different works. Next we have the liturgical colors; then we have a shelf and place of preparation for the cruets and the chalice. Next is a section for the Infancy Narratives. On the opposite wall we have two shelves for practical life and art and supplies for the atrium.

There is a space for the altar and sacristy shelf; in the middle of the room is a table with the Parable of the Good Shepherd. To one side is another table with the Parables of the Kingdom.

This year as a catechist has been a rewarding experience for me. I've spent much time preparing and making the materials. While I've done this, I've had time to contemplate and reflect on the materials and the catechesis. I feel that for my own faith and spiritual growth this work has been extremely powerful.

At first, and sometimes even now, I've wondered if my presentations of the work have been proper or effective. But each day I pray for guidance and wisdom from the Holy Spirit. Also, I do believe there has been a change in the children. On days when we work in the Atrium, the children seem quieter and calmer.

Mary Reichardt, 512 East Davenport, Iowa City, Iowa 52240.

## Napa, California

The atrium at St. Thomas Acquinas Church in Napa was recently the feature of an article in the Diocesan newspaper, The Redwood Crozier. Claudia Riordan is working in the class with the children, as well as conducting a two hour session each week for parents. Sister Patricia Cullen, who attended the course in St. Paul this past summer, is the Co-ordinator of the program. Claudia is a trained Montessori teacher and has also studied in Rome with Sofia.

They found a group of 25 children was too large to work together and allow for meditation while working, so it has been divided into two smaller groups which meet on two separate week days. Sister Patricia sees a great interest in the class and a great reluctance in the children to leave when class is over.

Claudia Riordan and Sister Patricia Cullen, St. Thomas Acquinas Church, 2725 Elm Street, Napa, California 94558.

## Oakland, California

Margie Wilkinson was the Co-ordinator of St. Theresa's Sunday School, a preschool religious education program that had been going for five years due to the good graces of the parents of several young families in the parish. However, she felt that the published programs they had been using were not very helpful in dealing with what was most interesting and most essential in the education of the children. She came to St. Paul for the Summer Course, returned home and gave a presentation to the parents on September 6th, 1984, and on October 7th welcomed the first children to the new atrium.

The atrium has been in session each Sunday morning from 8:50-10:00. They began with the first presentations of the Altar, the Liturgical Colors, a visit to the sacristy, and the Preparation of the Chalice. The pastor, Monsignor Bernard Moran, blessed the atrium the first time all the children were assembled. A dinner was held for parents and Margie presented the Parable of the Good Shepherd to them.

The atrium began, and continues, due to the efforts of many people. There are two carpenters; an 80 year old retired ophthalmologist and a trial attorney. One mother is an art major, another a seamstress who works with a mother of six on the chasuables and stoles. Some volunteers set up the library in the school every Saturday for the class, and another teacher/mother is making the relief maps of Israel.

Margaret Wilkinson, 5454 Hilltop Crescent, Oakland, California 94618.

# St. Paul, Minnesota

On Sundays I started working with Mary Koenigsberger at the Catholic Community of Christ the Redeemer in St. Paul. We expanded on the program of the year before of one presentation a month. Now we meet almost every Sunday and have 11 children age 3 and 4. We meet for two hours. We have a room where we can set out the materials each Sunday and a storage cabinet that locks especially for the catechesis. The children are full of anticipation and Mary and I found them a wonderful group to work with. We took turns doing presentations and preparing materials. The class moved along well but Mary became sick and had to retire from the program. I was asked to continue by the Religious Coordinator. Three people volunteered to assist on alternate Sundays so with their help and support from the parents the class was able to continue. When one of the children had a new baby brother who was soon to be baptized I did the Baptism presentation and we participated in the Baptism of the new sibling. The whole class was wide-eyed and happy to be invited to participate. They sang "this little Light of Mine". Since then they have wanted to be at every baptism and there are many. We also spend much time each Sunday lighting candles. The children are happy and I can hardly squeeze in a presentation. They want to work with the materials right away. I'm learning to sit back and let them come to me when they need something. I wish I could spend more time in this work. That is my future goal.

Carol Dittberner and I try to meet at least once a month to exchange our experiences and support each other. Of course we worked together on the newsletter. We build each other up when we need it.

Rose Marie Paul, 4901 West 114th St., Bloomington, Minnesota 55437

# Washington, D.C.

The atrium program at Christian Family Montessori School (which serves as part of the Center for the Association) includes a 3-6 atrium shared by two primary Montessori classes, a 6-8 atrium in the Montessori Junior class, and three afternoon atrium groups. In the regular school atrium programs, Cathy Maresca, Judy Walsh-Mellett, Jo Kendrick, Rob Soley and Rebekah Rojcewicz give weekly presentations to small groups of children in the 3-6 atrium, with the children being free to use the atrium at all other times during the school day. There is one 3-6 atrium group after school for which Rebekah is the catechist. In the junior class atrium Sr. Mary Elizabeth Klier and Rebekah work together in giving the weekly presentations, the children having access to the atrium at all times during the day. Rebekah also has two 6-8 after school atrium groups.

In December one of these 6-8 groups celebrated their First Communion (the first group to do so at CFMS and so, an extra special occasion). In preparation, there were five Sunday afternoon meditations (in addition to the weekly atrium time). Then there was a three-day retreat at the Oblate College December 7-9 culminating in a family service for the children's First Confession and the receiving of the white garment Saturday evening. First Communion took place on Sunday morning. One of the richest times of the weekend came after Mass and the reception, when families and guests had left and the First Communicants stayed on for a time together.

In addition to the atrium program at CFMS, Rebekah and Rob Soley (CFMS Staff and member of Sojourners Community) are working together to bring the catechesis to two groups, (6-8, 9-12),of inner city neighborhood children where the Sojourners live and serve.

Rebekah is eagerly awaiting the birth of her first child sometime around Easter.

Rebekah Rojcewicz, 3900 Hamilton St., F301, Hyattsville, Maryland 20781

# The Catechesis of The Good Shepherd

We wish to thank all the contribtuors to this newsletter, our second publication! Seeing its size, it seems we may be able to begin two issues a year for the 1985-86 season. We welcome information from the atriums around the country and invite you to send us a little report on your work. Also, art work by your children, or a particular photograph, some writing a child has done, will be nice to include. Bring these things to share at the courses this summer also.

We also invite members to be thinking of a name for our newsletter.

Newsletter articles may be sent to:

    Carol Dittberner
    1429 Portland Avenue
    St. Paul, Minnesota 55104

If you are interested in the association but have not as yet become a member, we welcome your membership and support. Membership fees are for one year and are as follows:

    Member......................................$30.00 per person
    Member joining with a group of 5......$20.00 per person
    Subscription to newsletter only.......$ 5.00

For further information and an application, please write to:

    Cathy Maresca
    INNAMORAMENTO
    3628 Rhode Island Avenue
    Mt. Rainier, Maryland 20712
    Phone: (202) 832-2477

Note to members: if you would like additional copies of the newsletter, please send $3.00 per copy needed to Cathy Maresca at the above address.

 This Newsletter was compiled by Carol Dittberner and Rose Marie Paul in collaboration with Dr. Sofia Cavalletti.

Published in St. Paul, Minnesota          Copyright (c) March 8th, 1985

# Catechesis of the Good Shepherd
## Spring, 1986

"Take this, All of you,
 and eat it:
"This is my body which
 will be given up for you.

"Take this, all of you,
 and drink from it.
 This is the cup of my blood,
 the blood of the new and
 everlasting covenant.

"It will be shed for you
 and for all men so that
 sins may be forgiven.

"Do this in memory of me."

(From the Eucharistic Prayer)

# Let us pray with the children. . .

Age 2½

This child was overheard my her mother while she sang to herself in bed:
"Jesus loves me, Jesus loves me, (several more times),
Holy Spirit,
God,
Jesus loves me,
Holy Spirit,
God.
Alleluia."

Age 4

This child is in her second year at the atrium. She was home baking bread with her mother.
Child: "Mommy, do you want to be in the kingdom of God?"
Mother: "Yes, I do."
Child: "Eat the bread."

A boy overheard singing to himself at home after the Presentation of the Mustard Seed. The prayer moved from reflection to celebration.
"The reign of God, (repeated like a chant many times)
Everything is the reign of God,
The Light,
Thank you, Jesus.
Lord, I want to walk in that number.
(He took out the guitar and began to strum)-Our Lord is our Shepherd,
(He took out the tamborine)-Jesus is our Shepherd
(He played louder)-O Lord, O Lord, O Lord,
O, Lord is our Shepherd,
He is Jesus.
One more song."

Age 5

A girl who is in her third year in the atrium dictated this prayer to be written down for her.
"God made the world.
He made the market so we could buy food.
He made the toys so we could play.
He made the house so we could live.
Alleluia. Amen."

Written prayer of a boy, third year in the atrium:
"I luv Geesus. Hee did. I am soree, Geesus."
I love Jesus. He died. I am sorry, Jesus.

A boy, third year in atrium:
"I wish Jesus would get off the cross."
This same child made a booklet on the Hidden Treasure in which he wrote: "He sold all he had and then joy came to him." He drew a happy sheep at the bottom.

Age 6

Written prayer of a boy who was in the atrium his first month:
"I like you. I'm six."

Age 7

During prayer in the atrium a girl began with a story:
"Jesus was on the cross and Mary looked at him and said, 'Are you crying? (pause) Are you crying because you are in the tomb?'" Then she asked us to pray for babies who have died.

Age 8

After the presentation of the True Vine this girl made up a song. It is her fourth year in the atrium; her first presentation of the True Vine.
"Vine, oh vine,
I love you so.
Vine, oh vine,
You're the prettiest one I know."

"For the children in El Salvador and the other people who don't have what we do and may we give them everything."

Written prayer of an eight year old girl:
"He is our place of rest.
His power is in us.
He is our shield.
He helps in making peace.
The kingdom of God is all around.

Do not be afraid for He is near."
She surrounded the prayer with crosses and lit candles.

Ages 9-13

This group of elementary children wanted to make something special for the First Eucharist children. After discussing many ideas they decided on a project which would take several weeks. After their first session of oiling wooden pieces for crosses, the children set their work aside and asked the catechist if they could pray about their work. They each lit a candle and asked that their work would go well and that the younger children would like their gifts. There was a beautiful atmosphere in the room and in their prayer.

Susie E. Ericson, age 9,
Minneapolis, Minnesota.

# The Characteristics of Catechists of the Good Shepherd

Dearest Catechists,

Last year we asked ourselves which are the characteristics of the catechesis of the Good Shepherd. I indicated some of them and I would be very happy to know if you recognize your work in them and which points you would like to add.

This year let us ask ourselves a more difficult and challenging question: which is the characteristic of the catechist of the Good Shepherd? I mean a characteristic that qualifies us from the spiritual point of view. We spoke about that during the meeting last summer, spurred above all by Betty Hissong who feels very deeply the concern to found our work on prayer and on the union with God, a concern shared by all of us, I think.

I asked myself if I had something to suggest to you; I am telling you here what emerged during the interchange we had in St. Paul and met the concensus of the ones who were present there. I am sharing this with you so that everybody may contribute to such an important discussion. The first point I think necessary to clarify is that, if a spiritual characteristic of the catechist of the Good Shepherd exists, the characteristic must be an expression of the soul of our work; if such a spirituality has to take some shape, this shape must emerge from inside our work and must adhere very closely to it.

The path is already indicated by the principal aim of our association: "To involve adults and children in a common religious experience, in which the religious values of childhood are predominant." The way by which the relationship of the child with God takes form is in some way the answer to our question. We have all seen the contemplative capacities with which the child is gifted and how capable he/she is of enjoying the presence of God in his/her life. The spiritual characteristics of the child can be expressed by contemplation and enjoyment.

If we want to reach a concrete form, let us ask ourselves when do we see these characteristics of childhood emerge in a more explicit way. I think that each of us had the experience of them on the occasion of first Communion. Long and prayer-filled silences, a deep and serene joy and peace that shines through the very pores of the children are among the best remembrances of many of us. Also, besides first Communion, the children are capable of enjoying Mass in a particular way and, often during the celebrations of Eucharist a very intense atmosphere is created and it lingers for a long time also after the celebration, so for many children it is hard to be obliged to leave.

All this makes us think that Eucharist is a pivot in the religious experience of the child and, if this is true, Eucharist is also the pivot of the spiritual life of the catechist. If we dare speak about a spirituality of the catechists of the Good Shepherd, we must speak about a eucharistic spirituality. And then the problem arises of how to nourish it.

Our work lead us to speak over again about eucharistic subjects with the children. These opportunities are precious for us in order to constantly meditate on some basic points. We must be very careful not to waste these opportunities, reducing them to a more or less mechanical repetition of things that seem to be known to us. These opportunities are a means to make us aware of how boundless is the Mystery we are speaking about; they help us to understand that we always are on the threshold of a "space" that has no limits and that attracts us just because of its unfathomableness, just because we know so little about it. If we feel some tiredness in these presentations, this means something is wrong with us.

In this general framework, the specific preparation of first Communion is the strongest moment. This is the moment when children prepare themselves for their first eucharistic encounter, and we prepare ourselves for our repeated eucharistic encounters. The preparation is both for the little ones and for the adults, because we never finish preparing ourselves. To stay with the children in this particular moment is a privilege because it helps us concentrate upon Eucharist and to do so in a close communion with the children.

The retreat of first Communion is *the* retreat of the catechist of the Good Shepherd. Not all of us had the opportunity to participate in the retreat Brother Ignatius gave us last summer in St. Paul. They were beautiful days of meditation and prayer that strengthened our interior life and will improve our work with the children; but, for many of us, the retreat with the children is the major opportunity. I know that in these days we have to face many organizational problems; we have to try to settle them beforehand as much as possible so that these days may be for us, also, days of peace and enjoyment together with the children. We know that during the retreat we do not have to give new presentations, but we have to try to create such conditions that make it possible to live, with peace and joy, what has already been received; we have to create the conditions capable of helping the child's enjoyment of the eucharistic event. We will not be capable of helping the children if we are tense; more than at any other moment we have to "abandon" the children to God and abandon ourselves to God.

Keeping all that in mind, I would like to ask you to let us know, if possible, the dates of the first Communion (and therefore of the retreat) of your groups so that they may be published in the newsletter. We live mostly very far from each other; it would be very good to create a kind of "network" of thoughts and prayers which unite us during these very important days.

I think, moreover, about the importance of meditating on the biblical and liturgical texts concerning Eucharist. Of course it is not possible to give a list of the texts that should be read, however, basic texts are certainly the account of the Last Supper in the synoptic Gospels, Ch. 13 of John, Ch. 11 of the First Letter to the Corinthians, and how many others? I would also like to recommend to you the meditation on the liturgical texts. We now have several Eucharistic Prayers; let us read them over and over again, meditating upon them also outside the celebrations. Let us compare the one with the other, looking for the common points, the differences and also- why not?- the lacunae and the defects. It would be very good to go to the celebration being already familiar with the texts. Hearing the celebrant repeat them (very often always the same) could make our listening just mechanical, without a previous meditation.

And, finally, I think that the most important and efficacious preparation for the participation in Eucharist is to participate in Eucharist. It is in Eucharist that all we have prepared beforehand becomes alive; it is in the Eucharistical encounter that Christ trains us in a very particular way. It is there that, little by little, day after day, He helps us to make our lives "an everlasting gift" to the Father.

I am waiting for your reactions to what I have said, and for your advice.

Much love,

# Celebration of First Eucharist

In response to the discussions last summer and the article preceding this, "Characteristics of the Catechist of the Good Shepherd," we are publishing the dates of the celebration of First Eucharist. Keep in mind that the retreats begin three days before the dates which are listed. Let us hold the children and each other in prayer.

First Communion in the atriums with the Catechesis of the Good Shepherd in Mexico:

| Chihuahua- | April 26th | May 10th |
| | May 3rd | May 17th |

There will be two hundred children more or less from different atriums in parishes and Montessori schools. Also, more children of those working with the books and manuals of this Catechesis. We do not know the number of them; God knows it and enjoys it.

Ciudad Juarez-   May 11th
                 May 18th

Children from one atrium in a parish church.

| Mexico City- | May 11th | May 25th |
| | May 17th | June 1st |
| | May 18th | June 8th |

Children from different parishes and a Montessori school. Also children working with the books and manuals.

Torreon-   December 13th

Children from the first atrium in Torreon. This will be the first group in this city.

                                                                     Instituto del Buen Pastor
                                                                     Mexico, 1986.

From Rome:

    Via degli Orsini-   May 4th

    S. Francesco a Monte Maria-   Ascension Day

    Instituto Maria Immaculata, Ciampino-   April 25th

From the United States:

| Cleveland, Ohio- | May 4th |
| Minneapolis, Minnesota- | May 4th-this is the first group in this city. |
| Chicago, Illinois- | May 4th |
| El Paso, Texas | June 8th-this is the first group in this city |

Please note that some groups have already made their First Communion. The group in Morelia, Mexico and another group in Washington, D.C. both celebrated in December of 1985. Let us keep all the groups in mind also whom we have not heard from and so are unable to publish their dates.

This is a holy card made by Julio, 6 years old, for the day of his First Communion in the first group in Chihuahua, 1979. It says: "Shepherd you invite us to your feast because you are our brother." On the reverse of the cards are printed the names of all the children, the date and the name of the atrium.

Reflections from the group making First Communion in Morelia, Mexico, December 8th, 1985. There were eight children, seven to ten years old.

On the eve of the first day of the retreat, the catechist asks Maria (eight years old): "Do you have a big desire for your First Communion? How big is your desire?" Maria replied, "Is from here to the infinite."

Heaven and all in heaven are waiting and preparing themselves for the Feast of our Confession.

The Feast of the Immaculate Conception is the Feast of the White Garment of the Virgin Mary.

As Mary is full of grace, so we will be with our White Garment; full of grace with the Sacrament of Reconciliation.

This story comes to us from Emilia Sandoval in Chihuahua, Mexico. She had sent this story to Sofia who adds her response at the end. This took place on the eve of the celebration of First Eucharist.

That night somebody called Martha, the catechist from the farm, to tell her that there was a serious problem. They had investigated and it looked like Monica and her sister Maribel (that has her story also) weren't baptized. They forgot to tell us. I looked for Father Padilla and could not find him until 9:00 in the morning. The First Communion was at 11:00 A.M. He told me that it was very serious, that he could not do anything about it, that he had to ask permission from the bishop, that it would take some time because they had to investigate, and that they should look for another person, the parish priest of San Juan.

I went to San Juan and Fr. Fierro was there fixing the microhpone. I told him what was going on and he told me that we had to arrange this as soon as possible. "Tell me what you know about them; they are girls who had suffered alot, we cannot give them a hard time." I told him what I knew. They were daughters of a prostitute, and when they were two and three years old their mother was put in jail on the charge of perversion of minors. The girls stayed by themselves in a low rate hotel and some people took them to the farm. It is probable that they have never been baptized. "We are going to do it now so that the First Communion starts on time; go and get them."

We got them, meanwhile the other boys were arriving in the Sacristy, and there in the Sacristy we held the baptism ceremony, very simply. The Father explained to the children what was going on and everyone participated in perfect order. There were thirty-six children, two girls. At 11:00 A.M. we started the Mass as planned. The children were filled with peace and everything transpired peacefully.

At the moment of giving thanks when the children were alone in the church, she participated at times. I don't remember all of what she said, she thanked (God) for her baptism, for the light that she had received, and she asked that this happiness never ends. Later she drew a picture of a house. It said, "God's house." In the center of the house she drew a candle and under it a label which said "the True Vine." She brought it to the catechist and the catechist asked her "are you going to draw the vine?" Monica answered, "I don't need to draw it-here it is," and she pointed to the candle. I don't think I need to say anything more.

Monica went back to her daily life but I keep thinking: "What can we do in order to help Monica so that her joy will last forever?"

Sofia responds: Emilia is asking this question to all of us and I think that each of us asks herself/himself such a question at the moment of first Communion. The children of the center of Via degli Orsini knew something about the story of Monica and about her prayer. They prayed with her words during the retreat of first Communion and during the celebration on Sunday morning. This was surely a way of answering Emilia's question.

# "Take this, all of you, and drink from it...."

A personal meditation on the Water and the Wine by Carol Dittberner

We are the water, a few drops which symbolize us, millions of people - wine which encompasses the water. We can no longer be seen (in the wine); we are mixed up in Jesus, we are all Jesus. The child said, "we are lost in Jesus."

This could be the total rest, to be so all surrounded you would not feel yourself any longer, you would not be aware of anything except God, you would not think anything except love. Everything stops.

To be "lost" in Christ is to think no more of yourself or your needs, your pridefulness, your anxieties. To be lost in Christ is really to be "found" within the immense love which says to us, "you are mine, live in me." To lose ourselves in this way is a very good thing for we also lose all our faults; we give ourselves up to someone who is greater than we are, some One who surrounds our very life - our whole life. This is union, "lost" (in the wine) and "found" in Jesus, united with divinity. I believe it is possible, truly possible, in our humanity to really feel God's essence; it is possible if we give ourselves to it.

To be mixed in the wine also reminds me of the Good Shepherd for the Shepherd gives support; we are no longer alone. Even to think about the properties of wine, to be buoyed up by this special liquid which has greater properties than water. (Though it is water which gives life, it is wine which gives spiritual life).

I am also thinking about a homily which I heard at a wedding in which the priest referred to us as "people of promises" and "people of forgiveness" because we live in commitment to each other (spouses, family, friends); we make promises. But we are weak and often break those promises so we have a need to forgive each other when this happens. He went on to say that, as Christians, the great keeper of our promises, and whose promise to us is covenant, is God. Since it is God in whom all promises are made, then it is God's forgiveness which heals our weaknesses.

The great forgiveness of God which contains all of ours for each other.... we are mixed in the wine which is total love and total forgiveness and total promise. We are buoyed up, held up, retrieved....we are "found."

# The Richness of Early Religious Experience

by Sofia Cavalletti

translated from the Italian
by Claudia Riordan

We have already had occasion on these pages to speak about the religious experience of the child and about how it seems to figure into early childhood. Today we would like to stop briefly on what an early religious experience can give to the child.

As we have said at other times, the religious experience is essentially an experience of love, of love received and returned.

It is well known that the person keeps on forming him/herself in a relationship, i. e., in the creative interchange, in a dynamic that involves in depth the gratifying experience of receiving, and the no-less-gratifying experience of giving. Both moments of such an interchange are at the level of being, i.e., they involve the person globally down to his/her deepest roots.

Such an assertion is perhaps clear for what concerns the first moment of the relationship (receiving), while more often than not the second moment is considered to be placed above all at the level of behavior, i.e., at the level of doing things, characterized by multiplicity. If the latter were true, it would be extremely serious in regard to early childhood (i.e., that period which precedes what used to be called the "logical/moral crisis" (which manifests itself at about six years of age). The child before the age of six, who is not so interested in things to be done or not to be done, would appear to us as lacking the capacity to truly live the relationship and therefore to form him/herself as a person. But such an interpretation of the aspect of response in the relationship is extremely limited and incomplete. Both the moments which constitute the relationship are based on the deep level of being that precedes and nurtures every realization on the level of behavior. If in the second moment the behavior assumes value, it assumes it only inasmuch as it is a manifestation of a state of being. Fundamentally, the second moment of the relationship is constituted by a movement that can be compared to the heliotropic movement of the plant that turns itself toward the sun; it is with a movement that involves it totally and orients it in a certain way. It is clear that it cannot be but one orientation that the multiplicity of behavior gets its value and meaning. Deprived of vital sap that comes from the roots, all human works can be an ephemeral blooming if the deep level of the person is not helped to form itself and to set its roots in being.*

The formation of the person is characterized by the need (exigency) of globality. It is from such a globality that the level of behavior, characterized by multiplicity, gets its value.

With such a vision, early childhood presents itself as the golden age for the formation of the person, because early childhood is the time when the child does not as yet open him/herself up to the multiplicity of the real; rather, in each of his/her experiences, all of the person is involved down to the very depth of his/her being. Free and clear from the preoccupation and worry of practical utility and the anxiety of doing things, the child goes to the relationship with all of his/her person. The child opens up to it with all of him/herself, both in that moment of receiving and in that of giving.

*translator's comment: see John 15.

EARLY RELIGIOUS EXPERIENCE continued

With this vision, early childhood appears as the age when the very structure of the child responds to the most essential <u>rules</u> of the formation of the person.

Dr. Montessori says something very similar when she speaks of early childhood as the "first place (level; stage) of education," and the harmonious establishment of it is indispensable to the construction of the planes that will follow.

We haven't yet answered the question we asked ourselves at the beginning: What does an early religious experience give to the child? In order to answer this, we observe that the child, who is in the ideally existential situation to establish the relationship, must find in it the adequate partner: a partner that corresponds to and is in harmony with the child's capacities of globality; a partner that satisfies the child's exigency (vital need) of a rapport where he/she is involved down to the depth of his/her being; a partner that, because of its own capability of giving of itself and loving without limits, could not delude (deceive).

At this point, to assert that such a partner cannot be but God - God is Love (1John 4:8) - might be asserting a principle that not everybody's willing to accept. But to look for those qualifications we spoke of in anyone who was not God would cause anybody embarrassment.

Anyhow, we are not going to answer the question we asked ourselves on the level of principles, but rather at the experiential level.

It is evident that it's not granted to the adult to enter the mystery of the first moment of the relationship, that moment when the child receives the gift from the Other. Such a moment cannot be in any way the object of experimentation from the outside.

Yet the value of such a moment can be evaluated by the intensity with which the child lives the moment of response. In fact he/she lives it with a feeling of joy so deep that any observer can notice that it involves the child down to the most intimate part of his/her being; the child answers with a joy that manifests itself in attitudes of serene and recollected peace which in words can be expressed with such a sentence as: "It makes me feel so good!" The child's reactions are those of a person who has found all that corresponds to his/her most vital, most essential needs (exigencies) and <u>all</u> the child's being rejoices in the satisfaction of such exigencies. Let us recall that "very great feeling of joy" that Dr. Montessori had noticed in the children during her first experience of religious formation in Barcelona.

We have spoken about this at other times and we don't want to wander from the subject. What we would like to stress here is that the feeling, the sense of complete satisfaction that the child shows in the religious experience, in our opinion, finds its reason in the fact that in such an experience two "globalities" meet. One is that of God who is Infinite and the other is that of the creature who, even within the creature's limitation, reflects the image and likeness of God. In the child who seeks God and rejoices in finding Him, we see "the likeness who seeks his/her Likeness." It is natural that, upon finding Him, the child feels satisfied down to his/her depths. In reference

EARLY RELIGIOUS EXPERIENCE continued

to the previous statement "God who is Infinite" a child from a school in Tuscany, raised in a totally areligious environment, said of Him after a long meditation: "Perhaps He is an infinite perfection."

Helping children to experience the presence of God in their life is helping children to form their person according to the exigencies of their deepest structure; failing to do this means to expose the children to delusion, which it cannot fail to derive from relationships which do not fully correspond to the child's make-up. We believe that we can say that an early religious experience is what can best help the formation of the person.

vocabulary clarification by Rose Paul

globally - totally or completely -encompassing all
multiplicity - manifold or multiferous - many
ephemeral - transient - short lived
reductive - limited
exigencies - vital needs

Gabriel Burns, age 5, with the Good Shepherd.
Oak Park, Illinois.

This article appeared in "Vita dell' Infanzia," Vol. XXXII, No. 1, September, 1983, Rome, Italy, and is reprinted with Dr. Cavalletti's permission.

# Experiences in the Atrium

**Knowing God with the children and learning how to listen to his word.**

Reflections from the atrium, 1984-85, by Maria Christlieb, Mexico City

For a catechist, to be in an atrium is a continuous and precious gift of God. It is a gift for which we will never be thankful enough, but will treasure and reflect in our hearts over and over again. It is a gift to share, as the prophets shared God's secrets with us. I want to share this treasure with our readers.

Diego-three years old. Diego is new to the atrium this year and is one of the youngest children. He has speech difficulties and yet he has no difficulty in communicating. For instance, after preparing the altar, he will ask to have the candles lit. Then, kneeling down in front of the altar, he clasps his hands together and says: "Jesus, Jesus" while pointing at the crucifix. He then bursts into a deep smile with his black eyes shining.

At the last session before Christmas, Diego was walking around and around the chasubles. I asked him: "Would you like to work with them?" "Yes, but I can't," he said. "Oh yes, you can," I replied. "We will begin together and then you can continue by yourself." "All right," he said. My help was very simple: I gave him the white chasuble and showed him how to place it on the holder. I watched him from a distance and after some effort he was able to do it by himself. Then something beautiful happened. Diego started dancing and jumping around the holder with the chasuble, clasping his hands and saying with incredible joy, "I can! I can!" He burst with joy for quite a while.

Diego is so small, that while we were meditating on the Nativity and the children were bringing figures for the scene, I asked him of he wanted to place a sheep near the manger. He said, "No, the sheep will eat Jesus."

Gabino-three years old. Gabino is a very small child with big blue smiling eyes and freckles. He is always happy, enjoying the presentations and beginning to do very simple drawings and pasting. But mainly, he is there. He has fallen asleep two or three times. He goes to the prayer corner, sitting on a carpet on the floor and reclining his head on the table where the statue of the Good Shepherd is placed. He sleeps until his mother comes. The other children watch him but no one disturbs him. While the others work, Gabino sleeps. Sometimes this is his "being" in the atrium. I watch him, enchanted and, remembering the scene, the Psalms come to my mind:

> As soon as I lie down, I fall peacefully asleep,
> for you alone, O Lord, bring security to my
> dwelling. How lovely is your dwelling place,
> O Lord of hosts! I set the Lord ever before me;
> therefore my heart is glad and my soul rejoices;
> my body, too, abides in confidence.

José-four years old. It was José's first year in the atrium. His story happened from December 6th-23rd, 1984.

December 6th: We lit the second Advent candle in the atrium. I do not remember how it happened exactly, but at a certain moment José said, "Jesus is God and He is the Son of God. Then there are two Gods." The comment surprised me very much and I did not answer it directly. We read the passage of the Annunciation. I only insist on the words: "This child will be great and He will be called the Son of the Most High. He will be Holy and will be called the Son of God."

When the session ended, I spoke with José's mother, Neither one of us had an answer and we were afraid of giving answers which would spoil the relationship of the boy with the mystery of God. We did not want to touch his wonder; we decided to wait and pray about it.

December 9th: José went to mass and, upon entering the church and seeing the altar and the priest, he said to his father, "I am going to ask the priest is there are two Gods: Jesus and His Father." The parents were afraid of any kind of explanation so they distracted him from asking the priest. In the meantime, I prayed and thought about José and his question. I asked God, "What should I say to José that will not impoverish the mystery for him and yet would answer him in some way?"

December 13th: In the atrium we meditated on the Nativity and, when we placed St. Joseph at the manger, José said, "Who is Joseph if Jesus is the Son of God?" We commented saying Joseph is the one chosen by God to take care of Jesus here on earth. And José says again, "But, Maria, are there two Gods: Jesus and His Father?" I turned to him in a very calm and serious manner and said, "José, your question is very, very important and big." Hearing these words, he looked at me fixedly and his dark brown eyes opened more and more. I continued: "It is so big that I can not answer it. I do not know the answer; I look for it like you." José looked at me even more. "I can only tell you that Jesus is God and His Father is God and that Jesus said once, 'The Father and I are one.' (John 10:30) I can not explain to you how this is, but I can tell you that He said that to us. He told us that secret: 'The Father and I are one.' In our whole lives we probably will not understand this fully. Jesus wants to explain it to you, to me, to everyone little by little. It is His secret: 'The Father and I are one.'" José did not say one word and I do not have words to describe his face and eyes while he listened to those words. I suggested to his mother that at a good moment she could read to him again the Annunciation, but with no explanation of any type.

December 23rd (Sunday): Ten days later, José goes to mass. He is happy. During the homily his mother tells him to listen and she adds, "Maybe it will help you for your question, your important question about Jesus and His Father." The boy looked at her and said, "No, mama, thank you. Maria already told me what Jesus said: 'The Father and I are one.' I do not need any more explanation. Jesus said: 'The Father and I are one.' There is nothing else to say."

José goes on living! Children listen in this way to the Word of God.

Christmas Day, 1985: José is five years old and in his second year at the atrium. The present he prepared for his mother was all his work from the first year in the atrium and some from the second year. He wrapped it in beautiful paper and gave it to her. José is asking now if Jesus really was a boy like him and if He was five years old, and what was He like at that age.

In the atrium the child has the opportunity of choosing his work each session. This permits him each time he is there to satisfy a particular hunger of that moment in his life of faith and relationship with God. Each time he is fed with the particular food that he needs, it is a source of immense happiness. The experience of the child with God is a global experience in which his whole self is involved. Between God, who reveals Himself, and the child who little by little grasps Him, a complete union is taking place. The Parable of the True Vine is being realized. God floods the world of the child, and the child has a "divine milieu." God and the child are the Vine and the branches.

This winter, of 1985, we saw how children answer to the Word of God with all their beings as they are living a particular moment.

Pablo-five years old. Pablo is at the sensitive period for the "Explosion of Writing." For him there is nothing more marvelous than to be able to write a word. We had the presentation of the Prophecy of the Light in Isaiah. Pablo copied the prophecy as beautifully as he could: "The people who walked in darkness have seen a great light." He brings it to me and I suggest that he draw something around it to make it more beautiful. He goes back to his place and after a while he comes back full of satisfaction. He made a frame with four lines and around the frame he wrote words and illustrated them: apple, orange, lemon, etc., with the corresponding drawing in small size. This is the exercise he does in the school when writing new words. Pablo had decorated his prophecy with WORDS WRITTEN BY HIM. This was the most precious decoration he could do at that moment. He is beginning to write and nothing is more precious for him now.

We had another boy, Felipe, seven years old, who decorated the prophecy with geometric figures.

Carlos Adolfo-seven years old. Carlos was born with the "bed syndrome." It is an illness in which the channels for respiration close. If the person falls asleep, he can die of asphyxiation. The first seven months of his life Carlos slept very, very little; he was kept awake. After this period he was always overprotected and his behavior was very upsetting. Even now, people are demanding order and discipline from him and the child lives in rebellion. He was invited to leave the Montessori school he was in and, he was, until last year, a terror in the atrium also. I met him without knowing this story.

This is the fifth week at the atrium. The last four weeks, Carlos was at the prayer corner most of the time. He said, "I am praying." When he left, there were matches all over. He participated happily in the presentation of "The Bible." In general he is restless, has a kind of lost look, and sometimes seems very sad. He is very sensitive and perceives immediately your attitude and feelings toward him. One day he arrived, went to the prayer corner and came to tell me there were no matches. I said, "If you want the candles lit I will do it for you." He did not like this and walked away. He went to his table and said to me, "I am going to write the life of Jesus." He worked for about an hour and a half. The director of the Montessori school was there and she could not believe she was seeing the same child. Carlos Adolfo in total work all this time! He had written this story:

> Once upon a time there was a virgencita (a loving way to
> call Our Lady in Mexico) and the shepherd, and the virgencita had the shepherd counting the sheep and one was lacking. It was the smallest one and quickly he went to look
> for her while the virgencita stay watching the others. And
> came back with the sheep, and gave her food and gave her
> water and she became satisfied and slept. And he counted
> them again and the others give food and gave her water and
> she became satisfied and slept. And he counted them again
> and the others gave food and they all slept. The end.

We read the story together. As I was reading it I saw him smiling and his eyes were happy, serene and tranquil as never before. His face corresponded to the description of "the sheep who became satisfied and slept." Comments are useless. Just read the story and see the elements in it: the role of the virgencita, the role of the shepherd and what He does, what she does, what happened with the sheep, and ask God ... maybe... to be able to write "The Life of Jesus" in the way Carlos did.

Daniela-eight years old. This is her first year in the atrium and at the end of the session the second week she comes to the catechist, radiant with joy, and says: "Good-bye, thank you. I had so much fun. Estuvé divertidísima."

Diego-eleven years old. He is working with the material for the children's work on the Unity of the History of the Kingdom of God. Diego is finding the greatest moments for him in this History and he points to the moment in which God says, "Let us make man in our image, after our likeness." The catechist asked, "What do you think this means?" Diego never answers immediately. After a while he says, "It means we are able to live the Maxims." Then he brought the box with the Maxims and under the words of Genesis he placed some of them:

## LET US MAKE MAN IN OUR IMAGE, AFTER OUR LIKENESS.

Be perfect as your heavenly Father is perfect.

Love your enemies.

Love one another as I have loved you.

Forgive, not seven times, but, I say, seventy times seven times.

You shall love the Lord your God. You shall love your neighbor as yourself.

From a group of children twelve to fifteen years old we have this reflection on the Parable of the Leaven (Matthew 13:33). "When all the flour ferments there will be the Parousia and God will be all in all. The daily living of the Maxims and of the Parables ferments us. When we die, we probably will not be totally fermented. After death the process of fermentation continues until God will be all, in each one of us and in all."

The meditation ended with a long prayer. I could not write the prayers right there; I did not dare to write them then. There was a deep silence between prayers and the environment was charged with the presence of God in each one in the room. Silence wrapped the environment.

These are some glimpses of an atrium. It is impossible to write down the joy of the children there and the hunger they have for God. They long for Him, to find Him is a source of immense happiness at all ages. The manifestations are different, but thirst for God and joy in Him is common to all ages.

I want to finish with some words from Sofia Cavalletti in her introduction to <u>The Religious Potential of the Child</u>: "For whatever good there may be in these pages, and above all for the work of which they are an expression, we thank God profoundly, Who has willed to place us in the service of His Word through the child, and Who has guided us toward a more essential penetration of it with the child."

"The Forgiving Father"-Michael Wagner, first grade, Bloomington, Minnesota.

# Catechesis as Celebration

A precious "moment" in the life of a catechist

A letter of Patricia Coulter to Sofia

Easter 1985

Introduction by Sofia

Very often it is hard for people to understand what we mean when we say that catechesis is a celebration, that catechesis either is a celebration or it is not catechesis.

It is also very difficult for us to explain it by words. Patricia makes it quite clear telling us what happened in her center with children preparing for first Confession.

Yesterday with the children was our confession moment - about the rite, which I did including cards for the actual celebration following the personal confession - the gown and light. Well we had the idea to do our own, very personal and private booklet and as we spoke about each part -- and they were as hungry as I have ever seen children be -- there was an alteration in the quality of the day. Somewhere, somehow Sofia it changed from being a sort of preparation/meditation (for it is still two weeks to the retreat) to actually taking on the dimension of celebration, and in the sense of "sacramental" celebration - if you understand what I mean.

The children would be together for a part, say on the "listening to the word" and would go and write/draw something, but it became the experience itself. I am faltering to find the words, but what I saw happening was, in fact, their living the sacrament. (had Fr. Paul been there I think they would each have confessed as if "now" was the right time) -- It was for me, at the outset, a time to "orient" them, more or less "present" the individual components of the rite; for them it was becoming immersed in the reality itself then and there.

The momentum increased, but not in "busyness" or "activity" but as in an almost imperceptible dropping down into the dynamism of forgiving love itself. I say almost unnoticeable because it was only after, on looking back, did I put the whole two hours together and see. Most of them came back saying "my mother/father say I can stay longer". They were in no mood to leave somehow. Moments like that - unasked (and, for me lately even unhoped for) and gratutitous are like something so peace giving it is marvellous.

---

Note: In last year's Newsletter we published an article by Sofia Cavalletti on the "Characteristics of the Catechesis of the Good Shepherd." We invite your response to that article, and to the one in this issue entitled "Characteristics of the Catechist of the Good Shepherd." Do you see the elements discussed in your work? The above is a response from Patricia Coulter, Toronto, regarding last year's article.

# Experiences in the Atrium
## The Nativity

I send my greetings to all! I miss everyone whom I had the pleasure of meeting this past summer in St. Paul. Yes, I am still "riding high" on the shoulders of the Good Shepherd. This is my first year in the atrium and it has been an incredible experience, especially our Christmas celebration.

Invitations to the celebration were handed out to the families of each of the sixty-seven preschool children to come and celebrate the "true meaning of Christmas." The morning of the celebration, while the parents were attending mass, the children prepared the school clubroom and arranged Christmas cookies on trays. Then, fifteen minutes before the celebration was to begin, the children "hid" in the library.

When mass ended, the families were asked to be seated in the clubroom and remain as silent as possbile until the children arrived. In the center of the clubroom was a large rug for the children to sit on, surrounded on three sides by chairs for the family members. The fourth side of the rug held a small table and directly behind that was a little larger table, just large enough for the stable containing the ox and the donkey and, next to it, the hillside.

The room was slightly darkened and silent. I went to bring the children "out of hiding." The first six children, in procession, were carrying the four Advent candles, the candleholder and the wreath. As all sixty-seven children entered, they began to sing:

> Candle, candle, burning bright,
> Shining in the cold winter night,
> Candle, candle, burning bright,
> Fill our hearts with Christmas light!

It was truly enchanting as they assembled the Advent wreath on the small table in front of the stable. The singing continued as the children took their places on the rug and the light from the candles seemed to make the stable come to life!

Then, I had the extraordinary privilege of presenting the Nativity and Adoration of the Shepherds to two hundred or more awaiting faces. My first time giving the presentation, their first time seeing the presentation. The children's responses during the presentation were endearing and I could feel that they had placed themselves "at the stable." At the end of our meditation I softly began to sing "Silent Night" and everyone soon joined in. As a conclusion, to express our joy, we sang "Happy Birthday, Jesus!" It was great!

I received beautiful compliments from every single family and phone calls from our Religious Education Director and Pastor also complimenting me. However, my biggest reward and greatest compliment came from a man who is uncertain in his religious beliefs and never attends mass. He did come to the celebration though, because of his children. In the first twenty minutes following the Presentation he came to me four times to express how moved he was by it. The last time he came up to me he had tears in his eyes and asked, "May I come to your class?" He's coming this Sunday for the first time.

> Love to All,
>
> Patti Orrben
> "The Lighthouse Atrium"-for
> children of the Light
> St. Kevin's Parish, Minneapolis,
> Minnesota

"The Nativity"-Andy Nelson, age 5,
Minneapolis, Minnesota.

The Lord is the only purpose to life; even the most learned men are shameful in His presence.

Joshua Spaulding, age 9,
Mt. Rainier, Maryland.

Jesus is TEACHER

Katrine Halbach, age 8,
Minneapolis, Minnesota.

John Dittberner, age 5, Minneapolis, Minnesota.
Editor's note: To me, this is an essential drawing. The church which this child attends has two floors, the sanctuary/chapel and the basement. He has drawn them and put in the most important features: the priest at the altar, the cross, the box at the bottom right is the "atrium"–and the stairs which connect the two. The small rectangle near the bottom center is the door.

# Working with Adults

Last summer in St. Paul, a proposal was made to send to the newsletter an article about our work with adults. It is not easy to write about it since it is still very new for most of us, but there may be certain facts that will help us to discover something in this field, to see what is happening in this area among the catechists of the Good Shepherd.

My first contact with adults as a catechist of the Good Shepherd was in <u>September, 1976</u>. After the first course with Sofia Cavalletti, in Mexico City, I went back to Chihuahua very enthusiastic and eager to work in this way with the children. The priest of my parish told me that I had to present the idea to the Parish Council and so I presented the Good Shepherd. The parents of several children were enchanted. "We knew these things," they said, "but never before have we seen them in this way." They themselves offered to make materials, chairs and tables, and the work began with twelve children.

In <u>October, 1976</u>, we started the first atrium in Chihuahua at the Parish Church of San José de la Montaña. After a few months three adults in the community were participating very intensely in the catechesis and were being transformed by it; the priest, another catechist, and myself. The children became our catechists and they were giving us a new look into the Mystery of God, and into the mystery of themselves and their relationship with God. Our priest, Father José Cereceres, after the first year of this work said: "I have studied the Bible, Liturgy and Theology in the seminary and on my own for many years, but I have never understood them as this year in the atrium, seeing the children. He used to go and sit in the atrium while the children were working. For ten years now, he has helped our work in Chihuahua. The Bible and the Liturgy shine for him now with a new light discovered with the children. He said once: "I wish I could see the Light of the Risen Christ the way the blind children of the atrium can see it."

<u>Holy Week and Easter, 1977</u>: Colonia Lealtad is a very poor neighborhood in the hills of Chihuahua City. Father Cereceres decided to prepare Easter, for the community, with some of the presentations of our catechesis. As Lent began we gathered in a very small room. More or less, fifty to eighty adults of different ages, both men and women, gathered. We meditated, just as the children do, on the Good Shepherd, the found sheep, the Eucharistic Presence of the Good Shepherd, the Cenacle, the Liturgy of the Light and Baptism.

That year, in the community, an Easter of Salvation was lived. Many came back to the sheepfold carried on the shoulders of the Good Shepherd, and there was feast (sic) and joy. Many knew and felt they were loved. We realized that the Light of the Risen Christ and the White Garment were offered again to all of us, and forever.

<u>September, 1977 to June, 1979</u>: A group of catechists met once a week to have a presentation. We meditated on Wednesday and on Saturday or Sunday we would see it again with the children. What happened to us in this catechesis? On Wednesday, many reactions came forth from enchantment and new insights to comments like: "This is impossible and ridiculous!" From great joy to a sense of "losing our securities," that is to say, we began to realize that the mystery of God could not be enclosed in fixed formulas and precise answers. The Parables, the Liturgical Signs and Gestures, opened to us an unlimited horizon in the grasping of the mystery of God.

On Saturdays and Sundays with the children, all our resistances were broken. As we had the presentations with them, their joy, their brilliant eyes opening wider and wider before the Proclamation, their capacity to see the invisible, their peaceful and serious work, their will to come and to remain in the atrium, showed us a new way in faith and relationsip with God.

In the <u>summer of 1978</u> Sofia Cavalletti gave an intensive course in Houston and we experienced there a new dimension in our work with adults: ECUMENISM. Deep relationships in faith, mutual respect and love were created there and still remain among different people from various backgrounds and traditions. Some of the highest moments of the month were lived as we meditated the History of the Kingdom of God and its unity, its vastness and its unique design of communion. Ecumenism, regarding understanding among Christians, flourished there, but also ecumenism towards the people of Israel rose and irradiated in our horizons after this course. It also extended towards people of Oriental beliefs.

In Houston I heard, for the first time, questions about how this catechesis could be used with non-Catholic and even non-Christian children. Does it have universal character? Are the Biblical presentations universal? Are the Liturgical ones universal?

From October, 1979 to June, 1982 I was part of a group of adults receiving the Catechesis of the Good Shepherd in Rome at Sofia Cavalletti's house. Hours and hours were given to me for personal and silent contact with the materials and there I was happily invaded, as an adult, by this catechesis. Little by little, with no activity of my own, a joyful harmony permeated my whole person. The treasure of the global experience of God, lived by the child, was transmitted to me by adults and children from the atrium in Rome at Via degli Orsini.

In July, 1984 I was invited to help as trainer in an intensive course with twenty-five adults in St. Paul, Minnesota. This was very different from my work with adults in Mexico. I had in my group several people with Masters degrees in Religious Education, Montessori trainers and teachers, married and single people, sisters, persons with long experiences as catechists in parishes or CCD centers, and four ladies from different Christian denominations: Episcopalian and Methodist Churches. ECUMENISM was again a characteristic of our work. The questions raised in Houston repeated themselves, and some answers began to appear. One of us said once: "In my tradition, during the celebration of Eucharist, we do not have the gestures of Epicelsis and the Offering. Yet, I see them as gestures of the Covenant and I will see how I can present them to our children. I really see them as essential presentations in a Biblical Faith." Comments like this thrilled the hearts of all of us.

A Director of a Montessori School, at the end of our courses, was planning an atrium with biblical presentations in the center and, around them, liturgical presentations according to various traditions.

Also, the MESSIANIC CHARACTER OF THE CHRISTIAN FAITH was rediscovered in the group and this brought us closer to the people of Israel. Another light was the growing consciousness of the REALITY OF THE RISEN CHRIST IN OUR LIVES. A PASCHAL CHARACTER was another aspect of Course I at St. Paul in 1984.

Two courses on the Old Testament and Typology, given to adults in Chihuahua in the Fall of 1984 and 1985, had also an ECUMENICAL GOLDEN THREAD, particularly towards the people of Israel.

July, 1985-Course I in St. Paul, Minnesota. Twenty-five adults were in our group again! Thirteen Christians came from the following Churches: six Episcopalians, two Presbyterians, two Lutherans (one of them working at the Congregational Church), two non-denominational Christians, one from the Church of the Saviour, and twelve Catholics.* Their ages ranged from twenty-three to seventy years old! More or less half of the group were Montessori people; there were married and single people, including a member of the community of the Order of Aaron.

Why such a group? What brought us together? What did we have in common that first morning of the course, on July 15th in St. Paul? THE CHILD. We all were there because of one common element: the child and his or her relationship with God. On our course an ECCLESIOLOGY was lived, a very real one, an alive ONE SHEPHERD AND ONE FLOCK in which each sheep had his or her own name, a name that only God knows and pronounces. That was a reality in our meetings every day.

The strongest moments of communion happened during some of the liturgical presentations like the Eucharistic Presence of the Good Shepherd. How was that possible? It was possible because of the essentiality and objectivity of the announcement in the presentation. The proclamation of the Good Shepherd, inviting all of us around His altar and giving Himself to us in the bread and wine, was for all.

*Editor's note: There was also a participant from the Greek Orthodox tradition in Level II.

Could it be that an essential Catechesis, as the one the child asks of us, is what will bring forth more and more Ecumenism and Communion? Could such Catechesis lead us to a Living Church in which the voice of the Good Shepherd, calling His sheep, will resound in seventy languages, as the voice of God sounded at Mount Sinai? It is possible to think that as we go nearer the Jewish people and the richness and vastness of their oral and written traditions, we will understand more what ecumenism among Christians could be? These and other questions are coming from our work with adults.

Going back to Mexico we have Magdalena, a catechist who, after at least five years of work with adults, says to us: "We said that the Catechesis of the Good Shepherd is for children, but it really has no age; it is for all." She has groups of adults using the Manuals and enjoying, just like the children, presentations and personal work with the objects of the Mass, the vestments and the Liturgical Calendar. "Their understanding of the Parable of the Good Shepherd," adds Magdalena, "has changed, in many homes, the family's relationships." The introduction to Maria Montessori and her vision of the child has also helped parents and children very much.

Since the beginning of the work in Chihuahua, in 1976, the Catechesis of the Good Shepherd has been a source of human promotion and social union. Some other methods were good for a particular social or economic group. This catechesis is for all. Around the different atriums or centers working with the albums, we have seen adults from very different social and economic levels being one and learning from each other. We have also seen catechists who, ten years ago, were practically incapable of expressing themselves, and now are blooming in their atriums or centers with children and adults, and are helping others to know and live the Catechesis of the Good Shepherd.

Olga, a catechist on a ranch in Morelia says: "People who are not sophisticated understand the meaning of the presentations much more." She is referring to her work with adults, parents and other catechists.

Reflecting on these and some other facts, could we begin to see certain characteristics of our work with the adults?

- The children are guiding our work with the adults:
    Adults come to us because of the child.
    Adults remain with us because of the child. (In most cases)
- The child, presented in the first course of the adults, opens to them new horizons and invites them to begin a new adventure in the relationship with God. Adventure guided by the child.
- The child brings essentiality and universality to our work with adults. In working with adults we are opening an ecumenical dimension in our Catechesis.
- The child brings wonder and global involvement, joy and peace to the adult's experience of God.
- The child takes away some of the "false securities" of our faith as adults, and throws us into the vastness of the mystery of God.
- The child becomes the catechist of the adult.
- The work with adults in the Catechesis of the Good Shepherd has had a dimension of promotion, liberation and social communion.
- In a certain moment of its process, the work with the adults becomes like a work in an atrium with the children. Adults become like children in presentations and celebrations.
- The work with adults is a source of hope and we trust that it may hasten the New Creation, the Parousia.

What do you think? Send your experiences with adults and your comments to the next newsletter. Thanks

*Maria Christlieb*

Maria Christlieb
Mexico City, Mexico

# Dear Association Members and Friends,

As we publish our third annual newsletter we rejoice in the growth of the Catechesis of the Good Shepherd, in the many rich experiences we've had with the children as we've listened together to God's word, and in the growth of our community as catechists. Our "fledgling year" as an association (since its formation in St. Paul during the 1984 summer courses) had its share of growth pains. As we gathered in St. Paul this past summer for a retreat and association meetings prior to the summer courses it was clear that some parts of our two-year experimental structure were thriving but that other parts had not proved to be truly compatible with the particular spirit and aims of our association. Therefore, some things were reaffirmed while others were restated or rennovated. During the time in St. Paul the board met twice, the committees on materials, newsletter and formation each met once, and there was an all day meeting of the general membership. We offer here a report of some of the fruits of these meetings (including a report of the November board meeting), particularly for those of you who were unable to attend.

ASSOCIATION MEETINGS - ST. PAUL - JULY, 1985

NAME: The name we adopted after a mail-in vote of members, "Innamoramento: An Association for the Catechesis of the Good Shepherd," had to be changed to "The Catechesis of the Good Shepherd: An Association of Adults and Children," because the name, "Innamoramento," has a connotation in Italian which is not appropriate to our identity as an association.

MATERIALS: It was reaffirmed that the nature of our work demands a certain approach to material making and distributing. We want to be attentive to the needs of people who want to equip their atriums but lack of certain skills or resources inhibit them. We recognize that the careful, prayerful preparation of one's own materials is an integral part of the catechist's formation; therefore, we feel the best help we can offer is that of helping the catechists to be able to make their own materials (drawing also on the talents and resources of the community built around the atrium...the parents, members of the parish, etc.). The materials manual which Sister Sheila Sentiff has prepared under the direction of Sofia and Gianna Gobbi is intended to serve this purpose. The manual is available to anyone who has participated in a 3-6 level training course and is for sale through the association. We also agreed that there might be some materials particularly difficult to make (such as the statue of the Good Shepherd, the model of Jerusalem, or the material of the Books of the Bible) which could be made available for purchase through an individual catechist (or through his or her "artisan connection"). Such materials would first be approved by Sofia. Catechists would be notified of their availability through the newsletter. It was strongly emphasized, however, that the association would not be in the business of producing and selling materials.

THE CENTER: During our first year as an association, Christian Family Montessori School served the association differently than other atriums. Its atriums were thought to be "the atrium of the center" in keeping with one of the original aims of the association that the work of the children be visibly connected to all our work, including administrative work. Thus, we began with the notion that "center" means office and atrium. There was also a financial link between the association and CFMS in that ten hours per month of Rebekah's paid time as association coordinator were spent in observing in the CFMS atriums and consulting with the atrium staff in order to help insure that the work there was truly representative of the Catechesis of the Good Shepherd (particularly since it served as a visitor center by virtue of being connected to the national office). In St. Paul this summer we recognized that this arrangement had been a divisive point in our community and was no longer appropriate. The CFMS atrium no longer receives any "privileges." The financial link between CFMS and the association was removed in order to help us understand that all atriums benefit equally from the association, that all atriums are an equally valuable representation of the Catechesis of the Good Shepherd, and that we are one atrium, one work. The board also voted to give up our rented office space at St. James Catholic Church (where CFMS is located) primarily for financial reasons. The office in now to be found in corners of Cathy's and Rebekah's homes. The association mailing address remains the same.

CATECHIST'S FORMATION: When we speak of formation of the catechist we mean much more that just the successful completion of a training course or even the preparation of one's album or a set of beautiful materials for one's atrium. More important than these particular aspects of formation is that of the on-going spiritual formation of the catechist. During the general membership meeting we posed the following questions: "How shall we call each other to a life of prayer? Should our work call us to a particular spiritual discipline, regular participation in Mass, a particular sort of prayer life?" We agreed that prayer and participation in the Eucharist are essential if our work is to remain under the guidance of the Holy Spirit. Sofia had given much thought to this matter over the past years. She suggested that if we are to have a particular spiritual discipline as catechists, it must not be superimposed from the outside, not mandated as in a religious community (such as having to say the rosary every day, etc.). Rather, it should be something that comes from inside our work. Sofia then recalled with us our aim as an association: "To involve adults and children in a religious experience in which the religious values of childhood are predominant, primarily those values of contemplation and enjoyment." She pointed out to us that First Communion is a central moment, an experience in which the children show us, in a particular way, these values of contemplation and enjoyment in the long, slow preparation and in the celebration of First Communion. She went on to say that the spirituality of the Catechesis of the Good Shepherd can be called a Eucharistic spirituality. Therefore, our preparation for First Communion with the children is deeply significant to our formation as catechists. The children's retreat for First Communion should also be truly our retreat. Sofia then proposed that we let each other know of the dates of our First Communion groups (via the newsletter) so that we can join in some way with what other catechists and children are living. Other catechists present at the meeting suggested that we pray for one another during the year and that we might meditate on particular liturgical texts or the Our Father during the year.

MEMBERSHIP: Several persons expressed their concern that our 1984-85 membership appeal letter too closely linked being a member with paying money (the $30.00 "membership fee"), although it was never intended to be mandatory that one pay that amount in order to be a member. It was decided that for the 1985-86 membership appeal letter we should stress that all catechists and children are considered members if they so choose, that a request for $5.00 should be made for mailings during the year, and that an opportunity for one's giving further financial support (via donation) be made available, since the association does have operating costs beyond mailings.

TREASURER'S REPORT: Barbara Kahn reported that, miraculously enough, we had been able to meet our expenses during the past year. Some of these expenses were part-time salaries for the Coordinator and Administrator, office rental and supplies, mailings, publication of the directory and the materials manual, publication of the newsletter, and scholarships for the summer courses. There was an additional appeal made for the scholarship fund which enabled nine persons to attend the summer courses on full or partial scholarships. During our meetings in St. Paul, it was decided that there should be an additional part-time salary for the Newsletter Editor. Financial statements were passed out at the general membership meeting, additional copies of which may be obtained from Barbara Kahn. To date, our income has been from membership fees, summer course tuitions, and donations. Questions were raised as to the possibility of grants. Are there reservations about applying for such funds? Sofia cautioned us about becoming too much interested in business and suggested that we must carefully consider each case where funds are being offered. It was agreed that, for now, it is best to keep our expenses as low as possible and to continue to rely on the above-mentioned income sources.

SUMMER COURSE SITE FOR 1986: We recalled our original intention (at the inception of the association) of moving the summer course site periodically in order to build community in different areas of the U.S. and Canada. The courses were in Washington, D.C. for two summers, and then they were in St. Paul, Minnesota for two summers. Several sites were mentioned: California, Phoenix, Houston, Toronto, Chicago. It seemed that Toronto might be the place best prepared at this point to sponsor a course. Patricia Coulter has been doing the catechesis there for the past ten years and is part of a larger community of catechists there in Toronto and surrounding areas. Furthermore, a bishop there, Marcel Gervais (whom some of you met at the summer courses in St. Paul in 1984), has been particularly interested in and supportive of our work. Decision on the course site was then left pending until after Sofia, Patricia, Maria Christlieb and Rebekah would meet with Bishop Gervais in Canada in mid-August.

NEWSLETTER REPORT: Carol Dittberner reported that 350 issues of the 1985 newsletter were printed. Because of the length, it did not come out until March. The newsletter paid for itself. It was decided that two newsletters a year would be too costly, both time and material-wise; that they would keep the same format for this coming year with one issue; and that they must ask for a separate subscription fee in order to cover costs. It was determined that a subscription would cost $5.00. The catechists were encouraged once again to send in prayers and drawings done by the children as well as a report on one's atrium for use in the newsletter.

MISCELLANEOUS CONCERNS: Several catechists felt that our retreat and general membership meeting did not allow enough time for us to share our experiences as catechists and that this kind of sharing is vital to building community among us. They asked, "How can our gatherings provide more of an opportunity for this sort of sharing?" Also, some catechists felt they had not had enough of an opportunity for input into board decisions during the previous year. The question was raised, "Do we need more formal avenues for association members to let their feelings and opinions be known?"

ASSOCIATION BOARD MEETING - NOVEMBER 22-24, 1985

In attendance were Barbara Kahn, Carol Dittberner, Cathy Maresca and Rebekah Rojcewicz. We regretted that Sandi Yonikus could not be with us due to illness. We were graciously given a home on Lake Erie (near Cleveland) by Frannie Murphy and her family where we stayed for the two days of our meeting. Our time together seemed particularly blessed with a spirit of love and trust. Our opening meditation, the reading of the Transfiguration, seemed to set the tone for the whole weekend. Here we would like to share some of the agenda items we discussed and decisions we made.

SUMMER COURSE FOR 1986: A large portion of discussions pertained to the summer course, retreat and community meeting for next summer, including location, staff, budget, structure, etc. Rebekah first reported on the mid-August meeting she attended in Canada with Bishop Gervais, Sofia, Patricia and Maria. Based upon the outcome of that meeting and input from other catechists, the board came up with the specific plans for the summer course and meetings as stated in the course/meeting announcement included in this newsletter. We agreed that the most suitable location for this year seemed to be Toronto. In view of our lack of approved course materials (Sister Sheila and others are now working on a "travel set" of materials but can only attend to the 3-6 level for this year), and our lack of trainers, it would be best to offer courses in only one location this year and at only the beginning level. By doubling the size of the group (from 25 to 50) we would better accomodate the need in Canada for training new catechists while also providing enough places for Americans. The board also decided to continue calling this course an introduction to the work with the 3-6 year old child...meaning a second summer would be needed to complete the 3-6 level work. We agreed that since Sofia was willing to come, she should be the one to select the teaching staff and work out with them the actual course format.

One of our bigger discussions came in regard to the proposed retreat and association meetings for next summer. Based upon input from many catechists, the board felt strongly that the greatest need was for more of an opportunity to share our experiences with each other and for more time to prayerfully discuss association matters than was allotted last year in a four day retreat and one day general membership meeting. We then proposed a sort of combination retreat/meeting experience following the course (Aug. 11-15) which would be called the "Community Meeting of the Catechists of the Good Shepherd" and would include each day a time for meditation (on themes from our work) and Mass, association meetings, and sharing of our experiences as catechists. It was also recommended that this meeting be dedicated to those already involved in the work (meaning that it would not be really approriate for someone just introduced to the work or to the community).

The board also felt it important to provide an opportunity for a limited number of "returning catechists" (those who've already begun training) to participate in the summer course for one or more weeks in order to hear the kerygma again, work on one's album or with materials, meet with Sofia or other catechists, etc. The only restriction would be in participating in the small group experience in the afternoons (the time in which new catechists are learning to work with materials, make an album, give presentations, etc.). Please see the course announcement for further details.

DIRECTORY: Our new directory will include a list of atriums as well as of individual catechists. The question of the children's membership was raised. They are considered members, but we feel we could not possibly list all their names in the directory. In essence, they are included as the atriums are listed. We hope the new directory will be ready in March. Thereafter, it may not be published more than bi-annually with an addendum of new members being sent out annually.

PROPOSAL TO SPONSOR TRAINING FOR CENTRAL AMERICAN CATECHIST: During last year's summer course we received a letter from Judy Walsh-Mellett and Millie Dosh which had been signed by many other catechists. It was a request for a scholarship to be provided by the association for training a catechist from Central America. They had discussed this with Maria Christlieb in terms of the person attending the training in Mexico, and Maria thought this would be possible. The board decided to encourage Judy and Millie to investigate exact costs and to find the right candidate. For our current budget we felt we could commit to $500.00 to start with and then seek ways to find the remainder.

SCHOLARSHIP PROCEDURE: In response to a letter from a catechist, Carol Dittberner asked that the scholarship procedure be explained. The scholarships are announced in the course announcements and newsletter. Anyone may apply and state their need, telling something about the group they are serving. Last year all the requests were held until the 15th of May and a summary of them was prepared. Rebekah, Barbara and Cathy each reviewed the requests and then jointly decided on the disbursement. As it turned out, they divided the money (the $1000.00 allocated in the budget) equally among all those who had requested aid. An additional $600.00 was obtained through a scholarship appeal letter which was disbursed as above. A catechist had proposed that we add a finance committee to the board or that we have people handle the finances who are not on the board or who are not receiving a salary. (Note: Barbara Kahn is the board's Treasurer or Finance Chairperson, and she receives no salary.) The board proposed that for this year Rebekah, Barbara and Patricia Coulter be on the scholarship committee. (Patricia has declined to be on the committee, so a third, non-board member person is being sought for the committee.)

EVALUATION OF ASSOCIATION STRUCTURE BY THE MEMBERS: As we are ending our two-year experimental structure as an association we feel it is very important to involve all the members in the process of evaluating where we've been and discerning where we need to be headed. The board proposed that some sort of evaluation form (not to thwart individual means of expression but only to be used as a tool) be sent to the members during the winter and that a group of catechists (non-board members) be asked to receive and collate the responses. Tina Lillig and other catechists from Chicago have agreed to do this. It is likely that there will need to be a second mailing before our meetings in Toronto, when we will be adopting a revised or altogether new structure.

With hopes that this summer will bring many of us back together again,

*Rebekah*

Rebekah Rojcewicz
Association Coordinator

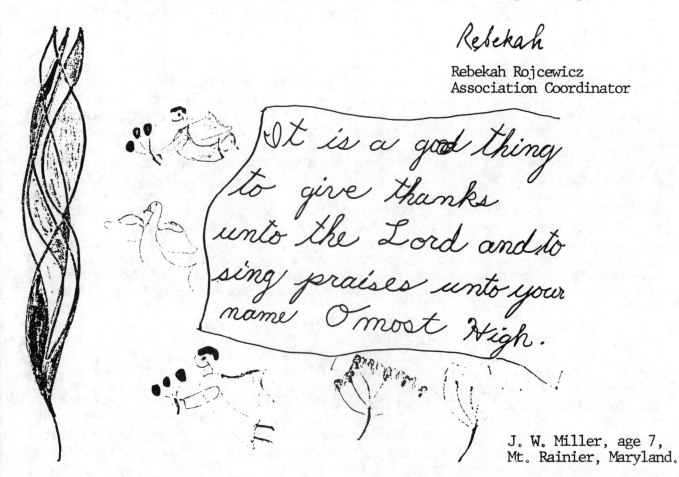

"It is a good thing to give thanks unto the Lord and to sing praises unto your name O most High."

J. W. Miller, age 7,
Mt. Rainier, Maryland.

# A Prayer for the Association

Bless this group that gathers here and in St. Paul, retreatants and students. Bless our prayers, our work and our meetings. Send your Holy Spirit to completely fill us with Light and Wisdom and Creativity. Bless our friendships and keep them Holy; keep our friendships strong throughout the process of organizing. Do not let too much organizing divide this community.

Help us to make decisions of the heart for they are always the decisions of truth. Hold us, this community which gathers for a month, in your arms and love us. We in turn will bless your name with thanks and praise.

Amen.

Maria Christlieb, trainer for the Level I Course, presents the meditation for Pentecost. College of St. Thomas, St. Paul, Minnesota.

Sofia Cavalletti and Lillian Lewis at the first course sponsored in North America; St. Paul, Minnesota, July, 1975. The course was sponsored by the Montessori Foundation of Minnesota.

*In celebration of the tenth anniversary of training courses in the Catechesis of the Good Shepherd in the United States begun by Dr. Sofia Cavalletti in St. Paul, MN July 1975*

*August 1, 1985*

Seven participants from the first course in St. Paul were reunited in 1985 for the Tenth Anniversary. In the back row, from left to right are: Alicia de Arocha, Mexico City, Mexico; Sofia Cavalletti, Rome, Italy; Chulanganee Fernando, St. Paul, Minnesota, and Anna Mae Guida, New Kensington, Pennsylvania. In the front row, from the left: Carol Dittberner, also from St. Paul; Sister Sheila Sentiff, Rochester, New York, and Mary Polta, Marshall, Minnesota.

Sopana and John Dittberner, and Father Cecil Roufs celebrate the publishing of our first Newsletter in January of 1984 in St. Paul, Minnesota.

Cathy Maresca, left, from Washington, D.C., and Tina Lillig, Chicago, share the last evening together in St. Paul.

Bert and Marty O'Bryan of Phoenix, Arizona.

The retreat in Prior Lake, Minnesota gathered 24 participants including 5 catechists from Mexico. Above are, left to right, Gloria Fourzan, Emilia Sandoval and Noemi F. de Lopez, all of Chihuahua.

# A Dream

by Maria Christlieb

Last summer we had our first retreat as a group of catechists of the Good Shepherd. The quiet atmosphere, near St. Paul, helped us to know each other a little bit more and to dream together.

One of the dreams born there was A TRIP TO ISRAEL as a group, with the company and orientation of Sofia Cavalletti. One morning, Mary Polta and myself began to imagine this possibility, later we talked with Sofia about it. She looked at us incredulous but happy. "Dream," she said, "it might be possible, why not?"

From August 1985 to the present day we have gone on dreaming about it, but also working on this project. Mary Polta has done lots of research in several travel agencies and airlines in the USA and she is now an expert in routes and plane fares to Europe and Tel Aviv. I have made several programs for the trip distributing twenty days in Israel and Rome. I have talked with Sofia and other catechists and they all enjoy the idea but it seems like a great dream.

Sofia says that she basically agrees with the idea and is willing to go with us, but she can not commit herself to a summer course and to make this trip in the same year, it is too much. Her position gives us more time for dreaming and planning, since next summer she will be in Canada.

I believe this dream can be realized if a good number of us have it, and with the help of the Newsletter I want to propose it to all of you, especially the Catechists of the Good Shepherd.

The trip would be to know the Land of Israel and to fall in love with her, to go back to the roots of our faith and to contemplate, at least for a little while, the people and the land where God, since so many centuries, is revealing himself to man, the land which, in the blooming of her desert, in the open doors of her Jerusalem and in her daily cry to the Lord WHO IS ONE, reminds us of the faithful love of God and opens before us the hope for the Day of the coming of the Messiah.

The land where the Word was made flesh in the Person of Jesus Christ and where death was conquered forever. Land who has seen the morning of the resurrection and land who proclaims the Parousia.

What can we do to make possible this dream, this TRIP TO ISRAEL OF THE CATECHISTS OF THE GOOD SHEPHERD?

1. Believe that this dream can be a reality.
2. Talk it over with God and dream with Him about it.
3. Decide if you want to go.
4. Talk it over with other catechists and dream with them about it.
5. Write to Mary Polta for practical information about it.
6. Save money.
7. Write to Maria Christlieb possible dates for the trip, the convenient ones for you: month and year you will prefer. 1986 is not possible.
8. It will be very helpful to have your comments on our dream by next summer, whatever you like to say. Send them to Sofia Cavalletti, Patricia Coulter, Mary Polta, Rebekah Rojcewicz, Carol Dittberner or Maria Christlieb.

In this Newsletter, I am throwing to all of you the small seed of this dream. May it be a reality. At the summer meeting we will talk it over again and its being will depend on our answers.

I hope that we will do it and that, one day, many of us, together, will see the Walls of Jerusalem, the empty tomb, the Garden of Olives and the Sea of Galilee.

I entrust this dream to the Lord God of Israel, to the Prophets and to David Ben-Gurion, the first leader of the government of the State of Israel in 1948 who said once: "He, who does not believe in miracles, is not realistic."

I also entrust it to all of you. Let's make it possible.

Katherine Goodwin, age 7,
Mt. Rainier, Maryland.

# Summer Course Announcements

The Catechesis of the Good Shepherd offers for the summer of 1986 COURSE I: AN INTRODUCTORY CATECHIST'S TRAINING COURSE FOR WORK WITH THE 3-6 YEAR OLD CHILD. This course will be held in Toronto, Ontario from July 21st through August 8th at St. Joseph's College. The course format includes lectures, discussions and presentations of materials. The participants receive assistance in the preparation of a teacher's album and guided practice with the materials. Subjects include: the religious capacities of the 3-6 year old child, characteristics of the child's religious experiences, Christ as the Light, Christ as the Good Shepherd, and Baptism. There are no prerequisited for this training.

Staff will be Sofia Cavalletti, Maria Christlieb, Rebekah Rojceqicz, Gianna Gobbi, and Sister Sheila Sentiff.

Tuition: $450 (U.S.); $550 (Canadian)
Housing: Rates at St. Josephs' College are $150 for a single, meals incu

Housing: Rates at St. Joseph's College are $150 a week for a single, includes meals. $130 a week for shared accomodation.

RETURNING CATECHISTS: There will be a limited number of places available for catechists who have already completed the Introductory Course for the 3-6 year old child who would like the opportunity to hear the lectures, work on their albums, and meet with the staff. A catechists may come for one, two or three weeks at a cost of $50 (U.S.) per week tuition. Housing would apply as above for a three week stay. Costs are slightly higher for short-term stays.

COMMUNITY MEETING OF THE CATECHISTS OF THE GOOD SHEPHERD: August 11th-15th. These days are dedicated to catechists already involved in the work. They will focus on personal enrichment and the building of community. The structure will be as follows: mornings-presentations for meditation or Mass; early afternoon-free time, siesta; late afternoon-Association meetings; evenings-sharing of our experiences as catechists.

Facilitators: Brother Ignatius Feaver and Rebekah Rojcewicz.

Fees: $150 (U.S.), $200 (Canadian). Includes room and board. Fees will be adjusted for those not staying on campus.

For further information and an application, please write to:

CATECHESIS OF THE GOOD SHEPHERD     or phone: Catherine Maresca
3628 Rhode Island Avenue     (202) 832-2477
Mt. Rainier, Maryland 20712

Donna Macklin, left, of Casper, Wyoming, is welcomed to the course by Carol Dittberner, Joan Miller and Mary Polta who, along with Rose Paul (not pictured), hosted the summer courses in St. Paul.

# Announcements

This summer we all celebrated the publication of the Manual which was prepared and written by Sister Sheila Sentiff. The Manual includes descriptions of the materials used with the 3-6 year old children. There are directions, diagrams, and well thought out instructions to aid the catechist in making his/her own materials. Sister Sheila has also included a section on the types of tools one will need and how to properly use those tools.

The Manual is available to all those who have completed the first summer course training for children ages 3-6 years. To order, please fill out the accompanying form.

Please send me _____ copy(ies) of the Manual at $20.00 each plus $2.50 each for postage and handling.

NAME_____

ADDRESS_____

CITY/STATE/ZIP_____

_____

Amount enclosed: _____

_____

Class photos were taken in the summer (1985) by Bert O'Bryan. If you would like a copy, please contact him:

Bert O'Bryan
1338 Culver Street West
Phoenix, Arizona 85007
Phone: (602) 258-9623

Last summer the E. M. Standing Montessori Center of Seattle, Washington gave the Association many copies of the hard cover edition of THE CHILD IN THE CHURCH. We thank them for their generosity and have distributed the books to the students in last year's courses. The book is a collection of articles written by Maria Montessori, Sofia Cavalletti, E. M. Standing, Mother Isabel Eugenie, R.A. and M. and F. Lanternier on the development of the religious life of the child and the materials used with children. E. M. Standing edited the collection. There are some copies still available. If you would like a copy, please send $4.00 (includes handling and postage) to Carol Dittberner at the address listed on this page
Carol Dittberner, 1429 Portland Avenue, St. Paul, Minnesota 55104.

_____

If you would like a copy of the Spanish edition of this newsletter please send $4.00 for each copy to:

Irma Chandler
10476 Seawood
El Paso, Texas 79925
Phone: (915) 598-4838

Additional copies of this newsletter may be obtained for $3.00 each. There are a few copies of the 1985 edition still available also for $3.00.
Write to:

Carol Dittberner
1429 Portland Avenue
St. Paul, Minnesota 55104
Phone: (612) 645-8917

_____

This past summer Cathy Maresca and Carol Dittberner conducted an interview with Sofia Cavalletti which will be appearing in SOJOURNERS MAGAZINE this spring or summer. Watch for it!

# Catechesis of the Good Shepherd

We wish to celebrate with all of you the publication of our third Newsletter! We are also happy to tell you that this issue is being published in Spanish in Chihuahua, Mexico. Thank you to the staffs in both locations that have made this possible. We also express our gratitude to all the contributors this year. Catechists are invited to send articles about their work, their centers, and prayers and drawings done by the children. You may mail materials or bring them to the summer course.

Newsletter materials may be sent to: Carol Dittberner
1429 Portland Avenue
St. Paul, Minnesota 55104

If you are interested in the Association and would like to receive our mailings regularly, please write to:

Catechesis of the Good Shepherd
3628 Rhode Island Avenue
Mt. Rainier, Maryland 20712

Phone: Cathy Maresca, (202) 832-2477.

| | |
|---|---|
| Single Newsletter Subscription | $5.00/year |
| Membership/Mailing List (does not include Subscription) | $5.00/year |
| Donation (A donation of $30.00 per year will help to support our financial needs and is tax deductible) | $30.00/year |
| Group Membership/minimum of five per group (includes Subscription) | $8.00/each person |

This Newsletter was compiled by Carol Dittberner in collaboration with Dr. Sofia Cavalletti.

Photographs in this issue were provided by Alicia de Arocha, Carol Dittberner and Bert O'Bryan.

Copyright (c) by:
The Catechesis of the Good Shepherd
3628 Rhode Island Avenue
Mt. Rainier, Maryland
20712

Published in St. Paul, Minnesota
April 16th, 1986.
Spanish Edition published in
Chihuahua, Mexico.

Staff in St. Paul, Minnesota:

Joan Miller
Rose Marie Paul
Mary Polta
Carol Stenborg

Claudia Riordan, Napa, California
    Translation from Italian

Staff in Chihuahua, Mexico:

Emilia Sandoval
Noemi F. de Lopez
Bertha Sofia Q. de Marquez
Ema Luisa Fuentes
    Translation from Italian
Maria Inez Lafone

# Catechesis of the Good Shepherd

## Spring 1987

but they constrained him saying,
"Stay with us, for it is toward evening
and the day is now far spent."
So he went in to stay with them.
When he was at table with them,
he took the bread and blessed,
and broke it, and gave it to them.
And their eyes were opened
and they recognized him;
and he vanished out of their sight.
They said to each other,
"Did not our hearts burn within us
while he talked to us on the road,
while he opened us to the scriptures?"
And they rose that same hour
and returned to Jerusalem;
and they found the eleven
gathered together and those
who were with them, who said,
"The Lord has risen indeed,
and has appeared to Simon!"
Then they told what had happened
on the road, and how he was known
in the breaking of the bread.

Luke 24:29-35

# Let us pray with the children ...

Age 2-1/2

Thank you for my mom and my God.

Age 3

A child in Mexico says to her mother who would like to pray with her: "I pray alone and in silence."

Age 5

Thank you, God, for me.
Thank you, Father, for you.
Thank you for the light.

### How God Sings

Ana is a Mexican girl, eight years old, who has brain paralysis. She has been coming to the atrium for two years. One day she was in the car with her mother and started singing a song that they used to sing in the atrium: "I have a friend who loves me; his name is Jesus." The mother was listening to her. At a certain moment the girl says to her mother: "Mommy, do you know how God sings this song?"
"I do not," replied the mother.
"Like that (and she says singing), 'I have a friend who loves me; her name is Ana.'"

### Prayers of some children from Chad

These prayers come from a group of boys, catechuminates and baptized, ages twelve to seventeen years.

Lord, I have sinned greatly against you. Put your hands on my head so that I may be perfect.

Lord, because of Thy redemption we have succeeded in being new persons and we are prepared to enter into Parousia. May your will be done and may we walk under your sun that lifts us up to everlasting happiness.

Lord, I give you thanks because I was lost in the desert and you made me return to the new life. Thank you!

The water that I received abundantly is not sufficient for me; I would like much more the water that is the source of life, that is the water which will purify me later so that I may resurrect like the Savior.

When the world ends, I think (because everything unnatural is made out of something natural) it will be renewed. Here is how: everything unnatural will go back to what it was made out of and it would be alive if ever it was alive. And it would be so that the going back couldn't hurt anything alive, and everything alive would be in one place. I don't know where that place would be; it might be sort of like the garden of Eden.

Peter, age 7, USA.

## Praise to God

The following prayer has a story: Stefano, ten years old, is a very boisterous boy and he belongs to a family hostile to religion. Once the parish priest had to scold him very severely. Stefano did not come back to the catechesis. When Christmas approached, the catechist went to visit him and to invite him back to the atrium. Stefano came back, sat at his table, and wrote this prayer:

*Sono nella tua strada o Signore dimmelo tu nel buio si ode un canto Angelico.*

*Sono forse ingannato dalla voce di Satana, non sono un eroe non sono uno che cerca la gloria.*

*Sono un uomo che cerca di farsi strada nel cammino di Dio.*

*Sono davanti a un cancello penso e ripenso mi sono deciso sento come un fuoco nel mio cuore i cancelli si aprono entro vedo Dio.*

*Sono arrivato*

*Lode a Dio*

---

I am in your path, Lord. Tell me yourself in the darkness an angelic singing is heard.

Am I deceived by Satan's voice; I am not a hero, I am not somebody who looks for glory.

I am a man who tries to walk in the path of God. (May also be translated "to open the path in front of you.")

I am in front of a gate I think, and I think again I am decided I feel something like a fire in my heart: the gate is opened, I go in. I see God.

I am arrived..

On March 21st, 1987,
L'ASSOCIAZIONE MARIA MONTESSORI
PER LA FORMAZIONE RELIGIOSA
DEL BAMBINO
( the Maria Montessori Association
for the Religious Formation of the Child),
celebrated its 25th Anniversary.

The organization was founded in 1963,
and all of the catechists around the world
and the children served are the fruit
of this association. We offer our
congratulations and thanksgiving
to all those in Italy who began and
sustained this work. We give thanks to
God for this work, and for all the
people who have taught and inspired
us through the Holy Spirit.

– With much love from
the catechists of Mexico,
Canada, the United States,
Argentina, Columbia, Japan,
Africa and Italy.

The parable of the Good Shepherd,
Western Samoa.

# Social Justice: A question of relationships

Translated from the Italian
by Joan Marie Parasine

Dear Catechists,

At various times I have been asked what we do in our catechesis (program) in relation to social justice. This matter is certainly one of the most talked about problems of our day and it is quite proper that a message in this area be required (from us). While keeping in mind this central point, the initiatives whose aim is to achieve it (social justice) are many, the tasks are multiple and diverse.

For example, there is the task of the trade unionist, and that of the catechist. Each must follow its own path to arrive at the same goal: the living together of humans in justice and harmony. I would also distinguish the work of the catechist who works with the "little ones" up to six years of age from that of those who work with the older children (over six years). As always, the task of the former is the fundamental one in that it is the catechist of the "little ones" who helps them to establish the foundation on which successive developments are grafted.

What is social justice if not a question of relationships? Social justice flowers in a climate of balanced relationships, of reciprocal service in respect and love toward one another. In a situation of unharmonious relationships, of over-bearing power of one over another, we have social injustice.

In the matter of relationships, we find ourselves confronted with a question which is rooted deeply in the formation of the "person." Everyone knows that the "person" is formed in relationships. Every educational work which aims to help the child establish relationships in harmony and love is, therefore, a work of social justice considered in its root.

At this point, we ask ourselves what WE do in this area. Let's consider for a moment the points of the Christian message which, according to indications given by the child, form the content of the catechesis with the little ones. With them we speak of the Good Shepherd who calls his sheep by name, and of the sheep who "strain their ears" to listen to the Shepherd's voice. We speak of Christ, the "Light", who transmits his Light/Life to every human creature. We speak of the gift of the Spirit, whom we ask the Father to send so that the presence of the Risen Christ might be effected in our midst, and of how we seek to respond to this presence.

We might also add a point that has greatly captured the children: the mingling of the few drops of water in the wine. These are all elements which make evident a relationship. To express it in biblical terms, they are all elements which make evident a <u>covenant</u>. The two biblical images of the <u>shepherd</u> and the <u>light</u> become visible in the sacrament "of the new and eternal covenant," namely in that act in which the relationship is realized and lives in a most particular manner.

The point of convergence of the whole catechesis with the little ones, therefore, is the covenant. This is a covenant in which the vertical dimension is, perhaps, the more important one with the little ones. But it is certainly not the exclusive one. If we study the drawings of the children, we see that the Shepherd always calls many sheep, among whom we can sometimes recognize the child's family and, more often, the child's class and catechesis group. "I love the Shepherd and I also love the sheep," was written on one picture of a five year old child.

There is only one Paschal Candle, but the little candles which receive the light from it are numerous, and the quality of light is always the same in everyone. And, finally, those hands which are moved vertically in the gestures of <u>epiclesis</u> and <u>offering</u> are later opened in the fraternal gesture of "peace."

We won't pause here to repeat what we have said so many times regarding the particular sense of joy which the children display in hearing these elements of the Christian message. That serene, peaceful joy which the child has clearly shown us leads us to believe that the Christian announcement resounds deeply in the soul of the child satisfying a vital, essential need. It is in such satisfaction that the child takes pleasure, and his "person" is being formed in a gratifying relationship with God and with his brothers and sisters.

In our opinion, in the catechesis with the little ones, the most essential basis for a formation in social justice is started. The most essential basis is to help the "person" open itself to the relationship with the "Other" and with others, in the certitude of being loved and being able to return love.

As we have said so many times, the educational work before six years is a work whose aim is to help the person in his origins. It is a "global" work which does not have as its target an immediate result, quantifiable in its moral and social yield. Without this (base), however, the numerous achievements of the older child would be devoid of life because they are detached from the tree from which they draw vital juices.

After the sixth year, the horizon of the child is widened. Maria Montessori speaks of "cosmic education." "Give the child the universe," she said. In addition, a new interest is born relating to what one should do and what one should not do. It is a new moral interest turned toward actions and the rules which ought to guide them. Social justice is, obviously, included in actions.

Catechesis ought to "follow" the child in these new dimensions of development. Let's see if the dimension of social justice is present in the contents (of the program) that we give to the child over six years of age.

The new capacity of the child, before it becomes set, is satisfied in the presentation of the biblical history, that history which begins with the creation of the world and will be concluded when "God will be all in all." This history begins with the search for an order of things so that a world is formed in which the human creature can live and work. The attention is noted that Montessori places on helping the child understand the links which join one element to the other elements of creation forming a mysterious net which holds the whole universe together in the inter-relationships of its various components. After all, this is what the ecology of our day is making evident.

When the human being enters the field, what happens? How is history developed? If we can look at it in a wide enough perspective, history shows us the existence of the invisible links between one human being and another, between one people and another. If a superficial glance is taken, we see the crises, the divisions, the wars and the violence. A more attentive examination, enabling one to scrutinize in depth, will uncover the existence of a deep current which leads toward community. At present, we enjoy the discoveries that people far distant from us have made and, yet, are essential in our modern life. (One thinks of the great discoveries of the Neolithic Era: agriculture, animal breeding, weaving. One thinks of the wheel, necessary even for flying.) The results of our efforts today are the springboard or the launching platform for the people of tomorrow. People are born, grow, vanish, but they leave the legacy of their work, of their human efforts, of their history to another people.

History is a history of relationships which intertwine through ages and millenia. Studied in depth, history shows within itself a force of cohesion which, beneath the sometimes tragic and deep ripples, has the formation of community as its aim. The Bible gives a cosmic dimension to such community. This cosmic dimension encompasses heaven and earth. The Bible speaks of the Covenant between God and Abraham, between God and the people of Israel. This is a relationship between the divine and the human which reaches its culmination in Christ and whose aim is to widen and to fill the world until "God will be all in all." We turn, then, to the covenant seen in an historical perspective. If this is history, it possesses within itself, by the sole fact that it is what it is (history), a very strong need for a certain human behavior in which social justice occupies a primary place. If this is history, then every division, every dissension is contrary to its own profound way of realizing itself, contrary to the plan of God. History is able to reach its goal only in community.

The child is being initiated into this reality of multiple and very vast relationships, helping him to become aware of himself as an important link, albeit a small one, in the development of history. It appears to me that in such a presentation of history, the problem of social justice is grasped at its roots. We are inserted into a history which is ongoing, despite all, toward a goal, and we are called to collaborate in its progress toward that goal.

In addition, the great Christological image which we give the children over six, that of the True Vine, is another way of attacking the question of social justice, dealing with it at its roots. Human relationships find their motivation in a real community of life: the same sap, the life of the Risen Christ, runs in every branch so that the richness of one is the richness of all; the poverty of one is the poverty of all. To speak of human relationships is not only a metaphor; it's an expression of a concrete reality, of a true "affinity" through which one can say that every human being is my brother and my sister.

This parable, the True Vine, which is added to the message of the parable of the Good Shepherd reinforcing the gratifying message with the invitation to "remain in his love," presents some very strong moral implications, proper to the meaning of human solidarity and, therefore, to social justice.

Basic for an education in social justice, as is basic for all moral education is, therefore, above all, the help which is given to the child to investigate reality, to know the rules so as to bring himself or herself into line with them, and so become an active agent in their own development.

Having situated the question of social justice on this broad and essential base, the scripture, then, offers us tools which we might call more than detail for attacking the problem. One thinks of the many maxims and parables concerning relations with others (love of enemy, the foolishness of accumulating things in Luke 12:15-21 and Matt. 6:19-20; the search for the precious pearl in Matt. 13:45-46, etc.). One could conclude, therefore, that the Christian message places within our hands some formidable implements for an education in social justice.

It is by using these tools, steeping ourselves in them and helping the children to grasp in them their great import, that we will fulfill that task which ought, certainly, to be central in all education: social justice.

So, at this point, I await your contributions and your reactions.

Sofia Cavalletti

# Ten Years of the Catechesis of the Good Shepherd

Translated from the Italian
by Joan Parasine

Lucia Cremona is one our catechists who has worked in Chad for ten years. Her activity was, above all, that of a catechist, but she also had to improvise as a nurse obstetrician to be involved with newborns who had lost their mothers. She had to give assistance of every kind and also fight off snakes who sometimes were unwelcome guests in her own house. (Afterwards) she had to return to Italy because her health was not holding up any longer, so much so that for a while we feared that she had given of herself truly to the utmost. Thank God she has recovered and we asked her to tell us a little about her work.

Sofia

### Ten Years of Work Among the Ngambay of Chad

When I arrived at Gagal in the Diocese of Pala (Chad) in August of 1968, I was immediately confronted by what a need there was there for a new method of evangelization. Indeed, the catechesis was pretty nearly the traditional type carried on not long ago everywhere in Italy: only questions and answers learned by rote without deeply searching out their meaning. The few and scanty available texts started with the Old Testament and eventually came to Christ who died and rose; but there was very little of the Gospel in these texts which were most often entrusted to unprepared persons, at times not even baptized persons, only because they were able to read them (the texts). In practice, the people came to the sacraments without a true and proper evangelization, without encountering the person of "the Christ."

What could be done to respond to the requests of the villages when only one missionary was available for such a vast area? The children of the Christians, baptized at birth, followed a brief course of preparation for First Communion and there was nothing else for them. Many adults, who had been baptized years ago, had not received Confirmation. The hard conditions of life for these people, the difficulties, the disease, the fears and such misery touched me deeply. I felt that all their valor, everything positive present in them needed a light, a spirit. It seemed to me that God was still a far-off God and that they did not feel the presence of Christ living and working in their midst (I am speaking about the Christians). One also felt the necessity for the Christians, who had been baptized for some time, to discover the Gospel. Baptism was considered a kind of "pass" or "permit." The Mass was neither known nor understood, mainly for the reason that many things are not adapted to the African mentality.

At Gagal (center) there was a small group of young people from 14-18 years of age, students, some unbaptized, who came to the course of the catechesis held by a young French woman using one of the only texts written in French. (It is noteworthy that the Ngambay language has been written for the first time by the missionaries and the Gospel was translated in part. The first announcement (of the Gospel) was carried out by a catechist who came from another diocese.)

From this young woman, who went back to France a few months later, I inherited this first group of young people and I continued with the program in progress, not without uneasiness. I discontinued using the unconvincing text; then I spoke with the missionary about the situation of the catechesis. From this conversation I came away resolved to begin the new catechesis, with a translator's help (because I understand little French) as the missionary left me free to do as I chose.

The language is certainly a difficulty, but not insurmountable, so great is the power of the word: "Do not concern yourself if you cannot speak our language; your words touch our hearts." All the written work in the materials sent to me from the center in Rome had to be translated beginning with the little Gospels (Infancy and Paschal Narratives, Parable Booklets), and so I began the work which I did every evening by the light of a kerosene lamp, first into French and then into the Ngambay language.

Very slowly I began with the children and the young people, dividing them by age and preparation into four groups. In each group there were baptized and nonbaptized children. Many came and were attentive. The materials which I had available were a very powerful attraction; in addition there was the pleasure of working with paper, pens, pencils and pastels which they did not have. Some of them took a pencil in their hand to draw for the first time. I remember a missionary who visited the school telling me that all these things wouldn't last long in the hands of these young people. I was very confident and I was not mistaken (in this).

However, it was not only the materials that attracted them, but the word of God which they remembered with ease, almost by memory. With the same ease, after they had listened and reflected, they composed the most beautiful spontaneous prayers, true responses to the Word, which they had heard and been attentive to.+ So the baptized children slowly became prepared for First Communion and the older ones for Confirmation.

Meanwhile, I had also begun a program of catechesis with the adult catechumens, of whom I spoke, so that I would always be helped by a Christian translator. The first was a boy, who moved to the city to continue his studies; then, in succession, some student catechists who came with their families to the Gagal Catechist School. For the little ones, I was also helped by two girls. For the translation into the Ngambay language, I had the help of the catechist Matthew, with whom I translated many pages of the Gospel for the first time; among these was the parable of the True Vine. However, I used another image for the vine since here the vine is non-existent.* Then I began with Leon who became a very effective helper and true collaborator, who not only announced the Gospel, but gave witness to it as well.

We gathered all the Christian's who had not been confirmed into a group of about 40 people and we gave a separate course for them. Also, we gave a course for the spouses of the student catechists.

+Editor's note: some of these prayers are included in the section entitled "Let Us Pray with the Children".

*Translator's note: I think here she refers to the grapevine, in particular, since there are certainly vines in Africa.

It is difficult to give an idea of the difficulties which we encountered in a place where having a meal assured every day was a problem which we did not always succeed in resolving. Added to that are the climatic conditions, epidemics, snakes and other poisonous animals. Many people came form a distance to participate in the catechesis (roads are non-existent, and where there are roads, they are often impassable). A person afflicted with leprosy came 7 or 8 km. on leg stumps to be present.

At the beginning, above all, I often heard the adults say, "But this catechesis is totally different." A boy, after hearing the parable of the True Vine for the first time, exclaimed, "Why isn't this parable given to us at the beginning?" Some of the little ones said, "I am going to stay here all the time, even at night...." A group of adults said, "We could stay here all night talking about these things." At the end of the catechesis course a woman was asked what thing was most well received during the year. "The word of God," was her answer.

I had to remake many pictures that are part of the materials to adapt them to the environment here. For the little ones, it was enough for me to ask them who the people were, when showing a picture. In this way, they would recount a whole story or parable to me. I even used some of the materials with the adults (except for the written materials since they were practically illiterate).

My sudden departure and the difficulty I encountered in trying to find someone prepared and available (that is, someone who can move easily from one village to another) didn't permit me to leave someone in place who could continue the catechesis in the same manner. However, Leon Majardet, who had always been with me and was somewhat prepared, remained. He continued as best he was able. I say "as he was able" because, having to divide himself between family, work and catechesis, it made even weekly classes too much for him to manage. His preparation and witness as a catechist was noted and appreciated even in the diocese and he participated at all hours at the meetings of those responsible for evangelization. He was later taken on as an official catechist and commissioned for the evangelization of several villages which he reached by bicycle.

Two years ago he told me that many of the materials were attacked by termites (very voracious insects). He said that the material of the Good Shepherd was the one he used most; he used the narratives of the Last Supper and the True Vine to talk about the Sacraments and the Mass, but only when he did the catechesis at Gagal.

Slowly some ideas made headway and, after a few years, they began to talk about a renewal of the catechesis in the diocese and they have begun to talk about the need to start out with the Gospels.

In my missionary experience, during which I did a bit of everything, I don't hesitate to say that the most beautiful experience was that of direct evangelization because, in evangelizing (others), I evangelized myself and my rapport with Christ increased from it daily.

I always think of Sofia with gratitude for the preparation and for the materials sent to me.

Rome, October, 1985                                                    Lucia

P.S. Today I received a letter from a young person who had participated in the catechesis and who was then 14-15 years old. Among the various bits of news said to me was, "Allow me to call you 'mama' instead of sister or miss, because you are dear to me and to Gagal, particularly for your continuing efforts for the Church at Gagal. Despite the distance which separates our spirits, which have been so close, they are united in the spirit of prayer and in the same faith of Our Lord Jesus, whom you came to teach about in the catechesis.

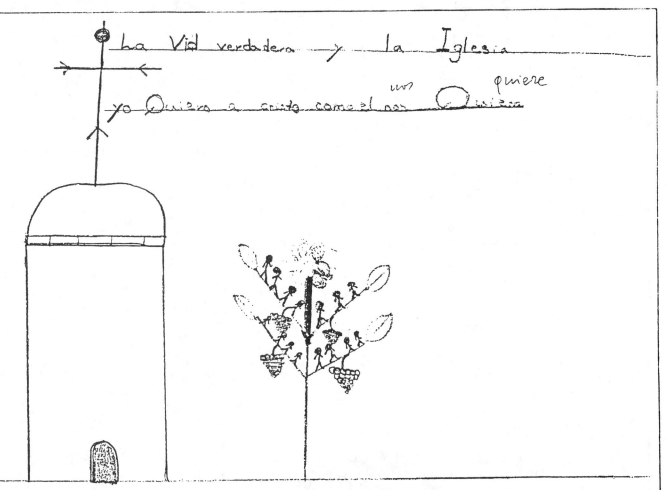

This drawing does not need any explanation. The written words say: "The true vine and the Church. I love Christ as he loves me." José Carlos, age 6, Mexico.

## In Memoriam

Leonard H. Lounder

May 17, 1912-January 21, 1987

It is with great sadness we announce the death of Mr. Lounder, the carpenter in Minneapolis, Minnesota. For four years he served the catechists in this area, and many of you outside of Minnesota have the Liturgical Calendar which he made. Many of the materials, furniture and shelves used in the 1984 and 1985 St. Paul courses were the "work of his hands." Please remember him and his family in your prayers.

The Tabernacle and the Ark of the Covenant made by Mr. Lounder -- presented to Sofia Cavalletti and Maria Christlieb, St. Paul. 1985.

# Celebration of First Eucharist

We recognize that the preparation and reception of First Eucharist is the high point of the year for the children involved and for the catechist. Last year we began publishing the dates of First Communion so as to gather all of us together in prayer during these important days. Please keep in mind that the retreats begin three days before the dates listed.

First Communion in the atriums in Mexico:

Torreon                             December 1986, 1987
                                    March 1987

Ciudad Juarez                       May 16th

Chihuahua and Mexico City           May 10th, 17th, 24th, 31st
                                    June 3rd

From Italy:

    via degli Orsini

        May 3rd

    Rome S. Maria in Apurro

        May 17th

    Scuola Montessori

        May 24th

From the United States:

    Chicago, Illinois

        May 3rd

    Minneapolis, Minnesota

        Holy Thursday

        May 3rd

    Bloomington, Minnesota

        May 17th

    Washington, D.C.

        December 1986, 1987

Drawn during preparation for First Communion. John, age 7, USA.

Reflections of Children during their First Communion Meditations and Retreat

From Chihuahua: A seven year old child was preparing for the mass during the retreat. The child began, "I give you Good Shepherd thanks because you are the lamb of God who takes away the sins of the world." The child paused and turned to the other children and added, "of the world, not only of all of us."
Emilia Sandoval

From Washington, D.C.: During the meditation of the True Vine we discussed its universality. The children were quite sure it included everyone, everywhere, so I asked, "What about the people who have died?" Emilia, age 6, said, "They're still on the vine because of the sap; the sap doesn't die."

During the first examination in preparation for First Confession the children are asked to think about the gifts of God in their lives. Lisa, age 7, said, "Me." Later she said, "My life." Finally she said with great joy, "My life: I know I keep saying that but that's what I keep thinking about."

While meditating on the parable of the Ten Bridesmaids the children are asked what God gives us to help us to be wise, and to enter the kingdom. Some responses were: John, age 6, "I have the gift of reading."
 Catechist: "What can you read that helps you?"
 John: "I have a children's Bible at home."
 Michele: age 8, "Our brains."
 Jennifer: age 6, "Our bodies."
 John: "Our hearts . . . love."
Catherine Wolf Maresca

From Minneapolis: The children were thinking about what the sap could be. All of the children are seven years old unless otherwise noted. Joel: "Jesus' blood," and later he said "all life." Erik: "Grace." Luke: "Light." Peter: age 6, "Loving love."
 Adriano: "Jesus is like a plant because he grows and grows."
 Joel also said the quality of the sap was "everlasting."
 The children felt the dead were also part of the Vine "because they are in heaven."
Carol Dittberner

A child who made her First Communion two years ago was asked by one of her parents (at that time) what receiving Eucharist meant to her. The child, 7 at the time, replied, "It means God is in front of me and behind me and on the side of me and holding my hand so I don't fall and get into trouble."
 This year, the girl's brother is making First Communion. He is 7 and was asked the same question. He said, "God is on my right side and Jesus is on my left side and the angels are all around me."

Editor's note: It is interesting to find these similar responses from children in the same family. The brother had not known what his sister had said two years previous. I would like to ask the catechists if they have similar responses from children about feeling all surrounded by God's love during this special time. As catechists we do not pose the question as the parent did, but I am wondering if, during meditations or while on retreat, the children say or write about it in this way. Please send your responses to the newsletter (address is on the last page). Thank you!

# The Children, the Eucharist and their Happiness

Translated from Spanish by
Carol Stenborg and Ruben Hernandez

A Letter from Emilia to Sofia

We had a mass to witness the Gospel with Fr. Gallo, and Lupita Villalobos' group of children. The children had prepared the Mass the preceding afternoon. They had chosen for the reading the parable of the Mustard Seed, and each knew what they had to do. There were 250 children from Montessori and 10 from San Rafael. When they came into the church, I noticed that the four most unruly children were seated together. I signaled to Lupita to separate them but she did not so they stayed together.

The mass began and the very intense atmosphere you've talked about was created. I noticed the children totally quiet and filled with peace, the four unruly ones never turned to look at each other. The peaceful atmosphere prevailed not only for those four, but for all. The celebration continued. Each received the Gospel in the same atmosphere of peace. They [the children] had brought their prepared prayers and read them. We finished with that happiness.

Lupita came closer to me and said, "Did you realize what happened here?" I only smiled. And then I noticed that one of the girls from San Rafael was crying on a bench, embraced by her mother. It was Estelita, a seven-year old girl who had one leg 20 centimeters longer than the other. You could never quite tell if she was looking at you because she was also cross-eyed and had some other mental deficiency. She was in kindergarten for three years and for two and one half of those she had been fighting with the other children. To me, she seemed like a lamb bounding around all day. But when we spoke to her of the First Eucharist and asked her why she wanted to do it, she smiled and said only, "Because the Good Shepherd loves me and wants me to be closer to him." I approached the bench and noticed that she was crying in silence. Tears were on her face and her mother told me, "Don't worry. They are tears of joy. She is OK."

We turned around at this and there was the mother of another child (The mother had cancer and was in a wheelchair). With tears in her eyes, the mother said to me, "Emilia, what happened here? What do you think? I don't know but there is something here...." And she said no more.

The next day, another mother went to the kindergarten and told my sister, "Teacher, come and tell me what happened yesterday at Mass. There was something in the atmosphere that I can't explain." And a bit later Marcelita's mother came as well. Marcelita is a girl who is not yet six years old that I had seen filled with peace at the Mass. She said, "Teacher, I came to tell you of something strange that I felt at the Mass. Then we got home and Marcelita asked if we'd read the Parables. She listened and her eyes filled with tears."

It really grabbed my attention -- the sensitivity of ordinary persons, but "Blessed be God, the Father, for he has hidden these things from the wise and experienced, and he has revealed (them) to the ordinary people."

Later, for the reunion with the mothers, I had prepared the Cenacle and, as with the children, we experienced their astonishment and long periods of silence... so prayerful that I could do no more than the memorial cards, and then we continued.

I don't think I need say anything more....

Emilia Sandoval<br>Chihuahua, Mexico

Drawn during preparation for First Communion. Michaela, age 8. USA.

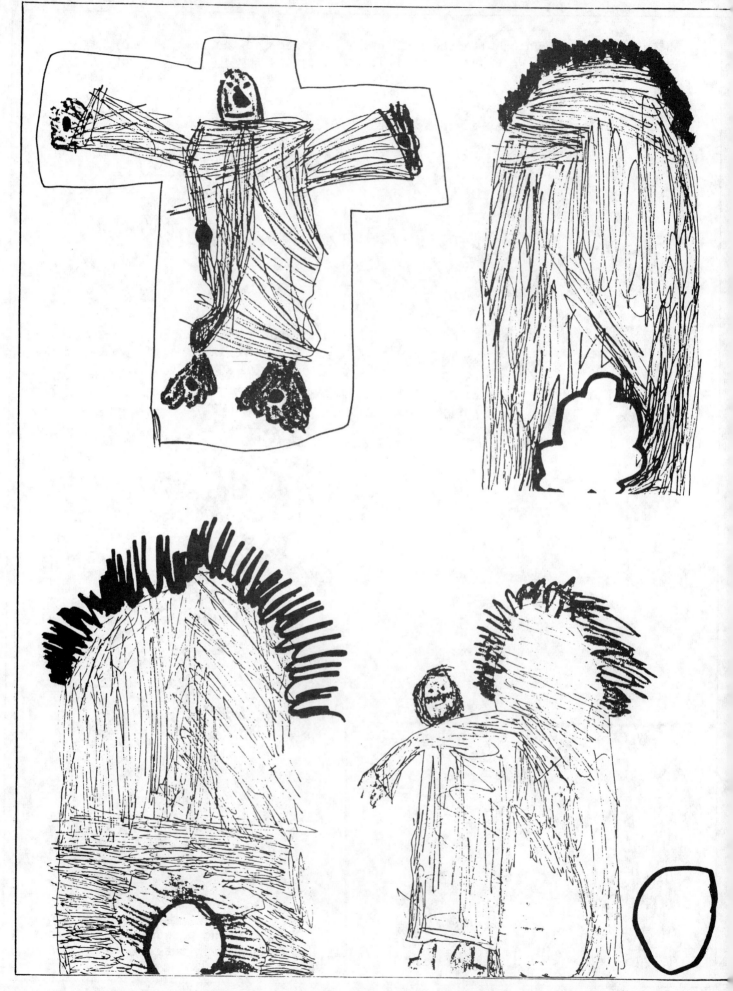

This series of drawings was begun after the tomb was presented. The boy sat down and did 4 of them: the tomb, the tomb with the stone (the tomb was brown and green grass on top of it), the tomb with the yellow light around the stone, the resurrection of Jesus (note how Jesus is still one with the tomb-again the color of the tomb and Jesus' garment is brown. The child drew Jesus first and then the tomb). The visit of the 3 women: the 3 women are shown just by their heads represented by the 3 arcs which were colored blue. The following week he returned and went right to the table and began adding to the series as if nothing had transpired since his last moment at that table. He drew the angel appearing to the women (now shown by 3 faces); note how the tomb has become larger and larger as we seem to go inside of it. Then he drew the Paschal Candle; the last drawing was the crucifixion. The child decided to adjust the order when he had finished and put them into a booklet form which he named "My Picture Bible." Ben, age 6, USA.

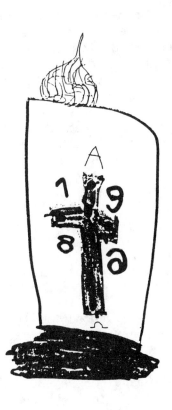

# Development of the Catechesis in a Lay School

Translated from the Italian
by Claudia Riordan

Lidia Celi is a directress of the Montessori School at Tito Livio Street (Rome), a school which has always given particular care to the spiritual and religious formation of children. This kind of thing managed to stir up many problems because of the presence of parents who were hostile to any kind of religious ways. Lidia, who is also a catechist, explains to us here briefly how she faced the difficulties, succeeding in overcoming them not only to the satisfaction of the children, but also to that of the parents.

Lidia's account: Our school is a lay Montessori school which began operating in 1962. Actually, it houses 180 children from one to ten years. It is divided this way: "nido"-about 20 children from 1 to 2-1/2 years; Casa dei Bambini-about 50 children from 3 to 5 years; and an elementary school (equivalent to the public schools)-about 100 children.

From the very beginning we prepared an organized environment for the religious formation of the child according to Montessori principles and we began with two classes of about 30 children, 4 and 5 year olds and 6 and 7 year olds. The classes, attended by children and parents alike who had accepted this undertaking, were held in the Atrium outside of the academic schedule, with two Montessorians trained at the via degli Orsini Center.

In 1972, for the first time, a group of 12 children was prepared and brought by us to the point of First Communion. That First Communion was lived in a very intense way and was participated in by both adults and children and brought about a leavening of new life in the school. Since that time, every year the children (about 20 in number) prepared themselves with us for Communion.

At the same time we were always more and more convinced that in a united and global educative project, aimed at the changing needs of children of different ages, it was necessary to help all of them to live the experience of God. We realized that, in our own reality, the families interested in the religious formation of their children were barely half of them; the others had chosen our school because it was a lay Montessori school.

What were we to do? Give up? Use force? An extended work of research clarified two fundamental ideas: 1) the school that realizes the thinking of Maria Montessori is by its nature spiritual. Consequently, the families that choose it, even if they are not interested in the religious formation of their children, know that their choice implies the adhesion to the content of the spiritual dimension of human beings. 2) The Gospel message, in its simplicity and essentiality, is a universal message acceptable at different levels by anybody.

We decided to extend to <u>all</u> the children the knowledge of the biblical message within the academic schedule, and outside of the academic schedule we continued to prepare the children for the encounter with Jesus. The preparation for Communion takes place within the confines of the school itself (in the Atrium). Even the days of retreat, i.e. those immediately preceding Communion, are lived out in the Atrium. All the school community participates joyously creating, a particular atmosphere of silence and of respect, and also offers an active participation: the children see to it that their friends find the prepared table decorated with flowers, their name plates and the short, personal Gospel messages. On the great day they help to prepare the Church and they offer their voices to the choir.

The parents, for their part, prepare the community food for the days of retreat and this is one of the ways of making them all feel united, besides naturally all the other individual participations. In this circulation of truth-life, in an atmosphere of trust and collaboration, some parents who hadn't had their children baptized had made the decision to do so. During these years we'd prepared and lived with joy the Baptism of 10 children.

Actually, four Montessori teacher-catechists working at the school full time had been prepared at the via degli Orsini Center. Their work is united in its various aspects: historical, biblical, liturgical and of the community life. It is articulated in the following way:

-one catechist during the academic schedule shares the Message once a week with seven groups of children from 4 to 10 years of age.

-one catechist follows two groups of children from 1 to 3 years of age.

-two catechists, outside the academic schedule, follow a group for two years preparing for Communion and continue to meet with these children even afterwards.

At the meetings with the children of the various groups, the respective teachers are actually present in order to be able to continue the topics even in diverse moments and circumstances.

We meet with the parents directly involved in the religious discussions three times during the year. Together we go over again the path covered by their children and we find that they react with interest and joy, as if the Christian message, seen over again through the eyes of their children, re-acquires its vital power.

With the other parents we discuss the subject at least once a year, in the class meetings, but we are available for individual discussions or with small groups if they request it. Moreover, the parents are invited to live some powerful events of the liturgical year with their children.

This picture was drawn by Christina, age 8, to show the "power of God" after a meditation on the leaven in which she realized that the woman was an image of God. USA

# Angelina and the Good Shepherd

by Catherine Wolf Maresca

"I will place my law within them, and write it upon their hearts; I will be their God, and they shall be my people. No longer will they have need to teach their friends and family how to know the Lord. All, from least to greatest, shall know me, says the Lord" (Jeremiah 31: 33-34).

How are "the least" able to know God? Is it possible for them to know God without adults? When a mother says to her child, "This is Jesus," is this a moment of introduction or recognition? Is God able to have a relationship with a child from the moment of conception?

These were the questions of a group of parents of one and two year old children. We met for some months to share our observations about the spirituality of these children, and to learn how we could encourage their spiritual development. We began with the work of Sofia Cavalletti and Maria Montessori which taught us that the spiritual life of the toddler is very different from that of adults. Our observations lead us to reaffirm their work with children as well as adding to our understanding of the relationship between God and the child. The following is an account of that experience.

Children are very comfortable with things of God and the metaphysical world, but the way in which they <u>enter this world</u> is not only through the mind (a method used by adults) but <u>through their whole being</u>, aided especially by the senses and the hands. My daughter, Angelina, showed me this after our second parent meeting.

> Two weeks ago I started making a Good Shepherd out of wood. It is for Angelina who is eighteen months. There are the Good Shepherd and two sheep in a sheepfold. Today I was nailing the Shepherd to its base while Angelina was watching me, so I gave her the statue saying, "Jesus," and "Jesus is the Good Shepherd." She took it in her hands and started running her fingertips over the surface saying, "Tseesa, Tseesa." This was the first time she tried to say Jesus although I have been using the word with her since March. (June 7, 1984)

With objects that the toddlers can see, hear, and above all touch, they have some aids to focus on God, which allow the Holy Spirit to inspire them. This is not a rapid process. Repetition is important, and time is needed for the child to absorb the world of God. After some months, they <u>know things which nobody has told them</u>. Another time, Angelina showed me this with the Good Shepherd.

> The Good Shepherd is broken and a few days ago I removed it to be repaired. Now, Angelina is here with the sheep while I am working on something else. And she is talking to the sheep: "Right back, the Good Shepherd will be right back." (December 15, 1984)

She knows that the Good Shepherd is always with the sheep, and that it is important that the sheep hear this. But she had never heard this from anyone else.

Another thing that children <u>know is what is spiritual and what is not spiritual</u>. Almost all the parents in the group said that their children recognize spiritual music, the cross, a church, paintings of Jesus and respond appropriately. One girl, when she heard spiritual music, began to dance and sing. Another toddler sang in a different manner songs of praise. One boy said "Jesus" everytime he saw a cross. His friend would say "Amen, Amen" whenever she entered a church.

All of these children are only one, two, or three years old, and see and hear many different things every day, but they are able to distinguish the spiritual things from the others. It is clear that the spiritual world is very important.

My son, Kevin, wanted to share this with his sister more than anything.

> Since Kevin was a baby I have sung the simplest songs
> from church to him, like "Alleluia" and "Amen." He
> often sings to God with great joy songs which he makes
> up; he sings up to thirty minutes. When Angelina was
> a year old and Kevin was two years old, I was upstairs
> and overheard Kevin saying, "Annie, Annie." Then he
> sang "Alleluia" to her five or six times very care-
> fully. This was the only time that Kevin taught
> Angelina a word.           (December 12, 1983)

The <u>prayers of the toddlers</u> were the last thing that we discussed. This is an age when children are able to learn new words rapidly, and therefore it is a good time to introduce to them the language of prayer. In music, in the blessing before meals, in the liturgy, the toddlers are able to hear and learn this language. It is not necessary to teach them formal prayers because their prayers come from their hearts and express their unique spirituality.

The prayers and songs of the children are not prayers of petition but of thanks and praise. The youngest children want to repeat words like "Allelu-ia," sometimes to a simple tune that they make up. Later, they want to sing longer songs and say longer prayers, like the following example:

> One day, when Kevin was three years old and Angelina
> was one and a half, Kevin came to me and said, "Annie
> and I were singing and praying. She is still praying.
> I said, 'Thank you for the food.'" (May 18, 1984)

<u>The children know the love of God</u>. Sometimes, adults find that the love of God is difficult to understand, especially God's personal love, but the toddlers are able to accept this without difficulty. They showed us this in the great joy of their songs and in their desire for the things of God. The example which follows was not the first time that I saw the faith of a child in the love of God.

> Kevin, who is two years old, is sitting on my bed
> tonight while I am feeding Angelina. He is "reading"
> a book about Jesus and on each page he stops and sings
> with different tunes, "Jesus loves me." Only these
> three words, repeated many times, for fifteen
> minutes.                    (October 6, 1983)

After our meetings, we parents had a little more understanding and much more respect for the spiritual lives of "the least." Indeed, God is able to have a relationship with the toddlers, a relationship which they enjoy very much. We are able to give them the words and the things of God, but this relationship is the gift of God alone.

Editor's note: This group was made up of parents, and their toddlers who were the siblings, of children attending the atrium. They were also joined by some friends with young children. A letter was sent out at the beginning of the year to invite the families to a monthly meeting. This could be an on-going group for centers and would encourage support for very young children.

I spoke with a CCD catechist a few weeks ago who had a mixed age group beginning with children as young as one year. She was amazed at the responses of the 18 month to 2-1/2 year olds to the lessons given. If any of you have experience with toddlers and their relationship to God, please share it with us.

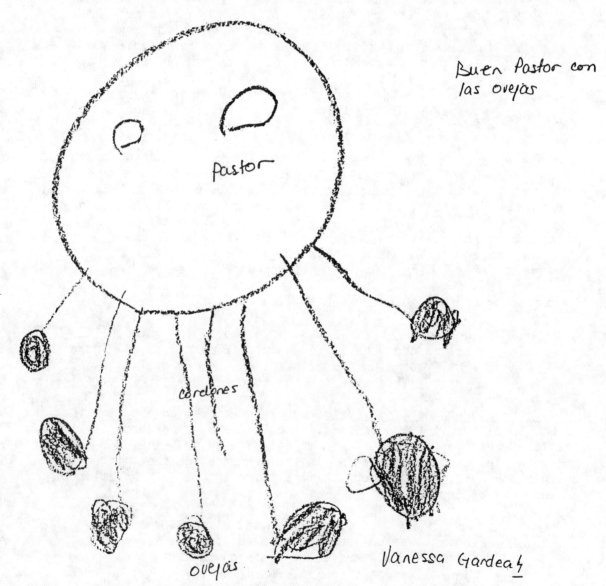

The intimate link between the Shepherd and the sheep is expressed by the strips that connect the big round circle (the Shepherd) and the smaller circles (the sheep). In the upper part of the big circle, the child put much light. Vanessa, 4 years old, Mexico.

# The Tent of Meeting

by Carol Dittberner

The Tent of Meeting is an artistic work created by Michele Zackheim to promote understanding and dialogue among people of many faiths. It is our usual experience that religion is the source of conflict among peoples but Ms. Zackheim hopes her work will be a gift which inspires peace. The idea for the Tent began during her own visit to the Middle East and her reflections on how Christians and Moslems shared the same spiritual journey.

The Tent of Meeting was exhibited in St. Paul, Minnesota this past year and was used by many different religious and civic groups as a meeting place for prayer, ritual, ceremonies, music and dance. The Tent is a black Bedouin tent forty by twenty-five feet in size. Inside the Tent the walls are painted with the symbols and traditions of Christianity, Judaism and Islam. Ms. Zackheim underscores each pictograph with the scripture from the Bible or quotations from the Koran. All three of these traditions trace their roots to Abraham. There are 250 vignettes: the wall of Islam is done in geometric designs with floral and stylistic symbols for Moslems do not depict any person images. They believe that only Allah can create people and animals. The vignettes on the Judaic wall are represented inside two large wings, the wings of the cherubim, the same wings which protect the Ark of the Covenant.

The vignettes on the Christian wall are set inside of four trees; beneath the trees sit the prophets and the gospel writers. The Christian vignettes begin in the Old Testament and then trace the major moments in the Life of Christ through the passion, resurrection and ascension.

I took a group of children from the atrium to visit the Tent. It was possible to reserve it for private groups, each group given an hour. A guide led the children through the explanations of the three religions and discussed with them some of the symbolism of various vignettes. On our own, we had a short meditation and prayer. When we came out from the Tent I gave all the children drawing paper and markers. One child, age 6, drew a series on the passion of Jesus: the Last Supper, the crucifixion, carrying the cross (his order), the tomb, Jesus resurrected with rays of rainbow colors around him. He continued the series with four more boxes: the Tent of meeting, the temple of Jerusalem, the Cathedral of St. Paul and his own parish church. These four buildings were each surrounded by the same rainbow patterns of lines. This series was drawn by the same child who, six months earlier, had done the series on the resurrection which is published in this issue of the newsletter. Ben has been attending the atrium since he was 2-1/2.

The picture printed here was drawn by Susie, age 4, Ben's sister. She has also been in the atrium since the age of 2-1/2. While at the Tent she drew a big picture of Jesus alone, on 12 x 18 paper. Her mother said she had never seen the child draw all those lines for details and must have really been influenced by that aspect of the Tent (which has everything outlined in black). The picture of Jesus was done in purple. Then the child went home and drew the picture shown here. She called the formation that looks like the Tent the "power of Jesus" and she colored that part yellow. Then she said that Jesus "made the father, the mother, the sister, the brother, and the animals." Note how they are all walking and facing the same direction.

For the most part, the other children drew their own versions of the various vignettes. One girl, age 8, drew a tree with four branches. At the end of the branches were the following things-the True Vine (she made First Communion last spring), a picture of herself, the Ark of the Covenant, and Jesus on the cross.

I recommend that you watch for the exhibit in your area as it is traveling around the United States. For further information about it, please write to:

        Tent of Meeting
        Union Theological Seminary
        3000 Fifth Street Northwest
        New Brighton, Minnesota 55112-2598

# Dear Association Members and Friends,

I greet you as one of the two members of our new communications committee. Carol Nyberg and myself have received, with joy and excitement, your letters, membership information, donations, phone calls, and news of much growth in the Catechesis of the Good Shepherd. We feel a closeness and connection to you all -- through prayer and also through the deepening of those spiritual themes we share with children in the atrium. As I write, in these early days of April, I think about the many children who are with us as we think together about the Cenacle, and about Jesus who gathers with his friends.

It is as friends that Carol and I have come to know you, and wish to share with you some of the communication that has taken place.

1. Correspondence: In addition to the large membership mailing last fall, we have sent out 65 individual letters. Some of these letters have been responses to those who are interested in the summer offerings, interested in finding THE RELIGIOUS POTENTIAL OF THE CHILD by Sofia Cavalletti, or Standing's THE CHILD IN THE CHURCH, or wanting to know if there is an atrium located near where they live. We also write frequently (and with the disadvantage of our letters often crossing in the mail) to members of the other three committees (formation, materials, and newsletter). Most of this correspondence has been about plans and details for this coming summer.

2. Membership: We have received and processed 73 memberships and 3 additional newsletter subscriptions. We opened a bank account in the name of the Catechesis of the Good Shepherd, and Carol's personal computer is where we store membership information.

As I wrote last November in the membership letter, "No one will be denied membership in the association because of inability to pay the requested $30.00 fee. We are appreciative of any donation you might be able to send -- large or small." Just send your name, address, phone, and anything you'd like to share (religious affiliation, courses you've taken, if you work in an existing atrium that serves a particular age group, etc.). Memberships can be mailed to Tina Lillig, 918 Wisconsin, Oak Park, IL 60304.

3. Directory: During the spring months we plan to prepare a directory of catechists, and mail a copy to all members, hopefully by early summer.

4. Incorporation and taxes: We now have incorporation, and are in the process of working out the bylaws with our lawyer. Carol's husband, Larry Nyberg, prepared our association tax return for this year.

5. Formation and gathering: Within this newsletter you will find an announcement of the two opportunities for the formation of catechists planned for this summer. One will be in Toronto, and the other in Phoenix, Arizona. In order to accomplish well these offerings, we had to lay aside any plans for a retreat or general association membership meeting in 1987. I will be writing to all the committee members regarding a less formal opportunity for planning the coming year.

I thank all of you, association members and friends, for your patience and understanding as Carol and I took up these tasks that were new to us. In particular, this has meant mailings that were a few weeks later than usual. We enjoy hearing from you, at any time, and rejoice in our connectedness.

Love,

Tina Lillig

# -- Summer Course Announcements --

THE RELIGIOUS POTENTIAL OF YOUNG CHILDREN: PART TWO

July 13-31, 1987

Location: St. Joseph's College, 90 Wellesley Street, Toronto, Ontario.

Workshop Description: Part II on the completion of the two-part adult formation experience relating to the religious needs of children 3-6 years of age. The morning sessions will continue the exploration of the biblical and liturgical themes which are most nourishing of the religious potential of young children. Topics will include: nurturing the children's prayer, the parables of the kingdom, "wonder" and religious education, Baptism and the Mass, moral formation and children, Jesus Christ, the True Vine, and the meaning and impact of "signs."
The afternoon sessions will explore the practical dimensions such as preparation of the atrium, understanding the meaning and use of various means to help the children's meditation, purpose and use of materials, compilation of a personal journal or album relating to Bible and liturgy for children.

For those who are interested in participating in Part II but who were unable to attend last summer, we encourage listening to the tapes from the 1986 seminar. These tapes, entitled "Being Called by Name," are available from the Daughters of St. Paul, Communications Centre, 3022 Dufferin St., Toronto, Ontario, M6B-3T5, (416-781-9131). A detailed listing of these tapes, as well as prices, is included in this newsletter.

Teaching Team: Dr. Sofia Cavalletti, Gianna Gobbi and Collaborators.

Tuition: For the full day, three week seminar the fee is $450.00 American dollars; $550.00 Canadian. $100.00 (U.S. Funds) is due with your application and is applied to the tuition.

Application: 1-Send a letter with your name, address, phone, and any background information on yourself regarding experience in religious education. Include how you came to know about the Catechesis of the Good Shepherd. 2-Include a check or money order for $100.00 (U.S. Funds) payable to: Catechesis of the Good Shepherd. This fee is non-refundable unless the application is not accepted. Send your applications to:

> Patricia Coulter
> St. Philip Neri Parish
> 2100 Jane Street
> Downsview, Ontario, Canada M3M 1A1
> (416) 241-3101

Housing: St. Joseph's College is a summer residence that offers room <u>and</u> board. Rates are established on a weekly basis with no refunds available for meals missed or days spent away from the residence.
   Weekly: $150.00 single room (meals included)-All fees are in U.S. Funds
           $130.00 (each) shared accomodation
   Short term: $25.00 single (overnight and breakfast)
               $20.00 (each) shared accomodation
               Lunch-$4.00......Dinner-$5.00
               Provincial sales tax included.

A CATECHIST FORMATION WORKSHOP

July 13-31, 1987

Location: All Saints Newman Center, Arizona State University, Phoenix, Arizona.

Workshop Description: Level 1: An introduction to the Catechesis of the Good Shepherd focusing on the religious world of the 3-6 year old child. The lectures and presentations will help participants begin the work with young children and instruct them in the preparation of the atrium (the prepared environment designed to help the child's encounter with God). Presentations will be given from the entire liturgical cycle.
Level 2: The completion of the 3-6 cycle and the beginning of work with the 6-8 year old child. Lectures will explore the characteristics of this child and there will be a focus on First Communion preparation. Participants in Level 2 must have completed a 3-6 level course.

Teaching Team: Rebekah Rojcewicz, Cathy Maresca, Sandra Yonikus, Bert and Marty O'Bryan, and Maria Reed.

Tuition: For either Level 1 or 2 the tuition is $400.00 (American dollars). A $100.00 fee (U.S. Funds) is due with the application and is non-refundable unless the applicant is not accepted.

Application: Please see the information listed for the Toronto course. Applicants for Phoenix, please make checks out to: The Arizona Corporation for Montessori Religious Education. Mail to:
>Bert and Marty O'Bryan
>721 W. Wilshire Drive
>Phoenix, Arizona 85007
>(602) 258-9623

Housing: Arizona State University campus housing offers apartment units which are equipped with a kitchen, private bath and air conditioning. Cafeteria meals are also available.
  Single: $119.70 per week        Triple: $59.60 per person per week
  Double: $79.80 per person per week   Quad: $51.50 per person per week

GENERAL INFORMATION

All participants in the courses are asked to read THE RELIGIOUS POTENTIAL OF THE CHILD by Sofia Cavalletti, Paulist Press, 1983, before they arrive. For more detailed course information, housing details, or any other questions, please write or phone:
>Tina Lillig
>918 Wisconsin Street
>Oak Park, Illinois 60304
>(312) 848-7992

Please note: Due to the efforts needed to sponsor two courses this summer, we will be unable to hold a Retreat or a General Membership Meeting. We feel a great loss in this and invite catechists who are interested in serving the association to contact Tina Lillig. Please let us know if you are able to serve on a committee, help to coordinate summer arrangements, or host the catechists in your city.

# Research in the Atrium

We would like to go deeper into a research that we already began; to go further we need your collaboration. We mean a research on the resonance of the image of the Good Shepherd in the child. We really hesitate to propose to you a method of research we always refrained from using: the inquiry.

We always refrained from such a method for two reasons: first of all, because asking questions of a child can be a lack of respect for what is fermenting in him/her, an unjust intrusion in his/her life. The second reason is the very limited value of inquiries because very often the question conditions the answer, and then deprives it of any value.

If, keeping in mind all these limits, you are willing to participate in the research we mentioned, we ask you to make copies of the form below and fill them in for each child.

Ask the question below <u>only</u> of children who have been familiar with the parable of the Good Shepherd at least one or two years and <u>not</u> before.

Ask the question during a conversation that happens with an individual child (not with the whole group), and allow the question to arise quite spontaneously from what you are speaking about with the child.

It would be particularly interesting if the answer would arise spontaneously from the child, without being asked.

Name of Center_____

Catechist_____

Girl _____     Boy_____     Age_____

Years child has attended the atrium _____

Question: "Who does the Good Shepherd make you think of?"

Response: _____

_____

Date: _____

Please return the forms to Sofia Cavalletti
                               Centro di Catechesi
                               via degli Orsini, 34
                               Roma, Italy  00186

# Book Reviews ...Book Reviews...

## Guiding God's Children    by Tolbert McCarroll

Paulist Press: New York, 1983.

This book is complimentary to our work in the Catechesis of the Good Shepherd. McCarroll discusses the psychology of learning in young children and how the traditional forms of religious education have not truly served the child. He speaks of the sensorial nature of the child and how important it is for the child to learn through the hands and not only the head; he uses the terms "head words and heart words." An example he uses from scripture is of the two on the road to Emmaus; they did not recognize Jesus through the words which he spoke but they recognized him in what he did when he broke the bread. McCarroll urges parents and religious educators to be aware of spiritual development through right-brained activity which means activities of hand and heart. Our society has become too heavily developed in left-brained functions which include reading, writing, analytical thinking, logic, and so on.

> It is the Western way to put down our great learning
> in complex thoughts wrapped in heavy books. (pg. 9)

> Therefore, no matter how highly we prize the religious
> aspect, without a unique sense of God there is an incom-
> pleteness that may be fatal to the continuation of the
> lived-out response to faith. We are left increasingly
> with the intellectual response of theology, which is
> not satisfying to the total personality. This is a
> major weak point in the general development of faith
> in our age, specifically in regard to our young
> children.                                         (pg. 30)

McCarroll also gives a concise history of the development of religious education in the United States, discusses various schools of psychology as they relate to the young child, and gives some practical suggestions to parents and educators in guiding the spiritual development of children.
Regarding the use of parables, he says:

> We cannot control the parable with our rational mind,
> but we can learn from it with our intuitive gifts. (pg. 39)

The author introduces thought from Eastern religions and notes the trend for our young adults to seek out these religions which are more "heart" focused than "head" focused. He asks us what we have missed in educating our own children and to look at what draws them into these other religious experiences. The young child needs to experience God in order to build a foundation of faith for his or her later adult life.

# Book Reviews...

## Puddles of Knowing  by Sister Marlene Halpin

Religious Education Division, Wm. C. Brown Co. Publishers: Dubuque, Iowa, 1984.

Sister Marlene Halpin, a Dominican, has been conducting a prayer room at St. Augustine's Cathedral Parish in Kalamazoo, Michigan. She meets with children from grades Kindergarten through Eighth for a half an hour at a time. This book is the culmination of one year's experience in the prayer room, how she set it up, the materials and meditations she used, and the responses of the children.

I would like to recommend this book because I found that so many of the childrens' responses, including their love for the prayer room itself, were similar to what we experience in the Catechesis of the Good Shepherd. The children asked often to return to the prayer room after school. Sister Marlene also encouraged children to find a place which was theirs at home and where they could "invite God into their hearts." She led the children in simple meditations for prayer and, at other times, used parables or the real life situations of the children, such as a death in the family, to help the children express themselves and their relationships with God.

Sister Marlene found that the most profound prayers and responses came from the youngest children. She stresses that young children need their experience of God to be validated by adults. Some adults will discount the young child's experience or ability to enter into prayer.

## To Dance with God  by Gertrud Mueller Nelson

Paulist Press: New York, 1986.

Gertrud Mueller Nelson is an artist who has also been a Montessori educator. Her book focuses on family ritual and community celebrations and brings carefully thought out ideas for celebrations for children and adults. She writes about the young child in terms of the developmental needs, such as the child's sense of wonder.

Ms. Nelson also tells us the history of many rituals and how they have developed and changed. She focuses on Christian ritual but discusses the psychological needs of ritual and celebration in general. The book traces the whole liturgical year and offers prayers, symbols, and rituals for each season.

by Carol Dittberner

# Course Tapes Available from Toronto (1986)

During the 1986 Course in Toronto, the following tapes were made and prepared for purchase by the Daughters of St. Paul through their Book and Audio Visual Centre. The tapes may be purchased by those who participated in the 1986 Course, by those preparing to attend the 1987 Toronto Course, by any persons who have taken the 3-6 year old training, and by those who are involved in the catechesis and want to gain a deeper understanding of the work.
Please place your orders directly with:

    Daughters of St. Paul
    Book and Audio Visual Centre
    3022 Dufferin Street
    Toronto, Ontario M6B 3T5
    (Telephone: 416-781-9131)

Lectures by Sofia Cavalletti:
1. History - Catechesis of the Good Shepherd
   The Child: Religious Potential

2. The Child: Religious Potential
   Unity of the History of Salvation

3. Questions - Answers
   Religious Potential of the Child

4. Drawings: Questions
   Unity of the History of Salvation
   The Incarnation
   Incarnation and Liturgy

5. Unity of the History of Salvation
   Resurrection
   People of God: Jewish
   Christian Expectation of the Messiah
   Questions and Answers

6. Speaking of God to Children
   Presenting the Parable of the Good Shepherd to Children

7. The Method of the Parables
   Children's Response to the Parable of the Good Shepherd

8. Questions - Answers
   Liturgy in History: Its Place and Function
   The Memorial

9. Bible and Liturgy
   Presenting the Eucharistic Presence of the Good
       Shepherd to Children
   Questions & Answers on Liturgy in History
   Doctrinal Content: Good Shepherd (Parable and
       Eucharistic Presence)

10. Passover Meal and Last Supper
    Presenting Last Supper to Children

11. Last Supper, Death and Resurrection: Paschal Mystery
    First Easter Sunday: Resurrection Gospels

12. Preparation of the Liturgy of Light
    Continuation

13. Infancy Narratives
    Brief Exegesis on the Gospel texts: Matthew - Mark

14. Infancy Narratives
    Exegesis on the Gospel texts: Mark - Luke

    Set of 14 cassettes.............$84.00 Canadian Funds
    First class mailing to U.S......$ 8.65 Canadian Funds
    Total..........................$92.65      "          "


Lectures by Gianna Gobbi:
1. Environment
   Atrium

2. Questions and Answers
   Religious Environment - the family

3. Adult Formation for Catechesis of the Good Shepherd
   Album

4. Questions and Answers
   Organization of a Centre of the Catechesis of the
       Good Shepherd

5. The material in the Catechesis of the Good Shepherd

6. Album
   Help and orientation for album work

7. Mystery of Death and Life (John 12:24)
   Silence in the Catechesis of the Good Shepherd

8. Questions and Answers
   The Three Period Lesson
   Liturgical Colors: Presentation and Children's Work


   Set of 8 Cassettes.............$48.00 Canadian Funds
   First Class Mailing to U.S.....$ 6.10 Canadian Funds
   Total..........................$54.10     "          "

# Announcements

The following books, newsletters and magazines are available:

THE CHILD AND THE CHURCH, Edited by E.M. Standing. This is a collection of articles by Maria Montessori, Sofia Cavalletti and other early pioneers in the Catechesis of the Good Shepherd.
Includes postage............$4.00

1985 or 1986 issues of the Catechesis of the Good Shepherd newsletters.
Includes postage.......each $3.00

Sojourners Magazine, January 1987 issue with Interview of Sofia Cavalletti and article by Carol Dittberner, "The Pure Wonder of Young Lives: Spiritual Growth in Children."
Includes postage............$2.50

Music for the Atrium composed by Tom Allen: a collection of 5 songs which were specifically written for the Catechesis. "The Pearl of Great Price," "The Mustard Seed," "The Parable of the Yeast," "The Annunciation," "Mary Had a Baby."
Music and lyrics.
Includes postage............$4.50

The above items are available by writing to:
Carol Dittberner
1429 Portland Avenue
St. Paul, MN 55104

Spanish Editions of this newsletter are also available at $4.00 each.
Write to:
Irma Chandler
10476 Seawood
El Paso, Texas 79925

MANUAL for the Catechesis of the Good Shepherd by Sr. Sheila Sentiff. This Manual includes all the material making information, directions and an introduction to needed tools for the 3-6 level atrium. The Manual is available to anyone who has completed the 3-6 level training; please specify your training location and year when ordering.
$20.00 each plus $2.50 postage.

Write to:
Tina Lillig
918 Wisconsin Avenue
Oak Park, Illinois 60304

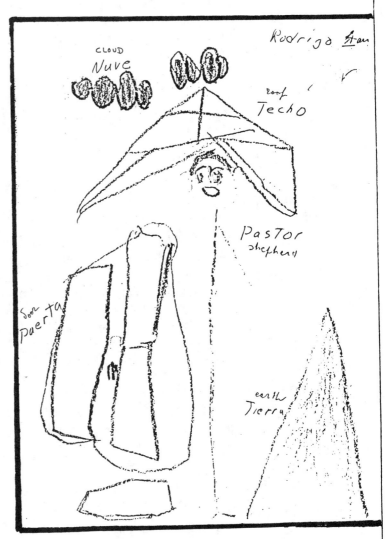

Everybody knows that the house in drawings of the children expresses a feeling of protection and security. In this drawing, Rodrigo, 4 years old, represents the body of the Good Shepherd as a house. The hat is the roof; at the left he put the door. Mexico.

# Catechesis of the Good Shepherd

We extend our thanks to <u>all</u> the people who have made possible the publication of our fourth Newsletter! Again this year we are publishing in Spanish with the staff in Chihuahua. We are also pleased to announce that the catechists in Italy have begun the publication in Italian, starting with the 1986 issue. Thank you to the contributors of this issue. We invite catechists to send us information about their children, their centers, the prayers and drawings of the children.
Please direct all Newsletter materials to:

    Carol Dittberner
    1429 Portland Avenue
    St. Paul, Minnesota 55104
    (612) 645-8917

If you are interested in joining the Catechesis of the Good Shepherd or subscribing to the Newsletter (published once a year in Spring), please contact:

    Tina Lillig
    918 Wisconsin Street
    Oak Park, Illinois 60304
    (312) 848-7992

Membership Rates/Subscriptions:

    Single Newsletter . . . . . . . $5.00/year
    Foreign rate for Newsletter . . $6.00/year*
    Mailing List . . . . . . . . . $5.00/year
    (this does not include the newsletter)
    Foreign rate . . . . . . . . . $6.00/year*
    Membership (tax deductible) . $30.00/year

Please note: no one shall be excluded from membership due to an inability to pay the $30.00 fee. We are appreciative of any donation you are able to send.
*Note: Foreign rates apply to Europe and South America due to postage expenses. All fees are due in American funds.

---

This Newsletter was compiled and edited by Carol Dittberner in collaboration with Dr. Sofia Cavalletti.

Copyright (c) by:
Catechesis of the Good Shepherd
918 Wisconsin Street
Oak Park, Illinois 60304

Published in St. Paul, Minnesota
April 30th, 1987.
Spanish Edition: Chihuahua, Mexico
Italian Edition: Rome, Italy

Staff in St. Paul, Minnesota:
Joan Miller
Rose Marie Paul
Carol Stenborg
Translators:
Joan Parasine, Herndon, VA
Claudia Riordan, Napa, CA
Carol Stenborg, St. Paul, MN

Staff in Chihuahua:
Emilia Sandoval, Editor
Noemi F. de Lopex
Maria Inez LaFone
Bertha Sofia Q. de Marquez
Translator: Ema L. Fuentes

# The Catechesis of the Good Shepherd

Fall 1988

O Lord, our Lord, how glorious
is your name over all the earth!
You have exalted your
majesty above the heavens.
Out of the mouths of babes and
sucklings you have fashioned praise
because of your foes,
to silence the hostile and the vengeful.
When I behold your heavens,
the work of your fingers, the moon and
the stars which you set in place —
What is man that you should be
mindful of him; or the son of man
that you should care for him?
You have made him little less than the
angels, and crowned him
with glory and honor.
You have given him rule over the works
of your hands, putting
all things under his feet:
All sheep and oxen, yes, and the
beasts of the field,
The birds of the air, the fishes
of the sea and whatever swims
the paths of the seas.
O Lord, our Lord, how glorious is your
name over all the earth!

Psalm 8

# Let Us Pray with the Children ...

God, the Savior, God of the Heavens, God of Light,
God of the world, God of the earth, God of love,
Holy God, God who sees us. **(7 years)**

Lord (I can't thank You enough - I think that's what I mean but I'm not sure) and I do not have anything to ask You because you give me everything and my praises are endless. **(7 years)**

Mary and God, thank you for Jesus **(3 years old.)**

I thank You that You have allowed us to see this light in our heart. **(6 years)**

I thank Jesus who hears us. **(7 years)**

### Prayer Before Meal

Thank You for Daddy; thank You for Mommy; thank You for John (his brother) and for me. (pause) God blesses us. All of us know what God is. Amen. Halleluiah. (pause) **(6 1/2 years)**

### Prayer During Advent

I want to be born in heaven and grow up with God then I will cry because God is so beautiful. **(4 years)**

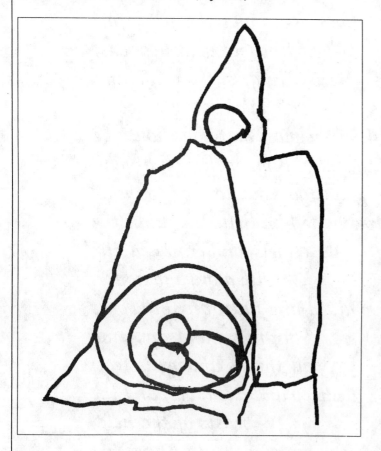

The above tracing was done by Michael Fox, from the Mary Help of Christians Atrium, in Toronto. The Catechist (Susan Furlan) explained that upon first look she thought it was an image of the child Jesus in Mary's arms or womb. When asked about the image, the child explained "I made a picture of where Jesus lived. He also made a second image, which is more clearly the land of Israel. Unfortunately, the second image was made on dark colored construction paper and would not reproduce well for the newsletter.

---

## Presentation of Our Newsletter

### Its Aims:

- An understanding of the child, particularly from the point of view of his/her religious potential.

- Knowledge of the Catechesis of the Good Shepherd: its global message which it proposes to the child, and its principal themes, examining them in the light of the psychological needs of the child and Christian tradition.

### In Accordance with these aims, it publishes:

- Doctrinal and psychological studies pertaining to catechesis with children (from 2-12 years of age, in particular.)

- Word and expression of the children (prayers, observations, drawings, "theology", etc.)

- The experiences of educators (stories through which the children reveal themselves in their religious spontaneity and in their encounter with the Christian message; gaps in the program, difficulties with the children and the environment in which they work.)

- Useful news regarding the material

- News of various centers in action, relating to the "rise" and development of the Catechesis of the Good Shepherd

- News of experiences in formation offered to catechists.

### The Newsletter has an Ecumenical Character

- The newsletter accepts, with pleasure, contributions of catechists who live the biblical liturgical tradition in their own varied branches.

*from the "The Mustard Seed" Atrium, Mexico*

# A Celebration of Light

**Contributed by
Maria Christlieb
Mexico City, 1987**

With the little ones the celebration of the Light was filled with wonder, joy, and fascination before the light.

At the end of the celebration, Alejandro, 3 years old, before the lit candles, said: "I'm staying, I want to kneel here." And there he stayed for the rest of the afternoon. Almost without moving all the time. He could only see the light.

The prayers and expressions of the children were:

- Thanks.

- We are happy because He has risen.

- What a beautiful party we've had today.

- The light of Jesus is in our hearts

- It's a light greater than the sun.

- Jesus, I love you and like you a lot. (David, after the celebration, 6 years old. II Atrio).

- Thank you for the light

**Drawing by Claudia Calderon Quiroz, 10 years old, of Chihuahua, Mexico, dated 19/2/87.**

*ed. note: The girl in the drawing is wearing a dress of several colors, and in her hands is a heart painted totally yellow, like a light.*

The text in the image reads:
**"I want to have a very brilliant light."**

The word "Peace" is colored over with green.

The image to the left was centered on a page. Around this image, Claudia had drawn lines and written the following words:

**"I am part of the white page and my mission is to build invisible bridges with other people and with people of other centuries. I am part of the light of the world as much as everyone who lives on it. I will build invisible bridges leaving my own wisdom to other people. God has given me many gifts and I have to make the most of them.**

**I do not know if I am more than others, but I would like to know for sure that in front of God and my neighbors I would be a good, noble, respectful woman, with a light that cannot be extinguished, as the light God has given me when I was born and which I reinforced in Communion. I know that some day, when Gods calls me, with my effort will be a messenger of peace.**

*ed. note: I would have liked have this girl's work appear with her own writing, however, when this image was duplicated, handwriting around the image, which was lighter than the rest of the image, did not reproduce clearly enough to be legible.*

---

The prayer card, left, was created by Ana Sofia, 6 years old, of Mexio.

This was done during her third year in the Atrium.

The words are **"God is the most important of the World."**

## In Memoriam
# Sandi Yonikus

**These thoughts about Sandi's presence among us were contributed by Carol Dittberner.**

Sandi was a great gift to us because her love of God and her essential nature were so apparent. We will remember well her quiet strength and her ability to give in spite of being in great pain.

Sandi served on the first board of our Association and was named "consultant" for she said her illness prevented her from holding an office. In fact, she was our very own contemplative and her prayer was always there supporting us when she could not come in person. When she was with us she could always go to the essence of any issue being discussed and recall us to the original vision for the Association.

It is a beautiful symbol, her death occurring on the old feast of Corpus Christi, and her burial on the new feast of Corpus Christi. Sandi lived the body of Christ, the one which is shared among many and the one which is made up of many. Sandi's own home was a symbol of community: One house built by many hands, the hands of her friends. Imagine how it would feel to look around and see each thing, be it structural or decorative, given by a friend. All of us knew about the house being built; I believe it was a house of harmony for one who loved God. We are thankful for Sandi's numerous contributions to the Catechesis in many cities and for her vision which aided the birth of our Association. We are thankful for her holiness.

### Sandi's house in Driftwood, Texas

*"The Laborer is Worthy of Her Hire."*

Bert O'Bryan found the image pictured at the left, in Sandi's home when he attended her funeral services. Bert kindly brought color copies of the image, along with the following explanation, for each participant at this summer's *"Time Apart"* retreat in St. Paul.

Unfortunately, the color copies did not reproduce well enough to be legible for the newsletter. The explanation which accompanies the image reads:

This is how I remember seeing it for the first time. It was carved into a picnic table in a little pavilion along the waterforont where the fishing boats are harbored across from St. Gregory's Church in Sitka, Alaska. I had gone there to give a workshop to the catechists when Fr. Ryan was there in November of 1976. Early in te morning on a very grey, cold day, I went across the pavilion to pray the Liturgy of the Hours and the little primitive but powerful drawing captured my whole attention with its symbolism and significance and remains with me still as the most perfect logo for the church ..... Community of God's people, imitating the community of the Trinity bringing forth "The Kingdom" ...."The new creation," into the visible world .... transforming the old into the new in the only way it can be done through our (Joint Effort).

*from Rome*

# 20 Years of an Atrium at Our Lady of Lourdes

**Contributed by
Tilde Camosso Cocchini
Rome, July 2, 1987**

This year marks the 20th anniversary of the founding of the Atrium at Our Lady of Lourdes in Rome. I wanted to tell you its history, to thank the Good Shepherd with you, and wish the atrium a long life.

In 1966 I was teaching art in the middle school of Torrancia, in the area south of Rome. This is an area of great contrasts, with a population of about 15,000 people, all with completely different economic conditions: businesses, clerks and workmen.

The pastor of Our Lady of Lourdes came to the school to bring Christmas greetings from the parish. We talked about Catechesis, and he told me that he had decided to close the oratory due to the lack of attendance by the children. At that time I was a Catechist trainee at the atrium at Via degli Orsini (this is the address of Sofia's Centro di Catechesi, also her home) and I asked him if I might try an experiment in Catechesis with the 3 and 4 year old children in his parish. I didn't have anything to use, he responded, and he gave me a large room that I was able to furnish in a few months with the necessary materials.

Our first meeting was on May 5, 1967 with fifteen children from four to 6 years of age. Some were the children of my colleagues, the rest were from the parish.

In the beginning I was assisted by a Montessori directress who wished to deepen her understanding of the spiritual and religious abilities of the child. She had worked for years in the Children's House (Casadei Bambini is the name given her preschool environment by Dr. Montessori, so it always means the Montessori preschool) directed by Flaminia Guidi, a co-worker of Maria Montessori. But what she observed in the atrium was, she told me, a source of revelation and help.

The pastor followed our efforts with a great deal of interest. He was amazed by the joy, the silence, the concentration in their work, and by the spontaneous prayers which the children sometimes expressed after the meditation.

The parents were astonished by the joy and profound peace that the children began to enjoy in the atrium right from the beginning. They found it hard to believe that these two hour weekly meetings became the moment the children looked forward to all week. The mothers were full of curiosity and questions.

It seemed to me that it was important and quite necessary for the sake of the children to answer these questions and satisfy that curiosity. It would be beneficial for the children if they could have a continuation at home of the religious experience begun in the atrium.

The parents took turns coming to the atrium with their children, and in the second year, meetings on Montessori education and Catechesis were established, first monthly and then every two weeks.

In the third year, the pastor was transferrerd and the new pastor planned to use our room for other activities. It was the parents who convinced him to continue the experiment.

New courses were started and my two daughters and one of the mothers, Mirella Casano, who had attended the course of Catechesis in Via degli Orsini, became Catechists. Then another three parent couples attended the course in catechesis and began to work in the atrium. A small religious community was being born guided by the children.

The newness of our work was ignored or barely supported because it involved small children, mainly, and because it didn't bring about large numerical results. These difficulties became apparent, especially when we needed a priest for celebrating First Communion liturgies and Confirmation retreats for the young people of the parish.

In 1974 the bishop of the south sector of Rome made a pastoral visit to the parish for the Holy Year. The episode is reported in Sofia Cavalletti's book "The Religious Potential of the Child." In his visit to the atrium, the bishop was particularly captivated and touched that children so young could speak so naturally and seriously about such profound matters. This consoled us and aided us in our talks with the parish priests.

An even more exceptional event occurred on February 13, 1983. During the pastoral visit to Our Lady of Lourdes Parish, Pope John Paul II came to the atrium while the children were at work with the Catechists. One group was working on the Parable of the Good Shepherd and the Eucharistic Presence; another group on the "Synthesis of the Mass". Other children worked on baptism and the Parable of the Precious Pearl. The Holy Father would approach each group and listen attentively, then ask a question and again listen, amazed and touched. He stayed in the atrium for 20 minutes, and the memory of this meeting still lives in us all. Carrying on the work of Catechesis that day were parent Catechists from the course of 1978, the year in which I left the atrium, and also some young Catechists, who were part of the first group from 1967 who had become Catechists on their own and now working in the atrium they had attended as children they continue to love the Good Shepherd and encourage others to love him.

At present, 62 children and young people from the age of 4 to 18 years, divided into five groups, attend the atrium. The fifth group is composed of 10 young people, 16 to 18 years of age, for whom this is the 14th year of catechesis.

The rapport with the parish priests has improved. For two years now thanks to the efforts of some young people and Catechists who have taken part in parish activities, the Catechists of the Good Shepherd have succeeded in working with all of the youth groups of the parish: the group for sacramental preparation, the boy scouts, and with those of the oratory. They celebrate Mass together on Sunday and the more important liturgical moments of the year. The whole atrium community benefits from the contribution that each group makes and from the fact that the children and young people feel themselves to be a living part of the parish community.

Now autumn, after summer vacation, we hope to trace all the "children" who have attended the atrium and together celebrate the past twenty years.

**Affectionate greetings to all!**

*from Sofia:*

# On Moral Formation

Rome, Mary 25, 1987

Dear Catechists:

Last year we tried to clarify what is done in our work concerning social justice. The dialogue we carried on is certainly insufficient, and I am hoping for your input.

The point we reached was this: since the problem is a social one in "relationship," then the relationship that the child establishes with the Good Shepherd is surely an element of great importance, also for formation in social justice. We want to pick up the discussion on "relationship" extending it to the total formation of the child from the age of three years onwards.

First of all, let's ask ourselves what we mean by the term *"moral"*, what do we refer to as "moral"? Do we use it to refer to behavior? To regulations? To a law? To a decision? To a person? All of these can be moral if they relate to a "moral" person. It is the person, then, in the first place, who is moral, and specifically the person in relationship. This is a point that recent studies underline strongly.

From this statement arise three questions:

1. What is a relationship?
2. With whom or with what?
3. What kind of relationship?

Point one:
**What is a Relationship?**

It is something that implies another person, someone other than myself and, therefore, a movement out of myself toward another who is different from me. A relationship is not established without a movement outwards, not only of part of me, but of my whole person. When I open a door or a window for myself air comes in, and an exchange takes place between the air inside and that outside; a beneficial mutual exchange is the goal.

This brings us to the second question:
**Relationship with whom?**

It is clear that the broader the horizon of my window the more enriched I become; the more enriched the person with whom I have established a relationship the more I am enriched myself. In our Catechesis we are called to help the child in the relationships that make up his/her life, and his relationship with God. It is clear that assisting in any relationship is a great help to the child's development; we have all seen the response of the child when s/he is enabled to encounter God. I'm not going to go back, now, over what we have already said repeatedly, what we have all experienced, which never ceases to amaze us. It is that special response of pure joy - different from any other manifestation of joy - which the child gives as he draws closer to God.

From what the child has allowed us to see, we are convinced that in his/her relationship with God the child find nourishment involving the inner being in an enjoyment quite special, intense and serene.

Point three -- This is an established fact in light of which we can ask ourselves a further question:
**What kind of relationship does the human have with God?**

There are two kinds of relationships: necessary ones, which are not the result of choice, e.g., being the daughter of my mother and father is not a choice. Other relationships are the result of choice, e.g., the relationship of marriage.

What kind of relationship is our relationship with God? According to the biblical tradition, God is Father: "Israel is my first-born son." (Ex. 4:22); Jesus teaches us to pray, saying "Our Father." (Matt. 6:9) In the Bible God is also Mother: "Like a child consoled by its mother, will I comfort you." (Is. 66:13) In these cases, the relationship with God is a fact; we come from God; it is God who created us; we received our existence from God; we are children of God who is mother and father to us.

But in the Bible, the relationship with God is also expressed in nuptial terms: God is the bridegroom, Israel is the bride. (Is. 54:5; Ez.

*Drawing by Joseph Kosowski, Atrium at St. Frances Cabrini, after the presentation of the Mustard Seed. This drawing contains the mustard seed, trees and birds.*

## Translated from Italian by Joan Parasine

5) In Matthew 25:6 we read "The bridegroom is here! Go out to meet him."

The two kinds of relationships with God are not mutually exclusive, but rather complement each other. I'm a child of God; God is a father and mother and must be recognized as such; to whom I must say "yes, I am your child because of an act of love." But for this to become a true relationship and not just a one-sided initiative, I must respond to this gesture of love in kind. The relationslhip with God which begins as one of necessity becomes one of choice and requires a response.

In the biblical tradition, the relationship with God presents a marvelous balance between the necessity and choice. I find myself to be a child of God; I must accept this situation as an initiative of God. But this is an initiative that has a "covenant" as its final goal. It is complete, therefore, only when it finds a response from the other partner, when the creature responds to God's choice with his/her own choice.

Forgive me if the premise is long and, perhaps, somewhat involved. What I want to make clear is the kind of relationship that the child is able to establish with God. S/he finds herself in the situation of being a child of God; but the child has the capacity to integrate this 'fact of life' into a relationship of choice. Does this relationship allow for a response on the child's part? In other words, does the child enjoy this situation as a creature of God only passively, or is s/he capable to responding actively to God?

Here, too, we need to agree on the meaning of active response. If we mean a response to the level of "What to do", of conscious effort, we must answer in the negative. But are actions the only way to the God who calls us? Underlying individual actions, individual conduct, there is, as we have mentioned before, a global response that involves the whole person, and through which the entire being turns toward the partner, similar to the way a plant turns toward the sun.

I dare say that we have seen a similar response in the child. Each time the child allows us to see the joy that s/he feels in drawing near to God, when s/he listens with rapt wonder to the message and meditates on it, the child is allowing us to see his/her response to the God of the covenant.

That special joy that we have seen in the children, that certain silence, intense and recollected, full of restraint, that certain glow in the eyes, are all signs of a relationship that has been accepted and enjoyed. Though not explicitly expressed in words, it is no less real or rooted in the inner person.

The child's response to the relationship with God that is offered to him is his "drinking" of the message, making it his own to relish and live in profound enjoyment. I believe this is the best response we can give to the God who searches out his human creatures.

I confess that it was surprising to me to realize that the greatest assistance we can give the child in forming himself as a moral person is the parable of the Good Shepherd. Some will say: but in this parable there aren't any indications of what to do and not do, no exhortations. But it is exactly for this reason that is so important for moral formation: it doesn't aim at doing things, but a "being" with the Good Shepherd, to enjoy his presence in our lives.

Have you ever noticed how frequently the children draw the "Good Shepherd" whose lips utter the name of his sheep? What part of the parable do they put more emphasis on than this very relationship?

Little Maria, two and one half years old, all alone in the hospital, sang softly to herself at night "He knows my name." In other words, he takes the initiative to bring about a relationship with me, and I receive and savor it. It is marvelous to see ones so young capable of opening themselves to a relationship in which they have the full dignity of a partner. The partner not only accepts the gift passively, but knows how to assume, in this partnership, what "flows" from the gift, an active role.

The vehicle of the child's response is on a level superior to any action or effort of will; the vehicle of his response is of a kind with the gift offered. It is a love that involves the whole person in the enjoyment of the one loved.

Each time we see the children absorbed and engrossed in listening and meditation, we should stop in reverence, for it gives us the privilege of catching a private moment in the union of God with his creature. And, perhaps, at these moments, in respect we should compel ourselves not to look so as not to interfere in a moment of such great intimacy.

We can say that the Church has always recognized in the child the great dignity of a partner in the covenant, baptizing them, even from very ancient times, at birth. Based on this wise premise, then, it doesn't make much sense when, in handing on the message, we neglect the little ones, saving it for the "the age of reason." For God there doesn't seem to be a human being too young to respond to his initiative.

I would like to conclude, therefore, by saying that the educator of the very young child has a fundmental role in moral formation. His/her task is not that of offering, urging or solicitation directed toward behavior. On the contrary, he/she needs to be careful because the time for that (moral exhortations) has not come yet; it will be done at the proper time. The educator of young children is called to make the "announcement", to introduce the mystery of the person to God, thus assisting the relationship with Him, and hence the basic formation of the moral person.

On this point, too, I await your reaction, wishing you a good year of work and sending the expression of my affection.

**Sofia**

Claudio prepares the altar every week. He delights in every detail and uses the vessels with great complaisance. From Susan Furlan's Atrium in Toronto.

*Catechesis of the Good Shepherd, 1988 Newsletter*

## from Lucia's letter to the Group in Rome:

# The Material

Translated from Italian by Joan Parasine

*Ed. Note: These comments are continuing Lucia Cremona's remarks on the Catechesis in Chad, Africa, from last year's Newsletter.*

The usefulness of the material is indisputable, especially that which is completely concrete, where there is no abstraction.

I used it for the adults, but only as a presentation. The little ones drew things easily and worked mostly with the miniature altar, the dioramas (for Infancy and Paschal Narratives, I would imagine) and the first parables.

The elementary aged children worked and drew. A few were able to trace and copy, some did not yet know how to read or write, though they attended school.

The older ones worked with the materials very little, but I noticed that the materials were well fixed in their memories. They drew, but most of all they traced and copied. The Parable and Narrative booklets and the maxims were very popular for tracing and copying.

They took their work home at the close of school, but they had a hard time keeping it in good condition in the house since there was no furniture and rain often leaked in. The materials proved themselves most useful on the levels of both sensorial and intellectual development.

### A FEW ANECDOTES:

Sometimes, when their reflections were solicited, they were marvelous. One seemed "to see" the work of grace opening them to the discovery of a God unknown and ever new. There were indescribable moments which seemed as fleeting and fragile as the air we breathe. One time I asked them why they don't go to confession before baptism. One woman answered, "Because we were like the blind, we could not see." At the recounting of the Lost Sheep (by the way, Sofia prefers the word "retrieved or refound" instead of "lost") one woman said with great simplicity, "I was a prostitute before. I lived like that because I didn't know any better. But the Lord called me and I felt something."

A woman who had twins, with one child in her arms and the other in her husband's arms next to her, meditated out loud, "When I brought these two children into the world, I was deeply struck by something: I, who am so frail, gave life to two creatures at the same time. I thought a lot about what life is, how God creates through us, and I came to know this God."

One time, at the vigil of a baptism celebration, I noticed that they seemed a bit tense and anxious. I asked them how they felt. I saw a smile on everyone's face, which a woman explained, "Before when I came to the preparation classes from the fields, my legs were heavy and I dragged myself along with fatigue. But now that I have arrived at the moment of baptism, I don't feel tired anymore; I feel full of energy," and, so saying, she sprang to her feet.

A woman recounted, "I was accused by my father-in-law of stealing his millet to make beer with it. I went to his house and explained how I got that millet. A few other people who were there spoke up in my defense, but he continued speaking to me in very harsh words. I got up to react violently, but then I remembered that now I am pledged to live the Gospel, which I had heard on Sunday, and so I said nothing. I said goodbye and went away happy."

### BAPTISM AT EASTER 1971:

I thank the Lord for the great grace of preparing the catechumens for baptism. This year was truly beautiful. There were 23 new candidates for baptism at the Easter Vigil. They made the retreat together at Gagal. I experienced this beautiful moment with them. There were moments of true emotion, I can assure you. The celebrations were followed with great devotion. There were many people who came from the "savana", but also many non-Christians from Gagal. It was very beautiful when the newly baptised received their "white garments" and went out to put them on, then re-entered by the central door singing a new song, in which everyone then joined. All were visibly moved.

At the point of the candles, which they don't use here because they would melt at this temperature, the priest took the light from the Paschal Candle and lit their oil lamps, and by this light they returned to their huts.

From these examples one has to believe that Lucia's path was strewn with flowers. Lucia continues, "I gave great expanses of time to the parables so as to send them (catechumens) forward on the search toward the discovery of the Kingdom in which they live, and are called to live actively with a response of love to the loving call of God."

I did my best to introduce them to personal prayer, to the liturgy as a source for life, but there were many difficulties. The truly converted were very few.

All things considered, it is thanks to the Lord that people have emerged from the phase of fear: fear of white people, fear of God, but even now, the way is not easy; this passage from fear to love through an avenue of discovery, of faith, of hope, is long and difficult. Who will help them?

We conclude with the prayer of a Christian of Chad: "Lord, have mercy on all people who are separated from you. Give them the strength to come into this fold."

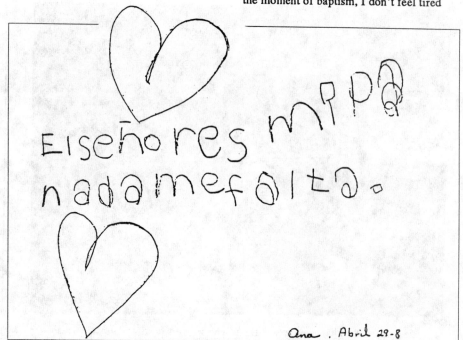

This prayer card was drawn by Ana Sofia (six years old) from an Atrium in Mexico. It reads " The Lord is my (Shepherd), nothing I lack."

## *A First Communion Retreat*
# The Children are not Angels

The days of the First Communion retreat are precious because they allow us to see the children for a longer time than the two hours weekly, when the work of the catechesis usually goes on. It happens, therefore, that we sometimes witness, not only moments of "grace" which one might expect during these days, but also the "normal" moments, and sometimes moments when the children argue with one another.

This year the quarrel happened on Sunday, just after the midday meal (dinner), while the children were playing in the garden. The girls were the ones involved in the argument. They had broken up into two groups -- three girls against two - because of some "secret" which the two had shared without letting the other three into it.

When I became aware of this rift, I sought to reconcile them, first by speaking with the two groups separately, then together. Nothing helped; the problem seemed unsolvable. Fortunately, I knew better than to insist. They stayed out in the garden, ignoring each other and teasing one another.

Finally I returned to the studio (or workroom). Then I thought of appealing to each one individually, and called aside the girl who seemed to me the most offended and least open. I told her that when the day came to an end and she thought about it, she would surely be sorry to have let that quarrel ruin the day.

The girl seemed convinced but unable to find a solution. She went back to the garden, and I called her friend Cecelia, who was the one certainly who had started the argument and kept it going the longest. I spoke with her in the same vein and she responded that she was agreeable to ending the rift, but she did not see how to make a positive gesture of peace. She asked me if perhaps I could talk with the girls in the other group, because she did not think she could do it. I told her that I would think about it and waited for a few minutes before calling anyone else.

When I decided to call Catherine, the leader of the other group, to my great surprise, she did not give me a chance to open my mouth, but said, "Don't say a word. I have been in the chapel praying, and I see everything."

I only said, "Can you tell the others what you have realized?" She said, "Yes" and went back to the garden while I went and got myself a cup of coffee.

On my return, more than a half hour later, Cecelia came to meet me. She hugged me and said, "I am so happy; we've made up." But it didn't end there. After a while I went to the chapel and found Cecelia kneeling before the tabernacle. When she noticed my presence, she asked me, "How do I ask the Good Shepherd for forgiveness?" I answered, "Have you any doubt he can forgive you? Don't you think it's enough to ask him? Just one moment is enough."

She was persuaded. She went back to the tabernacle for a short time. She blew one kiss to "Him" and another in the direction of the statue of Our Lady and then ran off. Everything was finally settled.

**I embrace you all affectionately,**

Francesca Cocchini
Rome, May 4, 1987

# An Experience of Lent

Berta Sofia Quiroz de Harquez
Chihuahua, Mexico

I would like to share with you the experience I lived with the children of the Atrium during Lent in 1987. The children were from 8 to 10 years of age.

We began Lent reading a message of Pope John Paul II, which is a meditation on the Parable of the Good Samaritan and an invitation to open our hands and share what we have with the poor, with the helpless.

Then we saw a film about the anguished situation of hunger and cold that the Indians in Chihuahua, the Tarahumaras, were going through as their daily life.

We invited the children to participate every Friday in a campaign which took place in the Cathedral. Its motto was: **"FAST SO THAT OTHERS MAY EAT."** People came to pray and fast, food and money were collected and given afterwards to the most needy people.

The children joyfully accepted the invitation, saying that they still had eight days to prepare themselves for it.

During the week they broke their piggy-banks, they asked for money from their families; some of them worked sweeping the streets; the girls made and sold cakes.

Friday at five in the evening we arrived at the Cathedral, each bringing whatever they had collected.

The Penitential Liturgy began and, to our surprise, the priest made the examination of conscience with the Maxims of the Gospel, just as the children prepare themselves for Confession at the Atrium. Some of them received the Sarcrament of Reconciliation. Then they placed the money which they had brought in a special box assigned for that.

As they were doing it, they saw a very poor boy bringing some food to offer it. They asked the priest if that child was giving or getting something. The priest answered them, "He comes to give food for the ones who need more than he does. When someone has felt hunger and cold, they are the first ones to come and help their brothers who are suffering."

The experience was lived every Friday during Lent, and I saw the children were very satisfied, as they felt capable of helping others, living the words of Jesus: "Give to the man who begs from you. Do not turn your back on the borrower."

## The Fishers

# Our Visit to Chihuahua, Mexico

by Martha Fisher
Jackson, Mississippi

Over a year ago, in Toronto, Maria Christlieb invited my husband and me to visit her in Mexico City and Chihuahua to observe the work there. As the time for the trip drew near, schedule conflicts made it necessary to shorten our itinerary, so we all decided that it would be best if we by-passed Mexico City and flew straight to Chihuahua. Maria met us at the Chihuahua airport, having arrived less than an hour ahead of us. Emilia Sandoval was there to welcome us all and to drive the three of us into the city.

As we soon discovered, many arrangements had been made for our visit. We began with lunch at the Sandoval's home. It was our great pleasure to get acquainted with the whole family over two delicious meals during our stay.

In three short days, we visited five atriums and a seminary where a first communion retreat was in progress. We were also taken on two shopping expeditions, as many hand-crafted items and printed materials are available in Mexico, and, of course, our hostesses knew just where to find catechesis treasures! As Red and I later reflected together on our visit, we discovered we were both impressed by several things:

(1) The sheer numbers of atriums, catechists, and children involved in this city. We visited five sites, but we were told of many more and we also had described to us an extensive catechist training system that is evolving to meet the explosive needs of the area. All of this has developed in a relatively short period of time, revealing great energy and responsiveness among the people.

(2) The wide diversity of settings. The Good Shepherd is shared in churches, schools, a store front, a small daycare center, and we were even told of a group that gathers on a sidewalk in the open air. Both catechists and children come from every part of town and every walk of life.

(3) The intense commitment and personal sacrifice of time/care/money made by the catechists and their families. The work of the catechesis is a real labor of love. We were impressed by their intiative and creativity, their confidence in their calling, and the commitment to each child personally. God has raised up a wide base of leadership among these women of all ages and backgrounds, and they work together with love and mutual respect.

(4) The liaison between clergy and catechists that appears to be growing. In the church family, gaps are slowly closing between clergy and laity, male and female, adult and child as we work together in the heart of the Good Shepherd.

Martha Fisher, far right, visited this Atrium in Chihuahua, Mexico, with her husband, Red. These catechists have been in an Atrium since 1976, 77 and 78.

(5) The gracious hospitality and generosity of the Mexican people. And yet we felt that it was more than the lovely manners of the culture that made us so welcome. It was, we believe, the Good Shepherd Himself, present in their midst, giving us all a deep knowledge that the Sheepfold of God encompasses all national boundaries.

Before we left, we were given many gifts to take back to the children in our church. Perhaps the greatest gift was expressed by Emilia at our parting. She embraced us and said, "Remember, you have a friend in Chihuahua."

Back in Jackson, the children received each gift with delight and were much impressed by the pictures of the Mexican children enjoying the Good Shepherd just as we do here. It was exciting to them to learn that they were a part of such a large international family. The children wished to make a tangible response, so it was decided that they would undertake chores at home to earn allowances from which to make gifts of love to our new friends. These offerings are gathered each week and placed in a special savings account. At the end of the year, all these fruits of the childrens' labors will be sent to Chihuahua with our love and prayers.

## Book Review: *A Human Being*

**Ed. Note:** *The following are Sófia's comments on Silvana Quattrocchi Montanaro's book., A Human Being. We were unable to find out if the book is available in English at the time of newsletter publication.*

We would like to bring Silvana's book to the notice of parents and anyone interested in the child. The reader will find helpful advice, easily carried out, yet of great importance to the life of the child.

It deals with things so simple and essential that in reading it, we are surprised that we did not think of it on own. But often the simple and essential things are what we need help with. Silvana gives us this help in good measure.

Most appreciated in this book is the impassioned consideration given to the potential of the child, from the first instant of life and throughout the life in the womb.

This book gives us a profound sense of the dignity of the child, dignity which Silvana presents to us with out frills, basing it rather on solid psychological and medical knowledge.

# The Catechesis of the Good Shepherd in Argentina

By Herminia Wasserzuc

In 1979, after many years of hearing about the Catechisis of the Good Shepherd I had first encounter in Rome with Sofia Cavalletti and Tilde Cocchini. Later, in January of 1984 I attended a few meetings of the course in Via degli Orsini where I could appreciate even more the profundity and essentiality of the catechesis and its adaptation to children of different ages.

When I went back to Argentina I tried to call the attention of people responsible for catechesis in schools or parishes with the purpose of organizing a first course in Buenos Aires. Following the suggestions of Sofia I got in touch with Nora Bonilla in Bogota, who agreed to conduct an intensive course of first level in January of 1985.

Twenty one persons attended and by March of that year we could initiate three Atrios. The necessity to train new catechists to reinforce the existing atrios became apparent.

We counted on the presence of Nora Bonilla during the months of July- September 1985.

It was repeated in Olion, Province of Buenos Aires, a course of first level with the participation of nineteen new people. Nora visited in different opportunities the Atrios of Olion, Villa Bosch, (Provincia de Buenos Aires), and Cordova.

Her presence and help permitted the continuation of the mission with higher confidence.

In 1985, around seventy children between the ages of three and five received the catechesis of the Good Shepherd assisted by five catechists.

In 1986, we had Nora again among us between April and June. She directed two intensives courses of the first level, one in Olion and the other in Santa Fe, capital of the Province of the same name. There, as in times before, we counted on the presence of the Bishop.

In the Olion's course, 285 catechists participated from schools that already had atrios and from other institutions.

In Santa Fe, forty five catechists from schools and parishes and two priests got together.

Up to now two Atrios have been organized in schools and one in a parish. Around two hundred and sixty from ages three to six attend and they are staffed by fifteen catechists.

In 1987, five catechists and one priest were able to attend, for about five months, to the course of the Catechesis in Rome.

We hope to be able to respond, little by little, to all the demands that the development of the catechesis of the Good Shepherd requries in Argentina, especially the need to help the Atrios already in existence and to train even more the catechists that may join.

As we count on more possibilities, the organization of new Atrios could be extended as to make it possible for other children and adults to receive the benefits of the catechesis of the Good Shepherd.

# Building up an Atrium

Ed. Note: *In these excerpts from her letter to Maria Christlieb, Carol Stenborg tells about her own experiences in the Atrium.*

In my own home material making was always in evidence. My husband, Fred, helped paint materials, draw posters, cut elements for the various collage exercises.

All the exterior preparation should not overshadow the interior work which was ongoing in the children, in ourselves, for me most particularly within my own family.

I may be the one that the parents and children recognize as the Catechist, but I feel that Fred is also deserving of the title. He has helped make so much of the material we use. In order to make the material, he needs an explanation of its use. He also helps me set up and put away our Atrium each week. (Carol, along with Millie Dosh and Dan McCarthy have an Atrium at the Minneapolis Newman Center. As their space, they may use a meeting room on Sunday morning. So before each session, the Atrium must be set up. And after each session, all the materials put away).

Our own two children found their places in what was not just a partnership of two - husband and wife - but a family work - the building of our family faith life and the building of an Atrium in our community, because other families also contributed with us in this work. Millie and her husband, Terry, and other parents - families were also involved. The growing sense of community amongst us was felt primarily focused on the children, but like ripples on a pond, growing outward in widening circles...

Though four of us usually set up the

Oliver does not speak much English but lives joyfully in the Atrium.

Atrium - my husband, my sons and I - it is not chaotic (though sometimes, I am sure, my husband will say differently). For me it is a giving order to our space. We move amongst each other, each going to their task, all in a quiet, reverent way. It becomes a meditation for me, a silent readying for the morning.

It is the same at the end of the morning. As we put the materials away, I have, again, a quiet time to ponder what we have done together.

And now to the most important time...our time with the children... It is all the things we've talked about in our classes. Though Millie and I are still developing and growing in this work. So are the children... Our Atrium experience unfolds and grows - like a plant - slowly, with much nurturing.

As we approach our third year, I feel we have accomplished so very much - yes, there will always be more work, but we have begun a precious journey.

## Reflections on Social Justice

# "Thy Kingdom Come ...."

*Editor's note: Emilia Gonzales de Sandoval continues the reflection on Social Justice initiated by Sofia Cavalletti in the 1987 Newsletter.*

My dear Sofia:

I read with joy and interest your article in the magazine "**Justicia Social, Problemas de Relaciones**." You know that justice is one of the values of the kingdom that I feel strongly about and I want to share a few reflections about it. To speak about justice in a country like Mexico, where all the political, social, and economical structures are unjust and make the rich get richer while the majority does not have the indispensable, is not easy.

But the Gospel clearly says: "Seek the Kingdom of God and its justice." (Matthew 6:33)

And this justice, will it be to give each one what he deserves? Will it be that, and only that? What meaning did that word have for Jesus?

We have said that the Bible can be understood with the Bible and it is in this way that I will try to find the biblical meaning of the word justice.

In the Bible the theme of justice is connected to three words:

**Sedeqah** - Justice in the most generic sense.
**Mishpat** - right, about realization of justice.
**Din** - Which usually translates as vindication which means the justice exercised in behalf of the one that is not only poor, but made poor and mistreated by others, that is defenseless.

Woe to those who enact unjust statutes and who write oppressive decrees (**Din**), Depriving the needy of judgment and robbing my people's poor of their rights(**Mishpat**), making the widows their plunder, and orphans their prey. **Isaiah 10: 1-2**

They do not judge according to right, (**Mishpat**); they do not defend the cause of the orphan, (**Din**) or sentence in favor of the poor (**Din**). **Jeremiah 5: 28**

Open your mouth in behalf of the dumb and for the rights of the destitute.
Open your mouth, decree what is just, defend the needy and the poor. **Proverbs 31: 8-9**

Did not your father eat and drink? He did what was right and just, and it went well with him. Because he dispensed justice to the weak and the poor it went well with him. Is this not true knowledge of me? says the Lord. **Jeremiah 22:15b-16**

This text really sounds like this: to know the Lord is to defend justice, to defend the defenseless (**Din**), the humiliated and the poor, is to vindicate the oppressed. (1)

And in the Deuteronomy, we read:

For the Lord, your God, is the God of gods and the Lord of lords, the great God, mighty and awesome, who has no favorites, accepts no bribes; who executes justice for the orphan and the widow, and befriends the alien, feeding and clothing him. So you too must befriend the alien, for you were once aliens yourselves in the land of Egypt. **Deuteronomy 10:17-19**

And in this way we could go on finding further examples in Isaiah, Jeremiah, Psalms, etc., but with what we have seen we can say that "God reveals himself in the Old Testament as the Liberator and the Protector who gives justice to the poor, the oppressed and the unfortunate ones: first as Liberator of the people that cry out in their oppression and later as the Liberator of the invalids or unfortunate ones who were oppressed by their own poeple." (2).

This way we arrive at the New Testament, where Luke places on the lips of Mary:

He has shown might with his arm; he has confused the proud in their inmost thoughts. He has deposed the mighty from their thrones and raised the lowly to high places. The hungry he has given every good thing, while the rich he has sent empty away. **Luke 1: 51-53**

I think that we have read this passage for so long without knowing what we are saying, but Mary shows us again the liberating and protecting God who brings justice to the poor.

I think that Jesus, totally integrated in the history of His people understands justice this way, as Luke 4:17 says:

He was given the volume of the prophet Isaiah and he found the passage where it is written:

"Therefore He has anointed me; He has sent me to bring glad tidings to the lowly, to heal the brokenhearted, To proclaim liberty to the captives and release to the prisoners, To announce a year of favor from the Lord and a day of vindication by our God, to comfort all who mourn." **Isaiah 61:1-2**

Then Jesus says: "This passage takes place today among those of you that hear listen to me."

I would dare to say that Jesus presents himself as Justice and with Him a new way of living enters into history: the Kingdom of God where everything can change, where all the structures turn around...

I think that all the catechists of the Good Shepherd have seen their lives changed with your presentations on the "History of the Kingdom." I think we all are more conscious of the responsibility that we have to contribute to that History, to write on the blank page as a response to God who is always seeking us so as to continue His covenant. However, have we given **Justice** an important place in our lives?

When trying to live the Maxims:

"**Say yes when it is yes, and no when it is no.**" Do we realize all the times that we have remained silent, when we should had denounced the injustice that surrounded us? The times that we have remained indifferent before the suffering of the weak and unprotected?

"**Give to the one that begs you...**" What do we give? To whom do we give? To the weak, the poor, or to those who can give us something in return? To give things isn't so hard but do we give our time, our knowledge to the Lord's poor?

"**Our body is the temple of the Holy Spirit.**" Do we remember all those bodies who are Temples of the Holy Spirit who live in inhumane conditions?

"**Love your neighbor as yourself.**" Do we realize that our neighbor is the one who needs help? And that the one that needs help the most is that one who is marginated, that does not have access to health, education, and goods.

Do we remember that saying "**Lord, Lord, is not enough to enter into the kingdom of God, but that you have to do the mission of my Father**"? Would this "mission" be justice?

"**Where your riches are there is your heart.**" Is our heart in *justice*? Do we strive so that the structures in which we live are more just? Or, on the contrary, do we help with our apathy and conformist ways to make and maintain more injustice?

Could Jesus say of us some day, "**Blessed are those who hunger and thirst for justice...**"?

I think that these reflections can help us to **"Seek the Kingdom of God and his justice"**...

For a long time I believed that this search was the most important in the life of a Christian, but the years and the injustices that I see growing around me have taught me that this is not enough...it is necessary, I believe, to ask the Lord constantly "Thy Kingdom come" because to beg "Your Kingdom come" is to renew our hopes, the most radical ones in our hearts, so this will not succumb to the prolonged brutality of the absurdities that take place in the social and personal realm.

How will the Kingdom of God come? For the Christian faith there is an infallible criteria to indicate the coming of the Kingdom: when the poor are evangelized, that is when justice begins to come to the disinherited, the dispossessed and the oppressed. Every time the ties of fraternity are established, ties of participation and respect toward the invaluable dignity of man... the Kingdom of God starts shooting forth new sprouts.

**Thy Kingdom Come**

"It is a shout that rises, borne from the most radical hope, constantly striving but without ever renouncing, regardless, to hope for the absolute revelation that God has to realize in all His creation. Who prays thus gives himself to Him who shows himself to be stronger than the strongest (see Mk. 3:27) and so has power to transform the old into new and to establish a new heaven and earth where reconciliation will be for all and among all." (3)

With a loving embrace,

**Emilia Gonzales de Sandoval**

Chihuahua, Mexico

Sources cited:

1. Jose Ignacio Gonzalez Faus, *Reflexiones sobre Cristologia y Lucha por la Justicia*

2. Josep Vives, *Reflexiones sobre Dios y su Justicia*

3. Leonardo Boff, *El Padrenuestro*

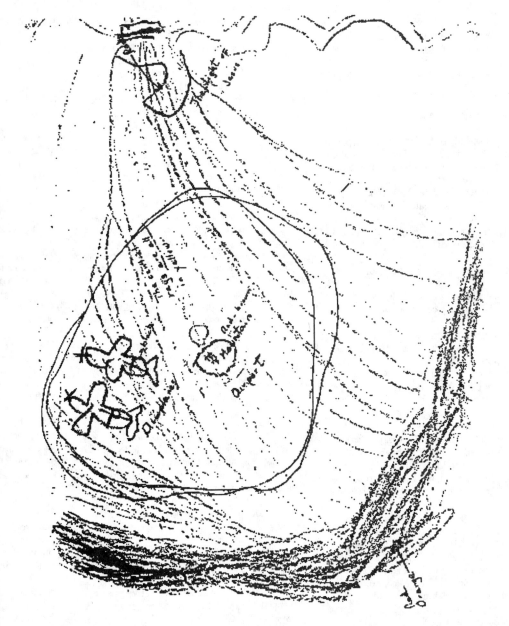

Drawing by Ernesto, five years old, Mexico; done during his second year in the atrium.

## Atrium of Saint Jerome

# A First Communion Journal

by Maria Christlieb
Mexico City, 1986

I go on learning that the period immediately before the First Communion, from the time they write their name, is a sensitive period particularly toward God. It is a period of extraordinary falling in love.

## March 20: The True Vine:
Today we start reading the text directly and helping each other to understand it. Without words from me. Better that way. The children immediately got involved, going deeper and deeper.

Diana: "God's own heart gives sap and life to the vine."

Ceci: "When will we know all of God's secrets?"

Bernardo: "Never, they are like numbers -- always more."

Manuel: "How much love!"

Christian and Mauricio insisted much on the union of the vine and the vineshoot, as of the vineshoots among themselves. They related the Vine to the mustard seed.... two plants in Jesus' parables. What is the Virgin Mary in the Vine? The most beautiful branch, no, the most beautiful flower. They insisted much in the Virgin. It was they themselves who asked about her and responded.

A long period of praying at the end.

They also stopped a lot on "I have told you this so that your joy could be fulfilled."

We now arrive to what is the most difficult, if not impossible to write about: **The retreat and First Communion...**

The reading in the first day's mass was: The Last Supper.

In spite of their restlessness, Mass was the most important feature of the day. Especially the moment of the breaking of the bread. The majority of the children, although they were only eight years old, were in their first year of Atrium and they had seen very few presentations.

Today, in the breaking of the bread, we heard his surprise and exclamation: "he is going to break it [or share it]." What did the child mean? I do not know, but Father Cereceres told us that since the First Mass for him it was very difficult to celebrate, to continue celebrating, when seeing the intensity with which the children were living it. He said that he sincerely felt touched by what was happening in them.

## The Third Day of the Retreat
Today in the morning we went back to the Maxims. I do not recall exactly what they said and we could not write it at the time. But for us, the three adults that were there, it was very special. We did it in the garden, for a good while in the morning, and from there we went to Mass. They had chosen the reading of the ten virgins.

When they came, the children immediately went into the classroom and Father, Lupita, and I went to the chapel to get what was needed for Mass. We were so impressed by what we heard about the Maxims that we started to talk about it in the sacristy. The children were by themselves in the other room. Nothing could be heard. Twenty minutes or more passed before we realized it. Lupita and Father stayed to arrange the altar and I went to the classroom to bring the children to the chapel... I couldn't...

When I went in the silence was perfect and each one was working at his and her own place. They had lowered the blinds and had little light. Each child had in front of him his candle lit. I stayed by the door paralyzed with emotion. God and they were there. Without making noise I went out and returned to the sacristy to explain to Lupita and to Father what was happening. "We cannot interrupt them," I told them. On the other hand it was the only time of the day that we could celebrate Mass. Father Cereceres came with me to the classroom. I don't know if the children were aware of us. We decided not to interrupt them and to prepare, without bothering them, there, in the classroom everything necessary for Mass. They continued in their work. Calmly and quietly we fixed a table as altar and brought everything that was necessary for Mass.

When everything was ready I gently said: "Children..." They turned to me and I proposed to them that we celebrate Mass there. They turned their chairs toward the altar and we began the celebration in the atmosphere as it was, with their candles in each place. The reading of The Virgins... They said that they were the Virgins and Christ the Spouse. They talked about the Light, the oil, etc.

After mass the morning went quietly, and so the rest of the day. We, the adults, didn't know where we were anymore. Everything happened, everything took place between the children and God.

In the morning of this third day, when we were in the garden, Cecilia stopped in front of the children and with her hands on her waist said aloud:

"Well, I still do not understand. How is Jesus the Good Shepherd and the Good Vine? Besides, what is more important? The lamb or the plant?" (She was still talking to herself and said) : "the lamb eats the plant so the lamb is more important than the plant."

**Elena, eight years old, told her:** "Ceci, the lamb eats the plant, but does so through the bread. The lamb eats the real vine."

**Cecilia:** "Ah, now I understand."
This conversation was the center of the homily of the First Communion Mass.

I don't know how to tell about the Celebration of the Light . As a catechist, it was difficult to be living such a marvelous experience. I didn't know what was going to happen each moment.

That was since the second day. Now, during all this the children organized everything. It was their retreat, their First Communion; songs, silence, spontaneous celebrations, everything came from them. Father Cereceres and Lupita had the same impression. The three of us were completely surprised by what was happening.

Father Cereceres told me, "I thought I was going to be bored. I never imagined what I would experience with those children. This has been my retreat for the year. What more could I ask! I was surprised at the depth those children reached."

He said he believed that three children had had a truly mystical experience, one with the "Light of God."

**A Mother commented:**

"I would have liked to hug and express my feelings to Diana. But the child, when she came to the house, asked to be alone and went to her room for quite a while." Then she came out, and she shared lovingly with them. Then she said:

"Mama, I know that many times you have things to say, things which you wanted to speak about with someone, but you knew that you didn't have a person to whom you could say those things. Now I know that that person is the Good Shepherd. Those things were to be said to him. And now I can do it."

The mother of Diana also spoke of the mystical experience of her daughter.

Catechesis of the Good Shepherd, 1988 Newsletter

# The Cosmic Vision of the Mass

The following two images on this page were drawn by two different children, from different Atriums. Notice the simliar themes represented in both the works.

The drawing at the right was done by a three and a half year old child from Holy Name Church in Toronto. This picture was drawn after only four sessions in the Atrium, including the presentation of the altar. He explained his work thusly: "The external line is the world. The internal one is the altar."

The external line is brown; the rays are red; the internal line is purple, and the lines at the center are yellow.

The drawing, below, with the hands was done by a seven year old boy from St. Francis Church, College Station, Texas.

The hands in the gesture of epiclesis extend themselves over the world.

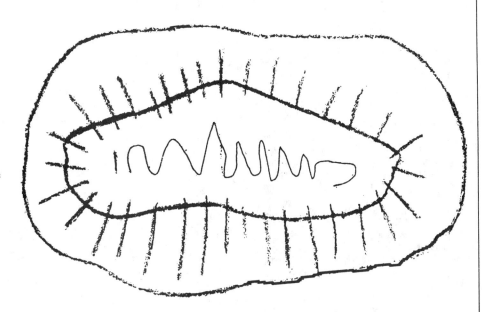

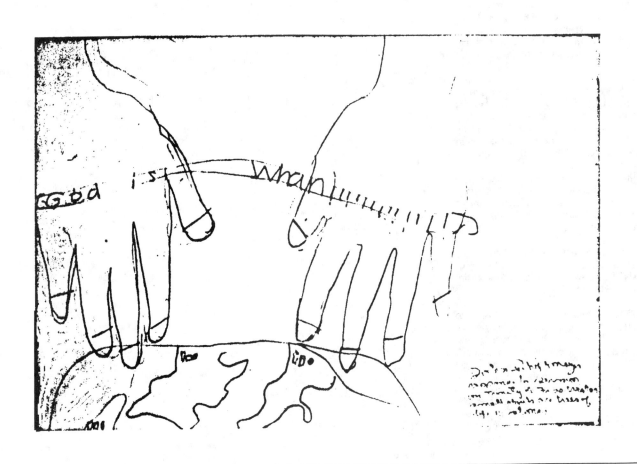

# Ten Years of the Catechesis in Rome

**Contributed by
Sandra Pollastri
Roma, June 28, 1987**

The tenth of June marked the 10th year since an atrium for the Catechesis of the Good Shepherd was opened in the parish of St. Lucy, Rome. On June 7, Pentecost Sunday, we celebrated first communions for the fifth time in these ten years. The date coincided with that of the first celebration that we held for the first group after we opened in 1977. That year the pastor, Father Sandro Plotti, now archbishop of Pisa after five years as auxiliary bishop of Rome, gave us the use of a large room at the top of the stairs alongside the belltower. We were a group of 4 catechists: Christina Giuntella, who had taken the course with Sofia in 1966/67; Nicoletta Lanciana and Alberto Biagi, who hadn't attended the course but had "experienced" the Catechesis of the Good Shepherd themselves since the age of three, and I, Sandra Pollastri, who was in the second year of the course with Sofia.

We prepared the environment*, though we had to take most of the materials after our meetings because a part of the room was used for other purposes during the week. The pastor gave us financial help to buy shelves; the small tables were donated from another center for the Catechesis of the Good Shepherd in Rome; financial help and some materials came from the Montessori Association. Some parents, parish catechists and friends met to present our future work.

This first catechesis meeting was held on Saturday, December 17, 1977. Only one child came; he was Francesco, a five year old, who was very timid and accompanied by his mother the whole time he spent at the atrium. He looked around the environment and Christina showed him the little altar while the other catechists observed. He watched with interest, but didn't pause to work. The catechesis resumed after Christmas vacation with four children. Their number continued to grow slowly throughout the year until it reached 11 children of 3 - 5 years of age.

This group made their first communion on Pentecost Sunday, June 4, 1981, after 4 years of catechesis. There were 6 children (one child, Silvia, decided to wait.)

We could not get permission from the parish to hold a celebration for so few children, so we contacted another catechist and worked out some meetings together with her and her children. (We did the Passover Meal and Last supper and the Liturgy of the Light.) These meetings laid the groundwork of reciprocal understanding and common language (between the two groups) for the retreat. This contact proved very beneficial, and the harmony between the two groups during the retreat was spontaneous.

A similar thing happened the next year for Silvia's first communion. We wanted to follow the same path we pursued for the group the previous year. We were in touch with a catechist, and the mother of one of our children, and with the parents, some of whom have supported our suggestions (the white garment, special meetings on the True Vine and Reconciliation, the three day retreat, the Saturday celebration for the conferring of the garment and the light.) The catechist liked these ideas, among others, so much that we wanted to propose them for and carry them out in her group, and she did so. The contacts we established that year raised some problems, though, due to lack of understanding on the part of some catechists and parents of other groups and especially the new pastor (on June 1, 1981, Dom Sandro was consecrated bishop) who was hesitant in the face of different experiments (or experiences) and worried about keeping uniformity in method. These problems turned to our advan-

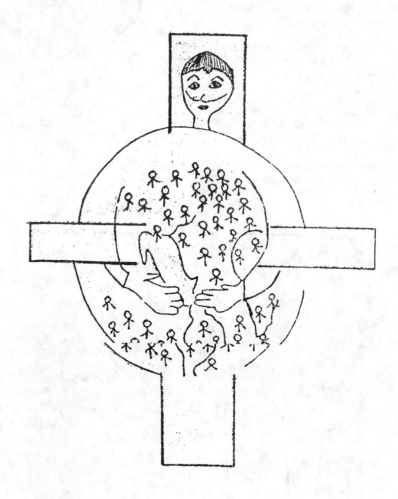

Drawing by Mili, eleven years old, Chihuahua, Mexico. The Cross, the world, the circle and the face were in brown. The hands were pink. The people were blue, green purple and red. This drawing was on the cover of the child's yellow work folder. The words below the drawing read: "God is risen and dead for us. The parousi God embracing us all and we united by love and joy.

# Parish of Santa Lucia

tage in the future: our experiment became better known and appreciated in the parish community and the rapport that we had on that occasion with the children and parents of traditional catechesis continued on other later occasions.

After the first communion, the children from that first group, with some dropouts and some additions, pursued the Catechesis for four years. Then, as we had started other groups of small children and found it impossible to work with them (older ones) they passed on to the parish Catechesis program for Confirmation preparation.

One of the major problems for the Catechesis of the Good Shepherd at St. Lucy now is mostly the restrictions on the space that we have at our disposal. In fact, we cannot use the large environment that the first pastor had assigned us; we have 2 smaller and less suitable rooms with unofficial use of a third.

The change of pastor has been a great loss to us. When Dom Sandro left we realized how much he had endeared himself to the children and that his silence and seriousness, which at times had perplexed us, was the expression of an attitude of real listening and readiness to understand the religious sense of the child. In one of the last Masses that he celebrated with us, the spontaneous prayer of thanksgiving after communion lasted a lot longer than the time provided. Although we were waiting for him at another meeting and someone had come to hurry him up, he didn't give any sign to speed things up. After the Mass one of the mothers said to him, "How beautiful you were." Dom Sandro replied, "But I am so comfortable with these children." And later, speaking with others, he spoke of the children as "theologians". Before he left he tried to see to it that we would be welcome in the catechist community so as to guarantee the continuation of our program. He confided to us that if our catechist experiment should be discontinued by the new pastor, he would be most displeased.

If lack of space and sensitivity to the religious potential of the child on the part of the present pastor make for objective difficulties, the positive aspects that have manifested themselves concerning the presence of the Catechesis of the Good Shepherd at St. Lucy are numerous enough.

First of all, there are the increasing requests from parents and children of all ages and the enthusiasm with which the children come and want to continue to come for many years after first communion, despite the inconvenient times that we are forced to meet in order to permit other groups to use the same rooms. Second is the support from the parents with whom we meet during the year on the subject of the "message" we give to the children. This support has been evident to us in different ways: by their help in material ways and in helping to prepare the atrium environment, tables and bookshelves; the cooperation in the preparation of liturgical celebrations; even in arranging contact with the pastor to resolve problems; or simply in their attitude of affectionate respect.

Third is the continual improvement in relations with other catechists of the parish. After some initial misunderstandings, one catechist, after bringing nieces, nephews and grandchildren to our group, decided to attend Sofia's catechesis course, and has decided to work permanently in the Catechesis of the Good Shepherd. A girl who had come four years ago in the first catechesis group has started to work with us as a catechist-helper.

There are other significant moments to remember in the course of ten years:

On the first of February, 1980, an interview that a journalist did with us was broadcast on Vatican Radio. He interviewed us and some of the parents on the rationale for a catechesis for children of preschool age and on the Montessori Method used, and the content of the message which we presented. They also interviewed the pastory about the pastoral choice of this type (of catechesis.)

On January 18 of this year, Pope John Paul II came to our parish on a pastoral visit. As we didn't have permission to have a specific meeting with him in the enviroment of catechesis, as we had hoped, the older children had the idea of preparing an album or notebook for him which would present and synthesize the most important elements of their catechesis work and of giving it to him when he would met all the children together. Their enthusiasm and involvement in this work was great. They decided to prepare a drawing of the Good shepherd since this is the point of reference for the whole catechesis, to illustrate the four sacraments which are "lived" in the atrium (baptism, reconciliation, eucharist, confirmation) unifying them under a large drawing of the gesture of epiclesis, to trace the card material from the History of Salvation, and to copy out an entire missal. The Pope sent a thank you note via the Secretary of State (for the Vatican).

Finally, on April 6, the bishop of the area, Monsignor Ragonesi, came specifically to visit the groups (children and catechists) of the Catechesis of the Good Shepherd. The children, especially the older and middle ones, wanted to show him as much of the materials and their work as possible so as to arouse his interest and admiration. In referring to the children, the bishop later commented, "These children have a capacity to intuit and grasp the truth that we don't have." He already knew Sofia and the Catechesis of the Good Shepherd and continues to help us not only with moral support, but also in his availability to support us in difficult moments in our relationship with the priests of the parish.

Recalling that day ten years ago, December 17, 1977, when we began the catechesis with one child, we can't help but think of the invisible and unexpected power of that mustard seed, before which the children always ask, "How is it possible?" Many times during these years we have lived through difficult situations and we asked ourselves "Will we still be at St. Lucy's next year?" And even today we must ask ourselves the same question. But, despite the memory of those precarious moments, we end the year with confidence in the immensity of the power of that seed, whose growth exceeds our greatest possible expectations.

---

\* For those not familiar with Montessori education, environment is a term used for the specially prepared place for children with materials and furniture specially designed. The materials and furniture, the whole environment must be orderly and beautiful so as to call to the child. It is a place where the needs of the child are met.

---

## *The Religious Potential of the Child*
## Spanish Edition Now Available

*The Religious Potential of the Child* by Dr. Sofia Cavalletti is now available in a Spanish Edition.

The book costs $12 (U.S. dollars) including postage and handling.

Copies may be ordered through:

Pia Cuside Lozano
Juarez 99
Tlalpan, Mexico D. F.
Mexico

For more information, call 52-5-573-4981 or 52-5-573-6918.

Catechesis of the Good Shepherd, 1988 Newsletter

## *Winter Meeting Recap*

# Our Association

February, 1988

**Dear Catechists and Friends,**

The sun is shining over Chicago as I write, but just a week ago today we were in the midst of a 45-hour snowfall. On Feb. 12, as the accumulated snow reached 17 inches, Carol Nyberg and I began to welcome to Chicago the representatives of our four association committees. They came to join us for a weekend of discussion, reports, planning, sharing, prayer and Eucharist.

This weekend gathering was proposed by the group at the committee members' meetings in Toronto last August. At that time we realized there was a little money left over in our treasury, which would make the weekend gathering possible, and there is much need, at the midpoint of the catechesis year, to reflect on our work and divide among us the responsibilities ahead.

Eight of us attended the weekend: Carol Nyberg and I (communications and finance), Bert O'Bryan (materials), Carol Stenborg (newsletter), Linda Kaiel and Nona Landon (formation), Susan Furlan (to represent Canada and add her wisdom from the Toronto formation experiences) and Marty O'Bryan (adding her wisdom from Phoenix).

Both Rebekah Rojcewicz and Father Cecil Roufs were unable to be with us as planned. Rebekah was responding to family needs and Father Cecil to his pastor's advice to continue recuperating in a slowed-down fashion from a recent heart attack.

We were very moved by the letters of support and promises of prayer that we received prior to our gathering. Telegrams arrived from Sofia Cavalletti and Maria Christlieb. Letters came from so many and even long-distance phone calls. Each letter and telephone message was shared and truly affected our weekend.

The weekend was essentially a time of listening — to our Shepherd and to each other. Each committee told of its work, and together we planned for the summer. We listened together to some psalms and to the scriptural texts of the true vine, the mustard seed, the leaven, and of our unity in Christ. We also shared abundantly the Good Shepherd's work in our different areas of North America.

The following items were discussed over the weekend:

**Finance** — Our treasury is in "fair" shape, with approximately $1,500. From this we will be able to cover the spring mailing, the newsletter/directory and its mailing, and provide some money for materials and a brochure.

**Formation** — For the summer of 1988, the association will not be sponsoring any training courses. Our goal is a simple gathering of catechists — three or four days set aside to be together, to nurture and strengthen the catechists and, through them, the atrium communities in North America. We realize there have been several requests for training courses (3-6, 6-9, even 9-12). But we see this gathering as a crucial time for all of us to deepen what already exists, and to hear the requests of the "training teams" for a sabbatical year.

Linda and Nona will be planning the "flow" of this gathering, and they welcome any suggestions. We accepted the offer of the Minnesota catechists to, once again, welcome us to St. Paul.

**Newsletter** — A committee of catechists from Mexico is compiling a newsletter this year. Its production takes place in Mexico and also in Minnesota (through Carol Stenborg). At our weekend we spoke of the various deadlines, some ideas for design, and we previewed its contents with excitement.

**Materials** — Bert reported that he and Sister Sheila Sentiff are both relieved to have the "breathing room" of a summer off. Their current project, the 6-9 materials set for training courses, is indeed a big one. Also, Bert volunteered to receive any questions about materials and, if necessary, he will forward them to the center in Rome.

**Communications** — So far, 72 people have responded to our membership mailing. We thank each one of you for your membership and/or subscription. Many additional letters are also received by the association. Most of them are either items of committee work or requests for information about the Catechesis of the Good Shepherd. People want to know where an atrium can be found or how to receive the training. So far, 60 response letters have been sent out to answer these requests.

Those gathered for the weekend previewed the work, begun by Barbara and David Kahn, on a brochure for the catechesis. This work is a slow process, involving much thought and consultation, but the result will be well worth their efforts.

A real highlight of the weekend was the presence of both Lech Kaiel and Devin O'Bryan — both under 2 years old. They walked and explored happily in our large meeting room. Their smiles and their expressions of need both blessed our work and gave it its proper focus. I had called so many retreat houses - none were able to accommodate the children until we found one run by the Sisters of the Holy Family of Nazareth. They truly lived up to their name!

All of us feel deep gratitude to the sisters, to all who have worked so hard for our association, to the children who lead us, and to our Shepherd for his immense love. We look forward to a rich and peaceful gathering this coming summer.

Love,
Tina Lillig

## *From Summer, 1987*

# Courses in Arizona

**Contributed by Marty and Bert O'Bryan**
**Holy Family Catechetical Center**

Phoenix, Arizona was the site for the National Association 1987 offering of two summer training courses (3 to 6 and 6 to 8). Sixteen participants were "called to the desert" where they were able to experience their faith through the eyes and sensitivities of the child. Their guides through this three-week journey were Rebekah Rojcewicz and Catherine Maresca of Washington, D.C. and Sandi Yonikus of Houston, Texas. What examples to us were these women of faith and deep love for the Good Shepherd!

During the second weekend of the course, participants packed up cameras, bags, children and nannies and travelled to the northern part of Arizona to see our greatest natural wonder: the Grand Canyon! What a perfect close to that week's lectures on the child's education to wonder!

Bert wanted to do the Fettucia and the history of the Gifts right there on the rim of the Canyon!

The small number of participants for these two courses came perilously close to forcing their cancellation. Yet in retrospect we were able to see providence in it, as the small numbers allowed the Phoenix hosts to be eased into and guided ever so gently through the "how-tos" of organizing a training course.

So, we'll be ready in 1989 to welcome even more. Come on down!

# The Power of God's Love

**Contributed by
Catherine Wolf Maresca
Washington, D.C.**

I have found that the 6-8 year old children in our Atrium are very concerned with power. And so I decided to discuss the power of God with them using the parables of the Mustard Seed and the Leaven. The meditation, however, was far more thought provoking than I could have anticipated.

In one group, after reading the parable of the Mustard Seed and talking about how the power of God is in us, but it is not ours (we cannot control it), Peter (age 9) said we do have a power that is ours. He was talking about free will, although we didn't use the term, and I agreed with him that we do have the power to make decisions and sometimes use it to do good things, and that we sometimes use it to do bad things. The children quickly began to use the language "good power" and "bad power". Annie (age 8) said, "We all use bad power once in a while."

The meditation continued on our use of bad and good power as the children contributed very concrete examples of the choices they had in regard to siblings and friends and the fights they sometimes had with them. Then I asked the question, "Which is stronger, good power or bad power?"

Some immediately answered "bad power", others were more thoughtful. We talked about what happened to Jesus. He was threatened by bad power, and had the choice of using violence against it. However, he chose to love, and was crucified. At this moment it seemed as though bad power is stronger.

But by the Resurrection, Jesus overcame bad power. We talked about the power of the Risen Lord, and then I asked, "Do you have the good power of Jesus?" The children said, "No." "What about Baptism? I asked. "We receive the light," said Peter. Shawn said, "But I'm not baptized." In fact, Peter is not baptized, either. We talked about the ways in which Jesus shares his Risen life with us: in prayer, in communion, in the Bible and so on.

## Our Association & the True Vine

**From a letter of Susan Furlan to
Maria Christlieb May, 1987**

If our association is like the true vine; it will grow. But, when it has grown to a certain point it will be pruned back. Not by the members of the association, but by the vine-dresser Himself. What happens when a vine is pruned back? It cannot bear fruit or leaves that year, but that's OK. The best thing that happens (and the only way it can happen is if the vine is pruned) is that the main stem of the vine gets stronger, more dense and the roots go deeper and spread. Although we don't get fruit this year, the new fruit will be better than before, and the vine will be stronger and richer than ever before. I think it's worth waiting for, and we must, because this is God's work and His hand and time will have the final word.

If catechists feel pruned back, then they should know that they are chosen for more growth. They should know that it is a blessing, and much good will come from it.

# Tapes from 1987 Toronto Course

Cassette recordings of last summer's seminar, "Being Called By Name, Part II" are now available from the Daughters of St. Paul. They are duplicated as recorded without editing and are 90 minute tapes.

The set of 14 (fourteen) cassettes covering the conferences (morning sessions) of Gianna Gobbi and Sofia Cavalletti costs $105.00 Canadian dollars. Please add the appropriate postage for regular or air mail delivery, for the United States or Canada.

Residents of Ontario should add $7.35, which is the tax imposed by the Province.

When ordering, please state clearly how many sets you want, and how you would like them shipped. Be sure to enclose payment in Canadian dollars with your order.
Further questions regarding the tapes, or orders should be directed to:

Daughters of St. Paul
Book & Audio Visual Centre
3022 Dufferin Street, Toronto
Ontario M6B 3T5

Telephone: 416 / 781-9131

SIDES A & B

1. July 13, 1987 — History/Psalm 23/ Two Paths in Education
2. July 14, 1987 — I Peter 1:3/Montessori: Developmental Stages
3. July 15, 1987 — Matt. 11:33/I Cor. 2:12-15/Montessori: Sensitive Periods
4. July 16, 1987 — Psalm 139/Sensitive Periods/Freedom and Independence
5. July 17, 1987 — Is.40:28-31/Heb.12:12/Psalm 91/John 6:1-15/ Freedom and Discipline
6. July 20, 1987 — Moral Formation Before 6 Years of Age
7. July 21, 1987 — The Cosmic Function of Liturgy
8. July 22, 1987 — Christological - Trinitarian Structure of Liturgy
9. July 23, 1987 — Signs in the Eucharist/Ecumenism
10. July 24, 1987 — Meditation on the Eucharistic Prayer 1
11. July 27, 1987 — Meditation on the Eucharistic Prayer II
12. July 28, 1987 — Baptism/The Method of Signs
13. July 29, 1987 — Meditation on Baptismal Rite/Questions Answers
14. July 30, 1987 — Parables of the Kingdom/The Mustard Seed

# Catechesis of the Good Shepherd

We extend our thanks to all the people who have made possible the publication of our fifth Newsletter! Again this year we are publishing in Spanish with the staff in Chihuahua. Thank you to the contributors of this issue. We invite catechists to send us information about their children, their centers, the prayers and drawings of the children.

Our next newsletter will be published in Spring/Summer 1989. The deadline for submission of materials is December 31, 1988. Please direct all Newsletter materials to:

> Maria Christlieb
> Hidalgo 21-1, 001060
> Obregon, Mexico D.F.
> Mexico

# Membership

Catechesis of the Good Shepherd, an Association of Children and Adults, welcomes members throughout the year. Our membership fee is $30 (tax deductible). The fees we collect go toward the expenses of our four committees - Communication and Finance, Formation, Materials, and Newsletter.

Members receive the annual newsletter, all mailings, and a directory listing catechists and friends of the Association. A newsletter subscription only is $5 within the USA or $6 for foreign mailing.

No one should hesitate to join the Association because of inability to pay the requested $30 fee. We appreciate any donation - large or small.

Mail memberships and donations to:

The Catechesis of the Good Shepherd
P.O. Box 218
Mt. Rainier, MD 20712

(All fees are due in US funds.)

---

This newsletter was compiled and edited by Carol Stenborg in collaboration with Maria Christlieb and Dr. Sofia Cavalletti

Copyright (c) by
**Catechesis of the Good Shepherd**
**P.O. Box 218**
**Mt. Rainier, MD 20712**

**Published in St. Paul, Minnesota**
  September, 1988

**Spanish Edition:**
  **Chihuahua, Mexico**

**Staff working on St. Paul Edition:**

| | |
|---|---|
| Editor: | Carol Stenborg |
| Translators: | Dianne and Nino Capoccia, Columbus, OH |
| | Ivan Nunez, Minneapolis, MN |
| | Sr. Eileen O'Loughlin, St. Paul, MN |
| | Joan Parasine, Herndon, VA |
| Proofreaders: | Carol Dittberner |
| | Millie Dosh |
| | Tina Lillig |
| Typist: | Lynn Linder |

**Staff in Chihuahua:**
  Maria de los Angeles Christlieb
  Noemi F. De Lopez
  Maria Ines G. de Lafone
  Bertha Sofia Q. de Marquez
  Emilia G. de Sandoval

# The Catechesis of the Good Shepherd

Number 6. English                                                                 1989/90

The Lord is my shepherd; I shall not want.
In verdant pastures he gives me repose;
Beside restful waters he leads me;
he refreshes my soul.
He guides me in right paths
for his name's sake.
Even though I walk in the dark valley
I fear no evil;
for you are at my side
With your rod and your staff
that give me courage.
You spread the table before me
in the sight of my foes;
You anoint my head with oil;
my cup overflows
Only goodness and kindness
follow me all the days of my life;
And I shall dwell
in the house of the Lord
for years to come.

*Psalm 23*

Catechesis of the Good Shepherd, 1989/90 Newsletter

## Contents

| | Page |
|---|---|
| Let us Pray with the Children | 2-3 |
| The Children speak to us about God | 3 |
| On Moral Formation *by Sofia Cavalletti* | 4-5 |
| Two Visions of Education *by Gianna Gobbi* | 6-7 |
| The Catechesis of the Little Ones *contributed by Gianna Gobbi* | 8 |
| Pili and the Sacrament of the Sick *contributed by Emilia Sandoval* | 8 |
| 10 Years of an Atrium in Santa Lucia, Mexico *contributed by Nora Maria Bonilla* | 9 |
| Washington Course / Summer 1989 *by Carol Dittberner* | 10-11 |
| The Catechesis of the Good Shepherd in Columbia *contributed by Nora Maria Bonilla* | 12 |
| Call for help with a Research Study *contributed by Sofia Cavaletti* | 13 |
| "Out of the Mouths of Babes" *by Cathy Maresca* | 14 |
| Remembrances<br>Sandi Yonikus<br>Massimo Nobiloni<br>Father Angelo De Angelis | 15 |
| Our Newsletter (deadline for next issue: March 1, 1990) | 16 |

---

*[Handwritten prayer:]*

Jesus and I

Jesus will walk with me and I will walk with him. He will talk to me and I will talk to him, he will be nice to me and I will be nice to him. he is a part of me and I am a part of him. The angels will sing and we will dance so I Love him and he Loves me we will walk in the flowers.

By Trevor
January 30 1989

This prayer was written by Trevor Trujillo, age 7, from Our Lady of Fatima Parish, in Casper, WY. He wrote this prayer after the infancy narratives had been given.

# Let us pray

Thank you for making me one of your sheep.
    (eight years old, Minnesota)

Emily is seven years old. She has been at the Atrium since she was three. She wrote this at home and even set it to music and immediately shared it with her mother and a friend. Emily's mother shared the prayer with Ruth Scheef. The music could not be retrieved.
    (From Minnesota)

"Cranking all the love up to God.
Down to us
Lays his life down for us.
All the love in the world
To everyone."

(From a nine year old girl: She is in her second year at the Atrium. This prayer was written on a day when there was no presentation given).

        Understanding
    We all shall know that God
      is a Jewel. The Lord will do
        His best on anything.
  Understanding is one of them, and
      Love and Kindness, too!

We had meditated on the Nativity of Jesus. The children entered into it with their whole being and with enchantment. At the end the prayers sprang out like a cascade. I only remember a few. (From children five and six years old):

Thank you
    for life,                for love,
    for the world,        for our beautiful country,
    for Daddy and Mommy,  for Christmas,
    for light,              for food,
    for all the things of the world, for us,
    for toys,              for our houses.

"I love Him very much."
    (Mexico)

**After the Parable of the Mustard Seed:**

Thank you
    for the world,        for life,
    for food,            for our families,
    for everything, for everything, for everything.
      (Mexico, five and six year olds)

After the Celebration of the Light and the Light received at Baptism:
    The Light of Jesus gives color, peace, love, life, light to the world.
    Thank you for the little flowers,
        life,
        light,
        water,
        food.
           (Mexico, five and six year olds)

# with the Children . . .

After the Celebration of the Light:
Thank you for giving us life,
    for fruits and nature,
    for vegetables,
    for love,
    for taking care of us and giving us life,
    for sharing your light with us,
    for rising from the dead,
    because you go on sharing your light with us,
    for the whole world,
    because you gave us life,
    because you gave your life for us,
    for what you have given us.
We pray that you keep on helping us (Mexico, seven and eight year olds)

The above drawing was created by a child, age 5, who has been in an Atrium in Mexico for one year. It says "God I love you, I love you. God is Risen." "I love you" can be said in two different ways in Spanish.

## The children speak to us about God

*The merchant met God and that is why he sold the other pearls. Could the pearl be bought?*
The pearl could not be bought because God cannot be bought.
    (4 years old)

Today is my fourth birthday and I am going to ask Jesus to bring me the Pearl material as a present.

Before the globe, Mariana, 5 years old: "How could a God so great be born in a place so small!"
    (Torreon, Mexico)

The Holy Spirit is color, the light of God is color.
    (5 years)

Mary was happy at the Visitation because now the Kingdom of Heaven would come to be, the Good Shepherd.
    (9 years)

Jesus is the Good Samaritan.
    (9 years)

The yeast brings growth and unity. In the kingdom we are united with God, unable to be separated. And united with each other.
    (10 years)

"Remain in me and I will remain in you," as the yeast in the dough and the dough in the yeast.
    (9 years)

The Father is the Vinedresser in the True Vine and He is the woman in the yeast and the dough.
    (9 years)

All Powerful God: What is the power of the Child Jesus? The power of doing good, of friendship, of loving, of giving life.

The power of the Shepherd is the power of the sheep: the power to give life: we can give life to others, our parents gave us life. (10 years)

The Parousia will be like the mixing of the water and the wine: God all in all, as the water and the wine become one. (11 years)

The publican before God is like the lost sheep. (10 years)

Confession is the Sacrament of:
    liberation    (Ines, 11 years)
    of the new way    (Diana, 11 years)
    of the new page to write    (Mauricio, 12 years)

**What is Lent?** Lent is a time of reflection, of preparing ourselves for the resurrection of Our Lord, of sacrificing ourselves by doing something that takes a great effort, of remembering the 40 days that Our Lord was in the desert, a time of sharing and giving ourselves body and soul to God and to the Holy Spirit.
    (Jessica, 9 years old, Chihuahua, Mexico)

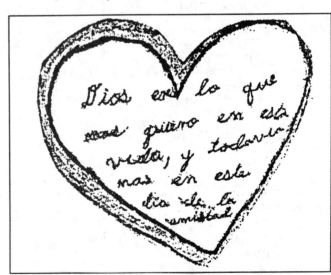

On Valentine's Day, Georgina came to the Atrium and asked, "Can I make God a Valentine's Card?" "Why not," said the catechist, "Is he or is he not our good friend."

Georgina spent the rest of the afternoon making the above card and a frame for it. The heart is red, and inside it says: "God you are what I love more in this life, and even more so on this Valentine's Day." Georgina's face was full of joy that afternoon. I wonder how God's face is with her card and her love? Georgina is seven years old, and has been attending an Atrium in Mexico for two years. (contributed by Maria Christlieb)

*Sofia continues the discussion*
# On Moral Formation

**Dearest Catechists and Friends,**

I am very grateful to Emilia Sandoval, who has further developed the reflections initiated by me on formation for social justice. I believe, on reading her letter, we all felt moved to implore him together, "Thy kingdom come." I hope that others among you might want to develop some of the points which are being proposed through this Newsletter.

I would like to resume the discussion on moral formation begun in the 1988 issue of the Newsletter, developing it and considering it in regard to children older than 6 years of age. I know that many of you feel a keen need to be helped in the work with the older children. It is an age for which there is still need for more documentation, and so I invite you to collect all the elements pertaining to this topic and, if possible, forward them to me, even if they are just photocopies.

I would like to link myself with what Emilia said with regard to the "History of the Kingdom" and its importance for us catechists so that we make it an object of meditation in its globality and dynamism. But I would also like to share with you what Millie wrote and her drawings, and also the work of Claudia Cecelia.

**Ed. Note**: The childrens' writing does not reproduce clearly. The texts Sofia speaks of are translated as follows. Cecelia's drawing was entitled **"I want to have a very brilliant light."** Her drawing was centered on the page, and around the drawing was written:

> "I am part of the white page and my mission is to build invisible bridges with other people and with people of other centuries. I am part of the light of the world as much as everyone who lives on it. I will build invisible bridges leaving my own wisdom to other people. God has given me many gifts and I have to make the most of them.
>
> I do not know if I am more than others, but I would like to know for sure that in front of God and my neighbors I would be a good, noble, respectful woman, with a light that cannot be extinguished, as the light God has given me when I was born and which I reinforced in Communion. I know that some day, when Gods calls me, with my efforts, I will be a messenger of peace."

Millie wrote the following:

> "We are awaiting the Great Arrival. We need to open our hearts.
>
> We are also waiting for Jesus, the savior. We live in the hope that his reign will grow ever deeper within us and around us.
>
> God, I thank you. There are no words to tell you.
>
> I always notice more and more how beautiful life is. What joy that a man, the Good Shepherd, the Saviour should give us such precious gifts, yes, love, the people, every person, a grain of sand half brilliant and sparkling with a little bit of black, the trees, all living things, intelligence, the flowers.
>
> Now, every day my intelligence reaches further. I think more. I try to enjoy the time as much and in the best way possible. I give you a thousand thanks and I wait for you
> ANXIOUSLY."

What do these children teach us? One thing struck me above all; I would like to share it with you while awaiting whatever else you can add.

The two children expressed very effectively how forcefully the message of the "history of the Kingdom of God" resonates even in the very young. The writings of Claudia Cecelia and Millie have captured the impulse to "do" (to build bridges, to share one's own wisdom with others). They are, indeed, very rich with this proclamation. In regard to moral expression at this level, it seems to me that the sense of wonder still prevails, the sense of "how beautiful it is," to be aware that "each day one's own intelligence goes a little further in exploring the world full of different people and beautiful things." The souls of the two girls are opened in wonderment to horizons which become even wider. It seems to me that what emerges first of all is the sense of enjoyment for the message received. This is different from what happens with us adults, who, for the most part, measure what our world still lacks in arriving at the fullness of the kingdom. In what Claudia Cecelia and Millie wrote one senses very powerfully the spring of hope - a fundamental Christian virtue - in the expectation that God is "embracing us" and that we are united in love and glory.

Emerging clearly from these writings is the importance of the message, the "kerygma," given assuredly with the purpose of making known the reality in which we live. Also it makes clear how our tradition is our guide, but in such a way as not to slip immediately into moral exhortation ("parenesis"), that is, the scholastic form of learning. (We must "deschool" catechesis.) The "kerygma" (the good news) is something that ought to be listened to in peace, so that it sinks into the depths of the person, heart opened joyfully. ("We have to open our hearts.") The "kerygma" is always — at whatever age — before and after the "so called " logic/moral crises — the basis for catechesis, because it is directed at the totality of the person, because the heart grows bigger when confronted by it, and delight and joy ensue from it. Joy, says Maria Montessori, is the indication of interior growth, like an increase in weight is a sign of physical growth. (**Auto-Educazione**, Garzanti. 1970, p. 83)

Joy has caused Claudia Cecelia and Millie to grow interiorly, opening their horizons to the boundless reality, a reality of which they are a part. The message has stirred a very powerful mainspring in them and has made them aware of a reality for which "there are no words" to say "thank you" sufficiently.

That the phenomenon of joy is produced in them means — in my opinion — that the theme of the kingdom, its history, responds to their inner needs. Existential joy is born when an interior need finds satisfaction.

We present the "history of the Kingdom of God" to children after the age of 6, the age at which Montessori speaks of "Cosmic Education," which means throwing open wide the doors of the universe before the children. "Let us give the universe to the child," she says. After the sixth or seventh year new capacities appear in the child, among them that of moving into a ever-widening horizon. The tool of this capacity is a new dimension of the imagination which has become capable of "seeing" things never before perceived (with the senses).

What does our tradition offer to satisfy this new potentiality of the child?

The history of the kingdom of God, as told in the Bible, is a comprehensive history; it includes all time and all space. The first page speaks of the beginning of time and of the world; the last directs our view, in hope, towards the completion or fulfillment of its history, when the "Long Awaited One," the Messiah, will say, in glory, "Yes, I am coming soon." (Rev. 22:20) It opens up for us the perspective of a world in which heaven and earth will be made anew, because "God will be all in all." (1 Cor. 15:28)

All humanity moves in time and space; all humankind makes its appearance with Adam in a world which God has already filled with countless animals and other things to help him live. Through successive stages, in Rev. 5:11, we find again a multitude of "ten thousand times ten thousand and thousands upon thousands of them" that together with "all living things in creation — everything that lives in the air, and on the ground, and under the ground and in the sea" sing the praise of God (from the Jerusalem Bible).

History has a direction and an orientation; it is like a great river that flows through time, engulfing every creature [and carrying each one] towards the river's mouth, where the river empties into the ocean: the fullness of the kingdom. In this river I, too, am a drop.

I believe we cannot find richer food for the growing hunger of the older child (6 - 12 years).

We need to find a means of presenting all this in a manner that corresponds to the grandeur of the theme and to the needs of the older child.

The materials, which we have elaborated and which have been presented in some courses, are attempts upon which we ought still to reflect further. What I believe clearly is that prior to introducing the children to particular moments of history, we should help them to capture its globality; we should help them open their eyes to the vision of the whole. We must assist them to discover in history a plan so vast and marvelous that it could not possibly originate in the human mind. The love of God that the little child has experienced most of all in his personal relationship with the Good Shepherd, now takes on a new dimension, a cosmic dimension, for the young person. The concept of God is enriched with a new dimension: God is the God of history, who is carrying out his plan of love, together with the multitude of his creatures.

At this point we might ask ourselves whether we have lost the discourse on moral formation along the way. What do you think? No, you know very well that every moral discourse begins with a relationship. Therefore we found it in the "kerygma" which has as its goal to establish and cultivate relationships. The "kerygma" responds to the question "Who are you?" It satisfies the desire to know the Other. Another question follows upon it: "What should I do?"

Before thinking about what "to do" in history, we ought "to exist" in it. We ought to situate ourselves in it within a network of relationships ever vaster, which link us to God, who guides history, to the men and women who, in time and space, live it, who are working and continue to build it up, and to the many creatures whom we encounter in this world.

It is in this broadening of horizons for the young person, in helping him discover himself as a point of receiving and giving in the broadest scale, that we effect the world of moral education in the profound sense, namely that of aiding the formation of the moral person. At this point I would like to reread with you a page from Montessori, in which she speaks of how to correct defects: "Correction is possible only by expansion, by giving 'space,' by opening up the means for the expansions of the personality.... Only the poor quarrel over a piece of bread. The rich are attracted by the possibilities offered to them by the world.... He who has the vision of a 'paradise' to be conquered, cannot be satisfied by the whole world, and he easily renounces transitory and limited possessions.... An education of 'vastness' therefore is the platform whereon certain moral defects can be eliminated. The first step of education must be to 'extend the world' in which the child of today languishes, and its fundamental technique consists in 'freeing him from the shackles which hinder him in going forward'." (**Formation of Man**, Theosophical Publishing House 1971, pages 49-50).

If we want to paraphrase what Montessori says, we could say that the essential elements of moral education are the formation of hope and humility. Hope: that dynamism that urges us to view the reality in which we are immersed in a positive manner. Hope is the essential mainspring of the human spirit, or better still a magnet which draws us toward a consciousness deeper still than reality, towards relationships and contacts that grow greater and greater. Hope is that dynamism that causes us to discover and awaken in ourselves the ability to become a part of and collaborate in God's grand plan. "Hope-Education" is an essential element in an education in which "you can be" prevails over "you must do."

Alongside hope we place humility, the virtue which is called "the cardinal Christian virtue," because the pagan world has little knowledge or appreciation of it. In the broad background of the plan of God we are able to make an honest evaluation of ourselves. We are very small in the great sea of history, a drop in the ocean; but the greatness of the ocean confers its own grandeur on each drop which forms it. At this point, we would like to search for the worlds of "thanks" which, according to Claudia Cecelia, will never be good enough.

I conclude with this, very aware of the difficulty of the subject which I have scarcely touched upon and I am waiting for your contributions.

**Sofia**

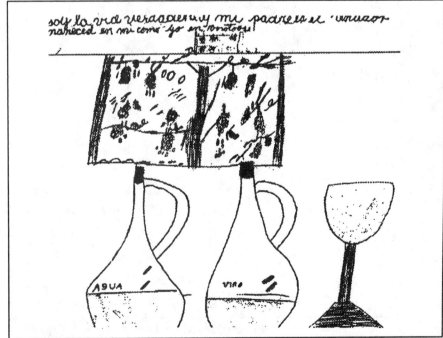

Bernardo, age 9 years, from Mexico, commented while working with the preparation of the chalice: "It is like in the True Vine." Then he made this drawing. On it is written: "I am the true vine and my Father is the gardener. Dwell in me, as I in you."

# Two Visions of Education

**By Gianna Gobbi**

*[Ed. Note: The following was one of the lectures given by Gianna Gobbi during the summer course in 1987. This lecture was published in the Spanish but not the English edition of last year's newsletter. Though it's taken an extra year to get to all of you, Gianna's comments are no less relevant today!]*

Our task as catechists and as believers is a special task which reflects on the field of education and commits us both as Christians and as educators. It seems to me opportune to offer some reflection on education, and education as Maria Montessori understands it.

This graph was presented by M. Montessori at the International Course in Perugia, Italy in 1950. It is a valid aid and can serve as a guide for our considerations on education. Looking at the graph we see represented two points of view on education: the two lines correspond to two different conceptions of education.

The upper line denotes the development of the person; This line goes from 0, and even before, from conception, to the age of 24.

The lower line represents the type of education used in the schools for many years, in which the teacher imparts knowledge to the students.

Both views of education share the same aim, that is, the realization of the personality of the individual, in the best possible way, to enable the person to fulfill his own function, and to carry it out in his social milieu.

In the upper line, it is evident that there exists a regular process of unfolding; four triangles are supported by the chronological line of life. These signify the four stages of development of the person, the validity of which is upheld by modern

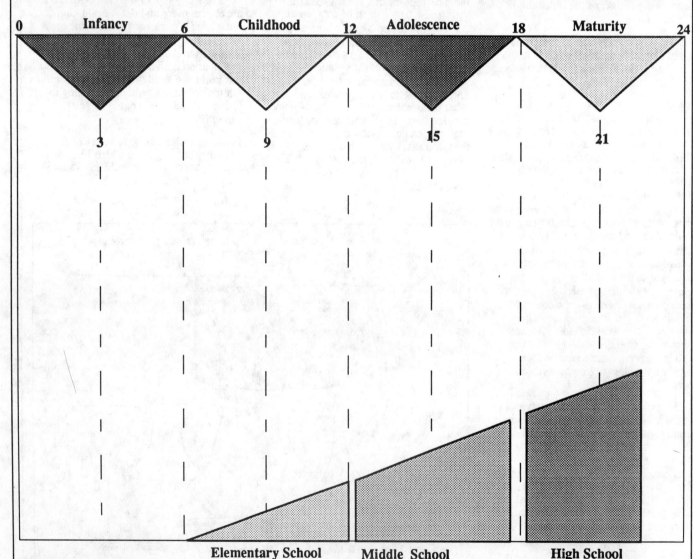

The dark triangles at the top of the chart are red, the lighter ones, blue. Please note, the school classifications on the chart do not correspond directly with our U.S. school system. The latter two categories at the bottom of the chart most closely correspond with Middle/High School and College/University.

psychology: infancy, childhood, adolescence and maturity. In the lower line it is obvious that the process begins toward the age of six, the age at which society pays attention to the individual. The vertex of the triangle widens with a progressive growth in size, which reflects the thought by which the intellect of the child is always increasing and which in relation to this growth must continue receiving an ever broader culture. There is no continuity in the divisions of the triangles; in fact there is a very definite dividing line, which marks the change from one sector to the other: elementary school, middle school, high school. The lower line must conform, according to Montessori, with the upper line which represents the development of life. All this has validity today. Those who are familiar with the school environment, know well how tedious the teaching programs can be and how far we are from applying scientific concepts that harmonize individual growth with progressive education. Although these two concepts of education have points of contact, the two are in opposition; nevertheless, they can come to an agreement. Through the development of the concept of education, the two points of view have been coming closer together. But they will not be able to be in harmony without totally eradicating certain preconceived ideas about education that still exist in our day.

Before going on to examine this graph, it is useful to reflect on and understand the meaning of the word education. And old Italian encyclopedia has this definition: "Under the category of Education, as its meaning is generally understood, is included the sum total of the customs of a particular community or a social group and the transmission of all that possesses the real or potential aim of protecting the continuity of its own existence and development."

This helps us to understand that there exists an educational process for all of human society — adults and non-adults. Today, more than in former times, the adult is called to reaffirm his own personality, character and abilities through constant contact. Freedom is being affirmed in the educational process. Today educators give more attention to working with those who are educating; that is, they are more involved in favoring, in the best way possible, self-education. Nevertheless, even though progress is being made, there are still many contradictions and set-backs and many programs still unaccomplished.

What the adult world is not yet fully aware of, and this concerns us as catechists and educators, is that the personality of the child is still buried by prejudices, practical interests, and utilitarian preoccupations. This prevents us from seeing the child from a different point of view than the usual way of thinking or than that of traditional education. This prevents us from seeing ourselves with humility in regard to the child, in order to learn his true nature and to learn the universal laws which guide and determine his development.

"If only we could manage to demonstrate the existence of these prejudices, we would have done something that would be of significant benefit to all." And: "Children are thought of as empty beings, suited only for playing, sleeping, and passing their time with fairy tales.... Any serious mental effort by those children seems a sacrilege. And in regard to the child's learning, we concern ourselves with protecting him from mental efforts and from intellectual exercises at an early age."

Even in regard to the physical life of the child, we are convinced that children do not have the ability to control their own movements; for this reason we avoid having them move by themselves or do things for themselves. Instead we do everything for them (dress them, feed them, etc.) and in doing so we prevent children from having experiences which are important for them, because they lead to independence and to self-confidence. In summary, as adults we are so caught up in our role as educators, that we forget to respect the child. Now, if we take these observations into the sphere of religious education, we find ourselves even more submerged by these prejudices, that have still not been overcome. If we as adults reflect on our relationship with the child, whether in the family, or in society, we can verify the existence of such prejudices, still today.

Some positive elements exist: the Church has recognized the dignity of the child as "a child of God," even from conception, and has offered baptism to newborn babies; the Orthodox Church permits very small children to receive the Eucharist, recognizing that the child is capable of participating in the most essential act of the Christian life. And in our day it is recognized that the religious world of the little one has its own aspects. In spite of this, the subject of religious education is taken up in the parishes - at least in Italy - around the age of eight, or when preparation for the Sacrament of the Eucharist or First Communion begins.

And even here, the concern regarding religious education is seen more in terms of instruction than of formation. If we look at the graph again with reference to religious education, the contrast between the two points of view will appear even more pronounced. We will see the same prejudices, for example, in the attitude that the deep concepts of theology are not comprehensible to small children. Our experience, on the other hand, in many countries and through many years, has demonstrated how very deeply rooted is the relationship of the child with God, even at the earliest age. How deep is the bond between God and the little one; how great is the ability of the child to see the "invisible" inside reality and how great is the capacity of the child to live in relationship with God as an experience and expression of prayer!

But it is precisely in this sphere of religious education where we must - and we will be able to more easily in the future - free ourselves from the point of view of traditional education based on an adult model of teaching oriented toward the adult, in order to be free to follow the potentials of the child. It is precisely in this religious sphere that education must be liberated from the idea of external casuality, and thus be free to follow the most constructive rhythms of Life, if we understand that Life belongs to God.

Maria Montessori, from the beginning of her work in 1907, in her experimental method conducted in a prepared environment, discovered new characteristics and unexpected capacities in the child, and it is on this discovery of the child that her educational work is founded.

The phrase that synthesizes the Montessori concept of education is: "Education is an aid to life." This is the aid which we offer in order that the potentials of the child may develop; this is the aid which we offer to Life (with a capital L) so that, by means of this very Life, the child may bring to fullness his task as a "builder of man," as Maria Montessori defined it.

And the phrase that completely summarizes her point of view on education is: "Help me to do it myself." The phrase that we as catechists offer as a summary of our own point of view on education is "Help me to come close to God by myself."

# The Catechesis of the Little Ones

Rome, December 22, 1988

From a letter by Gianna Gobbi to Maria Christlieb:

"The catechesis with the group of little ones must be very measured both in words and in the content that it announces.

At this age, the Mystery of God is received through feelings, through a global sentiment which is expressed by a single word, by silence, by movement, and not so much by things of the intellectual order. Children before age six are in the sensorial phase of religious feeling, intuiting the differences between similar things in both the lower and upper planes, those which refer to man and those which refer to God.

Maria Montessori says: "It is not so much a question of teaching, as of a vital development, which, occurring in the period of the absorbent mind, becomes character."

In the next stage of development, when a teaching is given, it will be built upon an already existing base and will be a clarification.

What do we do with the little three-year olds?

I wonder if we truly respect them?

When I see my children from last year — how big they've become, delighting in a small thing, in the light, in silence, in a sung prayer, in socializing, and in simple work, I wonder if it isn't too much to give them all that we propose in a program?

We must always be aware of who it is we have before us when we communicate something."

Ernesto, age 5 and 1/2, is from an Atrium in Mexico. In the drawing a square encloses the Nativity. Yellow rays are drawn around it. Notice the "Eucharist" beside the "Nativity." The writing says: "Christmas The light of God."

## *A child's faith is a lesson for us all*
## Pili and the Sacrament of the Sick

In the Assessment for First Communion, Claudia Felix arrived to tell us that Pili, her daughter, was still very sick; for a month she had had the same problem with her blood, and now cortisone was no longer effective. She had no platelets and the only thing left to do was to remove her spleen, but there was a 25% chance that the operation would not be successful. The child knew and decided in favor of the operation. If the operation failed, she could die with the first infection. There was also a risk that she could lose a lot of blood during the operation. She knew this too.

Today they went to El Paso, but yesterday Pili asked to speak to Father Careceres, and Claudia wanted me to make the appointment. I spoke with Fr. Careceres and we discussed the possibility of administering the Sacrament of the Sick. I told Claudia to tell Pili that it could be done either in private or in community within a Mass; she should decide. Pili asked her to explain the difference, and Claudia told her that the community reinforced the sacrament by prayer; she said she would prefer the community. Her friends and relatives were invited, and I invited the catechists that I could contact. It was only an hour before the Mass. I arrived at Santa Teresita and Pili was seated in a pew with her sister and friends. Behind her were Claudia and her husband (who at first didn't want this, but finally agreed when he listened to the child). Fr. Careceres spoke to me and I asked him if he had spoken with Pili. He said, with his eyes shining: "Yes, she is a very beautiful child." We were in agreement that the Sacrament would be after the homily; the readings would be a preparation. Then we began. Father explained what was going to happen, and the people were surprised. The readings were: one about a king, Eleazar, whom the prophet came to tell that he should make his will because he was going to die, and he cried out, asking God to let him live longer. Then the letter of James where it says that if any are sick, they should ask the priests to anoint them with oil and pray. Then the Gospel was, "Father, if it is possible, let this cup pass from me, but let your will be done." (Matt. 26:39) Fr. Careceres spoke very briefly but very beautifully; he was really moved.

Then Pili went up to the altar (she is 13 years old, but is quite tall), and during an imposing silence the Sacrament of the Sick was administered to her. The Eucharist followed; then she went alone to the altar for Communion.

At the end of the Mass all the people were deeply moved. In an atmosphere full of hope they all came up to congratulate her. (From a letter of Emilia Sandoval to Maria Christlieb, Jan. 1988).

[Note: Pili is alive and happy today.]

## *In Santa Lucia*
# Celebrating 10 years of an Atrium

**In the above photos, children are helping their parents to build the Atrium at Santa Lucia in 1977.**

contributed by
**Conception Hernandez de Sanchez**

On February 20, 1988 we celebrated 10 years of life in the Atrium of Santa Lucia in Mexico City. Santa Lucia was the first atrium to open in this city.

The first catechists were Nora Maria Bonilla and Guadalupe Palafox. Next to the atrium a "Children's House" was also opened. Forty families of the community were involved in beginning this work. The parents, along with the children, built the rooms and prepared the necessary material. The bishop, Msgr. Francisco Maria Aguilera, and the pastor, Fr. Jose Martinez, supported the work from the beginning and gave it their help and encouragement.

Many of the Mexican catechists received courses in this atrium, since Sofia Cavalletti, Gianna Gobbi, and Silvana Montanaro gave several courses here. In the early years of the Catechesis in Mexico, Santa Lucia was the place where we all went to copy materials, to observe the children, to get together with other catechists. Santa Lucia is a spot which is much loved by all of us in Mexico who live the Catechesis of the Good Shepherd.

Nora Maria Bonilla is now in Colombia. Regarding these ten years she writes us: "There is a lot of history in these ten years of the Atrium. Many bridges have been built to make present among us the Kingdom of the Good Shepherd. It is our task to prepare the environment for the encounter of Our Lord with his preferred guests. We are his servants; we are all pupils before one Single Master. How gracious of such a great God to have chosen us for this work with his most preferred flock, such as are the little ones! How small it should make us feel to think of the immensity of his Mystery that has passed so many times through our clay vessel!

**We can't do it without YOU!**

**Send us your experiences, letters, thoughts, children's work, photos of the Atrium.**

**Deadline for next newsletter: March, 1990**

# 1989 Course for 9-12 in Washington

**Contributed by Carol Dittberner**

This past summer, 32 of us gathered in Washington, D.C. for Part I of the 9-12 year old Course. Rebekah Rojcewicz did wonderful work in her presentation to us. The experience was rich: we listened for two weeks, every day, to the endless gifts we have been given by God. We all were reinspired in our work with children and our roles as parents.

Being together was like being with 32 best friends for two weeks. Many of us had met in Washington in the 1982 or 1983 courses: we saw both familiar faces and new ones. The level of work among us was absolutely frenetic! However, it was very well done, especially in our efforts to do well whatever we shared with each other.

A special compliment must be paid to the team of paper cutters: four catechists had to hand cut time lines from rolls of paper because we could not find a paper company who would handle it. This year, Greg Kerbawy was in charge of the taping, recording, and labeling. As always, there are so many small pieces which make up the whole.

The Washington hostesses were Jane Scheuermann and Marilyn Krause. Cathy Maresca, with a Washington team, was behind the time line preparations and material making. We were housed at the Center for Educational Communication and Design (CEDC) which is run by the Sacred Heart Sisters. Since they ran a Communications Center, all of the course tapes were made right on the premises. The second part of 9-12 is already scheduled for the same location for next summer. The CEDC is off the beaten path and so some of us drove the taxi drivers crazy looking for it!

The families of the Christian Family Montessori School were very supportive also in providing airport connections (those of us who forgot to inform others of our arrivals were the ones in the taxis). They hosted a picnic for us half way through the course, and also sent goodies for all of our snacks.

We were very happy to have Maria Christlieb with us for most of the course. She had many ideas and experiences to share about her work with older children. We also had a meeting to discuss the First Communion preparation.

Some of the new faces were Kathleen Alman, from Houston, Texas. Kathleen studied with Sofia in Rome for two years: this was her first "course" in the U.S. Martha and Red Fisher were accompanied by two catechists who work with them: Mary Nell Prichard and Laurie Dowdy. Gayla Bergren, who is from the Washington area, worships in the Moravian Rite. A priest from her church, Father Mark, who is a trained puppeteer, came and showed us how to make and use puppets in a liturgical setting.

Mary Ann Keshner has long worked with Tina Lillig in Chicago, but this was her first course experience. She and Tina work together as coordinators for the Catechesis in their community. Donna Macklin brought Jo Ann Williams who works with her. Donna and Jo Ann, and Laurie and Mary Nell, as well as Marjorie Farhat, were the ones most likely to be found working on materials at any time of the night.

We also renewed friendships with some people who haven't been able to meet at some of the courses outside of Washington: Joan Gilbert, Kathleen Sweeney and Jo Kendrick. The children present this year were: all the O'Bryans, Joshua Fisher and Annie Keshner. It is good when children can join us: there is continued discussion about how to make the intensive summer courses workable for families.

Another wonderful profile of the group was that one third of the participants were Episcopal. In fact, they had to have their own meeting! Kathleen Alman, who is also Episcopal, had worked with Sofia on the liturgy materials, making the appropriate changes for their needs.

Most of each day was filled wtih lectures and presentations on the materials. Then, we scheduled meetings according to our needs from 3:30 into the evening. Some days we would have a presentation given, such as the Good Samaritan, or a discussion on Art in the Atrium. Sr. Mary Elizabeth Klier gave the presentation "The God with No Hands," which is given to children in the elementary level Montessori program.

Activities around Washington included trips to the museums, especially the National Gallery of Art to collect all the religious art prints. We would run into each other there! Many of us visited the Washington Episcopal Cathedral and found a sculpture of the shepherd and the sheep. After several purchases, the

Laura, 6 years old, is from an Atrium in Mexico. The image above is a collage. She cut the cross, chalice, paten and stars from gold paper. Next, she drew the elements of the Nativity. The color in the space between the stars, down to the chalice is soft blue and orange. Also the back of the Nativity is orange. It was made in January. Laura wrote "the light of Jesus" by the stars at the top and "Nativity" at the bottom. The catechist added the English text.

saleswoman remarked, "What is all this interest in the Good Shepherd lately?" We must give the Most Books Purchased Award to Judy Schmidt. However, there are a lot of runners up!

We worshipped at the Prayer Meeting of the Christian Family Community, which meets every Wednesday evening at Cathy Maresca's. We also attended services at Washington Cathedral, the National Shrine, and St. Aloysius. The latter is a black community church which several of the catechists have joined. We sang at many more parts of the liturgy, eg. various times throughout the Eucharistic Prayer.

Prior to our arrival, there was an overview course for the 6-8 year old level. Seventeen catechists came for this refresher which was conducted by Cathy Maresca, and assisted by Jane Scheuermann and Marilyn Krause.

It is such a good feeling when our community is able to meet, and, in this case also study together. At the "Time Apart" in St. Paul, in 1988, the theme was the grain of wheat which falls to the ground and bears fruit. We had the realization of this tiny seed bearing fruit in the many places our catechists work and worship as we shared our stories and experiences. We were also keenly aware of all those who could not join us: our prayers were, and are, always with you.

Participants for both the 6-8 overview and the 9-12 course were: Kathleen Alman, Gayla Bergren, Maria Christlieb, Kathy Dahl-Bredine, Carol Dittberner, Millie Dosh, Laurie Dowdy, Marjorie Farhat, Red and Martha Fisher, Joan Gilbert, Nicolina Gleasure, Betty Hissong, Pam Hopton, Helen Jablonski, Linda Kaiel, Jo Kendrick, Greg Kerbawy, Mary Ann Keshner, Sr. Mary Elizabeth Klier, Janice Kral, Marilyn Krause, Tina Lillig, Donna Macklin, Cathy Maresca, Joan Miller, Carol Nyberg, Marty and Bert O'Bryan, Rose Paul, Mary Nell Prichard, Rebekah Rojcewicz, Ruth Scheef, Judy Schmidt, Jane Scheuermann, Diane Schaffer, Kathleen Sweeney and Jo Ann Williams.

Drawn by Ana, age 6 years, in her second year at an Atrium in Mexico. The catechist writes: "When we see Ana's drawing we are surprised by an amazing similarity with a drawing done by a Roman girl, aged 5 (See figure 10 in *The Religious Potential of the Child*).

In both drawings, the flowers take the place of the Shepherd's hands. In the published image, the sheep are represented following the Shepherd; in the above image, they appear as flowers following the Shepherd.

Other similarities: in the published image, a semi-circle, sign of protection and security, embraces the sheep. Above, a yellow cross dominates the scene. The mountains embrace all and the blue of the sky comes from the sun and goes into the mountains.

What else are these two girls dwelling on? How do they help us to understand the essentiality and universality of the Kerygma and of the child in front of it? - Maria Christlieb.

# The Catechesis shared in Colombia

Nora Maria Bonilla got in touch with the Catechesis of the Good Shepherd in 1976, in Mexico City. She began this work in Santa Lucia. Then she proclaimed it in Argentina and now in Colombia, her country, where she lives.

*(From a letter from Nora Maria Bonilla to the Catechists of Santa Lucia, Mexico)*

I want to tell you a little about the Catechesis of the Good Shepherd in this country, Colombia, which has so much beauty, but also so many problems.

In January - February, 1987, I gave the first course.

In February, 1988, I began the first Atrium in a Girls' School. 125 girls, 4-6 years old, attended two hours a week. They were divided into six groups. It went very well, thanks be to God.

In June 1988 and in December 1988, we gave another first level course. These courses were supported by the Xavierian Pontifical University in Bogota.

Also I am giving a course to cloistered nuns, in the Monastery of the Visitation, two hours a week. They pray a great deal for the Catechists of the Good Shepherd everywhere.

A few days ago I received a letter from Sofia. She told me something that I want to share with you, so that it will be for all of us:

"To be each day more able to see the light of God in its smallest manifestations, I believe should be the characteristic of the Catechists of the Good Shepherd, or rather, I should say, the privilege of the Catechists of the Good Shepherd. Each time we see and glimpse the delighted response of a child in the presence of God, we are seeing the light of God in one of his smallest creatures. To see God manifesting himself in that which is small seems to me a marvelous thing."

(This completes the letter from Nora. We hope you will send us news from your Atriums for our next newsletter. Deadlines are listed on back cover of this issue. -Maria Christlieb

Becky is 5 years old and attends an Atrium in Minnesota.

She began by drawing "Jesus on the Cross." Then she drew her and her mom with sad faces. Next she drew "Mary" with a sad face. All these were in red. Then she switched colors to draw baby Jesus and then His mother smiling.

This image was made around Easter time.

# Help with research sought

We would like to extend in depth a study already begun. In order to carry it forward we need your cooperation. The main point of the study is: What is the response in the young child to the Parable of the Good Shepherd. It is not without some hesitation that we propose a method of research here, from which we have always refrained purposely (in the past). We did this for two reasons: to ask questions shows a lack of respect for what is fermenting (like leaven) interiorly; it is an undue intrusion into the inner life ( of the child).

The other reason is the relatively small value of the research, since quite often the question conditions the response, and so deprives it of all value.

Therefore, keeping these limitations in mind, should you be disposed to participate in the study we propose, we ask of you the following:

- to ask the question only to children who have known the Parable of the Good Shepherd for at least one or two years,

- to ask the question in the course of a conversation which you hold with one child at a time, not with the whole group, and only when the question arises spontaneously from what is being said.

It would be of particular interest if the response could be arrived at from what the child says spontaneously without being questioned directly.

**Ernesto, aged 5 1/2, attends an Atrium in Mexico. He explained his drawing to the catechist: "Beside the chalice it is written, 'The Light of God'." Also, pointing to the lines around the cross, he said again "The Light of God."**

Catechesis Center: _____

Catechist: _____

Boy _____ Girl _____ Age _____

Years of Attendance at Center _____

Question: "Of whom does the Good Shepherd make you think?"

Response: _____
_____
_____
_____
_____
_____
_____
_____

Date: _____

Notes:  1. You may duplicate this form.
2. Mail responses to: **Sofia Cavalletti,
Via degli Orsini, 34, Roma, Italy 00186**

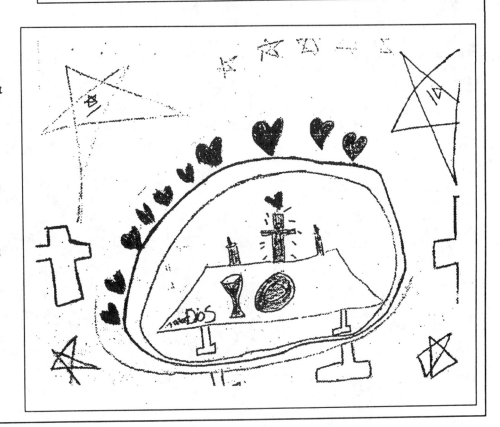

## Reprint
# Out of the Mouths of Babes

*[Ed. Note: The following article was published in* Catholic Evangelization *May/June 1988. It is reprinted here with permission.]*

**by Cathy Maresca**

Unfortunately the words "evangelization in the family," only bring to many minds the image of parents sharing faith with their children, initiating them into the traditions and mysteries of God and the Church. Some add to the picture: parents, sharing faith with one another, or aunts, uncles and grandparents passing their faith on to the youngest members of the family.

There is another part of the image: children sharing faith with each other, and with the adults in their families.

The newborn infant enters life unable to speak. Yet she clearly proclaims the wonder of God. Her home becomes for a while a holy place, where family and visitors speak softly, sit quietly, and with awe regard this new creation. She is the one who announces with Mary, "My being proclaims the greatness of the Lord." (Lk 1:46).

While adults are struck by the closeness of the newborn to God, they become skeptical about this closeness as the child grows. Soon the child is one who must be evangelized, as though she has never known God, nor enjoyed God's loving presence. And yet we read in Jeremiah 31, "No longer will they have need to teach their friends and kinsmen how to know Yahweh. All, from least to greatest, shall know me, says Yahweh."

John, even as an unborn child, recognized the presence of Jesus and leapt in his mother's womb. Jesus, while yet a young boy, began to recognize his mission in the temple and told his parents it must take precedence over family matters. Both these children witnessed to their parents with joy and with authority. Children today also recognize the presence of God in the world, and can witness to it with joy and authority. From them, adults can learn what is most essential about evangelization: a relationship with God.

Even before children use language, parents communicate with them. God is also capable of doing this. And children are capable of responding to the love of both their parents and God. It is from this love between God and children that their particular type of evangelization springs.

A group of parents met with me several times to talk about the spiritual potential of their very young children. While their children were barely walking, hardly talking, these parents were already eager to foster their toddlers' spiritual growth. I suggested that they go home and observe their children for signs of their relationships with God. All of these parents returned with anecdotes about their children's dancing responses to religious music, their repetition of prayer words like "Jesus," "Alleluia" and "Amen" and their recognition of Jesus in a great variety of art as infant, grown man and risen Lord.

Toddlers singing "Alleluia" spontaneously called their parents to prayer. One two-year-old boy was overheard calling his one-year-old sister. He then sang "Alleluia" to her five or six times very carefully. This was the only time he deliberately "taught" his sister a word. For these parents evangelization in the family had changed from an adult responsibility to a mutual proclamation — from child and adult — as well as to pure joy in witnessing God's presence in their families.

Parents who respect the relationship between God and their children are able to pray with their children instead of in front of them, and to listen together to the gospel instead of speaking without also listening. We may repeat to a seven-year-old child, "Love your enemies" (Lk 6:27). But then that child may show us how sinful our own exceptions and excuses are. We may say to the ten-year-old, "Do not live in fear, little flock. It has pleased your father to give you the kingdom" (Lk 12:32). But then she may show us what such trust is like, and lead us back to it. This is the kind of mutual evangelization possible in the family, and ultimately in the Church.

Children lack the education and sophistication to evangelize from anything but their own true relationship with God. Yet this lack is the strength of their witness to us. It is spontaneous, honest and without ulterior motives. The community of faith which is open to the evangelization of its children is greatly blessed. Its members may learn to evangelize from the wellspring of their own relationships with God and to truly share in the joy and authority of its youngest members.

*[Cathy Maresca is the mother of five and a founding member of Christian Family Montessori School in Mt. Rainier, Maryland. She works as a catechist of children ages three through nine. Her training with Sofia Cavalletti in the Catechesis of the Good Shepherd helped her to become attuned to the depth of children's relationships with God.]*

**Sofia Cavalletti, left, Monsignor Francisco Maria Aguilera from Mexico City and Silvana Montanaro visiting and helping the Catechists. 1982**

*from Sofia*

# We remember our friends . . .

## Sandi Yonikus

Now that the presence of Sandi has become invisible among us, we ask ourselves: Who was Sandi? That answer is not easy, first of all because of the richness of Sandi's personality, because the field of her work was very wide, and because she was very silent and discreet.

To try to answer this question I prefer to quote some passages from the last letters she wrote to me:

For us who had the privilege to have her as a companion, it is good to know how great a part the work of the catechesis had in her life. It was a new start in her life; about getting in touch with it she wrote: "I felt that my real life, my real work had just begun"; and she had been a catechist her whole life. In the same letter she said that the love of God for us "must be great, indeed, for Him to share such secrets with you." (Oct. 15, 1987)

She participated with all her being at the course in Phoenix in Summer 1987, and she thought it meaningful that it took place in the desert of Arizona: "I think the Lord has chosen a desert place again to speak to His people. The course has gone very smoothly and there is a real peace abiding in our midst. I feel a gentle, spiritual binding, has occurred which will strengthen each of us as we return to our work." (July 23, 1987)

At that moment her health was already extremely delicate, but the courage she faced with her sickness was astonishing: "I am able to walk now with a cane. I have learned so much through this experience with disease and pain. I hope I accomplish whatever the Lord had in this plan for me. I am eager to be well and working again. At the moment I am trying to practice patience while I wait on the Lord." (Dec. 30, 1985)

Her love for our work was such as to ask the Lord "for an extension of life... to continue in this work." The Lord had different plans, but Sandi keeps teaching us: Marty O'Bryan told me on the phone that Sandi passed away on the day of the celebration of Corpus Christi, according to the old calendar, and that she was buried on the day of Corpus Christi according to the new calendar. The feast of Corpus Christi is very important for us, the catechists of the Good Shepherd, if we accept the idea of the Newsletter 1986: the pivot of our spirituality is Eucharist. The feast of Corpus Christi is the celebration of the gift the Lord made of his whole self. The Last Supper is the way by which Jesus transformed his death into a gift acceptable to the Father and into an act of love for each of us.

Sandi's life has really been a gift for everyone who approached her, and we do not know how far the "waves" of her gift will reach.

Sharing with you all the sorrow for the distance death has created between Sandi and us, and deeply grateful for what Sandi has been and is for us and what she gave and gives to us, I would like to conclude with the words that Sandi prayed in one of her letters:

"I continue to pray that these of us who gather in Toronto and Phoenix are being gathered into a oneness with each other and the children we serve by our Shepherd and that that unity will spill over abundantly into the larger community of faith."

## Fr. Angelo De Angelis

A person we remember in our work with much gratitude is Father Angelo De Angelis.

We met him in 1966 when he was a parish priest in Colonna (Rome), a small farming community about 12 miles from Rome. One day, by chance, he saw one of our catechists in a store buying the small models of the articles of the Mass. He inquired into what this was all about and came immediately to observe a session with the little ones at Via degli Orsini, and to sit in on a lesson at the adult course (for catechists).

Catechesis was always at the center of his pastoral thought. The Catechesis of the Good Shepherd was organized at Colonna, first with a person sent from Rome and later with local catechists, who — not without some effort — came to Rome to take the course.

Father Angelo was a man of prayer and he particularly appreciated the atmosphere of prayer in our work, created during the meetings ( of the children). He found a similarity there to the Exercises of Saint Ignatius.

But Father Angelo also dreamt of being a missionary and decided to go to Brazil. We handed over to him the materials we had prepared. Our hands trembled with emotion as we said farewell.

From the time he arrived in Brazil in April 1973 we remained in touch by letter and so we were able to follow his untiring pastoral activities.

Overcoming health problems which caused him to lose about 20 kilos, Father Angelo had, by July, already organized a course for catechists. He supported the need for a remote preparation for Confirmation beginning in early childhood at the bishop's meeting for discussion of this sacrament.

He became a parish priest in the diocese of Candido Menides early in 1974 and began the catechesis work with children from the ages of 4 to 14 years old and a weekly course for catechists. He also initiated a translation of "I am the good shepherd," adapting it to the different rhythm of the school year in Brazil.

The catechists responded well and Father Angelo left for the interior (of the country) where no missionary had been for more than a year — "for the grafting (so to speak) of our kind of work."

Father Angelo was transferred to a parish in San Luis in January 1975 and he immediately devoted himself to the catechesis with children from the ages of 4 years on "with the goal of the integrated formation of the person" and also the preparation of catechists. At the Christmas Mass, celebrated with the children, the atmosphere was alive with a sense of simplicity and peace. He also worked with "exceptional children" (with learning disabilities and physical handicaps).

He also had an intense interest in and kept in touch with the Montessori World. In 1976, at the Montessori Congress at Rio, he proposed a course of religion for educators according to Montessori principles. In 1977, he participated in a Montessori training course himself, and in 1978, in the course held at San Luis, he was in charge of the religious education part of the course.

The end of 1978 found him at the San Jose Carmel of Rio de Janeiro, where he was being spoken of as person responsible for the catechesis of the diocese.

The Portuguese translation of *The Religious Potential of the Child,* published in 1985, was begun by Father Angelo in collaboration with a Carmelite sister.

**Continued on next page**

## Massimo Nobiloni

Massimo was a member of the very first group of four children with whom the Catechists of the Good Shepherd began in the spring of 1954. If our work did not end after a brief number of meetings, as we planned, we owe it to the response, full of enthusiasm, solemn joy, serenity and depth of these four children and in particular of Massimo (who was 6 at the time). It was he who, at the end of the first meeting, said he would like to come everyday. To his mother, who remarked that then he would have to abandon the music he loved so much, he replied, "But this is more important."

Again we recall Massimo as the one who organized a playlet of the Miracle of the Centurion's Son; he decided that he would play the part of the Centurion, reserving the part of Jesus for Francesco "because he is younger and has fewer sins." When he threw himself at the feet of "Jesus" asking for the miracle, he did it in an outburst of faith so real that we all found ourselves with tears in our eyes.

Massimo was lost at sea in a violent storm, on the 9th of December 1988. He will rest there forever.

I remember him here because we all, as catechists of the Good Shepherd, owe him so much.

## Our Newsletter and Our Association

Our newsletter was born to be a link of union and communication among the Catechists and friends of the Catechesis of the Good Shepherd in different parts of the world. It wants to be the place where we all meet in spite of distance and oceans.

The life of the Newsletter depends on our articles; it is nourished with the news of what each Atrium, each Center of Catechesis lives.

In 1989 we received almost no material, and partially for this reason this issue comes so late in the year. "Always waiting for more to come."

**Do not forget your newsletter.** Send your news, comments, experiences, reflections, dates of First Communions. All is important and interesting. All that you live and experience with the children and adults.

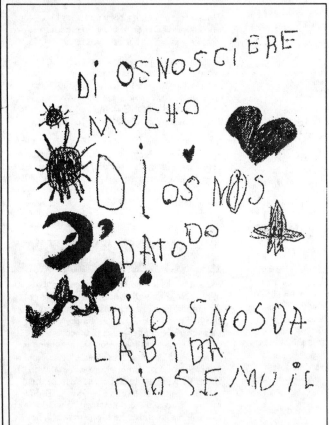

The above image was drawn by a child aged 6 1/2 years, who attends an Atrium in Mexico. It reads "God loves us very much, God gives us all, God gives us the life, God is very nice."

### Remembering Fr. De Angelis
*continued from page 15*

In March 1979, Father Angelo wrote to me from a hospital in Rio, mentioning "some health problems." Unfortunately, he was suffering from leukemia. He returned to Italy, where he died May 14 of that same year.

When I visited him for the last time at the hospital, Father Angelo, with a big smile, received the statue of the Good Shepherd which I brought him. Though dying, he continued to infuse the atmosphere around him with serenity and tranquility, which was always characteristic of him. He always seemed to live at a level higher than everyday events.

I know there is a lot to share; when we meet one another there is never enough time for telling each other "about our Atrium." Use the Newsletter and share with many, in different countries, the richness you find in your way with God and the child.

We are all busy -- but it is essential for the growth of our organization, for the support of those beginning the Catechesis with the children, and for those who haven't met others of us personally, to share your experiences in this newsletter. So, please take a moment to let us know about your experiences. Call, write, share with us!

Our next Newsletter will be published in Spring/Summer 1990. The deadline for submission of materials is **March 1, 1990**. Please direct all Newsletter materials to:

> **Maria Christlieb**
> **Hidalgo 21. Casa 1**
> **001060 Villa Obregon**
> **Mexico D.F.**
> **Mexico**

Staff in U.S.A.
  Carol Stenborg
  Carol Dittberner
  Italian Translators Joan Parasene and Nicolina Gleasure
  Spanish Translators Kathy Dahl-Bredine and
        Margarita Giner
  Proofreaders Kit and Jim Pfau

Staff in Chihuahua:
  Bertha Sofia Quiroz de Marquez
  Emilia G. de Sandoval
  Noemi F. de Lopez
  Maria de Los Angeles Christlieb

### Membership

The Catechesis of the Good Shepherd, An Association of Children and Adults, welcomes members throughout the year. Our membership fee is $30. The fees we collect go toward expenses of our four committees: Communications & Finance, Formation, Materials and Newsletter. Members receive the annual newsletter, all mailings and a directory of catechists and friends of the Association. A newsletter subscription only is $5.00 U.S. or $6.00 foreign.

No one should hesitate to join the Association because of the inability to pay the requested $30 fee. We appreciate any donation large or small.

Mail memberships and donations to:

> **The Catechesis of the Good Shepherd**
> **Box 218**
> **Mt. Rainier, MD 20712**
> **(301) 927-2015**

# The Catechesis of the Good Shepherd

Number 7, English     Winter 1990

*Therefore the Lord himself will give you a sign. Behold, a young woman shall conceive and bear a son, and shall call his name Emmanuel.*

*Isaiah 7:14*

## TABLE OF CONTENTS

| | |
|---|---|
| Let us Pray with the Children | 3 |
| "and a little child shall lead them. . ." by Sofia Cavalletti | 5 |
| The Development of the Catechist by Millicent Dosh | 9 |
| The Rainbow by Catherine Maresca | 11 |
| Letter from a Catechist, Houston by Anne Pechacek | 12 |
| Maria Montessori & the Religious Education of the Child by Dr. Silvana Montanaro | 15 |
| The History, continued | 17 |
| "The People Walked in Darkness" A song by Joel Rainville | 20 |
| History of the Research on the Mass by Sofia Cavalletti | 21 |
| Reflections on a Course, 1990 by Rose Paul | 24 |
| Announcements | 28 |

This quotation by Genelda Woggon, a church educator and member of the national Episcopal task force on Children's Ministries, appeared in "The Church News," published by the Episcopal Diocese of Mississippi, Jackson, July, 1990.

"The Catechesis of the Good Shepherd is not for the weak-hearted, yet the weak are actually strengthened through their commitment. It is not fun-filled and cute, but is filled with deep joy and great beauty. It doesn't offer simple answers; it creates wonder. Its teachers are not recruited, they are called. It's not something you learn "how-to-do," it is more of a process you enter into. It's not just another curriculum, it is a taste of the Kingdom itself."

Reprinted with permission.

"For to US a child is born to US a son is given and the government will be upon his shoulders. And his name will be called Wonderful Counselor, Mighty God, Everlasting Father, Prince of Peace."

A birthday cake for Jesus.
Red hearts, yellow stars,
yellow & blue candles.
The circles are brown.
Martina Mohn, 6-1/2,
St. Paul, USA.

# Let us Pray with the Children

Isint the world full of collers like god. Briana, 7 years old, USA.

God, on this day, when spring begins, I wish that the sun would bright as your love does. Georgina, 9 years old,
March, 1990, Mexico.

"God." The outline of garment & rays are red. Cross is outlined in brown, yellow inside. Juliana Fruzzetti, 6-1/2, USA.

Translated from the Spanish by Kathy Dahl-Bredine.

FOR GOD ULYSSES I love you
Jacobo Meyer, nine years old, Torreon, Mexico

god I love you I adore you you are my salvation without your light and you I cannot live you are my heart my love and you cause me to love my neighbor you are my love you are the one and only in the world and the best without you the world would not exist for you I live you love me and want me to be your child I declare before you that I am your child and I swear it by you yourself I will love you forever you are my father and I am your child you love me I love you I will be your child forever you my life my love my heart let me help my neighbor God I love you with all my soul and all my heart you gave me everything my mother my father my heart my life from god from my lord and my love you are my salvation my mother loves me and adores me she gives me everything I ask her she is a good mother and my father gives me everything he adores me and loves me papa gives me whatever I ask him for god without you I don't know what I would have done you are my soul my heart my life my will you my father you adore me my soul you are better than we are my past [words not recognizable] my father loves me and my mother too you are my king my sun my moon my water my earth my bread of the gift you are my love my fruitfulness my world you are Mexico yes the most beautiful land your mother is queen of Mexico and empress of America thank you for listening.

**Ed. Note:** *This was written by a child living in an environment so poor and underdeveloped that the catechists were discouraged and thought they (the children) did not "understand anything."*

Some prayers from the children at the Good Shepherd Center, St. Paul:

After Altar II (The Tabernacle) a four-year-old boy said, "Thank you for the altar and the food we eat." (His father is a Romanian Orthodox priest.) A three-and-a-half year old girl said, "Love, love, love."

Something that has struck me this year (1989-90) is that the prayers of the children are more global. I expect the five-and-a-half year old to share such prayers as, "Thank you for the whole world," which she frequently shares, but I am surprised that the young four-year-olds and the four-and-a-half year olds pray with more global interests. There was a boy named Jacob who was kidnapped in St. Joseph, Minnesota, who was in the news a lot in St. Paul. A four-and-a-half year old girl prayed, "Please give me Jacob home for Christmas." She said this a few weeks before the feast and there was no familial relation. Two other four-year-old boys have shared, "Thank you for the whole world," each without ever hearing an older child or each other say it in the atrium. Also, with all the problems in Romania around Christmas 1989, the little four-and-a-half year old boy shared prayers for his relatives there, but the surprising thing was his little friend, who is a four-year-old girl, also prayed for "the people over the sea who had war." This same little girl had also prayed after the San Francisco earthquake: "Thank you for the people and the buildings that aren't broken in the earthquake." All of these events were not once brought up by the adults in the atrium. I've found it amazing.

Also, a four-and-a-half year old boy shared during Advent: "Thank you for the light Jesus made. Thank you for the atrium."

A three-and-a-half year old girl's repeated prayer is "Thank you, God." It is her second year in the atrium and she is known to regularly set the altar, gather some others, get the Bible from the baptism corner, and "read": "Jesus is risen from the dead." As you can see, it's been a very fruitful year.

-Mary Lou Mohn

Additional prayers of the children:
Joseph and Mary had a son and his name Jesus. Jesus was a king. It was wonderful having him around. -Joseph, age 6-1/2, Fall, 1989, USA.

The Annunciation.
Briana O'Brien, 7,
USA.

# "and a little child shall lead them ...."

Dear Catechists and friends,

Patricia asked Gianna and me: "What are the essential guidelines which could assist us as catechits in helping children in their relationship with God?" In trying to respond to this request, I realize that it is anything but easy to highlight the principle points. Nonetheless I will try, and invite you to clarify and integrate these.

The first point I would focus on is the inner disposition to change what is our common attitude, as adults, towards children. This attitude generally takes two persons into consideration: the adult and the child. attributing the active role to the adult as the one who gives, and the passive position to the child as the one who receives. Yet in doing so we forget that, in the formation of the human person, there is a third person involved, the one who holds the absolutely primary position: the Inner Master. And it is He alone who teaches, both the adults and the children. The Christian message will be received in our listening together - adults and children - to the Master, and in a constant interchange among the hearers, big and small.

We also need to deschool catechesis, as we have mentioned so many times.

I think two texts from the Gospel will be able to help us in our search together.
"We are unprofitable servants." (Luke 17:10)
To be a "servant" means to be ready and willing to work in different ways. The catechesis of the Good Shepherd demands considerable effort in many areas. It calls for a personal commitment to learning, and a continual broadening of our own understanding in the fields of doctrine (bible and liturgy), psychology and pedagogy. A catechist may never consider that one's preparation in any of these fields is complete. We are called forward on a journey which leads us to go deeper and deeper in the heart of knowledge. In this way we become ever more capable of transmitting the Christian message, with fidelity to its sources and in its most essential form. so as to respond to the child's needs and touch the child's level of profundity.

As well as this, the catechesis of the Good Shepherd asks us to make a commitment to manual work. Making the materials and preparing the environment can not and must not be viewed as a secondary activity, one that we casually delegate to others, while keeping for ourselves solely the direct contact with children. The preparation of the material and environment is an integral and vital part of the catechist's task; in manual activity the catechist finds an instrument for indirect service to children in their relationship with God.

The environment and materials are truly a means of helping the child's meditation and prayer. They are a help that allows the adult to really be "servant," that is, one who is predisposed to do what is necessary and assists the child's encounter with God, and then steps aside once it has begun. "Help me to come close to God by myself."

Working with our hands is a help for us as catechists as well. We will discover that manual activity is a way for the message to enter more deeply into us by absorbing it within ourselves, and on more levels than the intellectual plane alone.

"Unprofitable." When sharing religious experience with the child, we will continually see that whatever contribution we have made as catechists is exceeded by the child's response. We will come to the awareness that children, in their relationship with God, reach a depth of knowing and an intensity of feeling that surpasses by far anything we have been able to offer. So it happens, that in being with children we will sense the presence of a force, mysterious and silent, which does not belong to us, and we will treasure it as an inestimable privilege to be granted at times to "see it" working within the child. As Elijah did, on Mount Horeb, when he heard the "tiny, whispering sound," at moments like this we too will want to "cover our face" in beholding the presence of God (1 Kings 19:13).

In this way we, as catechists, learn an enriching poverty: what comes from our hands and mouth is so poor in the face of what God works in his creatures, and in his littlest creatures, young children.

The other Gospel passage I would suggest for reflection is: "Unless you change and become like little children, you will not enter the Kingdom of Heaven." (Matthew 18:3).

Much superficial writing has been done on this text. But let us try to read it in the light of our experience with little children. How do children appear to us in their relationship with God? The most striking qualities that emerge are essentiality and enjoyment.

Essentiality. We have spoken together often about these two elements in the religious life of the young child. In seeking to understand more about what is meant in speaking of essentiality, and where adult and child differ in relation to this, I asked myself: Is there a connection between being essential and being simple? If so, what is it? And, how do the qualities of simplicity and essentiality mutually clarify each other?

Simplicity. Something that is simple is something I can contemplate, as concentrated in the space of a single point. This focal point, however, is endowed with such essentiality that the greatest realities can be discerned in it, and from this single point I can advance towards ever expanding horizons. Would you like an example? The mustard seed. And an even more overwhelming example? The Eucharistic Bread.

Is there anything simpler than a seed - which is the "smallest of all the seeds" - or a piece of bread? And yet within these is encased the most essential secret of Life. Can we say that the content is essential and the container is simple? I do not think it is possible to so divide the seed and the bread from the Reality they represent. Perhaps it is more precise to say that the container is simple because it is adequately suited to the essentiality of the content.

Simplicity and essentiality are, in my view, two aspects that merge in the greatest Reality.

And now let's turn to little children and the need for us to become like them. Children accept things that are simple and essential without any difficulty: in fact, as we have so often said, it is only in these that children find true satisfaction. When we adults are faced with such radical simplicty, we get lost, and we go astray in trying to complicate and multiply things. In our meeting with what is "simple" we seem to find a denial of our own importance as adults. In complicating things, we create a sort of smokescreen which covers our own inability or our own difficulty in being present, naked and poor, to Reality.

Let us seek to simplify ourselves, even though it is not easy, because in order to accept the essential in its simplicity, we need to be really poor inside ourselves. We need to let go of our own trappings, such as, for example, our erudition or experience as adults can become for us. In saying to "let go," I mean to say that we should give to trappings like these the weight -- so very light -- they actually have when measured in terms of the grandeur of Reality.

Twice we have centered upon, from different points of view, the theme of interior poverty. Could this be the most profound lesson the child is giving us? Could this be the meaning of "becoming like little children?"

Enjoyment. I will not stop to dwell on the capacity of the young child for enjoying the presence of God because we have done this many times together. However, I have been reflecting on the interconnection that likely exists between the child's capacity for enjoyment and the qualities of essentiality and simplicity. Perhaps it is only when we place ourselves in the presence of essential realities with a spirit of simplicity that we will find that type of enjoyment we have seen so often in the young child. And I have been reflecting on the privilege that is given to us sometimes to be able to be witnesses of such enjoyment as this.

I have also been thinking about the "training school," challenging and at times very demanding, that catechesis with young children provides for us. If this is true, then our direct contact with children can never be abandoned. There is not a time when, having "gone beyond" the point of working with children, we apply ourselves exclusively to the formation of adults. The moment for solely "teaching teachers to teach" will never come, because if we lose our contact with children we will distance ourselves from the most significant source of our own personal formation.

There is one final reflection, which is related to the preceeding one. If we are aware of how important a "school" the catechesis with children can be for us, then we will even be willing to share with them the low estimation that young children basically receive, in spite of all the discourses on the wealth of early childhood. There is no doubt that if we were occupied in catechesis with adolescents we would generate much more interest, and that many draw away in disappointment when we speak about catechesis of children two and three years of age. But it is precisely in the littlest children that there is not only the greatest religious richness, which we must serve, but also the best possible "school" for us.

The little child is truly "one of the least" in the kingdom (Matthew 25:40). Let us remain close to the child in enjoying the presence of God, and also in accepting that "being one of the least" is not always valued.

For the moment, here are the reflections I am able to offer. I will leave it to you to continue the dialogue.

Enjoy your work.

With much affection,

Sofia

P.S. Sofia has already communicated my reflections on the "guidelines."

I would also like to add the words Maria Montessori wrote in her book, <u>The Absorbent Mind</u>, in the chapter entitled "The Teacher's Preparation."

> The children take us to a higher plane of the spirit and material problems are thereby solved. Permit me to repeat, as a form of farewell, some words which have helped us to keep in mind all the things of which I have been speaking. It is not a prayer, but rather a reminder, and for our teachers, an invocation, a kind of syllabus, our only syllabus:
>
> "Help us, O God; to enter into the secret of childhood, so that we may know, love and serve the child in accordance with the laws of thy justice and following thy holy will."

An affectionate embrace,

Gianna

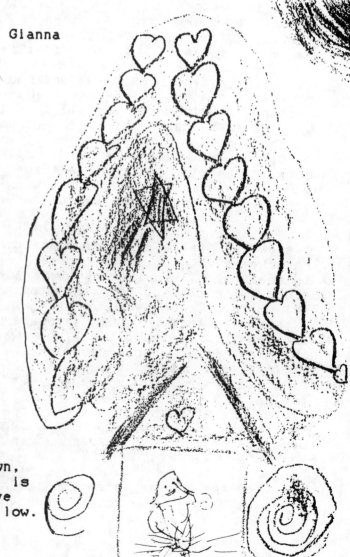

The Nativity. The stable is brown, Mary is wearing purple, the straw is yellow. The hearts and area above stable are red. The star is yellow. Rainbow in upper right corner.
Nicole Paul, 7-1/2, USA.

# The Development of the Catechist

This past summer, Millie Dosh attended the AMI/USA Summer Institute at Vail, Colorado. The theme of the conference was "The Inner Development of the Montessori Adult." She attended the workshop presented by Dr. Silvana Montanaro and Maria Christlieb. Following are her notes from the workshop.

> There exists a period specially sensitive to religion. The age of childhood seems to be bound closely to God.
> Maria Montessori

For the last three days we have been looking at ourselves as a very important part of the earth in which we live. We have been trying to be conscious of our inner selves in order to experience communion with ourselves, with others, with our planet and with the universe.

In our discussions, listenings, walks of these days we have focused on the adult. We have pondered over different aspects of our being and of our lives, the human being who creates with his/her hands, who thinks, who is religious and capable of playing and enjoying life. We have seen ourselves as political beings and beings capable of love, of a universal love.

This morning we are going to explore the religious person in our inner self. But no, I shouldn't say the religious person, which might be totally or partially deviated for different reasons. What we want to do this morning is to see the religious nature of the child within us. The religious nature of the original child, of that creative human being capable of developing physically and spiritually.

Let us look at the religious potential of the child who has the <u>power of life</u> at the service of the <u>project of life.</u>

But how? How can we do that?

It is difficult to arrive at the child within us, the original child full of religious potential. One way to gain access is to ask help of other children: what have children shown me? I would like to share with you what the children have shown us about their religious potential. (This is the original child who has not been deviated.) The silent plea of the child is, "Help me to do things by myself." He can and wants to act from the power and creativity within himself. We are only helpers.

We have observed several important things in children:

<u>Joy in their relationship with God.</u>
Children experience with God a profound, deep joy. It is peaceful, secure joy, inner joy which goes out to reach others. An eight year old child said, "I feel a joy inside of me." This joy involves their whole being. "My body is happy," said another child. This joy does not tire the child. He enjoys remaining with Someone he has met who fulfills his whole being. This sense of fulfillment comes not by the creation of many ideas, but is a global involvement.

### The child knows God by himself.

Children have this experience of God without anyone telling them about it. It is the work of the Holy Spirit. The child has intuitive, unconscious knowledge long before a conscious knowledge of God. A child once said, while moving her hands over her whole body, "I want to be full of God."

### A child is capable of seeing the invisible.

Through the help of signs, the child is aided in seeing the invisible. A child prepares an exercise with yeast and says, "I am seeing how the kingdom of heaven grows." A seven year old said, "The Kingdom of God is the food and the water and mom and dad and John and Sopana and home and Bear (the dog)."

Children penetrate the veil of signs without effort. They easily see the transcendent as though there were no barriers between the visible and invisible. A child once said, "I wish I could see the LIGHT like the blind children."

### Children pray.

It is alright to teach "prayers," but they are the words of someone else that a child learns to repeat. Children pray spontaneously. They are also silent. They show a radiant face; they are in wonder. They abide, remain in God. They say, "I love you." These are all prayer. Children pray with praise, with thanksgiving. Their prayers reveal their closeness to God and yet a God who transcends them.

A six-year-old prayed, "Jesus, you put in our hearts a light more beautiful and bigger than the light of the sun. I like the sun. I love you because you are good and you are more beautiful than the sun."

Another prayer: "Let me do, Lord, something like a bath in your light."

An eight-year-old girl prayed, "He is our place of rest. His power is in us. He is our shield. He helps us in making peace. The Kingdom of God is all around. Do not be afraid for He is near."

"I pray alone and in silence," by a three-year-old child.

A child is not satisfied with little stories. The child wants the _nucleus_ of revelation. If you move to non-essentials, you lose the child. We as adults can make a jungle for the child. We must show the child what is essential, and yet sometimes the child is clever in already knowing the essential. The younger the child, the deeper and more essential must be the message.

Who is the child? The child is the POWER OF LIFE, THE POWER OF LOVE at the service of THE PROJECT OF LIFE. God is the same. God is LIFE, and LOVE. Real love is creative energy, creative power. Religious experience has to be the experience of life, love, and creative energy.

True religious experience is the encounter between life, love and the creative power of the child and that life, love and creative power of God. Two plenitudes, two fulnesses, of God and child meet.

A brain paralyzed child prayed one day:

"God sings, 'I have a friend who loves me. Her name is Ana. I have a friend who loves me. His name is Jesus.'" This child does not need to know anything else.

# The Rainbow

by Catherine Maresca

Holly Tosco, who works in an atrium in North Carolina, described to me a remarkable insight of a six year old girl. She had drawn a rainbow and entitled it "God's World." On the back she wrote, "God's world is 5,000 religions." I have learned much from this child.

Sunlight. A light so bright our eyes are not capable of looking at it. But water refracts that light and makes it not only visible but beautiful in the array of colors we call the rainbow.

God. A light so bright our eyes are not capable of looking at it. But people refract that light and make it visible and beautiful in an array of religions like a rainbow.

Each people of the world, due to the particularity of their time and place in history, are able to offer to every other people a hue of the mystery we call God. It is all light, but what a variety, what wealth, what beauty.

We see most clearly at first the hue of our own religion. And in our faithfulness to that religion we refract for every other people its greatest gifts.

But we also live in a time in which we can know and appreciate the refraction of God which other religions make evident for us. A time in which we can know the limitations of our own band of religion and find it complemented as part of a greater whole.

The rainbow in Genesis is a sign of the covenant between God and all the people of the earth. Let us be faithful to our part of the whole, and grateful for every other band.

---

The circular figure inside was drawn with many colors; yellow rays surround it.
7 years, Nostra Signora d. Lourdes, Rome, Italy.

Text: "The shepherds saw a great light; it was God become man. The magi also saw a great light. The people of the time of Jesus saw a greater light, because he was risen. I too saw this great light at baptism; someday a light will come in the whole world."

# Letter from a Catechist, Houston, Texas

Dear Child of God, Companion Sheep of the Good Shepherd!

In the summer of 1983, from what seemed to me to be a miraculous decision, I was sent to Washington, D. C. for three weeks to experience the Catechesis of the Good Shepherd. More than seven years before, I had dedicated myself to the work and spirit of Maria Montessori and I had been sure I would find a lifetime of work in Montessori schools. But in working as an assistant in a Montessori environment, I remember being overwhelmed by the experience of serving children; in this work I felt I knew for the first time what Jesus meant by *service*.

An act of true service begins with a profound experience of the most fundamental needs of the other person. Out of this compassionate communion comes the ability to offer only that assistance which frees the other person in his or her journey to perfection in God. In this environment, I also noticed how meditative the children's concentration was; how together they lived the life of a real community; and how through conscious choice of work, they laid the foundation for a great adult contribution to building a more beautiful world. How could these foundations for adult Christianity in a "secular" Montessori environment be affirmed and nurtured more consciously by a believing Montessorian? In the summer of 1983, God led me to the answer.

As with all "answers" God offers, the Catechesis of the Good Shepherd has provided me with more questions than I can even express (much less attempt to understand). However, during my first four-and-a-half years, the greatest question has been: How do I recover the childlike humility which I, of necessity, buried under an ever-increasing mound of rationality when I was a growing girl of six or seven? Where is that path by which I can return to that garden of simplicity and let Jesus hold me in His arms and **love** me all the day? To reach this place the ultimate is required of me.... I must trust Jesus with EVERYTHING I thought was mine.

"The Good Shepherd calls His own by name and leads them out." Over and over I have read the words: over and over I have helped to move a sheep, struggling within and without to become, in fact, a sheep who listens to His voice and thus comes to know Him as intimately as the Father.

To be loved so well by Jesus is not an easy thing to experience. The moments when I humble myself enough to accept this ever-present love are not only painful, they are also the most healing, peaceful, and joy-filled moments. They are beyond imagination or compare.

During our third week in the summer of 1983, I remember how Sofia fed us with scripture each morning, scripture that was filled with love letters from God. And each morning, for five consecutive days. we failed to recognize (let alone begin to comprehend) this love. You would think after a day or two we would have at least "caught on," but we were so far from the child's experience of God, that even on the fifth day we still heard all kinds of other (more superficial) things when His love was so clearly proclaimed through the Word.

After I left Washington, I worked with a group of twenty children for a year. Then I was given the materials that had been made, and I worked with a new group of children in a different parish for three more years. Two children (both in the atrium two years or more) had profound personal experiences of recognizing the sheep. Many other children were visibly touched in some other way. I, a very poor and struggling catechist, remain wonder-filled for what I have seen and heard.

Sean, who was presented the first presentation of the Eucharistic Presence at age five, turned to me with a voice full of reverence, slowly making the profession: "We ... are ... the ... sheep." The sound came from his living, love-touched spirit.

Bonnie, who was four, was part of the group when Sean made this statement, but did not feel it too. Twice more in that one-hour session, she got the work out and asked for a personal re-presentation. At the end of the third presentation (in a single hour), she turned to me with earnest, round blue eyes and said, "These are **holy** sheep." It was a statement I knew would re-echo in her spirit whenever the day came that she discovered just who these "**holy**" sheep were.

The day came over six months later when, after a long time away from the lesson, she set out the altar, candles, small Good Shepherd statue, paten and chalice and asked me to come and talk to her about it. I sat down beside her and asked her where the sheep were. She chuckled at herself, but before she began to reach for the basket she said, under her breath, "Two are already here." I didn't believe my ears, so I asked her to tell me again what she had said. Clearly, she repeated the statement. Still not wanting to jump to conclusions (especially with a child at such a critical moment), I asked her what she meant. Happily she told me that the two sheep were "Ann and Bonnie."

I asked her how she knew and she said that I had told her. "No," I insisted, I had never told her that. She reflected carefully, then said she guessed she had just "grown up."

Other moments are poignant in my memory:
John and Stephen were brothers who came to the atrium for two years. I first knew them only in the atrium, but I discovered later that they were so undisciplined everywhere **outside** of the atrium that I could not even have a conversation with them!

One day, as the children were quietly arriving and waiting to begin work, John said to his brother (deep appreciation in his voice), "This is the place where things are always so silent."

Then there was Dennis who, at the tender age of five, was always in trouble at kindergarten and nursery school. His grandparents were obviously struggling to raise him. He came to the atrium for one year and he is the only child I ever moved to an isolated table because of the way he disturbed the other children. But Dennis had hopeful moments as well as difficult ones in our atrium. That year I had to cancel the last scheduled class because of illness. When I called his grandmother to tell her, she took the opportunity to tell me they thought I was "an angel," and they had never seen their grandson so peaceful as he was in the atrium and he had looked forward to it every week!

My first four years in the Catechesis were spent in once-a-week, hour-long sessions in a Catholic Church. In April of 1987, I became director of a private Montessori school.

Then I again went to Washington, D.C., this time to take the AMI Primary Training. I began once again enjoying the blessings of the daily Montessori classroom community, with the added dimension of encouraging the meditation implicit with the "Walking on the Line" exercise. (This central exercise was not part of the environment I first worked in, but it is beautifully emphasized by the Washington Montessori Institute.)

The owner of the school is a deeply committed, Christ-centered woman who asked me to begin the Catechesis of the Good Shepherd in her school. We began by introducing the parents to the materials.

After leaving the church for the school position, I had the Good Shepherd materials in my home. My third youngest daughter, Rebekah, then three- and-a-half, engaged in a relaxed, informal exploration of the materials. On Saturday and/or Sunday mornings, she chose a material (before breakfast or anything else) and we worked with it for as long as she wished. Rebekah has lead me to understand the child's life of praise better, and I have also learned much about just relaxing, listening, and enjoying from her.

One final story. I received a card from a fellow catechist (Sean's mother) who worked in the atrium with me at the church. In part, she said, "Thank you for introducing me to the powerful and prayerful lesson of the Good Shepherd...Your work and the time I spent learning from you will always be a special part of me." Praise the Lord for making His ways known to all of us! Let us make this work a of prayer of praise that calls **ALL THE WORLD** to His incredible sheepfold.

I love You,
Anne Pechacek

The Nativity, the risen Christ, the road with the shepherd and sheep. Perhaps another risen Christ, with hearts. Upper right says, "Jacquelen loves God."    4-5 years, Rochester, NY, USA.

# Maria Montessori and the Religious Education of the Child

contributed by Dr. Silvana Montanaro

<u>1907</u> - The new "scientific pedagogy" comes from the "discovery of the child" through observation in a prepared environment. Dr. Maria Montessori discovers a new child, not an empty container, but a very rich human being with the enormous capacities of the **absorbent mind** and **sensitive periods**. The prepared, suitable envirnoment reveals the child.

Maria Montessori said of her method: [It is] "a help to the independence of human personality, a way to free the human being from the old prejudices on which is based education (sic)."

The method is "the defense of the child," and this starts with the scientific knowledge about his/her development. "The human development is not only a social and world-wide matter but a cosmic one." Dr. Montessori talks of "the internal teacher" who pushes the child to self realization, and also: interest - work with materials - concentration - knowledge - love - service.

The first material is the external teacher because it is his/her love and respect for the child that will awaken the child's mind: there is a voice to call him/her to work.

In the prepared environment there are special fruits that come from inside the child: silence, discipline, and obedience. The children in the Montessori schools **"love what they do"**, (not "do what they love").

<u>1909</u> - Father Casulleras, a Spanish priest, thought that the Children's House should be attached to the Church.

<u>1910</u> - Pope S. Pius X made a decree about giving communion to young children, seven years old, and educating people actively through the liturgical celebration: to know through living.

<u>1915</u> - Liturgical Congress in Montserrat, Spain: Anna Maccheroni presented a paper on "Liturgy and its Pedagogical Teaching," in which she suggested to try to explain to children the Christian doctrine. Refer to <u>The Discovery of the Child.</u> chapter XXIII.

<u>1916</u> - In Barcelona, Spain, Dr. Montessori starts the "**Iglesia de los Ninos**" (Church of the Children) with the appropriate furniture in scale, and the children repsonsible for the environment: to clean, to arrange flowers, etc. Talking about this experiment she said: "It was that the church is almost the end, up to which leads a great part of the education which the method sets out to give. . . . there exists a period specially sensitive to religion. The age of childhood seems to be bound closely to God . . . ."[1]

Adele Costa Gnocchi was saying: "God and the child understand each other."

In Barcelona, the children cultivate the wheat (putting seeds into the ground) and the grapes for the mass celebration. They had two great festivities: one at the end of the school year for the harvest, and another at the begining for the vintage.

---

[1] Maria Montessori, <u>The Discovery of the Child</u>, (Madras: Kalakshetra Press, 1966), pgs. 343 and 345.

**1922** – First edition of the book, *I Bambini Viventi nella Chiesa*, (*The Children Living in the Church*).

**1929** – Second edition of the same book with results and observations.

**1931** – The book, *The Life in Christ*, is published, in which Maria Montessori explains the meaning of time in our life. Before Christ, the time was marked by the sun; now it is marked by the presence of the Person who created the sun. The years are counted starting from the presence of Christ in this world, and every year we go through a spiritual itinerary. The Liturgical Calendar material.

**1939 to 1946** – Dr. Montessori lives in India.

**1946** – In France, Dr. Montessori writes, "*Education Religieuse*" with a Missal which has not been published.

**1949** – *La S. Messa Spiegata ai Bambini*, (*The Holy Mass Explained to the Children*).
We know there are sacred plays on the seven words of Jesus, said while on the cross, and a drama of the Missa which can be presented by the children. They have been in the property of Miss Sorge, who died recently and, hopefully, these plays will be published in the near future.

**1951** – May 18th, IXth Montessori International Congress in London. Maria Montessori talks on the religious education of young children.

**1952** – Dr. Montessori dies on May 12th, at the age of 82.

**1954** – In Rome, Sofia Cavalletti and Gianna Gobbi are put together by Adele Costa Gnocchi in order to combine the Bible's knowledge with the child's knowledge, and the catechesis of young children with the Montessori method begins.*

**1957** – In Rome, at the Montessori International Congress, Dr. Cavalletti presents a lecture on "Catechesis and the Montessori Method."

**1961** – Sofia and Gianna publish *Educazione Religiosa Liturgica e Metodo Montessori*, (*Teaching Doctrine and Liturgy*).

**1965 to 1967** – Sofia and Gianna publish *Io Sono Il Buon Pastore*, (*I am the Good Shepherd*), 5 volumes with a guide for the catechist. They are translated into Spanish in 1981.

**1979** – Sofia publishes *Il Potenziale Religioso del Bambino*, (*The Religious Potential of the Child*). Published in English in 1983; in Spanish in 1987.

*Editor's note: It is a real point of interest to know that Dr. Cavalletti never met Dr. Montessori. She attended a lecture of Montessori's just before Montessori's death.
Dr. Cavalletti has an extensive background in biblical studies; Gianna Gobbi is a trained Montessori directress. Together, they have developed the catechesis from Montessori's corpus. At the Centro di Catechesi, in Rome, Sofia and Gianna meet with children, ages 3 - 12, each week. There is also adult catechist formation. At the present time, one year is devoted to the study of each level, 3-6, 6-8 and 9-12.

# The History, continued

As Dr. Montanaro began this historical review for us, it seemed fitting to continue the documentation of the growth of the Catechesis of the Good Shepherd. Following are a list of lectures and seminars given by Dr. Cavalletti about the spiritual life of the child. Afterward, there is a list of the intense, short courses presented since 1975, when they began in the United States. This material was compiled by Sofia Cavalletti, Maria Christlieb, Betty Hissong, and Carol Dittberner.

SEMINARS AND LECTURES

Dublin, Ireland- 1958

Dusseldorf, Germany- 1961

Como, Italy- 1962

Brescia, Italy- 1964

Nazareth, Israel- 1965

Domodossola, Italy- 1973

Paris, France- 1973

Foggia, Italy- 1974

Geneva, Switzerland- 1984

London, England- 1984

Amsterdam, Holland- 1984

Bendorf Koblenz, Germany- 1986

Munchen, Germany- 1990

Lectures presented at the Fondazione Centro Internationale Studi Montessori in Bergamo, Italy - nearly 15 seminars since 1962, and
The Centro Internationale Maria Montessori of Perugia, Italy

<u>In Rome, Italy:</u>

Regina Mundi

Angelicum

Ateneo Salesiano

Fondazione Besso

Universita Pontifica Lateranense


In 1975, Mr. A. M. Joosten, a Montessori trainer in India and the United States, was instrumental in arranging Dr. Cavalletti's first course in America. Dr. Cavalletti gave a lecture at the International Montessori Congress, held in Minneapolis that year. Then a five week course was sponsored by the Montessori Foundation of Minnesota. It covered children, ages 3-12 years. Participants came from Mexico, Canada, and the U.S.

**1976**
Mexico, City Mexico
   3-12 years, 4 weeks: Sofia Cavalletti and Lillian Lewis

**1977**
Chicago, Illinois
   3-12 years: Lillian Lewis

**1978**
Toronto, Ontario
   Toronto Faculty of Theology, 3-12 years, 3 weeks: Sofia Cavalletti and Patricia Coulter

**1979**
Mexico, City Mexico
   3-12 years, 4 weeks: Silvana Montanaro

**1980**
Mexico, City Mexico
   3-12 years, 4 weeks: Sofia Cavalletti and Silvana Montanaro

**1981**
Mexico, City Mexico
   First level, 3-6 years: Silvana Montanaro, Gianna Gobbi, Lupita Palafox
   Second level, 6-8 years: Sofia Cavalletti and Nora Bonilla

Chihuahua, Chihuahua
   First level, 3-6 years: Francesca Cocchini and Maria Christlieb

**1981**
Cleveland Ohio
   One week overview: Patricia Coulter

**1982**
Mexico City, Mexico; 4 weeks
   Third level, 9-12 years: Sofia Cavalletti and Nora Bonilla

   Seminar for parents - one week

Washington, D.C.; 3 weeks
   First level, 3-6 years, Part I: Rebekah Rojcewicz, joined by Sofia for the third week

**1983**
Chihuahua
   Seminar for priests: Sofia and Maria
   Second level, 6-8 years, 2 weeks: Sofia and Maria

Washington, D.C.
   First level, 3-6 years Part II, 3 weeks: Rebekah Rojcewicz, joined by Sofia for the third week

   Retreat/Meditation on the Mass: 2 weeks Sofia and Rebekah

   First formal meetings to begin Association

**1984**
St. Paul, Minnesota
   First level, 3-6 years, 3 weeks: Maria Christlieb and Nohemi Palafox
   Second level, 6-8 years: Sofia Cavalletti and Rebekah Rojcewicz
   Association meetings - election of first Board for a two year term.
   Publication of first newsletter

**1985**
St. Paul, Minnesota
   Retreat and Association meetings, 1 week
   First level, 3-6 years, 3 weeks: Maria Christlieb, Sr. Sheila Sentiff and Betty Hissong
   Second level, 6-8 years, 3 weeks: Sofia Cavalletti, Cathy Maresca and Carol Dittberner

Buenos Aires, Argentina
   First level, 3-6 years, 8 weeks: Nora Bonilla

**1986**
Sante Fe, Argentina
   First level, 3-6 years, 5 weeks: Nora Bonilla

   Courses continued by: Herminia Wasserzug, Padre Hector Francesconi and Amalia Gioino

Bogota, Columbia
   First level, 3-6 years, 6 weeks: Nora Bonilla

Toronto, Ontario
   First level, 3-6 years, Part I, 3 weeks: Sofia Cavalletti, Gianna Gobbi and Patricia Coulter

   Publication of the newsletter Spanish Edition begins

Catechesis of the Good Shepherd, 1990 December

**1987**

Merida, Yucatan, Mexico
   Third level, 9-12, Part I, Maria Christlieb and Francesca Cocchini

Bogota, Columbia at Pontificia Universidad Xaverniana
   4 weeks - Nora Bonilla

Toronto, Ontario
   First level, 3-6 years, Part II, 3 weeks: Sofia, Gianna, Patricia, Betty Hissong, Sr. Sheila Sentiff, Anna Mae Guida and Tina Lillig

Phoenix Arizona
   First Level 3-6 years, Rebekah
   Second Level 6-8 years, Cathy Maresca and Sandi Yonikus

**1988**

St. Paul, Minnesota
   "A Time Apart," 4 days of retreat and meetings

**1989**

Washington, D.C.
   Third Level, 9-12, part I, 2 weeks: Rebekah Rojcewicz

**1990**

Washington, D.C.
   Third Level, 9-12, part II, 2 1/2 weeks: Rebekah Rojcewicz

Jackson, Mississippi
   First Level, 3-6, Part I, 2 weeks
   Regional course sponsored by the Episcopal Diocese of Jackson. Carol Dittberner and Cathy Maresca

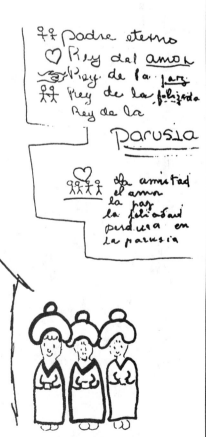

Joseph Kosowski, 6-1/2, Minneapolis, USA.

Text:
"Eternal Father
   King of love
   King of the peace
   King of happiness
   King of the Parousia

   the friendship
   the love
   the peace
   the happiness
   last at parousia."
9 years old,
Chihuahua, Mexico.

# The People Walked in Darkness

The people walked in darkness They've seen a great light.
Walked in darkness all of their lives.
People walked in darkness They've seen a great light.
The light shining brightly is Jesus.

Joel Rainville, written on October 5th, 1986
when he was 8 years old.
Newman Center Atrium,
Minneapolis, USA.
Printed with permission.

The Nativity and the Eucharist. On the left, perhaps the map of Israel. 7 years, Via degli Orsini, Rome, Italy.

# History of the Research on the Mass

Rome, July 1990

My dearest ones,

Translated from the Italian
by Nicolina Gleasure & Joan Parasine

This time, just like a good grandmother, I would like to tell you something about the past, while taking you back briefly along the path of our work through the development of the materials of the Mass. The evolution of the material in our catechesis marks a gradual clarification of the themes that the children themselves have indicated to us to be essential in their relationship with God.

The Christological image of the Good Shepherd has always been, as you well know, the biblical core of our catechesis from its inception. Unfortunately, I cannot remember how this image emerged in our catechesis, nor what the reaction was of the children who indicated to us that is was central in their lives. I am not expanding on this theme here because there have been many opportunities to talk with you and to write about it (as recently as the 1988 Newsletter).

You are also aware how laboured was the research to find a liturgical link to the parable of the Good Shepherd. The close union between the Bible and the liturgy (the Bible coming alive in the liturgy) has always been the foundation of our work. However, it has taken us 20 years for this union to be realized with regard to the parable of the Good Shepherd and the Eucharist. And it was so plain to see: the Eucharist is the time and the place when the Good Shepherd calls us to a special relationship and when we respond to Him in a special way. I think it took us so long to achieve this idea because it is so natural and essential. And the material which concretizes it (this idea) without adding to it, besides the little statue of the Good Shepherd - later removed - and the bread and wine, must be simple, almost poor I might say. Great things are simple; nevertheless, simplicity - true and essential - opens up horizons so limitless and profound that we feel almost lost when confronted with them. Unconsciously we create "complications" around simple and grand things. The child, on the other hand, does not do this; s/he seems to move in the most natural way into the greatest realities. This is why it is very educational for us, the adults, to live with the child.

During the 20 years required for us to come up with the Eucharistic Presence of the Good Shepherd, some fundamental ideas about the Eucharist came to light. In July 1964, Michel Lanternier, founder and principal of the Rennes School in France, and my dear friend, paid me a visit. Together we attempted to select some key ideas linked to a gesture of the Mass which could illustrate the profound meaning of the celebration. Thus we focused on the moment of the offertory, accompanied by the words or phrases "Through Christ, with Christ and in Christ . . ." and the breaking of the bread.

The following November, I presented the gesture of the offering to the children for the first time, with excellent results. As soon as I performed the gesture slowly, in silence, I saw all the children become perfectly still. The silence deepened. My presentation took place in an atmosphere of intense concentration, and was prolonged as each child, in turn, repeated the gesture and the words.

Thus we had isolated the second moment of the Covenant, the response to God's gift. The first moment had not yet emerged. This was due, in part, to the fact that the Latin theology did not yet focus on the effect of the Holy Spirit in the Eucharist. Therefore, the gesture of the epiclesis, the imposition of the hands accompanied by the words which explicitly say "Send your Spirit. . . ." were not yet emphasized. I do not remember when the gesture of epiclesis was presented to the children for the first time. However, sometime in the sixties we had focused on and presented the three gestures which clearly reveal the Mass to be the sacrament of the Covenant: the Epiclesis, which is the moment when we receive the gift of the Spirit, of the power of God -- that is the power of love -- that power which transforms the bread and wine into the presence of the Risen Christ, and the doxology at the end of the Eucharistic prayer. These two gestures stress the vertical dimension of the Covenant: everything comes from

God and everything returns to God. The third moment of the Covenant, which is its horizontal dimension, emerges from the gesture of peace and the breaking of the bread: we become united in the gesture which reveals the intimate relationship which comes from the one broken bread.

Was this the moment when we could state that we had arrived at the essence, or heart of the matter, concerning the Mass? No, we still felt an empty sensation. Something was still lacking that could transfer all these ideas, obviously very rich in meaning, from the mind to the heart. Something was lacking which could firmly anchor the Mass in the affections of the child, as well.

Finally this occurred in 1974 when, as we said earlier, we succeeded in linking the liturgy to the Bible, through the parable of the Good Shepherd. I won't spend too much time on this topic because we have spoken about it often and I wrote about it in the "Religious Potential of the child." (cf. Chapter on the Mass.)

Another element which has proved to be very important in introducing the littlest ones to the Eucharist is the mixing of a few drops of water into the wine during the preparation of the chalice. When did we begin to give it to the children? I don't remember, but what I do remember is that it was Massimo Lugli who made us understand its importance. It was 1962-63, or thereabouts; Massimo, who was 7 years old, kept coming back to this activity with a serious and concentrated attitude. Only towards the end of the cycle of meetings was he able to express its meaning clearly: there are only a few drops of water because we must "lose ourselves in Christ." It is best not to comment at such moments.

It is through this activity, which appears to be an exercise in control of movement, that the children become more aware of our participation in the offering of Christ to the Father. It is obvious to them that we are included in the offering: "We are in the drops of water" is a statement I have heard from the children many times. I should add that the mixing of the water and wine is a symbolic element found to be present even in the ancient tradition, as shown from research by Francesca Cocchini published in **Patristic Dictionary**, column 34.40, Marietti Publishers. As long ago as the second century AD, Irenaus writes about it and it recurs with the Hippolytus and Cyprian (third century AD); the latter says that the water mixed with wine is the people who join themselves to Christ (Epistle 63:13). Once again the children have guided us towards an idea that has demonstrated its importance in the church's tradition from the earliest times to the present.

The Cenacle, the narrative of the Last Supper, has been present in the Catechesis, I believe, from the beginning of our work, although I can't remember since when exactly. The words of Jesus focalized in "Take, eat . . . take, drink . . . ." emphasize the total gift that Jesus makes of Himself, once more presenting the Mass as the "sacrament of the gift."

Keeping in mind the points I listed, it is incredible to see how all the essential theology of the Mass can be understood by children before they are six years old.

What we do with children older than six years is not a deepening, because the central nucleus is already given, but rather a broadening, an ordering of what was already given. But the most profound and fundamental idea was arrived at prior to the age of six.

In 1978, the "memorial" was born, a material which helps to visual the Mass as the actualization of the actions it is founded upon, namely, the Last Supper, death, resurrection, and the gift of the Spirit; this material develops that of the Cenacle.

What was still missing? An idea of the structure of the Mass was still lacking. We had isolated some points, certainly essential ones, but they were disjointed. This was fine for the little ones, but not for the middle group of children older than six. So at a meeting with catechists on January 15, 1980, the "synthesis of the Mass," as we call it, came into being. In it the different individual moments, already known to the children, are organized and ordered in accordance with the sequence of the celebration.

Together with the catechists, we arranged on a large carpet all the materials we present to the little ones and there in front of us was the "synthesis of the Mass" we were seeking. It was necessary, however to reduce the size of the material so that it would fit into the box.

Gradually the work with older children (9-12) became clear. From the beginning we had worked with them on the materials of the Missal that goes back to Dr. Montessori's "The Open Book." Montessori suggested it for children older than 10 years. We have used it with younger children (8-9), but were not able to obtain individual independent work from the children. Obviously this was a sign that they were not oriented sufficiently to this work.

We had devised many different formats of the "guides" that are meant to help the children in preparing their missals. The good "guide" came about in 1981, 27 years after the beginning of this work. It is a material almost for adults, which leads one to the knowledge of the individual prayers which accompany and surround the essential moments of the mass. The material with which the children work at Via degli Orsini is still the same one that Rebekah wrote about during her Roman stay. The box with its drawers, where it is kept, is a gift from the Mexican carpenter, Jose Luis.

In 1983, the "Mystery of our Faith" was born. For a long time, I thought, "Is it possible that we are not able to prepare a catechesis (presentation) around the moment when we relive and express the essence of our faith, the synthesis of the Christian faith?"

This material is an outgrowth of the "Eucharistic Presence of the Good Shepherd," which we spoke about earlier. The presentation aims at helping the children think about the mode of the presence of the Good Shepherd NOW in celebration and how his presence SHALL BE among us at the completion of salvation history.

As you see, the path did not have a linear unfolding which would have been the case if it had been planned at a desk. We have worked, observed, met the needs of the children and become aware of the gaps in our presentations. Some attempts were too complicated, too intellectual, originating too much in our minds and did not adhere essentially to the reality of the Eucharist. The children were our exigent guides and inexorably "dropped" what was not strictly essential.

This story of our research has not been driven by nostalgic feelings for the purpose of keeping a record of our memories. I did it because I think there is an educational element in becoming aware of how slow, how attentive, alert and patient our research has been, It is important to be conscious of the fact that the results are good when one achieves a level of extreme simplicity and essentiality, even poverty, as I mentioned earlier. The results are good only when we find them before us as an unexpected gift, a "let down" when compared with the convoluted researches which have preceded it. So gradually we have reached the point you are acquainted with. Have we finished? I should say certainly not. One topic to be researched urgently with older children (9-12) and improved upon, is the link between history, as presented in the "Plan of God," and liturgy. We research, observe and look forward to a further gift.

Sofia

# Reflections from a course, 1990

by Rose Paul, a Minnesota catechist

Here I am again at 2:00 A.M. making materials! This "habit" started this summer at the course in Washington, D. C. I must admit TV has nothing as wonderful to offer as the late night conversations and antics of sleepy catechists working late, trying to make a dent in the vast amount of material to make. I am becoming satisfied with my own handwriting after spending so much time tracing other people's. It is much faster to do "free hand" work than it is to copy, I heard a catechist explain late one night.

In spite of late night activities, we were attentive and able to concentrate each day as Rebekah Rojcewicz drew us ever more deeply into The History of Salvation. We met Abraham and Isaac as if for the first time in the realm of the Nomadic Life, Worship, and the study of Typology. Reluctantly, we moved on to Moses, The Sojourn in the Desert, The History of His times, The Exodus, and The Gift of the Law. We realized that we could have spent the whole two weeks on any one of the subjects.

National Geographics became priceless possessions and we paid $5.00 each for a back issue with an article about the life and times of Abraham. In addition, a list of all available issues was compiled with topics pertaining to our study.

Having Rebekah's translation of The History of Salvation in hand proved invaluable, and so much easier to refer to than the previous year's work of translating during the course. I know I can speak for all of us: we are so grateful to Rebekah for providing us with this translation. We all look forward to the completely translated book which we know will be of the greatest help to all catechists as they continue this work. Thank you, Sofia, for sharing your many years of hard work, study, and inspiration with us in this way. We hope to express our gratitude by reading, studying, and carrying on the work with children.

We were close to being filled to capacity but the first week was not over! We carefully reserved our resources to continue as the prophets beckoned us to glean their secrets of listening to God. We understood the struggle of being called by God and responding with fear and looking for a way out, but we soon saw how God seduces, purifies and strengthens His prophets to fulfill His mission.

Filled to the brim with Old Testament life, history and wisdom, and ready to spend the rest of my life dwelling in Hebrew study, my bleary eyes and swimming head called out for "basta," a word I recalled hearing Sofia use many times after long sessions with us Americans. It means "stop," or perhaps, "enough is enough!"

I welcomed the retreat day away to a place called "Dayspring." We drove in a caravan of cars through heavy, gray mist, like the cloud I felt I was in or, perhaps, a reminder of the cloud that followed the Israelites. "No," I told myself, "none of that!" I let myself feel like I was in the protection of a cocoon that blocked out any more words. A peacefulness filled me as I participated in eating, singing, voting for the Association board members and listening to plans and dreams for the future being shared.

I participated in the Eucharist presided over by an Episcopalian priest, and I was blessed by an Episcopalian Deacon, both catechists of the Good Shepherd. Truly we are the Body of Christ. Peace and joy pervaded the mist and dispelled all darkness. I felt rested and refreshed and in contact with myself once again. I thank the people who worked so hard to plan this "Time Apart." It was a welcome break for me during the intensive 17 days.

We returned to the course on Monday and were saddened to hear of the death of Rebekah's grandmother and the news that Rebekah would leave us for a day or so, but her confidence in the fact that we could carry on while she was gone encouraged us to reach inside ourselves and take on new roles. We studied, did presentations and dialogued as catechists, used to the procedure of many training courses over the years. We worked on the Doctrinal Points, Direct and Indirect Aims. We stayed with a predetermined schedule that would keep us from getting behind on the work to be done; Cathy Maresca helped us stay on track.

We welcomed Rebekah back and shared in her grief and appreciation of a very special person in her life who will be sadly missed. I have the feeling that this person imparted much knowledge, love and wisdom to many. This was her legacy to them: Rebekah is truly a recipient and a conveyor of this legacy.

We moved on to the the Moral Parables (I am looking forward to trying to make the "talents"), the Mass, which we soon fully "clothed" with all of its prayers and symbols, and the Sacraments. We took time to look at specific prayers: The Preface, Intercessory Prayer, and a deeper view of the Mystery of Faith. I was glad and relieved to observe the presentation of the Memorial which I had vaguely seen presented by Maria Christlieb and Sofia in 1983, at the Retreat held after the 3-6 course.

This was the first course (1983, Washington, D.C.) I attended and I was drowning in the richness of the Good Shepherd and the Mustard Seed. My mind and heart were full at the end of this course and I had no room for more. I was looking forward to the Retreat. To my wonder and surprise the retreat participants, veteran catechists who had been with Sofia for many years, clammered for work! They were making materials and asking questions as if this were another course, not a retreat. I found myself caught up in their urgency and I proceeded to trace all the prayers and colored bases for The Mass and I took many pictures of material that was layed out but not officially presented, including the Memorial. I had no idea what was going on and my head felt full of cotton, but my hands kept busy. I am relieved to know what they are all about now, and I can put those tracings and pictures to good use.

We moved on to the Sacraments and covered Baptism which was my album page. I wonder if I will ever forget the sequence of pictures and prayers of the Rite of Baptism since I copied, cut and arranged them so many times! Reconciliation took on new meaning as we covered the meditations and participated in acting out the celebration during our retreat. Our shared revelations and the washing of each other's hands stand out in my mind as a time of healing and community.

This course has inhanced my appreciation of the Hebrew Scriptures. I read <u>The Liturgy of the Hours</u> each day and the prayers are from the Psalms, the prayers of the Israelite people. They make more sense and I can understand their pain, struggles and triumphs much better since I have tasted a little of Sofia's wonderful book, The History of Salvation.

When I returned home I asked my daughter, Jodie, who is presently job hunting, to help me with material making. She has beautiful handwriting and I hate to trace. She completed the Parousia material for me and she is working on The Peoples and the People of God material. I have finished all the typology cards and one chart. I am presently embroidering the felt material.

I know I must put all this aside soon and concentrate on preparing to open a Montessori preschool with an atrium by 1991. I do appreciate this work and the material and I pray that the Lord will help me find a way to use it. Nicole, my granddaughter, is just the right age (11) and history is her favorite subject.

I know we all have the habit of making materials. I wonder what we would do without it?!

At the top: "Advent, a voice which calls." On the left: "Jesus passes on the straight road, and comes into the heart." On the back: "Jesus comes into my heart. I put the straight road, and beautiful and shining. In the desert the glory of the Lord every man will see the magnificence of Him; the Lord promised it with his mouth."
Martino, age 7, Via degli Orsini, Rome, Italy.

Laurie Dowdy, of Yazoo City, Mississippi, and Cathy Maresca, of Washington, D. C., confer on methods of making boxes. The two have become quite skillful carpenters in order to fulfill the many needs in material making.

A group of catechists from the south and west who attended the 9-12 formation experience in Washington, D. C. this past summer. First row: Teresa Sears & Donna Macklin of Casper, WY, Marty O'Bryan, Phoenix, AZ, Jo Ann Williams, Casper. Second row: Kathy Dahl-Bredine, Silver City, NM, Linda Kaiel, Portland, Or, & Kathleen Alman, Houston, TX. Third row: Bert O'Bryan, Phoenix, Rev. Randall Trego, Houston.

## Our Newsletter

Please submit your articles, prayers of the children, and their art work for the next issue of the newsletter. Send materials in care of:

    Carol Dittberner
    1429 Portland Avenue
    St. Paul, MN 55104 USA

This issue of the newsletter was compiled by Sofia Cavalletti, Maria Christlieb and Carol Dittberner.

In the circle, figure seems to be the risen Christ; in the rectangle, the Nativity; candles, crucifix, and the world. Source unknown.

**Staff in U.S.A.**
Carol Stenborg
Carol Dittberner
Italian Translators Joan Parasine and Nicolina Gleasure
Spanish Translators Kathy Dahl-Bredine

**Staff in Chihuahua:**
Bertha Sofia Quiroz de Marquez
Emilia G. de Sandoval
Noemi F. de Lopez
Maria de Los Angeles Christlieb

## Announcements

Our set of figures for the Cenacle was carved in Haiti. It consists of 13 figures of Jesus and the disciples. The cost is approximately $85.00. These figures are hand-carved by Haitians who earn money through this work to send their children to Trinity Episcopal School in Port-au-Prince, Haiti. Other items available are Lamb of God cross, $20.00, Nativity Set (11"), $11.00, wooden goblet, $5.50. Orders and inquiries should be directed to:

    Myra Arnold
    1631 Ford Parkway
    St. Paul, MN 55105
    phone: (612) 698-2590

## Our Association

### Membership

The Catechesis of the Good Shepherd, An Association of Children and Adults, welcomes members throughout the year. Our membership fee is $30. The fees we collect go toward expenses of our four committees: Communications & Finance, Formation, Materials and Newsletter. Members receive the annual newsletter, all mailings and a directory of catechists and friends of the Association. A newsletter subscription only is $5.00 U.S. or $6.00 foreign.

No one should hesitate to join the Association because of the inability to pay the requested $30 fee. We appreciate any donation large or small.

Mail memberships and donations to:

**The Catechesis of the Good Shepherd
Box 218
Mt. Rainier, MD 20712
(301) 927-2015**

(c) Copyright, December, 1990.
Catechesis of the Good Shepherd
Box 218
Mt. Rainier, MD 20712
English edition published in
St. Paul, Minnesota.

# The Catechesis of the Good Shepherd

Number 8, English                                                                                     June 1991

*My heart is steadfast, O God,*
*My heart is steadfast!*
*I will sing and make melody!*
*Awake, my soul!*
*Awake, O harp and lyre!*
*I will give thanks to Thee, O Lord,*
*among the peoples,*
*I will sing praises to Thee among the nations.*
*For Thy steadfast love is great above the heavens,*
*Thy faithfulness reaches to the clouds.*
*Be exalted, O God, above the heavens!*
*Let Thy glory be over all the earth!*

*Psalms 108: 1-5*

## Contents

| | Page |
|---|---|
| **Let us Pray with the Children** | 2-3 |
| **The Bible in the Prayer Corner** | 4 |
| *An album page by Nora Bonilla* | |
| **Communal Prayer** | 5 |
| *by Sofia Cavalletti* | |
| **Reflections on Prayer** | 6 |
| *by Sofia Cavalletti* | |
| **Outline for Communal Prayer** | 6 |
| **The Liturgy of the Hours** | 7 |
| **The Catechesis in Munich** | 8-9 |
| *by Deborah Presser-Velder* | |
| **News from the Minnesota Catechists** | 9 |
| **Catechesis with Adults** | 10-11 |
| *by Eva Elesa Quiroz* | |
| **The Children Show Us How to Pray Joyfully** | 12 |
| *by Carol Dittberner* | |
| **Catechist Formation Class Listing** | 14 |
| **Association Meeting** | 15 |
| **On Taking Photographs of the Children** | 15 |
| *by Sofia Cavalletti* | |
| **Our Newsletter** (deadline for next issue: Oct. 1, 1991) | 16 |

# Let us pray

*The following prayers are from the First Communion Retreat in Torreon, Mexico, 1989.*

God, I thank you because I am going to make my first communion, and for the mass which I like very much. Thank you for loving me.

*First day of retreat.*

Hello Jesus, I am Peter, your sheep; I have so many things to tell you. I am going to receive you; I want so much to make my first communion. I think I am very well prepared. And You, how are You? I pray [to] you for my grandparents. They are coming by bus from San Luis Potosi; bring them safely.
Tomorrow we will celebrate another mass, like today. Today the priest read to us the ten bridesmaids. There I discovered many things of you;
I hope tomorrow will be also.
Goodbye, Jesus. Peter is writing You. Your sheep.

*Written on the second day of retreat*

Thank you, Lord, for all these days with you. Your sheep, Peter.

*Written on First Communion Day.*

*Childrens' Prayers continued on next page*

*Susan Schweigert, age 9, of St. Frances Cabrini Atrium, Minneapolis, MN drew this picture after the celebration of the Liturgy of The Light.*

*The colors she used were red, orange and yellow for the flame. God is dressed in blue.*

# with the Children . . .

*First Communion Prayers, continued.*

God gives us all. Thank you, God.
God made me. This is true.

Jesus, thank you for having received your bread and wine and also your light. Today I have been very happy.

O, thank you Jesus. Thank you for everything you have given me: life, love, bread and wine. Also because you have allowed me to live this moment of retreat.

Jesus is the "king of the universe."

Jesus is my heart.

Lord, I love you.

Hello Mary, Mother of God. You are the only mother.

The light of Jesus is precious.

Lord, you are the Shepherd and I am your sheep.
You the vine and I am the branch.
You the Father and I am the son.
I have sinned and I am not worthy.
Say your word.

Hello, dear Mary, I am very happy to be with you. Mary, I am happy because very soon God is going to hold me on his shoulders.

*Above, a drawing by Andria Gannon, age 10, of The Good Shepherd Center in Cleveland, Ohio.*

*Matthew Brown, age 9, of St. Frances Cabrini Atrium, Minneapolis, MN created the drawing at the right.*

# The Bible in the Prayer Corner

An Album Page prepared by Nora Bonilla

Translated by Nicolina Gleasure and Joan Parasine

**Age:** 3 years onwards

**Doctrinal Points:** The Bible is the book of the Word of God.
Jesus is the light.

**Presentation:** The group sits in a circle in the prayer corner.

The catechist says: "The most important book in the whole world is the Bible, the Holy Bible. This is the book where we find many of God's secrets for us. These secrets are for all the people in the world, both men and women. We know this because this precious book, the Bible, is written in every language and idiom spoken by human beings. This book can be found in different sizes, large or small, in all colours, but it always says the same thing."

Solemnly and lovingly, the catechist places in the children's hands various bibles in as many different sizes, colours and languages as possible. This most precious book, the Bible, is displayed on the book stand and children are told that it will remain in this corner where they can come, filled with love, to listen to it, to become familiar with it and little by little to read it. Nearby, are placed the candles which are to be lit when we come to read the Bible which is the Word of God who is speaking to us. The catechist asks: "Would you like to read something from this precious book, the Bible? Then we should prepare ourselves to listen to this Word, because even though I read it with my voice, it is the Word of God. Let's all stand up (or all sit down). We should fix our socks or shoes, or whatever might distract us. Now let's create an atmosphere of silence and listen intently. I will begin when I see that we are all ready to listen."

The catechist calls 2 children and shows them how to hold the lighted candles in their hands. The catechist then reads John 8:12 (or some other text) directly from the Bible. When the reading is concluded, depending on the group, one might say: "What does Jesus say He is? The light of what? This is the reason we light the candles; they help us think about Jesus as the light. He is the light of us all, of all the persons in the world."

*Note:* *This presentation is appropriate after introducing the Atrium, before the presentation of the altar model.*

**Direct Aim:** To know the book of the Bible

**Indirect Aim:** To initiate veneration and love for the Holy Bible in the child; to initiate his love for listening to it; to prepare the child for the celebration of the Word; to introduce the child to prayer.

**Material:** Various Bibles, 2 candle holders and candles, matches, prayer table and tablecloth

*See Reflections on this presentation by Sofia, on Page 6*

# Communal Prayer

An Album Page by Sofia Cavalletti

Translated by Nicolina Gleasure and Joan Parasine

**Age:** 8 years

**Doctrinal Point:** Prayer is listening and response.

**Material:** An established prayer corner is a prerequisite. The Bible, copies of collections of psalms (as many as there are children and **adults participating**), a book of songs, an outline **for group or common prayer** (based on the "Liturgy of the Hours"), a bell.

**Presentation:** Gather the children. The catechist announces that we want to organize the prayer (time), that is, that time when we pay greater attention to the presence of God in our lives. A child is invited to stand next to the catechist; later that child will assume the role of leader, together with another child, during the time of group prayer. The child who helps needs a piece of paper, a red and a black pen. The catechist indicates the various items which are needed and their location.

S/he begins to read the first page of the outline* (*see note below*) and asks in what order to organize the elements listed. The child writes them with the red pen in the chosen sequence. The catechist asks which preliminary prayer they wish to choose. Their number is written on the paper with the black pen, and so on for all the other elements: reading, song, etc. It's a good idea, at times, for the catechist to suggest some readings so as to introduce new passages. When we get to the psalms, we practice a reading with 2 "choruses" (or choirs), e.g. one group of children recites the first verse and the second group says the second verse, and so on. At the end of each psalm, everyone recites (or sings, if possible) the "Glory to the Father, etc." This preparatory work may be carried out by 2 children in later sessions while the other children are busy with other activities. When everything is ready, the 2 children ring the bell, wait for silence and then announce that the prayer is prepared; all are invited. The children who wish to do so will go and participate.

**Children's Activities:** In successive meetings, 2 children may decide to prepare the prayer according to the plan already discussed in previous meetings. When they have finished preparing, they review the outline with the catechist, then they inform the other children by ringing the bell. They (the 2 children who prepared the prayer) lead the celebration, and announce the individual titles one by one. If the catechist is not busy at the time, she also participates.

**Direct Aim:** To support the prayer with the help of a structure; to enrich it with new elements.

**Indirect Aim:** To nourish the religious life with prayer

*\*Note:* *The outline noted above is listed on the next page.*

## Reflections on Prayer

by Sofia Cavalletti
Translated by Nicolina Gleasure and
Joan Parasine

The presentation of "The Bible in the Prayer Corner" prepared by Nora Bonilla (Bogota, Columbia) seems to me very helpful to the children, even when very young, in linking prayer and the Bible.

I would like to add some thoughts on the prayer of the older children. Everyone is acquainted with the extraordinary riches of the spontaneous prayer of the little ones. Certainly, I don't wish to propose methods of prayer, nevertheless, I think that the older children (from 8 years onwards) can find help in their expression towards God in a particular form of structured prayer. It appears to me that providing an outline to be followed in prayer, although this is done freely, responds to the needs of that age, an age which is seeking support in rules that are to be followed. I think that you too may have experienced a certain fatigue in spontaneous prayer, a repetition of words already said without much involvement of the heart. The structure I propose should overcome these difficulties. I am proposing this together with an album page based on the "Liturgy of the Hours," albeit in a simplified format.

I would like to add that in the Rennes School in France, directed by my dear and ever remembered friend, Michael Lanternier, I saw children (10 years old and older, I think) saying group prayer following the book of the "Liturgy of the Hours" of the Taize Community, if my memory doesn't fail me.

I would also like to add that the children may not always be available for the preparation of the prayer. In this case, the community prayer does not take place. In the Rennes school, the children attended every day; obviously, therefore, the situation differed from that in an atrium where attendance is limited to 2 hours a week. In an atrium the problem arises that the children, in order to go and pray, must interrupt the work they are involved with. Often they are so engrossed in it, that they do not want to leave it. Usually the group prayer is enjoyed by the children very much, but it is often difficult for them to choose between prayer and work.

**Sofia**

# Outline for Communal Prayer

When we want to focus more on the presence of God in our lives, we address our prayer to God. We can organize it with the following elements:

   a. An introductory formula *(see Details, below)*
   b. A reading from the Bible and a period of reflection
   c. Psalms
   d. Silent prayer *(see Details, below)*
   e. Prayer of the faithful
   f. "Our Father"
   g. Song or prayer to Mary

### Details on a. and d.

a. The introductory formula can be chosen from the following:

   1. The Lord be with you and with your spirit.
   2. The peace of the Lord be always with you and with your spirit.
   3. Oh Lord, open my lips and my mouth will declare your praise.
   4. Our help is in the name of the Lord who made heaven and earth.
   5. Let the words of my mouth be pleasing to you, O Lord, and the meditation of my heart. Lord be my rock and my salvation.

d. The introduction to silence can be initiated with one of the following phrases:

   1. Let us offer a silent prayer to God.
   2. We make a gift of our silence to the prayer to God.
   3. We pray to the Lord in silence.
   4. We pray to the Lord with our whole heart within ourselves.
   5. We thank the Lord silently in our hearts.

## *The Religious Potential of the Child* being revised, reprinted

***The Religious Potential of the Child***, as published by Paulist Press, is currently out of print. The book is being revised and will be coming out in a second edition. The new publisher will be Liturgical Training Publications of Chicago, Illinois. The second edition will be available in 6-8 months.

# The Liturgy of the Hours

We thought it would be helpful to include here the following information on the Liturgy of the Hours. *The Complete Liturgy of the Hours* is available in four volumes, or in a shorter one volume, abridged version.

## The Celebration of the Hours

## Introduction

The first Hour of the day (Morning Prayer or Office of Readings) begins with the Invitatory:

> Lord, open my lips, and my mouth shall proclaim your praise. (without Glory to the Father and Alleluia)

The antiphon with the invitatory psalm (95, 100, 67 or 24) follows.

The antiphon may be said first and then repeated after each strophe of the psalm.

The Glory to the Father concludes the invitatory psalm.

The rest of the Hours begin with the verse:

> God, come to my assistance.
> Lord, make haste to help me.
> Glory to the Father. Alleluia.

Note: The Alleluia is omitted during Lent.

## Office of Readings

Introduction as above
Hymn, from the Four Week Psalter or from the Proper of Seasons
Three psalms with their antiphons
Verse
First Reading: biblical, with its responsory
Second Reading: patristic or hagiographical, with its responsory
(Te Deum, if prescribed)
Prayer, proper to the day (with Let us pray and the long conclusion)
Let us praise the Lord. And give him thanks.

## Morning & Evening Prayer

Introduction as above
Hymn—from the Four Week Psalter or from the Proper of Seasons
Morning Prayer: psalm, O.T. canticle, psalm, with their antiphons
Evening Prayer: two psalms and N.T. canticle, with their antiphons
Reading
Responsory
Canticle (Canticle of Zechariah or Canticle of Mary) with Antiphon
Intercessions
Lord's Prayer
Concluding Prayer (without Let us pray and with long conclusion) is proper except on weekdays in Ordinary Time.
If a priest or deacon is presiding, he dismisses the people; otherwise the Hour concludes with:

> May the Lord bless us, protect us from all evil and bring us to everlasting life. Amen.

## Daytime Prayer

Introduction as above
Hymn suitable to the time of day
Three psalms with their antiphon or antiphons
Reading
Verse
Concluding Prayer (with Let us pray and short conclusion) is proper except on memorials and weekdays in Ordinary Time.
Let us praise the Lord. And give him thanks.

## Night Prayer

Introduction as above
Examination of conscience
Hymn
Psalmody
Reading
Responsory
Antiphon and Nunc dimittis (Canticle of Simeon)
Prayer from the Psalter
May the all-powerful Lord grant us a restful night and a peaceful death. Amen.
Marian antiphon.

From *Christian Prayer: The Liturgy of the Hours*, Daughters of St. Paul, St. Paul Editions, 1976

*Robert Arnold, age 9, of the Good Shepherd Center, St. Paul, Minnesota, drew the figure of Jesus, and the rays (all in yellow) in celebration of Easter.*

# The Catechesis in Munich

*Letter from Munich
translated by Janet Griffing*

With much joy I would like to share with you my first experiences within the atrium which opened October 19, 1989 in Feldafing, near Munich, Germany.

A few years ago, Betty Hissong gave me a gift, *The Religious Potential of the Child*. Its contents fascinated me so much, that within me was born a desire to do this work. I met Sofia on one of my trips to Rome and that visit opened the path for me to start learning the catechesis. It is, and has been, a time of intense but marvelous work and, more than anything, a time of spiritual growth.

Four months before beginning the work in the atrium, I invited families from the parish, interested in religious education for their children, to a meeting to explain the program. Before this meeting, I had many talks with our priest explaining the methodology, the environment, showing him pictures and translating the material into German. I asked for his help and support. Little by little, his doubts disappeared and 2 days before the meeting he informed me that the parish would give us a chapel-like space for an atrium. The meeting with parents went well, although the group was small. The parents who registered their children spontaneously offered to help in material making. From this work grew the interest, the understanding and the support of the parents.

I prepared the environment with a friend, also a Montessori directress, and we transformed the space into an inviting place for the children, without it losing its sacred atmosphere.

I started with a few children, giving the exercises on control of movement. In a short time we had an atmosphere of respect and tranquility, in which we could joyfully work. This nucleus of children has continued to grow and at this date we have 12 children. The kerygma, and the presentations of the material continue to enrich the life of the atrium week by week. I realize how difficult it is to proclaim the gospel with the essentiality that children demand! The children responded in fascination and joy at the Good Shepherd parable. The afternoon in which this presentation was given, a great feeling of peace existed in the atrium.

One of the more beautiful experiences in this first year, was the presentation of the Light of Baptism.

Annette, a 6 year old, who was not baptized yet, said: "I am fed up."

"Of what?" I asked.

"Of waiting and waiting and waiting for my mom to have me baptized. I want to be, and I've told her but the only thing I do is wait and wait!"

That afternoon, I spoke with her mother and she, perplexed by her daughter's determination, said: "I guess the time has come."

We baptized her last week and all her friends from the atrium were there. In November we baptized a five-year-old boy who had had a similar reaction. Its beautiful to see a child receive baptism so consciously.

This year we celebrated the Liturgy of the Light with Sofia. She was in Munich to give her first course at Kinderzentrum. It was a beautiful moment for the children.

This course which Sofia gave in Munich in April of 1990 was very successful. There has been so much interest, that a second course has been organized for the weekend of November 30, 1990. We have great hopes that this work will continue to grow in Germany. This year, Claudia Schmidt will train in Rome, so as to start the work at Kinderzentrumand in the course for Montessori training.

The ability to do this work for me is a gift and a serious commitment at the same time.

I am profoundly thankful to Sofia, Gianna, and the group of catechists in Rome, for guiding me, teaching me and feeding the fire, and to Betty for having put me on this road.

**Deborah Presser-Velder**

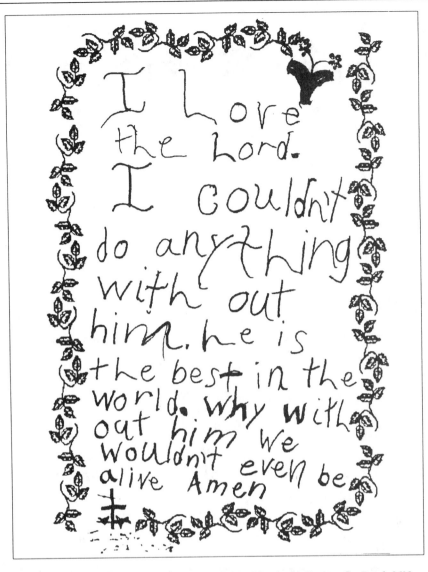

*Prayer by Martina Mohn, age 7, of the Good Shepherd Center, St. Paul, MN.*

# News from the Minnesota Catechists

We are happy to announce the start of several atriums in our area. In January, we celebrated the opening of our first Lutheran atrium. As far as we know, this is the first Lutheran atrium to open anywhere. It is located at St. John's Church in Northfield, Minnesota. The catechist, Mark Gleason, has just completed the 3-6 level course and began his atrium with 13 three year olds!

This past year, one of our existing Montessori schools added the catechesis materials to their program. Ethel Smith, of Morning Star Montessori has begun the first Christian school in our area.

In the fall, a second Christian Montessori School will open under the direction of Rose Paul, Bloomington, Minnesota. She is naming her school the Little House Montessori Center and Atrium. Both these Christian schools are at the preschool level.

Also in the fall, the Pax Christi Catholic parish will open a "pilot" atrium. This parish numbers 2,000 and it will be their first experience with the Catechesis. The catechists, Vicky Shields and Janet Griffing, will begin with just 15 children. They are hoping that the parents will respond to the Catechesis and more people will come forward to receive instruction and make the atrium available to more children.

This is our first local experience with the catechesis in such a large parish. It would be helpful to all of us if those of you who work in large parishes, which have already solved some of the problems of numbers, would write in to the newsletter about your decisions. Do you use the same atrium at different times during the week? Do you have multiple atriums?

As an example, at St. James Episcopal Church in Jackson, Mississippi, a decision was made to make the Catechesis the sole method of religious education. They built a facility specifically to house the several atriums. Since the Jackson community has so many children, they decided to divide the atriums according to age level: There is a three-year-old room, a four-year-old room, and so on. It is most ideal to mix three age groups together, and the catechists hope to do this in the future. However, in order to make the catechesis available to all the children, as soon as possible, they have begun in this way.

If you have something to share about how your atrium works in relationship to your parish or school, or within a very large parish, please let us know. Write in care of the newsletter.

*A Letter to Sofia*

# Catechesis with adults

Dear Sofia

A few weeks ago, we had a profound experience with a group of migrants. You had a part in their formation, and that is why I would like to share this with you.

I believe that Tatina has spoken to you about a priest, a Scalabine missionary, Italian, whose name is Flor Maria. He has favored us by presiding over our recent first communion celebration, and is distinguished for his devotion in that celebration.

Lupita Palafox was here, and we talked and decided on 10 lessons. Annunciation, Good Shepherd (complete), Parables of the Kingdom (Pearl and Mustard Seed), Baptism, The Virgins, The Gifts [of the Holy Spirit], Articles of the Altar, Epiclesis and Offering, Eucharistic Presence and Cenacle, Father and Son, True Vine, Maxims, Reconciliation and History of the Kingdom (could be creation).

I submitted the plan to Father just before I left on a trip. He was to review the plan while I was gone. On my return (October

*One of them said to me, "for me what has the most meaning are the last words 'because for God nothing is impossible'."*

*God couldn't have said it to me more clearly than this, that within my sin, my lack of trust, my limitations ... he would overcome!!*

A few months ago, he started a "Home for the Migrant," in this city of Juarez. "Cristos Peregrinos" arrive here: Here in the frontier come men, women and children from all over. From Central America to North, coming to find a better life, and others coming back from the north, deported for lack of documents. In general, all have suffered a lot and arrive with a heavy heart from the bad experiences....

I was led to this community by God. Father gave me the breakfast group [to work with], and all went well. It was easy, interesting and very simple. I decided to cut back my work at the parish, and focus on promoting catechesis for the young children.... Father knew that I was part of the group at Sacred Family and one day he commented that he had special permission from the archbishop to prepare a short course on first communion for the migrants. [He asked if] I would prepare a plan. I took advantage of the fact that

9), I found a message from him. He was out of town until the 19th, but could I prepare them for first communion on the 20th at 7 p.m.

The group consisted of 14 people: a young girl, 11 years old, and 13 men, ranging in age from 16 to 42 years old.

I believe, Sofia, that I have never felt so great a responsibility and almost an impotence. I began to understand how we are only instruments and in my case a very overwhelmed one.

I felt strongly the call and strongly also the fear ... After praying, I was ready to say "I can't" because [there was so much to be done]. Some worked by day, others by night, so it was necessary to have two classes: one from 12 to 2 and another from 6 to 8. The house [we used for our classes] was on the outskirts of the city.... Nothing was prepared at the house. But [somehow] He led the way and I started that very day... Later, Rosa Eugenia

became responsible for the young girl and at night Ofe would accompany me. Later still, Tatena, Mari Ortega, Makie, Elizabeth and Regina helped me with the presentation and the ceremony.

The first day, I found a group of sad men, tired, yet hungry for something more, some with resentment, that they didn't delay in voicing. I only had time to ask the Virgin Mary, "that these too are your children!!" I tried to meditate with them [on] the Annunciation.

"How difficult it is to be a messenger!" I thought. But they were quiet and they watched me... in those moments I felt their contempt, scorn, their questioning, and when we read "The Word," one of them said to me "for me what has the most meaning are the last words 'because for God nothing is impossible'."

God couldn't have said it to me more clearly than this, that within my sin, my lack of trust, my limitations ... he would overcome!!

The days passed, like on a spiritual retreat, I forgot all else, my husband supported me without question, my almost living with the migrants, (6 hours with them, plus the prep time).

Tatena allowed me to use materials of the school; they wanted to write, to save all the work. They were worried that they would get to tape everything, some had had very negative experiences as children with memorized catechism, with test and other things...

I started to use the album, first by taping the pages on the window of the dining room, which all of the migrants would read and comment on. Later we made copies for all of them, which they crammed into their notebooks and pocket New Testaments, which they never let go of. They reviewed and studied in all their free time. Each session was two hours long, but it was never enough time. They waited for us promptly each time and did not want class to end.

Each class was a unique experience. The Baptism Light, it was truly a bath of tears of those men, and of course, with the help of the light .... one of them who had experiences with parts of the United States, would ask a million questions and couldn't restrain his joy.... With the parables we saw how little by little they started to smile, to change, to trust.... and to have discussion amongst themselves reading again the New Testament and meditating.

Two days before first communion, Father Flor Maria arrived. He couldn't believe what he saw and he was very happy. He arranged reconciliation for Friday at two different times. We tested our conscience with the Maxims; there was an air of recognition, happiness, expectation, confidence.... Everything was set up in a room with two windows: one overlooking the chapel and the other facing the temple. On a table was a white cloth with a Bible, opened to "The Father and the Son," a candlestick, a Good Shepherd figure, a vase with a shaft of wheat, a bunch of red grapes and two chairs at each side. It was truly a celebration of Love! Father said that it was for him an enriching experience to hear confessions without blame, resentment but rather pardon.... He wasn't in agreement to open old hurt feelings and stir up pain, and the blame, and there wasn't any other way.

Saturday, almost at daybreak, we had our Reconciliation Celebration. The full sun came up just at the place where Father gave them each a white shirt, then the light, then the cross; to see those men whose hands shook and whose eyes shown with tears receive and accept, as one of them said to me "To be son of the Light." And [to see] Father who presided with that simple and profound respect and the ceremony.... Afterwards we had a great breakfast, followed by the presentation of the History of the Kingdom, using the whole length of the church. They didn't go to work that day, they didn't cease to amaze me, the happiness. (My choice of words are inadequate to express the feeling that was present.)

At seven that evening, the Eucharist had three different celebrations, First Communion, Fr. Flor Maria's birthday and the Feast of Mater Admirabilis, patron of our school and whose spirit accompanied us.

The church was full and decorated; for many, it was the first time they participated in the celebration and from the moment the men entered with their candles, who Julia, their Godmother, helped them light from the Easter candle, and who so carefully carried to the altar, caring for the "light" so nothing would extinguish it, this was the first reason for amazement, emotion and lots of tears among the assistants. The men never stopped smiling although there were moments of tears as well.

They participated in everything, lecturing, offering, etc. One by one they were called by name to receive communion and then go to the chapel to give thanks while the rest of us took communion. Later, they returned with a flower and their "work" to offer to the Virgin (that was what had been decided) but they, on their own initiative, knelt a few minutes and then stood, left their flower, their work, and each one gave the statue a kiss.... Maria won their hearts, she is truly Mother.... while La Maya (a friend) sang "How I love thee, Mother Admirable, O how tranquil my spirit feels...."

We left, wrapped in a joy too difficult to express but one that I know you recognize and understand! God has shown his presence once more.

I have later seen some of these migrants in the city and they return to the home as though to visit their family... and that is what we are, God our Father's family. This shepherd who takes care of us, protects us and over all, loves us.

Bishop Talamas referred to this group as the fruit on the road to Parousia.

*continued on the next page*

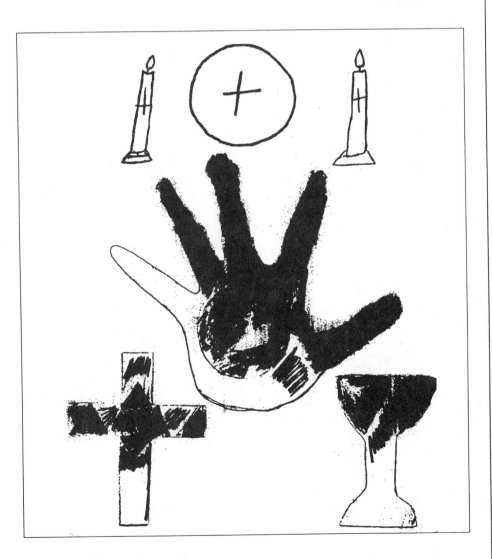

*Alissa Fortune, age 8, of the Good Shepherd Center in St. Paul created this drawing. The cross over the chalice and hand were done in many colors. The hand of God with the "whole world" was how Alissa explained the drawing.*

# The children show us how to pray

> *Blessed are the people*
> *who know the festal shout,*
> *who walk, O Lord,*
> *in the light of thy countenance, . . . .*
>
> Ps. 89:15 (RSV)

by Carol Dittberner

When I think about this scripture, the people who come to my mind are the children and their prayer. We have spoken so often in these pages, and in our work, about the nature of the child's prayer, particularly the young child, and so I will not go into detail here. Let us remember that the prayer of the youngest children, from 2-1/2 to 6 years, is praise and thanksgiving. It is only around 6-1/2 to 7 years that the child begins the prayer of petition.

The young child is filled with wonder and awe and joy, and so are their prayers:

Thank you for the Light.
Thank you for my mom and my God.
Thank you for rainbows.
Mary and God, thank you for Jesus.
God bless God. God bless the sun. God bless everything. Bless even the dragons. God bless space. Bless us.
Thank you father God for making the universe out of nothing. Thank you father God for making me out of nothing.
Thank you for light.

(*Compiled from childrens' prayers, as published in earlier issues of the newsletters*).

The children are the ones who truly "know the festal shout," the shout of praise and thanks to God. A festal shout, meaning celebration, festivity and joyousness! This shout of joy is the one which comes from deep within our spirit; we are moved emotionally, and sometimes physically, to exclaim.

The child is close to God, and the child's prayer is filled with the continuous acknowledgment of God's gifts. How can we understand these gifts? They are an endless mystery, unsolvable until we see God face to face.

The child seems to walk, and even to live, easily in the light of the Lord's countenance.

I also think of the child in relationship to the psalm we have used for the cover of this newsletter issue: "My heart is steadfast, O Lord, my heart is steadfast." (Ps. 108:1) The child has this steadfast spirit; we see it in their ability to love unconditionally. We see it in their joyfulness, their ability to return to a happy state after facing upsets in their lives. They are true to their words and their emotions.

When I think about how children pray, I also think of the Greek word panegyria. In Greek, "pan" means "all"; "ageiren" means "to bring together." It is defined as "the assembly of a whole nation," the bringing together for a public festival. It also has the meaning of a high festival, or "festal assembly" which gathers for the purpose of high praise.

How might we imagine this festival? In his book, *Eucharist*, Louis Bouyer discusses the time when "God would be praised unendingly by the people of God . . . "[1] We begin to participate in this through the

## Catechesis with Adults,

*continued from page 11*

Sofia, I want to share this experience with you and ask your forgiveness for not consulting with you beforehand, to know your thoughts, and feelings on the subject. I think of many other ways and every time I study or prepare I feel that there is nothing like what you have done to give us a focus; the material is even helpful to adults. How can we add to it? What changes would you recommend? Your direction and guidance is paramount.

Soon I will begin a project, the Nazareth House, for Mexican minors apprehended in the U.S., whom the government is turning over to Father Flor Maria, and he is opening the door to us and asks us to do an atrium for them (11-18 year olds). Would this be possible?

Your reply would be most valued on this "Divine Adventure" that the Lord has allowed me to live, I would like to thank you for the special way in which your dedication and spirit with which you work, setting the example with your guidance and teachings.

**God Bless You.**
**Eva Elesa Quiroz**

# joyfully

Eucharist, through the breaking of the bread and the blessing of the cup. We acknowledge the sacrifice of Jesus, "giving thanks with him and through him for his body broken and his blood shed which are given to us as the substance of the Kingdom . . ." "Thus we inaugurate the eternal glorification of God the creator and savior who on the last day will make the Church the panegyria, the festal assembly, in which all of mankind will join in the heavenly worship . . ."[2]

We have heard that in heaven, perhaps, our only "labor" will be one of great love, i.e. to continuously give praise and glorify God. We will be called together for the purpose of high praise. The prayers of the children may be a glimpse of this for us. In the atrium, we present the gesture of the Epiclesis, and we read the prayer to the children which asks the Holy Spirit to "make them (this bread and wine) holy . . . that they may become the body and blood . . . of Jesus Christ." One day when this material had been presented, we gathered at the end of our time together and we sang some songs. One of the songs I use often is a spiritual, "Oh Lord, shout for joy!" The children can easily add their own verses to this, e.g. "For the earth, shout for joy; for the people, shout for joy."! When I asked for verses, a five-year-old boy said, "For the blood." At first, I did not realize what he was saying, and so I repeated it to him. He said, "Yes, for Jesus' blood, shout for joy."

As an adult, this was hard to sing because the association with the blood of Christ first connotes the suffering. In the eyes of the child, this was not so. The "body broken and . . . the blood shed . . .are given to us as the substance of the Kingdom." This is something to shout about! The children who prepare for First Communion also sing, "For the bread, shout for joy; For the wine, shout for joy!"

The children will help us to rekindle our joyfulness. They will help us to learn how to pray. "Blessed are the people who know the festal shout . . ."; blessed are the children.

[1] Louis Bouyer, *Eucharist*, (Notre Dame, 1968), pg. 464.
[2] Ibid. pgs. 464-5.

*This drawing by Susan Schweigert, age 9, of St. Frances Cabrini Atrium, Minneapolis, MN, shows the bread, and a shaft of wheat (lower left), as well as the cup of wine and grapes (lower right). The drawing was done in very bright colors.*

# Catechist formation classes offered at various sites

Due to the great demand for formation of catechists, we would like to make you aware of the following information. The Association is unable to host numerous workshops, but there are many regional and local people working to bring the Catechesis to their own areas.

**South Bend Indiana - Association Sponsored Course**
**July 15-26          3-6 Level, Part 1**

This summer, from July 15th -26th, the Association is sponsoring two courses at St. Mary's College in South Bend, Indiana.

**Rebekah Rojcewicz**, of Hyattsville, Maryland, will direct the catechist formation for the 3-6 level.

Her assistants will be **Betty Hissong**, Cleveland, Ohio, **Linda Kaiel**, Portland, Oregon, **Marilyn Krause**, Alexandria, Virginia, and **Claudia Riordan**, Danville, California.

The 3-6 level has full enrollment.

**South Bend Indiana - Association Sponsored Course**
**July 15-26          6-8 Level, Part 1**

The 6-8 level will be conducted by **Maria Christlieb** of Mexico City, Mexico, and **Carol Dittberner**, St. Paul, Minnesota.

The assistant for this course, **Judy Schmidt**, of Glen Ellyn, Illinois, is currently studying in Rome with Dr. Cavalletti.

**The 6-8 level still has openings.** Contact Jane Scheuermann (202/544-5433) if you would like to attend.

These courses are Part I of each level, with Part II being offered in the summer of 1992.

**Phoenix Arizona - Regionally Sponsored Course**
**June 3-14          3-6 Level, Part I**

**Bert** and **Marty O'Bryan** are again teaching a regional course in Arizona. For more information contact them at 721 West Wilshire Drive, Phoenixx, AZ 85007. (602)-258-9623.

**Pottsville, PA- Regionally Sponsored Course**
**June 14-19          3-6 Level, Part I**

**Carol Nyberg**, of Chicago Illinois and **Rebekah Rojcewicz**, of Hyattsville, Maryland, will be conducting this course.

**Jackson, Mississippi - Regionally Sponsored Course**
**June 17-28          3-6 Level, Part II**

A regional formation experience for Part II of the 3-6 level will be meeting again in Jackson, Mississippi from June 17th-28th. The Episcopal Diocese of Mississippi is sponsoring this course which has had approximately 40 participants.

The instructors are **Cathy Maresca** of Washington, D.C., and **Carol Dittberner**, St. Paul, Minnesota.

**Springfield, Minnesota Workshop**
**July 29-August 9**

A workshop in the catechesis will be held in Springfield, Minnesota from July 29th -August 9th.

During this workshop, **Claudia Riordan**, Danville, California, and **Anna Mae Guida**, of Mt. Pleasant, Pennsylvania, will work with children. Participants will observe the children in an atrium.

For information about this workshop, please contact **Mary Polta**, 112 W. Van Dusen, Springfield, MN, 56087. (507)-723-4727.

**NY Catechists planning 1992 course**

There is a local course in the planning for New York City for this July, a weekend in September, and Part II in the summer of 1992. The instructor will be **Cathy Maresca**. For information, please contact Sr. Lucy Sabatini, (262) 243-1881, at Nazareth Nursery Montessori School.

**Milwaukee planning 1992/1993 courses**

There is also a course in the planning stages for Milwaukee, Wisconsin for the summers of 1992 and 1993. For more information please contact **Kathy Shea**, 2815 South 149th, New Berlin, WI 53151.

The seed that has been entrusted to us is spawning to many parts. Please remember in your prayers our growing catechist community. We thank all those who give of themselves to make these courses happen, and are glad for the growth of our work.

# National Meeting - July 20th

Since a national course is being offered at St. Mary's this summer, we have chosen to hold the Association meeting at that site as well. It will be in the Stapleton Lounge on Saturday, July 20th, from 9:00 A.M. to Noon.

Those not attending the course, who wish to attend the meeting, should contact Jane Scheuermann immediately.

By the time you receive this newsletter, the deadline for reserving housing will have passed. However, if you would really like to attend the meeting, please contact us so we can let you know what other options are available.

Presently the agenda includes: sharing information both amongst individuals and relaying regional information. We will also be discussing some present and future goals, and holding elections to fill three board positions.

At the "Time Apart" meetings in 1988, five board members were elected to three year terms. Last summer, because of board resignations, two new board members were elected and have served for one year. They are Carol Dittberner of St. Paul, Minnesota, and Barbara Searle of Niles, Michigan.

At this time, Tina Lillig, after many years of service to the catechesis, including the last five as service to the membership, had offered her resignation.

Rebekah Rojcewicz, of Hyattsville, Maryland, and Linda Kaiel, of Portland Oregon, end their terms this summer. Both are willing to serve the Catechesis board again if they are chosen.

The election will take place as part of the July meeting. Absentee ballots will be available by mail and *must be requested* from the national office by June 15th, and *returning ballots must be postmarked no later than June 30th.*

Registered members have received election information in a separate mailing.

We ask that those of you who are unable to join us for the annual meeting will keep all of those present in your thoughts and prayers.

---

*During a discussion on the gesture of the cross, Matthew said he saw it in the gesture the priest made (at the offering). He continued, "And that looks like the (branches of) a tree, and that comes from the mustard seed." Later, he drew it. Matthew Brown, age 8, is from St. Frances Cabrini Atrium, Minneapolis, MN.*

# On Taking of Photographs

## by Sofia Cavalletti

We have always been against the taking of photographs during the (eucharistic) celebrations but only now do I think I understand why.

First I thought we should avoid it so as not to disturb the children. But technical progress has overcome that inconvenience: There are now cameras which can be used without a flash, or from considerable distance.

So we should then accept the taking of "pictures" during celebrations?

I say "No!" And for a much more valid reason. The Eucharistic celebration is a very private moment in our relationship with God; it is a moment shared within a community, but also a profoundly personal one, and should be respected as such. Our relationship with God has a nuptial character and any interference whatever in such an intense moment seems to me to be trespassing into that "sanctuary" in which (according to the words of the council) the creature finds him/herself alone with God. It seems to me a violation of the boundaries of the "interior conversation" between Creator and creature.

# Next Newsletter to be Published January 1992
# Next issue to feature First Communion
# Next Deadline: October 1, 1991

Our newsletter was born to be a link of union and communication among the Catechists and friends of **the Catechesis of the Good Shepherd** in different parts of the world. It wants to be the place where we all meet in spite of distance and oceans.

The life of the Newsletter depends on our articles; it is nourished with the news of what each Atrium, each Center of Catechesis lives.

**Do not forget your newsletter.** Send your news, comments, experiences, reflections, dates of First Communions. All is important and interesting. All that you live and experience with the children and adults.

I know there is a lot to share; when we meet one another there is never enough time for telling each other "about our Atrium." Use the Newsletter and share with many, in different countries, the richness you find in your way with God and the child.

We are all busy -- but it is essential for the growth of our organization, for the support of those beginning the Catechesis with the children, and for those who haven't met others of us personally, to share your experiences in this newsletter. So, please take a moment to let us know about your experiences. Call, write, share with us!

**Our next Newsletter will be published in January 1992.**

The deadline for submission of materials is **October 1, 1991**.

We are planning to devote the next issue to First Communion, so please send us stories about your retreats and the children, as well as any special things that occur in your community. Don't forget childrens' artwork, childrens' prayers and photographs of children from your First Communion Experiences. (We can return all photographs to you.)

Please send all Newsletter materials directly to:

**Carol Dittberner
1429 Portland Avenue
St. Paul, MN 55104**

**Staff in U.S.A.**
Carol Dittberner
Rose Paul
Carol Stenborg

| | |
|---|---|
| Italian Translators | Joan Parasene |
| | Nicolina Gleasure |
| Spanish Translators | Kathy Dahl-Bredine, |
| | Margarita Giner |
| | Joan Griffing |

**Staff in Chihuahua:**
Bertha Sofia Quiroz de Marquez
Emilia G. de Sandoval
Noemi F. de Lopez
Maria de Los Angeles Christlieb

## Membership

**The Catechesis of the Good Shepherd,** An Association of Children and Adults, welcomes members throughout the year. Our membership fee is $30. The fees we collect go toward expenses of our four committees: Communications & Finance, Formation, Materials and Newsletter. Members receive the annual newsletter, all mailings and a directory of catechists and friends of the Association. A newsletter subscription only is $5.00 U.S. or $6.00 foreign.

No one should hesitate to join the Association because of the inability to pay the requested $30 fee. We appreciate any donation large or small.

Mail memberships and donations to:

**The Catechesis of the Good Shepherd, Box 218, Mt. Rainier, MD 20712**

# The Catechesis of the Good Shepherd

Number 9, English                                                          Winter 1992/1993

**B**lessed be the Lord, the God of Israel; he has come to his people and set them free.

He has raised up for us a mighty savior, born of the house of his servant David.

Through his holy prophets he promised of old that he would save us from our enemies, from the hands of all who hate us.

He promised to show mercy to our ancestors and to remember his holy covenant.

This was the oath he swore to our father Abraham: to set us free from the hands of our enemies, free to worship him without fear, holy and righteous in his sight all the days of our life.

You, my child, shall be called the prophet of the Most High; for you will go before the Lord to prepare his way, to give his people knowledge of salvation by the forgiveness of their sins.

In the tender compassion of our God the dawn from on high shall break upon us, to shine on those who dwell in darkness and the shadow of death, and to guide our feet into the way of peace.

*Luke 1:68-79*

# Contents

- Let us pray with the Children .................................... 3
- The Mustard Seed is planted in Japan ................... 4-6
- The Montessori Cosmic Vision and the Bible ......... 7-11
- First Communion Dates ........................................... 11
- A visit with Sofia and Jerome .............................. 12-13
- Formation experiences compared ........................... 14
- Sofia reviews Berryman's *Godly Play* .................... 15
- In Memoriam: Mark Searle ................................. 16-17
- from Tanzania: First courses given .......................... 18
- from Argentina: Thanks for the Catechesis ............. 19
- A Story of Hope – The Story of Israel ..................... 20
- Book Review: *Messengers of God* .......................... 21
- Course Announcements ...................................... 22-23
- Books and Tapes for Sale ......................................... 23
- About Our Association ............................................ 24

Dear Friends,

We are pleased to publish the ninth issue of the Catechesis of the Good Shepherd Newsletter. We would like to continue publishing on an annual or semi-annual basis. This newsletter contains major articles, news from catechists, childrens' prayers and artwork. The themes for our next newsletter will be First Communion and Reconciliation. If you have any stories or artwork for this issue, please submit these by the June 30, 1993 deadline.

Another topic we will be addressing in a future issue is material-making. We welcome articles and photos on this topic as well.

Some of you have been receiving a briefer newsletter called *Gathered Grain*. Millicent Dosh has been publishing this since 1988 and will soon be producing a final issue. We want to thank Millie for her work and for keeping us connected.

Please continue to send your articles, children's prayers, etc. to:

**Carol Dittberner**
**1429 Portland**
**St. Paul, MN 55104**

Our wishes for love and peace to each of you in 1993.

*Drawing by Matthew Hanson, age 11, St. Phillip's Episcopal Church, Jackson, MS.*

# Let us pray with the Children . . .

*The following prayer was written on Christmas day, by Amy Smith, age 9, New Zealand.*

Listen to all the lambs and Sheep calling for Jesus Christ the best Shepherd who ever lived the loving Shepherd that looked for his lamb if it got lost.

So Christmas is powerful, powerful, by the glory of the lost lamb and being found –

by angels singing - God loving - people sharing and Jesus keeping Christmas joyful for ever and ever.

---

*The following prayers were prepared by a group of elementary school children for their prayer service.*

| | |
|---|---|
| Response: | Lord bless our prayers |
| Alissa: | for the homeless and the hungry, we pray to the Lord. |
| Anna: | for the Twins that they may win the World Series, we pray to the Lord. |
| Erin: | for our brothers and sisters, we pray to the Lord. |
| Briana: | for the people closest to us, we pray to the Lord. |
| Maria: | for the people who have died for their faith, we pray to the Lord. |
| Brendan: | for our pets at home, we pray to the Lord. |
| Christina: | for creatures everywhere, we pray to the Lord. |
| Kata: | for the world and its people, we pray to the Lord. |
| Analisa: | for all people and living things everywhere that they may live under the arms of Christ, we pray to the Lord. |

---

*from Mexico, a child, age 6, wrote:*

Jesus, I love you very much.
I hope that your sheep (sic).
You are the best
Thank you for all you have given me: water, bread, cheese, soup, rice, beans.
Virgin Mary, I love you very much I hope.

**Diedre's Prayers** (age 6)

I love you God.

Thank you for this food.

Thank you for Mom and Dad and Eleanor.

Thank you God.

I pray for poor people. Amen

And people that are hurt.

**Supper**: Thank you God for the food we're eating tonight. Thank you God.

**Bedtime**: Thank you for this Day. Make tomorrow another day that's nice, please God.

**Supper**: Thank you for the supper we're having. Hope it will be good, please God.

---

*From Cristina, age 6 ½ Rome:*

"At night I tell him the beautiful things of the day."

*This prayer card by Silvia Giannone, 9-12 atrium, Via degli Orsini, Rome, reads: "We praise your coming. We acclaim the rock of our salvation." The Hebrew letters on the rock are "Yahweh."*

# The Mustard Seed is Planted in Japan

*by Patricia Coulter*

*Editor's Note: During the summer of 1991, the Association Montessori Internationale (AMI) held an international conference in Japan. Sofia Cavalletti was invited to speak and prepared a talk called "The Montessori Cosmic Vision and the Bible." Sofia was unable to attend the conference and asked Patricia Coulter to present the speech in her place. Patricia is a catechist in Toronto and translator (with Julie Coulter) of* **The Religious Potential of the Child.** *These are Patricia's reflections about her experience in Japan (as written in a letter to Sofia).*

Now we are at the eve of the talk, which was to take place at 9:00 am the following morning. Up to that point, I had been reflecting on Monday's readings for the feast of Mary Magdalene. The impact of the fact that Jesus had chosen her to be the first to "go and tell" the Good News of his rising really touched me then. For my part, though, I felt so poor a "messenger," particularly in light of the fact that I was here to offer a Christian proclamation in a country where only one percent of its people are Christian, formed in a "Western" culture but given in a culture that was not Western, to a group of people coming from so many varied religious backgrounds and traditions in which I was in an obvious minority.

Then, as I wrote you, I turned to the readings for that day: "We are the earthenware jars that hold treasure...." Time to turn in trust to the Message itself, to believe in its power even in such a 'challenging' context as this.

Being there made me appreciate more the openness, perhaps courage, of Maria Matsumoto and the Congress to make room for a specifically religious subject. And I appreciated more, given the range of religions represented there and the often-contested topic of spirituality—particularly such an "incarnated" one as ours—, the welcome of the international Montessori community to communicate your reflections. Unusual to say the least.

**Though wanting to trust, it was a wakeful night.**

Phrases from your talk would run through my head: "...instruments that Western tradition, contained in the Bible, offers us." What can that mean for non-Western ears? "In our Judeo-Christian culture we have a fundamental book, the Bible...." How does that sound to those whose spirituality flows from other streams?

Thoughts like these came from the brief but intense exposure to such a plurality of visions and belief systems.

New horizons had opened and the Message appeared in a different light. And when morning came, so did another sort of light, if I can call it that.

**How to describe it?** It "felt" like joy. While I walked from the hotel to the mini-bus waiting for us I became, unexpectedly, happy. Not the euphoria that comes from "it will soon be over and what a relief that will be," but the sense that something so-long-waiting to be born was about to "come forth." And not that "I" was doing it, as your representative, nor even that you were doing it, in the writing of those words; the time had come for the Message itself. Maybe it was a realization that, in itself, it has power. You had put so many words of scripture into the address, and the 'timelines' were a testimony to the Bible lived in liturgy and life; now I was aware that it was those words which were meant to be said here.

**When it began, Sofia, peace came and the rest went away.** A dear friend, Sister Olga, directs me to depend on "the manna" that is promised to be given each day, and is given in a way that meets that day's needs. So it was,

*Drawing by Becca Anderson, age 11, Guadalupe Montessori School, Silver City, NM.*

and then some. It can only matter to me that I felt a gentle strength, strong enough—if I may use the reference to Magdalene, to drive out the "demons" and give me a personal experience of the power, living and active, in God's presence through the Word.

What I had not given any thought to was if or how it would call forth a personal response on the part of the listeners. So I was unprepared for those who came up to me that day and the following—the last of the Congress—to speak of their own traditions or to share about their own situations at home or school or parish.

This was the most moving aspect of the whole Japanese adventure, and the time when I missed you most because you were often asked for and about, and also because what you said echoed in their hearts. All the same, I was so touched and I will tell you a couple of the exchanges. In that sense an "extra session" was given, and more than one.

Some of the people did not speak English but they conveyed a mutual understanding whether by a smile and gracious bow, a small token or gift (usually representing their culture), or just tears. At the reception held that evening, for example, Esther Takanohashi said that a Japanese woman who was Christian had been very moved to tears in fact. I went to meet her and we looked at each other, bowed towards each other, both with tears in our eyes (her simplicity and transparency were that touching to me). Or a Taiwanese trio came who were evidently communicating appreciation for the Message but, since we hadn't a verbal language, one offered, as all she had then, a coin. It was a genuine gesture much like a child will do. Or a woman from Korea who is a minister in the Presbyterian community there; two Montessori directresses from a school in New Delhi who wanted advice on how to introduce some religious influence in their school of "six religions", Hindu and Buddhist among them; a priest from Spain who is a missionary in Japan; the Montessorians from India who wanted a copy of your talk; a Japanese professor of philosophy studying in Germany; and, so many who indicated an appreciation for the overall theme "though I am not Christian." The reverence for the religious reality, regardless of the specific "differences," went beyond notions about "ecumenism," into a deeper level about the need for, and meaning of hope for, children in our civilization as a universal concern. In some way, there appeared a recognition and respect for this reality that is not so clear in our own Christian culture, but this may be due to the fact that the "Montessori vision" incorporates the dimension of the human spirit and its potentials and most people participating there valued that vision.

Four Japanese women came up to me the night of the reception. They are all mothers with young and older children, some of whom are in the same school in Tokyo. Yoko, who acted as interpreter for us, explained that the night before (the talk) they had been talking about the present state of affairs in the world generally and wondering where it is all heading and what to tell their children that would offer them some true hope about the future. The talk, she said on her own and their behalf, answered that question they had been worrying over. They wanted to know more concretely about the catechesis and, as they were leaving to go home at midday tomorrow, we set up a sort of meeting time before 9:00 am. It lasted until we were called away about two hours later. Maybe the plentiful programme and the intensity that

> The reverence for the religious reality, regardless of the specific "differences," went beyond notions about "ecumenism," into a deeper level about the need for, and meaning of hope for, children in our civilization as a universal concern.

can engender accounted for some of the earnestness of our dialogue together; I can't say for sure. Yet, the five of us sat there, looking out onto the lush green surroundings: they spoke of their longing, for themselves and their children with a simplicity of spirit that recalled the atrium atmosphere, if you know what I mean. I brought along the booklets describing the catechesis and highlighted some aspects, all new to them, as they questioned about certain points. All four had some knowledge of English, but Yoko elaborated when asked, either by them or myself, with a sort of "ah" resonance in them. One said in Japanese when she saw the cover picture of the American booklet: "Tell her that my son loves the Good Shepherd." Eager to know more, they asked about books, courses, help of some kind, any kind: "Tonight I will tell my daughter what I have heard." It is not easy to convey the deep and immediate rapport established in a brief time. "What is your motivation for doing this?" one mother asked me. How is that for a searching question?

Shared hunger creates bonds. It made me think of Weil's comment which, at the risk of misquoting, goes something like: "They may tell me there is no bread, but they cannot tell me I'm not hungry."[1]

*continued on next page*

## The Mustard Seed is Planted in Japan, *continued*

There is much more to say, but I've told you what—for me—is most significant. There was a reception one evening that became a celebration of different cultures with spontaneous songs from different countries, beautiful costumes worn by people from different nations, and opportunity for more exchanges among us. The closing ceremony ended with everyone in the auditorium linking hands while a poignant Japanese song was sung and translated for us. The goodbyes were tearful.

As I prepared to leave, Reiko, who had been so helpful and assisted me during the talk (moving the microphone, etc.), took off a pendant she was wearing and gave it to me. Earlier we had spoken of our backgrounds and although she is "not baptized" as she said, there seemed a particular openness in her to the theme of the talk. As she gave it to me, I realized it was a single, beautiful pearl. What a symbol of the whole experience, and I tried to tell her about the parable but time ran out.

On Monday, Maria Matsumoto took Renilde Montessori and me to Osaka airport. Since it is a two-hour drive, it gave me the chance to know her better. The day before, Mary Hayes and I had attended Mass in a nearby church; taking off our shoes (they have cubby-holes containing slippers by the entrance), we went in and were offered a Mass book, with English, Latin, Japanese in Roman letters, and in Japanese characters. There, those graceful gestures common to the Japanese become explicit gestures of prayers. The song, too, seemed gentle, not unlike—to my ears—a form of melodic chant. I wondered: if in a country of over 150 million, only one percent are Christian, then how many are Catholic? Those gathered were so present to the Eucharistic action, so reverent in their demeanor, as if this were not something to be taken for granted. It seemed more painful to hear, as Maria Matsumoto mentioned in passing during our conversation of many topics, that Hiroshima and Nagasaki—targets for the atomic bombs—were predominately "Catholic" cities. I can't remember her following words exactly, but they were to the effect that perhaps the Lord had allowed them to suffer for their people. The Montessori Method started to really take root after the war. Maria Matsumoto explained that after the devastation the war had wrought, the way it had dispirited the people, the Montessori vision of education represented a "little flame" of hope for the future, and the children who are its chief creators.

All the "trappings" of the Congress, the superb organization, the presence of dignitaries local and foreign, the painstaking preparations for adequate communication systems there — were all a tribute to that attitude towards education and the immense value of the child. It was an eloquent testimony.

Attending the various talks, covering all the ages of development from birth to adulthood, reaffirmed my conviction that the Montessori approach offers a profound pedagogical basis based on the enduring nature of the human spirit and the still unmeasured potential of its spirit.

Listening is the "key" in the religious formation of the child. That question of many years ago surfaced again; what about the child as a religious person? How can we help the child's life grow in that dimension? Of course it was that question that drew me to St. Paul in the summer of 1975, and I was inwardly happy to have come to know what I have since that time through the "catechesis" as it has since been named. The gratitude for these intervening years spent with children and adults is something that deserves savoring.

Sofia, this has taken more than a day and more than one cup of coffee to write. I hope it tells you some of the background. Sitting here, I think the overall impression personally was the surprise that individuals came and exchanged with me their own "spirituality," their own search to help children in this vein; that seemed, and seems still something gratuitous. Maybe it is a little like being allowed to have a glimpse, as you say, into the way God establishes and celebrates his covenant with the child. To be given an opportunity to witness that is not something one can necessarily expect; it comes, if it does, simply as a gift.

I told you that when working on your address, I found I needed to participate in its theme: that we need vast horizons that place personal interests and immediate concerns in a broader perspective, so as to be summoned forth into a space where one's "true stature" is discovered, where one experiences the "dignity of being a collaborator." Of course, I believe that for the child. But the richness of this catechesis is that in consenting to offer the Message to children or adults, we too put ourselves in the position of being touched by the same truth and feel the desire (is it any less strong than the child's?) to be transformed by its power.

I will send some of the memorabilia from the Congress soon. For the moment, the story is told. If anything here strikes you as suitable for the Newsletter, do feel free to edit as you wish. Finally, thank you for the invitation to go to Japan and all that it meant.

---

[1]"Here below we must be content to be eternally hungry; indeed, we must welcome hunger, for it is the sole proof we have of the reality of God who is the only sustenance that can satisfy us, but one which is 'absent' in the created world. 'The danger is not lest the soul should doubt whether there is any bread (God), but lest, by a lie, it should persuade itself that it is not hungry. It can only persuade itself of this by lying, for the reality of hunger is not a belief, it is a certainty'."

Weil, Simone, ***Waiting for God***, (New York: Harper Colophone Books, 1973), pg. 35.

# The Montessori Cosmic Vision and the Bible

*by Sofia Cavalletti*
*presented at the AMI conference, Japan, 1991,*
*and translated by Patricia M. Coulter.*

There is a well-known page in Maria Montessori's book, *The Formation of Man* (Kalakshetra Publication, 1975, p. 37) where she speaks of "expansive education." Montessori saw the necessity for an education which is not centered on "direct correction" because "correction is possible only by expansion, by giving 'space,' by opening up the means for the expansion of the personality."

Dr. Montessori speaks of the need to broaden the horizons so that the older child can be drawn towards higher goals. "Only the poor quarrel over a piece of bread." The human creature is anything but "poor". And the young and older child need to be helped to the journey in the spaciousness of vast horizons. Thus only an education which "amplifies" will carry the individual beyond immediate interests and lead that person towards one's true stature.

The expression "expansive education" coined by Montessori has a particularly prophetic resonance for us today, living as we do in a time of the "expansion" of the world. It is therefore even more urgent that Montessori's concept be realized in our own age.

I would like to describe what we do with children between the ages of six and twelve in relation to Montessori's vision, using the instruments that Western tradition, contained in the Bible, offers us.

In our Judeo-Christian world, as many know, we have a fundamental book, the Bible, a book whose redaction has taken more than a thousand years, gathering together traditions dating back some four thousand years.

Obviously it is difficult, or rather impossible, to give a summary idea of the content of a book such as this. I will risk limiting what I say to a single theme: the Bible tells a history that originates in primordial times, includes the moment we are living, and is oriented towards a future conclusion, which we await. It is a history made of memory and hope; between these two poles is poised the now moment. It is a history which starts with the beginning of time and concludes—but does not end—when the plan which is being realized in it comes to completion. It is a history with a clear orientation whose single stages are linked together by a "golden thread," the thought of God. God desires to lead men, women and all created things to reach the fullness of life in a relationship with one another and himself, a relationship that the Book calls "covenant." The biblical covenant is all-inclusive, a covenant that embraces both time and space, although time is the prevalent category in the biblical world.

The first page of the Bible tells of the creation of the world. The Creator places man who is his "image and likeness" in the world in order to care for and work in the world, that is, so that man and woman may enjoy all the elements of creation, and preserve and develop them.

If we pass directly from the first to the final book of the Bible, called Revelation, we read about the renewal of creation described as "a new heaven and a new earth"; about a new presence of God in the world, and the victory of the negative forces of suffering and death.

> Here God lives among men. He will make his home among them; they shall be his people and he will be their God; his name is "God-with-them." He will wipe

*continued on next page*

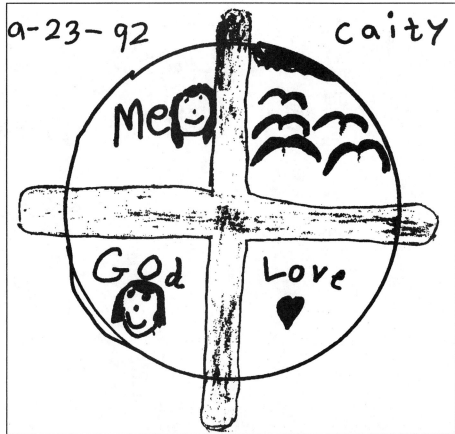

*The cross extending over the earth is the symbol of the Parousia used in the Atrium. Drawing by Caitlin Cain, age 6, Good Shepherd Center, St. Paul, MN.*

## The Montessori Cosmic Vision and the Bible, continued

away all tears from their eyes; there will be no more death, no more mourning or sadness. The world of the past has gone." (Rev. 21ff)

Other biblical passages, written in highly poetic language, speak about the cessation of all war: people

"will hammer their swords into plowshares, their spears into sickles; nation will not lift sword against nation, there will be no more training for war." (Is. 2:4)

They speak, moreover, of a time when harmony will reign between people and animals, a time when

"the wolf lives with the lamb; the panther lies down with the kid; calf and lion cub feed together, with a little child to lead them" (Is. 11:6)

Though my brief sketch hardly does justice to it, this is the vision of reality the Bible presents.

*How can we help children to enter into this vision and to enjoy its message?*

The elements are plentiful and immense in their scope. In presenting them to children, we have followed the Montessori principle of "isolating the difficulties." In this instance, we could paraphrase it as "isolating the various aspects of the covenant."

*The first aspect is the unity and globality of the history the Bible narrates.* It is a history that includes all time and all creation. When the first page of the Bible tells of *adam*, meaning the human being, it is speaking about the whole of humanity. When we turn again to the final book of the Bible, we read that God will make "all things new," that there will be a cosmic chorus of praise to God composed of

"all the living things in creation—everything that lives in the air, and on the ground, and under the ground, and in the sea." (Rev. 5:13)

Certainly it is not easy for children to embrace such a vast framework. They need, therefore, to be helped by means of tools which strike the imagination and provide incentives for activity so that gradually they will be able to absorb the message—the well-known function of the material.

### La Fettuccia — The Time Line

To give an example, we will describe the first presentation we offer to children on this theme, one which is designed

*Drawing by Joseph Kosowski, age 6 ½, St. Frances Cabrini, Minneapolis, MN. When Joseph drew the ribbon, he enclosed the white section in yellow. This speaks to Sofia's remarks about educating children about hope. Joseph wrote the words "White is the best part," around his drawing several times. See above, **La Fettuccia** for a description of the ribbon.*

precisely to capture the child's imagination. This material consists of a long (gross grain) ribbon 50 meters in length; each rib represents a time span of one thousand years (obviously the proportions are approximate).

The ribbon is in four colors. The first part is blue, representing the period when the inorganic world was formed. This is followed by a beige section, representing the period which begins with the appearance of vegetation on the earth. Further along the beige part of the ribbon, there are figures to mark the appearance of man—hominid and *homo sapiens*. This latter figure is accompanied by the image of a hand to illustrate that we are referring to the human person who begins to transform the world by the work of his hands. The beige is followed by two ribs that are yellow—the color of light—representing approximately two thousand years from the time of the coming of Jesus Christ to the present. The last segment of the ribbon is colored white, indicating the time from tomorrow onwards, that is, the page of history that is still yet to be written. This white segment ends with a yellow fringe. The fringe is to illustrate that we do not know when history will be concluded with the full establishment of the kingdom of God. Yellow, the color of light, is to illustrate that light will overpower darkness, the positive will overcome the negative.

## What are we saying in this presentation?

If it is permissible to express it this way, we are giving the "measure" of God and the human creature: since the beginning of history God is always present in this age-old process of development, a process in which we are immersed and whose fulfillment we await; the human creature is small and great at the same time. What does the life of a single person represent compared to the vast sea of history? What does it represent in the immensity of a plan that embraces all time and space? And yet the human person is an integral part of that sea, a crucial collaborator in that plan. The great history is also my history. It is the history of each one of us. Each one of us is present in it and in some way contributes to it.

A vision of this kind corresponds, I believe, to a fundamental need in the child after six years of age because this is the age when the world begins to open up for the child. It is essential to help older children to orient themselves in this "ever expanding" horizon so that they know how to walk ahead, drawn forward by the grandeur of a reality in which they are conferred the dignity of a collaborator.

*Drawing by Andria, Cleveland, OH.*

**This presentation leads us to ask ourselves another question: What must each of us *do* in history?** We remain faithful to the principle of isolating the points to be presented, and this question of "doing" follows as a second moment. Furthermore, we are convinced that *before* any emphasis on the plane of "doing," and thus of responsibility, first there is a time for *enjoyment*. The first plane—enjoyment—will later be expressed on the level of doing as well; the time for enjoyment must precede and accompany every action (and we shall return to this later).

We mentioned that the message of the Bible is made of memory and hope. This presentation recalls the mighty creative works God does for the human creature (a point emphasized in a subsequent presentation), and at the same time it offers a message of hope. The history we are living is not a succession of disconnected events; it is the realization of a plan which will have a positive conclusion. As we said earlier, we are awaiting a time of universal peace, a time when even death, the "last enemy," will be vanquished (1 Cor. 15:26). This is the hope held by Jews and Christians alike, which is to say the hope of those who belong to two branches of the biblical tradition. **This perspective of history certainly does not mean that we ignore the many contradictions encountered in life's journey, but Jews and Christians hope and know that the outcome of history is positive**.

*continued on next page*

# The Montessori Cosmic Vision and the Bible, continued

I believe this is the biblical value most needed in our modern day world. Theology speaks of three fundamental "virtues": faith, hope and charity, which are three modes of being, three ways of approaching and relating to reality. Today everyone talks about love (even if we are not always able to actualize it). Many speak about faith; witness the numerous spiritualistic movements making vigorous inroads in a materialistic world. Very few speak about hope. In fact, most often we are presented with a rather pessimistic vision, where life is viewed in terms of its negative elements. The negative is surely present, but that is not all there is to reality.

Seeing the darkness in our history is a manifestation of a new sensibility, attentive to injustices, a "darkness" to which the world that preceded us was blind. The error resides in focusing on the darkness and the pre-eminent and inevitable reality. Darkness itself can be blinding. To fix our gaze solely on it can prevent us from seeing the shafts of light reality reveals and thus prevents us from beholding life with eyes of hope.

**We must educate children to open their eyes to the positive elements in reality, not to encourage illusions, but to enable them to see the whole of reality.** Education is to help create persons who are capable of looking beyond the surface agitation of the waves, so as to catch sight of the current flowing deep beneath the movements of history.

It should be noted that we are not dealing with the progressive vision of modern thought, which post-modern thought rejects. We are speaking about the capacity of knowing how to catch hold of the positive, along with the negative, in the certainty that the positive will prevail. In the Judaic tradition, this certainty is based on the Word of God that flows like a promise throughout the whole course of history. In the Christian tradition, this certainty is founded not only on the Word, but on the event as well: the event of the resurrection of Jesus Christ. Christians await the victory of light over darkness, of life over death, because this has already begun to happen in the person of Jesus Christ who, in his resurrection, has attained the fullness of life. In him this has already happened as the "first fruits" (1 Cor. 15:20), that is, as the first step that others will follow.

**After the presentation we have just described, we highlight another aspect of the biblical message: in this great adventure of history in which humanity is involved, it is God who takes the initiative.** The covenant relationship presupposes two partners; however, one must take the first step. And in the Bible, the one who takes the first step is God.

*Andrea of Guadalupe Montessori School, Silver City, NM, wrote this prayer, and created a decorative border for it.*

"God in search of man," writes Abraham Heschel. The God of the Bible is a God who gives. The God of the Bible is a God who prepares an environment for human creatures, puts into our hands a world rich with everything necessary to live as well as beautiful things for us to enjoy, fills it with people to live and share our lives with, and even gives us his very self in the person of Jesus Christ, the gift that is meant to bring fullness of life to the entire cosmos.

The title of this material is "The History of the Gifts." Once again this is designed to help children experience the moment when the message is enjoyed. The dimension of "gift" stressed here is offered primarily to help children enjoy all that has been given and, in going beyond the gifts, to enjoy the love of the Giver. Moreover, "gift" is an eminently dynamic element: precisely because it is gratuitous, gift calls forth a response, but in an indirect way. Again, it is important to note the moral dimension is only approached in an indirect manner and at a later moment. Actually, the impact of this presentation—its power to evoke the child's personal response—is all the more valid and compelling to the degree that we do not spoil the time for enjoying the message by an untimely intrusion of the moral dimension.

**Now we come to the third aspect of history we propose to older children. We mentioned early that biblical history has a clear orientation, a history within which a plan is being realized. What kind of plan?**

The material we will show indicates some of the acquisitions that humanity has brought about across centuries and millennia, which we still enjoy today.

For this presentation, we have made use of one of Montessori's historical materials, familiar to many of you; however, we emphasize a particular aspect.

**The message of this presentation is quite obvious, yet we will try to encapsulate it in a few points.**

At various levels within the history we are living, there is a plan being actualized—with enormous difficulties, resistances, contradictions—a plan for communion that encompasses heaven and earth. This would seem to be the plan of God: this is what the Bible calls "covenant." This plan meets with so many obstacles. Nevertheless, to return to our previous analogy, the development of history is like a river. There are ripples, whirlpools, and eddies, but there is a deep current underneath which—despite everything—flows slowly along its course until it reaches the sea.

**The first and fundamental aim of this presentation is, yet again, to proclaim the message, to offer an orientation towards reality.**

All of us here recognize that the purpose of education is to make known the "workings" of reality so that the person can enter into and live it. This is the principal aim of the human learning process and of every educational undertaking.

Once we know the inner "workings"—even if only approximately—we need to live in the light of that knowledge. How?

And this is the second aim of this presentation: if this is the movement of history, if this is the plan of God, if we are living in a reality whose most intimate meaning is the creation of a cosmic communion embracing the whole of humanity and creation in their entirety—how do I become a part of it? How can I align myself with this reality so as to be able to live it fully? How can I foster its growth so that it develops and comes to fulfillment?

Therefore we can see that human action is woven into the framework of a plan that enfolds heaven and earth together in a cosmic communion. In the context of this plan, I can offer my own support and contribution, but I can also hinder or delay its growth.

Anything that creates peace is according to the movement of history and the plan of God; anything that makes for division and generates war is contrary to the movement of history and the plan of God.

And so, this presentation contains a profoundly evocative moral dimension, although it is secondary with respect to the proclamation of the message itself. Its moral evocation is all the more powerful insofar as it sounds the depths of a plan of such grandeur, a plan that calls forth our own personal involvement.

I believe that here we have an example of that "expansive education" which Maria Montessori spoke of so effectively.

## First Communion Dates

It is our custom to list the dates of First Communion so that all of us, as a community, will keep the children and catechists in our prayers during their retreats and celebrations of Eucharist.

| | |
|---|---|
| April 18 | Good Shepherd Center St. Paul, MN |
| April 25 | St. Frances Cabrini Minneapolis, MN |
| May 1 | Mexico City |
| May 2 | Via degli Orsini Rome, Italy |
| | St. Giles Community Chicago, IL |

*We ask you to send us dates for First Communion, as well as relevant artwork, pictures and articles.*

# A visit with Sofia and Jerome

*by Carol Dittberner*

The Association asked Sofia Cavalletti and Jerome Berryman to provide further clarification of their work. Providentially, I was in Rome in November of 1991 while Jerome was also visiting Sofia. We had some very good discussions in Sofia's study. I would like to highlight here some of the points which were made. However, it is difficult to discuss here the depth of their work in such a brief article.

Sofia and Jerome stressed that they both consider their work as experimental and not yet finished. They both seek ways to help the religious presence in the child, and have followed the child as a guide during their years of observation and research. Once, Maria Montessori, pointing toward a child, said, "Do not look to me, the one who is pointing, but to whom I am pointing." Sofia and Jerome also work from this premise.

Each of them brings a wealth of experience and research to their work. Sofia's background is in Hebrew and biblical studies, theology, and Jewish-Christian relations. She has worked with children since 1954. Gianna Gobbi, her collaborator, brings the Montessori expertise in the development of the materials.

Jerome is an Episcopal priest, and, in addition to divinity studies, also has degrees in history, literature, law, and Montessori education. He is a member of the Family Law Section of the American Bar Association. He has also spent many years working with children who are hospitalized or in crisis. Jerome met Sofia in 1971 in Bergamo, Italy, while taking the elementary Montessori Training. He later studied with her when she began giving courses in the United States. Through his own research and observations of children, Jerome developed the Worship Center, a special place for children to work and pray.

**The Worship Center and the Atrium have some similarities and some differences.** Some catechists have studied both approaches, but we have received requests to give a clearer picture of what these similarities and differences are. Both the Worship Center and the Atrium follow the principles of the Montessori Method; they provide an environment which has been especially prepared for the religious life of the child. Both provide an atmosphere of recollection which can lead to meditation and prayer. Concrete materials are used to aid the child's work.

**Sofia and Jerome saw the differences in their approaches mainly on the practical level, not the doctrinal content level.** Sofia added that there could be many ways to aid the child's spiritual life; these are only two.

Sofia and Jerome have developed the presentations given to children according to the age and developmental needs of the child. At the preschool level they both give the following parables: The Good Shepherd, The Mustard Seed, The Precious Pearl and The Leaven. Sofia also gives The Corn Seed and The Hidden Treasure. Jerome includes The Sower and The Good Samaritan.

**One of the differences in their approaches regards the works with the Old Testament.** Jerome begins Old Testament scriptures with children from the age of three years. He focuses on the most important events and uses a larger quantity of texts. Sofia feels that children need to possess a greater knowledge of time and historical perspective before introducing the Old Testament. She begins with children at age six and introduces the Bible as one global history of salvation. She emphasizes the unity of our history, and focuses on the moments of Creation, Redemption, and Parousia. The study of scripture is then related to each of these moments.

In Liturgy presentations, Jerome has worked with a wide variety of denominations and so presents here a global view which includes Holy Eucharist and Baptism. He stresses principles which will aid the catechists in the development of materials based on the child's denomination.

The Atrium materials for Liturgy are very detailed and include the language of gestures; there is a special focus on the Mass, Baptism, and the preparation for Reconciliation. However, the Liturgy materials are also open to ecumenical adaptation, and are being used in the Byzantine Rite, the Episcopal and Lutheran denominations.

Another area we discussed was the structure of the children's meetings. In the Atrium, Sofia has recommended two hours as the ideal amount of time which allows the children sufficient personal work time. Also included during this time would be presentations by the catechist, community and/or individual prayer. Jerome has modeled the Worship Center structure to more closely resemble the Eucharist. Children begin with a presentation (the proclamation of the Word), then have personal work time, and end each meeting with a "feast." The feast is a sharing of food together.

The amount of time any catechist can schedule for children varies greatly, depending upon worship schedules, Sunday morning church School, and so on. Some people are able to schedule the time for children during the week which allows it to be a longer time. Montessori always stressed that it is during the child's personal work time that the greatest development and concentration occurs. Sofia and Jerome both value this time for the children. If the meeting time is short, perhaps some weeks it is advisable to hold back on a new presentation so that the children are able to really work with the materials. Through their work comes their prayer.

**One of the differences between the Worship Center and the Atrium is the materials themselves.** Although some of the presentations are the same, Jerome has developed simpler versions of the materials made out of felt. This especially pertains to the parable materials which, in the Atrium, are made from wood. The felt materials have enabled the Worship Center model to be adopted easily in many churches. The Liturgy materials are similar in both settings, each being made child-sized and used as models to introduce the articles of Eucharist and Baptism.

**In both of these methods, adult formation is required.** This is a change from some of the traditional approaches in which catechists have simply been given a guide to work from in planning their weekly lessons. Catechist Holly Huisken has taken both formation experiences, and gives her own evaluation in the next article.

**I would like to add here one of my own observations about this work.**

In my work with adults, I have heard and experienced many stories about how this Catechesis has touched adults as well as children. With adults, there has been a deepening of faith, sometimes a transformation of spirit, and sometimes great healing. This comes from presentations given in the Worship Center and the Atrium, whether the materials were made from wood or from felt. The gift in this Catechesis is the way in which we meditate on the Word; it is in the questions that are asked, the reflections that are shared, and, most especially, in the silence we are called to.

It was a privilege for me to be in Rome and to share in this conversation between two friends and colleagues. Through the work of these two very special and gifted people, we have seen the recognition of the child's spiritual nature, and the growth, in a few short years, of many, many environments that truly serve the child who says, "Help me to come closer to God by myself."

*Drawing by Charlie Pate, age 7, Christ Church Episcopal Atrium, Nashville, TN.*

# Formation experiences reviewed

*by Holly Huisken*

In reviewing a former newsletter, I see that I promised to report back on my experiences at the Children and Worship training workshop.

The workshop is much more affordable than a Catechesis formation course. Two of us attended for $250.00 and the cost of one night in a hotel room. Additional church members were $50.00, and churches which had previously attended a training paid only $50.00 per person. Of course, the experience is completely different, as implied in the terms "formation" and "workshop."

The workshop sessions ran for two and a half full days (8:30 a.m.-9:00 p.m.), with some individual work time and meal and snack breaks. Food was not included in the price, but we all went home with a copy of *Young Children and Worship* by Sonya Stewart and Jerome Berryman, a packet of music and other materials, and a parable box which we had made during the workshop. There were a few lectures, but presentations of the stories in the Stewart/Berryman book comprised the bulk of the workshop.

The stories begin with Creation and follow some of the main Old and New Testament themes, as well as a baptism presentation. Parables are made one-dimensional, usually consisting of felt figures and laminated pictures, and are kept in gold-wrapped boxes on the "parable shelves."

In many ways, the "worship center" approach is different from the atrium. It is tempting to be able to bring parents or pastors into a room and say, "Look, here is a time line. We move from the Old Testament to the New. We follow the same general order of worship as the congregation. This is a special place for the children to be with God."

There is a certain mystery in the parable boxes, and enjoyment of learning God's stories through the materials. A catechist in a Worship Center would not be quizzed, "What does bean pouring have to do with Sunday School?"

Yet, "Children and Worship" lacks the wonderful mystery we experience in the atrium in the preparation of the chalice or seeing the yeast increase the flour. It includes a prayer corner, but lacks the invitation to prayer and meditation present in the altar presentations and work.

"Children and Worship" provides more structure for the time children spend in the worship center. Children are given time to "work" within this structure, which generally follows the order of worship of the congregation. This structure, the relative ease of preparing materials, and the fact that the curriculum is written down with lesson plans are other tempting aspects of this program.

The training itself was not as well organized as even the compacted sessions I have experienced in the Catechesis. If I had not had previous training, I think I would have been confused. As it is, I still do not have a clear sense of the **order of the Worship Center** because the presentations were given one after another and were rarely placed in context. There was a session with children that did follow the Worship Center order, which gave us a picture of the way a center would work.

Another drawback is that most of the presentations were given without background or enriching information. I appreciate the philosophy in the Catechesis of filling ourselves up so that our presentations will be richer as we give them to the children. We were encouraged to do further reading and research in one of the brief lectures, but it was not stressed.

In many ways, the underlying philosophies of the Catechesis of the Good Shepherd and the Worship Center approach differ. There are elements of each that recommend themselves. Churches and catechists must decide which program best fits their needs and goals.

*Drawing by Erin Bettendorf, age 7, St. Frances Cabrini, Minneapolis, MN.*

# Sofia reviews Berryman's *Godly Play*

*by Sofia Cavalletti*
*translated by Nicolina Gleasure and Joan Parasine*

It is a true joy to find a book which displays the religious capabilities of a child. There are many books for children written by adults. However, it is quite rare to find an author who explores the relationship between a child and God; one where the child is an important religious subject.

One such author is our friend Jerome Berryman, author of the book *Godly Play*.

**The joyful aspect of a relationship with God is stressed in the expression "Divine play."** Within a roughly authoritarian formation, with feelings tinged by fear and guilt which darken and distort, this aspect is lost. This is an "omnicomprehensive" game where the "players" are God, ourselves, others and nature. All of these elements interact and awaken us to new ways of seeing ourselves and reality, and our involvement in it. The fundamental rule of the "game" is that it is played for its own sake, without looking for a set, limited goal. It must be played for its own sake, for the pleasure of playing, without ulterior motives which could hinder its enjoyment.

That which Jerome recounts in this book is the result of his prolonged work with children. (This idea which was born during his attendance at the Bergamo Montessori course, of which we have so often spoken; and in particular, during the 1978 course in Houston which he organized and attended.) He is responsible for religious education at the Houston Medical Center, where he has been assisted by psychologists, child psychiatrists, medical doctors, social workers and pastoral ministers.

Since Jerome has often times referred to our work in the most flattering terms (for which I wish to thank him), it is my pleasure to state that the point at which his work and ours is closet is in the observation that the child's relationship with God is of the highest quality. The same quality as that of the gift God grants his creatures; the same quality as love. It is a relationship which precedes the so-called age of reason, and which expresses itself in a particular joy and a profound satisfaction of the entire individual.

It is obvious that Berryman's approach allows for his methodology and the corresponding tools for practical application, which examine instruction/formation through time, space and persons, particularly described in Chapter 5. However, that which we wish to stress here is the fundamental thesis of the book: Jerome states, "be children if you wish to mature into adults … join the divine game with imagination, awe and laughter if you wish to become new without end." (page 17)

The "divine game" in fact liberates creativity, that process which is present in the creator, "who renews all things," and in every creature who lives the life of love (p. 156). The "divine game" is to embark upon an adventure without knowing how it will unfold; it is leaving for an unknown land, like Abraham, just gazing at the stars.

Jerome writes, and we probably all concur, that when adults and children permit themselves to participate in the "divine game," a "joyfulness" is present in the air, a feeling of fulfillment and joy that one seems able to breathe.

In addition to his narration of, and reflections on, his experience carried out for so many years and with so much love, Jerome includes ample and abundant sources (readings) which he has used to research his arguments, spanning the ancient Greek philosophers to the contemporary scholars.

Space constrains me to a very limited review of this work; however, I hope that I have at least roused your curiosity enough so that you may personally experience the book.

I wish to conclude by expressing my joy at considering Jerome my dear friend, and a person who struggles for the proper recognition of the child's notable dignity in the Kingdom of God.

*"Me talking to God herself."* This drawing was done by Cecelia Bardy-Gagner, age 7. Cecelia has attended Atrium since age 2½. However, this drawing was made during after-school day-care, Minneapolis, MN.

# IN MEMORIAM
## Mark Searle

**b. September 19, 1941, England**
**d. August 16, 1992, Niles, Michigan**

—Graphic by Barbara Searle

If ... we were to learn from the celebration of the paschal mystery to surrender our lives to God in Christ, the death of the Christian would be but the further and final rehearsal of a pattern learnt in life and practiced over and over again in a lifetime of liturgical participation...
...for those who have learnt from the prayers and rituals of the Christian liturgy how to let go of all that we cling to to save ourselves from the void, the final surrender of death will be a familiar and joyous sacrifice.

—**Mark Searle**

*Mark Searle will be remembered among the catechists with great affection. Mark was a professor of Liturgy at Notre Dame University in South Bend, Indiana. He wrote the new introduction to the recently reprinted* **Religious Potential of the Child***. He gave strong support to the catechists and he will be dearly missed. Even though he was fighting the late stages of liver cancer, he gave a wonderful talk on liturgy for our Association Retreat this past July, 1992. Mark died at home in the presence of his wife, Barbara, and his children, Anna, Justin and Matthew. Mark gave the following homily at the closing liturgy of the Notre Dame Course in July, 1991.*

# Does God have a sense of Humor?

It is a delicate theological issue and one you have probably managed to avoid during your two weeks studying the Catechesis of the Good Shepherd. But, just as you thought you might escape having to confront the matter all together, here we are celebrating the feast of St. James and the question can no longer be postponed.

*Does God have a sense of Humor?* Well, consider St. James, known as St. James the Great to distinguish him from the other apostle of the same name, James the Less. Consider the fact that, of all the passages in which he is mentioned in the Gospel, that one is read on his feast where his mother puts in a bid for him and his brother to get the best seats in the coming Kingdom and where Jesus tells him explicitly that whoever would be greatest must make himself the least. We are then left with the conundrum of whether St. James the Great is really great, in which case he would be less than James the Less, or whether it is the lesser James who is really the greater. I imagine the pair of them laugh about this quite regularly.

But God's sense of humor, God's love of incongruity, goes a good bit further than such hagiographical trivia. It reaches to the very heart of the work of the Kingdom itself. God's joke is that the precious, life-giving gift of the Kingdom has been entrusted to the least likely people: us. St. Paul tells us: We possess a treasure in earthen vessels. Clay jars. Fragile containers. The Kingdom of God does not come well packaged and it is not well marketed. Its success has been entrusted to those least likely to succeed: those who are afflicted and full of self-doubt and harassed and unable to whip up support or raise a budget or even make the children stay on the line every week. And we ask whether God has a sense of humor!

"We possess a treasure in earthen vessels," says St. Paul, to make it clear that its surpassing power comes from God and not from us. We know that, of course, but it doesn't stop us worrying about success and failure. We continue to fret and fuss as if it all depended on us. In so doing we both miss the joke and obscure the very treasure we are so keen to share. Jesus told James and John: Forget about seats in the Kingdom, can you drink the cup I am to drink? Can you do what I have to do: namely lay aside all concern about success and failure and just do what God has entrusted you to do, leaving success and failure to God? Can you empty yourself of your fears and ambitions and allow God to find full scope in your life?

The great work of the Hindu scriptures, the *Bhagavad Gita*, puts it this way. The Lord Krishna tells his disciple to act without seeking the fruits of action:

You have the right to work, but for work's sake only.
You have no right to the fruits of work.
Desire for the fruits of work must never be your motive in working;
Perform every action with your heart fixed on the Supreme Lord.
Renounce attachment to the fruits.
Be even-tempered in success or failure.

Can you do your work for the Kingdom without seeking its rewards? Can you do what you have to do, for its sake only, not for the sake of something else: not to make an impact on the children, not for the satisfaction of knowing you have succeeded, not to win recognition, not even to earn a seat in the Kingdom, but just because it is God's work? "Desire for the fruits of work must never be your motive: perform every action with your heart fixed on the Supreme Lord." "You do not know what you are asking. Can you drink of the cup I am to drink of?"

The cup, in biblical language is a symbol of one's lot in life. For those who love and serve God, their head is anointed with oil and their cup is overflowing. Those devoted to God's service can speak of God as "my portion and cup." For the enemies of God's Kingdom the cup is a bitter one: "The cup of horror and desolation is the cup of your sister Samaria," Ezekiel prophesied. Isaiah spoke of the cup of God's wrath being poured for the nations to drink. The cup is what God has in store for you.

In the garden, Jesus prayed: "Father, if it be your will, let this cup pass me by. Yet, not my will, but your will be done." That was his sacrifice: to act with his heart fixed on the supreme Lord, the one he called "Abba." "Can you drink of the cup I am to drink of?" Can you do what God asks you to do, without worrying about success or failure? Can you make the sacrifice of acting without seeking the rewards of your actions? Can you make the sacrifice of doing the catechesis for its own sake, and leave it at that?

The cup comes into all our lives in one way or another, sometimes sweet, sometimes bitter. Sacramentally, symbolically, it is set before us at every Eucharist: the hollow container, the empty vessel, with the blood of Christ poured out for us.

Of course, the cup is also a symbol of feasting, and wine a symbol of joy, and the Eucharist an anticipation of the feast that is spread for us at the banquet of the Kingdom of God. But it has its dark side, representing suffering, failure and death: "Can you drink of the cup I must drink of?" "Let this cup pass me by." When we drink the cup and say "Amen," we say "Amen" to God's will for us, to our vocation to drink of the same cup that Christ had to drink, so that God's will may be done on earth among us, as it was in Christ, as it is in heaven.

To drink of the cup, then, is to share in the sacrifice. It is to sacrifice our own ambitions, to be part of the divine joke whereby our foolishness is the medium of divine wisdom, our weakness the place where God's strength is made manifest. To drink of the cup is to recognize that, for us as for Christ, to fail is to succeed, to be weak is to be strong, to be foolish is to be wise, so that God's power and wisdom may be made manifest in us. It is to abandon worldly criteria of success or failure, and to allow the heady wine of God's Spirit to fuel us instead.

As if to underline this basic principle of the Christian life, God has played one more joke on the world. In seventh century Spain the Christians won a notable victory over the forces of Islam and attributed their success to the intercession of St. James. Two centuries later, at a place called "the field of stars" — Compostella — they found what they believed to be the body of the Apostle and erected a great church over the site. For centuries, it was the biggest and most popular center of pilgrimage, apart from Rome and Jerusalem, in the world. Penitents walked there to find forgiveness and peace; the sick were carried there and were cured in the thousands; prayers offered century after century at the tomb of the saint were invariably heard. And yet...

We know that the bones dug up in the ninth century and venerated at Europe's most glorious shrine couldn't possibly be those of the man Herod had decapitated nine hundred years earlier. *Does God have a sense of humor?* For over eleven hundred years, the bones of some unknown person were venerated and kissed and carried and incensed and prayed over and touched for healing, while the real bones of St. James the Great turned to dust in unredeemable obscurity. But, the point is the healing did not cease, the prayers were still heard, the penitents were still consoled, even in the absence of the great St. James.

When we take the cup at the Eucharist we have to know that the work of the Kingdom goes on in us and around us and among us and in that, in drinking of the cup, we dedicate ourselves to the world without seeking its rewards. Let the memory of St. James be a warning to us not to take ourselves too seriously, for God has a sense of humor. On a bad day in the atrium, and even more so on a good day, that might be worth remembering.

— contributed by Mark Searle

## from Tanzania

# First Catechesis course given

*You may make a decision without knowing why you made it. Yet, you have the unshakable conviction that what you said or did was right, or that your decision was authentic. These are completely spontaneous actions done under the guidance of the Spirit. And this consolation without previous cause, it is a mystical gift.*
—from *Being in Love: The Practice of Christian Prayer* by William Johnson

*by Claudia Schmitt*
*translated by Janet Griffing*

I begin my letter with this introduction because it defines very well my lifestyle. I spontaneously decide on something and do it – even though there may be 1,000 unknowns. And this is how my adventure with Tanzania began!

I didn't know what awaited me, because no one could tell me. I didn't know what to prepare to present to them, the Montessori Method, or the Catechesis of the Good Shepherd. On one hand I was tranquil because I knew I had the ability to present something. But to whom? And how to structure the classes.

And so, on July 20, 1991, I was in Rome in la Via degli Orsini, so pale I was whiter than the wall (from nerves). Sofia Cavelletti loaned me "traveling" materials for the following presentations: the Good Shepherd, the Eucharistic Presence, the Objects of the Altar, the Pearl, and the Mustard Seed.

Sofia gave me lots of Mustard Seeds to take to Tanzania and I was really taking them spiritually too!

After a few days of traveling we arrived at Dar es Salaam and later – and after 8 hours by Jeep. Seeing monkeys and elephants, we arrived at Mafinga. We arrived at the mission, a solitary post - in the jungle! The welcome from the nuns was friendly and happy! I couldn't believe that such a place existed. With so much love. A town which expresses its happiness and love so spontaneously.

The first part of the seminar was to give an introduction to the method and the central focus of the mystery: the child!

The group consisted of more or less 60 people (all African except three Italians) who were very open to taking in all that was said.

Finally the day for the presentation of the Good Shepherd arrived. Step by step we reviewed the parable. My listeners were impressed. They didn't have a profound relationship with this parable but realized how rich it was. This reaction impressed me very much, for it was the same reaction I had when I realized the role the Good Shepherd plays ... and it was this awareness which changed in a certain way my life.

It certainly is difficult to describe the atmosphere when I gave them the statue of the Good Shepherd which Sofia had given me for them. They clapped for a long time and our happiness was great.

To top it all off they read the 23rd Psalm in Swahili. It was beautiful.

Surely you must ask yourself in what language I spoke. I spoke Italian and an African nun – who spent three years in Rome and spoke perfect Italian – translated for me. Sister Maria did a very good job. I thank her very much.

We also worked with: the Lost Sheep (they had never made the connection between this parable and the Good Shepherd parable), the Mustard Seed and the Eucharistic Presence.

At the same time, I gave classes to a small group of nuns who worked with a kindergarten - which they were building - on the Montessori Method and its integration with the Catechesis.

I don't want to give you the impression that I went to Tanzania, taught classes, and that was it!

My presence there started very early [in the morning] with the nuns in their work ( in the camp and with the animals, etc.). It ended with them in the nightly prayers, and the whole time we lived the theory we spoke or learned in our classes.

Oct. 8, 1991 was my last day there. Sad for the farewell, but happy to know that in '92 I would be back.

I'll explain: this first time was an introductory preparation to continue later. Since the materials were not ready, we couldn't work with the children, something which will happen in the future!

Now, at this moment I am enjoying the Catechesis work here in Rome, the children, and, every now and then seminars in Munich. I wish happiness to all and inspiration in the work with the Catechesis.

*from Argentina*

# Thanks for the Catechesis

*translated by Janet Griffing*

**Dear Sofia,**

We are seven from the Cathedral of San Isidro, whom by providence have come to know the Catechesis of the Good Shepherd.

Father Alejandro Bunge, pastor at the Cathedral of San Isidro, proposed to us to begin a course in the Rosario School with Ms. Herminia, who has since then become our "exterior" teacher, so we owe her for having revived our capacity for amazement and astonishment at knowing in such a special way our Good Shepherd.

We were all catechists of family catechism of Father Oeyen, and we felt very comfortable and efficient. At finding the Catechesis of the Good Shepherd, we felt — to the last fiber of our beings — useless. And I dare to speak this way — in plural — because as we were getting to know a little more the spirituality of the Good Shepherd, we all felt that each time, we were less.

And we *efficient* catechists, were left poor and desperate, and it was there in that empty space in ourselves, that our "interior teacher" began to live and act. It's truly wonderful to feel this way.

In these past few days, we've had the honor to have Francesca*, a wise and generous person who shared with us in great simplicity, profound things. With her, the Bible has turned into something new, infinite, and we hope that God permits that all her speeches reach our hearts to get to know the Good Shepherd a little bit more. On Tuesday (August 8), she visited our atrium where we have 50 children in 5 distinct groups, four of them are from 3 to 5 years, and four are children from 6 to 8. Since almost all of us had older children, and it made us very sad that a part of them, the smallest, had the opportunity to meet the Good Shepherd and the older ones - no.

---

*Francesca Cocchini works with Sofia in the 9-12 atrium in Rome.

And so once more the Providence acted. And one of the Catechists, Maria Sara Conale, under the direction of Herminia took the group, with such success that all of them want to go every day, the meeting is once per week and they wait with patience for the great day.

Sofia, we send you all our love and thanks, since your inspiration has opened the possibilities with future questions to celebrate the love of the Good Shepherd in the Liturgy and will get to know and love him more through his word.

The other day, talking amongst ourselves, we felt that each presentation was like the tip of the iceberg, that you can only slightly see above the water, and yet invisibly underneath are many revelations.

A big kiss and we ask that you remember us in your prayers.

*Maria Sara Conale, Fernanda Diáz, Laura Briosso, Monica Billoro, Virginia Conale, Stella Mara Haches, Celina Diáz Pumora.*

*Drawing by Mark Eskro, age 4, of the Good Shepherd Center, St. Paul, MN. He explains that this is the heart of Jesus with Mark inside praying to Jesus.*

# A Story of Hope – The Story of Israel

*by Sofia Cavalletti*
*by Nicolina Gleasure and Joan Parasine*

When I first presented the story of Israel to children (ages 9-11), I got such a marvelous response that I myself remained enchanted. At the conclusion of my somewhat lengthy presentation, having presented all the material, I believed I had fulfilled my obligation. However, I sensed that the children were not satisfied. I felt they did not want more details; rather, they wanted to reflect on what had been said. They wanted to listen, to be assisted in staying on the subject that was presented. Consequently, the two hours which transpired were dedicated to a leisurely reflection of the subject matter with the children, and were filled with a deep peace and great joy.

*Afterwards, I asked myself what had been the source of their enchantment, what had so captivated them.*

I believe the answer lies in the fact that the story of Israel is one of hope. As with the histories of all peoples, there are times of light and times of darkness; but, both light and the darkness are preceded by the Word. This Word is a promise; a promise of a happy end, a message of hope. A promise that the light is mightier than the darkness; that good is mightier than evil.

This can be asserted, not because I feel so, or because this consoles me.

For the Jews this hope is based on the Word its Saviour has always transmitted to his people, the one for which even at Auschwitz they said, "I believe with all my faith that the Messiah shall come, and despite his delay, I shall wait."

For us Christians this hope is grounded on the Word, and on an event: the Resurrection. It has already happened that in one Person life overcame death; there is, in our history, one Person who has achieved the plenitude of life.

*continued at the bottom of next page*

*Drawing by Briana O'Brien, age 9, of the Good Shepherd Center, St. Paul, MN. The lettering is in black, with a rainbow over the word "Lord." At the top right is a bright sun (colors did not reproduce well). Along the bottom are drawn a fisherman, a swing (below the "L" in Lord), a paten with bread, a chalice and bouquet of flowers.*

## BOOK REVIEW
# Wiesel's perspectives on Old Testament

*Messengers of God*
by Elie Wiesel.
Summit Books, New York. 1976.

*by Carol Dittberner*

While attending the 9-12 course in Washington, I read the book *Messengers of God*. It is a wonderful book, and I recommend its reading to all who study the Old Testament. Wiesel examines the Midrash surrounding the scriptures on Creation, Cain and Abel, Abraham and Isaac, Jacob, Joseph, Moses and Job. Each chapter addresses the legends about these people, and each ends with a collection of "Parables and Sayings" about these scriptures.

We are continually making an attempt to understand more deeply the mysteries before us. Wiesel's book, as well as all the others in this series, add the perspective and wealth of the Jewish tradition. Sofia has already fostered within us a deep respect and gratitude for this tradition.

In ending the first chapter on "Adam or the Mystery of the Beginning," Wiesel says: "According to Jewish tradition, creation did not end with man, it began with him. When He created man, God gave him a secret – and that secret was not how to begin but how to begin again." (pg. 32)

"To begin again," it is the secret; it is a gift we've received. It is the right perspective in front of all the gifts. Wiesel also says: "It is not given to man to begin: that privilege is God's alone." My impression of the 9-12 course was that, for two weeks, I listened daily to the litany of gifts, to all that God had created and given. How can we be so rich! And, in the face of God's compassion, we are able to continually pick up the pieces of our mistakes and start over. How many beginnings are there in each person's life, real and symbolic?

When we present the Kingdom Strip to the children, we ask the question. "Who has prepared all this for me?" Who has created this environment, with every piece so carefully planned and well made? Who has created the mystery of human life? In the Midrash, it is asked why God waited until the sixth day to create man and woman. The answer is that God wanted to prepare a place for us first.

Wiesel, while discussing Adam and Eve, says that all of us are like Adam; we all contain the same characteristics. He goes on to discuss the contradictions within us, our abilities to be both strong and weak. He wonders if "God intended to begin his work with a question. Perhaps God sought, through Adam, to continuously interrogate his creation." When I read this, what came to me were the myriad of questions God has left with us. How were the heavens and earth created: how did God form human life? How do we continue to live through the power of love? When shall we see God face to face? When shall the mystery be totally revealed?

The legends and Midrash surrounding the other people in scripture, mentioned above, are revealing and very helpful for us in our studies. As we study the Typology materials at the 9-12 level, as well as other events in the Old Testament, I hope you will refer to this book.

Other books by this author include: *Souls on Fire, Somewhere a Master, Five Biblical Portraits*.

---

## A Story of Hope,
*continued from previous page*

The reaction I experienced from the children makes me reflect on the importance of educating them about hope.

We all know the great virtues, which we label "theological" — faith, hope, and charity — which are the three fundamental means of placing ourselves in our existence. Today, we all talk about love, even if few know how to realize it. The discussion of faith is also somewhat scattered; nor do the various spiritual movements create faith. But the matter of hope is barely touched upon. Children are immersed in an environment where the negative elements are those most noted.

We have been entrusted with the biblical message, which is fundamentally optimistic. Biblical optimism is not the progressiveness of modern thought, which post-modernism refutes.

Biblical optimism is deeply realistic; it does not close its eyes to the negative, rather it looks elsewhere and seeks the depth of reality, noticing the sparkles of light, even if hidden. Biblical optimism knows that a small shimmer of light carries more weight in history than extensive darkness — in fact, because it is light. Biblical optimism knows that even if the times of darkness cause chaos, the softness of light — as light — is more powerful.

**Let us preach hope.**

# Catechist formation initiatives offered at various sites

The following are 2-week intensive courses (each level meets for two summers).

## Part I of Levels 3 - 6, 6 - 8 & 9 - 12 and Level 3 - 6 in Spanish

*This is an association-sponsored course.*

**Location/Dates:** Houston, TX, July, 11-23, 1993

**Staff:**
- 3 - 6   Carol Nyberg, Chicago, IL
  Betty Hissong, Cleveland, OH
- 6 - 12   Rebekah Rojcewicz, Mt. Rainier, MD
  Judy Schmidt, Chicago, IL
  Maria Ludlow, Mexico
- *3- 6 Spanish*   Maria Christlieb, Mexico City

**For details, contact:**

Marilyn Krause
PO Box 218, Mt. Rainier, MD 20712
(703) 971-7146

## Part I: 3 - 6 Level

**Location/Dates:** Denver, CO, July 5-15, 1993
**Staff:** Carol Dittberner, St. Paul, MN
**For details, contact:**

Linda Robertson
St. John's Episcopal Cathedral
1313 Clarkson St., Denver, CO 80218
(303) 831-7115

## Part I: 3 - 6 Level

**Location/Dates:** Tulsa, OK, July 7-16, 1993
**Staff:** Catherine Maresca, Washington, D.C.
**For details, contact:**

Bert Bibbons
Office of Trinity Episcopal Church
(918) 582-4128

## Part I: 3 - 6 Level

**Location/Dates:** Amarillo, TX, July, 19-30, 1993
**Staff:** Catherine Maresca, Washington, D.C.
**For details, contact:**

Laura Higgins
St. Andrews Episcopal Church
1601 So. Georgia, Amarillo, TX 79102
(806) 379-9738

## Part I: 3 - 6 Level *(offered in two 1-week sessions)*

**Location/Dates:** Phoenix, AZ, June 7-11, 1993 & July 19-23, 1993
**Staff &, contact person:**

Marty O'Bryan
721 W. Wilshire Dr., Phoenix, AZ 85007
(602) 258-9623

## Part II: 3 - 6 Level

**Location/Dates:** Milwaukee, WI, Aug 2-13, 1993
**Staff:** Carol Dittberner, St. Paul
**For details, contact:**

Kathy Shea
2815 So. 149th St.
New Berlin, WI 53151
(414) 784-1719

## Part II: 3 - 6 Level *(offered in two 1-week sessions)*

**Location/Dates:** Phoenix, AZ, June 1-5, 1993 & Aug. 2-6, 1993
**Staff &, contact person:**

Marty O'Bryan
721 W. Wilshire Dr., Phoenix, AZ 85007
(602) 258-9623

## Part II: 3 - 6 Level *(offered in two 1-week sessions)*

**Location/Dates:** Pasadena, CA, July 5-9, 1993 & July 26-30, 1993
**Staff :**

Marty O'Bryan

**Contact Person:**

Tracy Gaestel
1275 Church St.
Pasadena, CA 91105
(213) 258-6370

## Courses, *continued*

### 3 - 6 Level *(offered as 4 separate 1 week sessions)*

**Location/Dates:** Hickory, NC
Week 1 - June 11-15, 1993
Week 2 - Nov, 1993

**Staff:** Rebekah Rojcewicz, Mt. Rainier, MD

**For details, contact:**

Genelda Woggon
118 Macon Ave
Asheville, NC 28801
(704) 253-1748

### Part II: 6 - 8 Level

**Location/Dates:** Jackson, MS June 14-25, 1993

**Staff:** Carol Dittberner, St. Paul, MN
Catherine Maresca, Washington, D.C.

**For details, contact:**

Mary Nell Prichard
St. James Episcopal Cathedral
3921 Oak Ridge Dr.
Jackson, MS 39296-4463
(601) 982-4880

### Catechesis Workshop

**Location/Dates:** Springfield, MN Aug. 2-13, 1993

**Staff:** Anna Mae Guida, New Kensington, PA
Claudia Riordan, Detroit, MI

During these two weeks, there will be a combination of lectures and observation of children working in the Atrium.

**For details, contact:**

Mary Polta
112 W. Van Dusen
Springfield, MN 56087
(507) 723-4727

# Books & Tapes

Dear Catechists and friends:

In April 1992, I had the wonderful opportunity to hear Maria Montessori's granddaughter, Renilde Montessori, speak in St. Paul on "The Child's Quest for Discipline." Although her one-day talk was not directly related to the Catechesis, I found it very helpful. I am a catechist who has done several different training courses, but I am not Montessori-trained. She addressed many issues about the "whole child" and these fit very well into our Atrium work. She discussed some general issues, which gave me some very good ideas on how to handle some of the practical issues that come up, such as what to do with a child who continues to draw pictures of airplanes and robots, and resists working with the atrium materials.

Her talk is available in two forms from the Montessori Training Center in St. Paul. In addition, the Training Center has available a number of books by Maria Montessori, and about Montessori Education.

—Contributed by Carol Stenborg

**Renilde's Talk:**
   **Set of 4 tapes**    $40.00 + $3.00 Shipping/Handling
   **Transcript**    $15.00 + $2.00 Shipping/Handling

**Books:**

*The Discovery of the Child*
by Maria Montessori    $16.50

*The Absorbent Mind*
by Maria Montessori    $16.50

*The Secret of Childhood*
by Maria Montessori    $9.75

*Understanding the Human Being*
*(The Child from Birth to Three)*
by Dr. Silvana Montanaro    $14.75

*Maria Montessori: Her Life and Work*
by E.M. Standing    $9.70

Handling and Shipping charges:

(**Note:** These charges are based on Book Rate. First Class or overseas shipping would require additional charges).

| | |
|---|---|
| For 1 book | add $1.50 |
| For 2 books | add $2.00 |
| For 3 books | add $2.50 |
| For 4 books | add $3.00 |

To order, send your request, along with a check for the correct amount for the items and the shipping/handling charges to:

**Montessori Training Center of Minnesota, Inc.**
PO Box 16272, St. Paul, MN 55116.

# Next Newsletter to be Published: Fall 1993
# Next issue to feature: First Communion & Reconciliation
# Next Deadline: June 30, 1993

## We welcome your articles, questions, concerns and comments.

Your articles about your experiences in the atrium, about training, book reviews are what make this newsletter an important communication vehicle for Catechists throughout the world.

We want to address issues of importance to our work. Please let us know how we can help you by writing us about the newsletter or with your questions about our work with children.

## A note about children's artwork and photographs.

We want to reproduce photographs and artwork in the best way possible. For this reason, we ask that whenever possible, you send us the original artwork rather than a photocopy. We will return all work as soon as possible. Since this is a black and white newsletter, black and white photographs are ideal; however, color photographs are also acceptable. Again, we will return all photographs.

With artwork or photos, please tell us who the artist is, how old and if possible tell us a little about the child, and the drawing or picture. This information should be written on a piece of paper attached to the artwork with a paper clip or carefully printed on the back. Also tell us the name of your atrium, and in what city and state.

With any materials that you would like returned, please be sure to include the address. Thank you.

Please send all Newsletter materials directly to:

**Carol Dittberner**
**1429 Portland Avenue**
**St. Paul, MN 55104**

**Staff in U.S.A.**

Carol Dittberner
Millicent Dosh
Carol Stenborg

Italian Translators:   Joan Parasine
                       Nicolina Gleasure

Spanish Translators:   Kathy Dahl-Bredine
                       Janet Griffing

**Staff in Chihuahua:**

Maria Ines Gonzalez
Bertha Sofia Quiroz de Marquez
Emilia G. de Sandoval
Noemi F. de Lopez
Maria de Los Angeles Christlieb

---

## *Membership*

**The Catechesis of the Good Shepherd,** An Association of Children and Adults, welcomes members throughout the year. Our membership fee is $30. The fees we collect go toward expenses of our four committees: Communications & Finance, Formation, Materials and Newsletter. Members receive the annual newsletter, all mailings and a directory of catechists and friends of the Association. A newsletter subscription only is $5.00 U.S. or $6.00 foreign.

No one should hesitate to join the Association because of the inability to pay the requested $30 fee. We appreciate any donation large or small.

Mail memberships and donations to:

**The Catechesis of the Good Shepherd, Box 218, Mt. Rainier, MD 20712**

---

© Copyright 1992, 1993: The Catechesis of the Good Shepherd, Box 218, Mt. Rainier, MD 20712

# The Catechesis of the Good Shepherd

*Editor's note: On the eve of her death in 1952, Dr. Maria Montessori sent this message to Catholic teachers gathered at a meeting in London, England. This message is as relevant today.*

Never, as in this moment, has the Christian faith needed the sincere effort of those who profess it. I would like to ask all of you, who are gathered in this meeting, to consider the great help that children can bring to the defense of our faith.

Children come to us as a rain of souls, as a richness and a promise which can always be fulfilled but which needs the help of our efforts for its fulfillment.

Do not consider the child as a weakling: the child is the builder of the human personality. That this personality be Christian or not depends on the environment around him and on those who guide his religious formation.

Do not think that because the child cannot understand in the same way that we adults understand that it is useless to allow him to participate in our religious practices. The staunchest and deepest faith is generally found among unsophisticated people whose women take their children to church while they are still breastfed: the child's unconscious absorbs divine powers while the conscious reasoning of adults is only human.

You who enjoy the great gift of belonging to the Catholic faith must intensely feel the great responsibility you have for the future generations because, among you, there are those who have renounced the world to bring the world to God. Take then, as help in your task, with faith and humility, "the all-powerful children" (Benedict XV). Take as your special task to watch that their limpid light be not dimmed. Protect in their development those natural energies implanted in the souls of children by the guiding hand of God.

May God be with you at this meeting and may God guide you in your conclusions and decisions.

—*Maria Montessori*

# Contents

- Let us pray with the Children ................ 3
- "O Taste and See that the Lord is Good" ......... 4-6
- First Communion Dates ..................... 7
- In Everything Give Thanks .................. 7
- The White Garment for Eucharist ............. 8-9
- *The Story of Bread* ........................ 10
- Booklet for *The Story of Bread* ............. 11
- Enjoying the Gift:
  The Communion Retreat in the Episcopal Church ...... 12
- First Eucharist Liturgy Planning Forms ....... 13
- Songs for First Eucharist ................... 14
- *The Mystery of Faith* Booklet .............. 15
- Reconciliation for the Older Children ........ 16-18
- Resource Materials ......................... 18
- Book Review ................................ 19
- 1994 Catechist Formation Courses ............ 20-21
- About Our Association ...................... 22

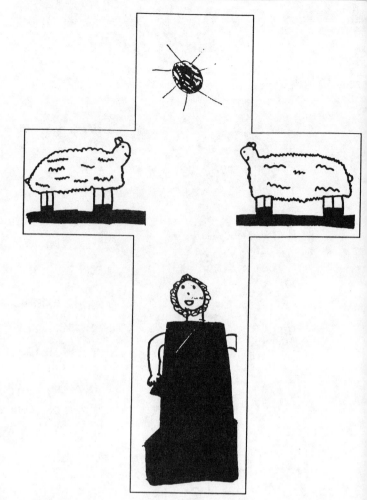

*Throughout this issue are drawings which were done by children preparing for First Communion. The cross by Erin Bettendorf, of St. Frances Cabrini Church, Minneapolis, MN, shown above, and the other similarly shaped images in this issue were decoupaged to wooden crosses and varnished. The crosses are one of the keepsakes from First Communion preparation.*

---

Dear Friends,

It is a great pleasure to publish our 10th newsletter and to focus on the theme of Eucharist in this issue. We began in a small way with the newsletter in 1984 here in St. Paul, Minnesota, and have produced one issue a year. However, there are so many more atria and catechists now, that all of our work is growing. The Board has discussed more frequent publication of the newsletter.

Carol Stenborg and I will pass on this ministry now. We wish to thank all the contributors over the years: Those who wrote articles, the children for their prayers and art work, the translators, and many who helped with typing, proofreading, mailing and distribution.

The first newsletter staff consisted of Rose Paul, Mary Polta, Fr. Cecil Roufs and myself. Maria Christlieb was our editor for two years. Joan Parasine, Patricia Coulter and Nicolina Gleasure deserve extra thanks for all their translating as there were Italian articles from Sofia in *every* issue!

And our thanks to Sofia and Gianna and their work which has planted a beautiful seed for so many of us. Those of us who have watched the Catechesis grow—slowly but with such richness—appreciate how beautiful this plant has become, reaching so many children, and extending through many denominations.

It is good that in this issue we have the *Story of Bread*, the seed which grows, becomes wheat, becomes bread through human hands, and becomes Jesus Christ through God's blessing. It is how our work has grown, from tiny seeds, worked by human hands and abundantly blessed by God.

There is a drawing by a child of the *True Vine* which has grown from the *Mustard Seed*. We need say no more!

Happy Anniversary to all for our 10 years!

Alleluias and Easter Light to each of you throughout 1994!

Spring 1994 Newsletter

# Let us pray with the Children . . .

*by Cecilia Bardy-Gagner, age 9, Minneapolis, MN.*

*This prayer was written by Cecilia in her best cursive for her mother for Mother's Day.*

God is a mother that is gentle and kind.

God can cook for the rich and poor.

You shall never die in the hands of God.

You are the daughter of God,

and every girl is the daughter of God.

---

*by Santa Caballero, age 8, years, after hearing the presentation of the True Vine.*

God will be with me. I will share the love with many other people. God is my best friend no matter what. The light of the world will always glow. It will glow every day of my life.

---

*by Sara Jo Brownlee, age 8*

Thank you Lord for everything you have given me.

Thank you Lord for treating* the true vine.

Thank you Lord for giving the sap to the vine.

And thank you Lord for sending Jesus down to earth.

(* meaning "to care for")

*This cross was drawn by Sara Jo Brownlee, age 8, from St. Frances Cabrini, Minneapolis, MN. The cross was pasted onto dark colored paper, so the text could not be reproduced. The following four pieces of text were written at each corner of the page: "The grape vine holds all arms of life...", "We are all of the life for it", "Time comes and time goes," and "as our people come and go."*

---

*by Andrea Piescik, age 7, in her third year at Sacred Heart Church Atrium, Southbury, CT.*

How a river flows is how your love spreads across the land.

---

*by Colleen Perry, Age 9, at Christian Family Montessori School, Mt. Rainier, MD.*

God I may forget you this day. But please don't forget me.

*(written in many colors over a picture of a rainbow)*

---

*from Christian Family Montessori School, Mt. Rainier, MD*

A child asked her mother after both had gone to confession, "Is everything alright?"

Mom said, "Yes."

"Then why aren't you smiling?" the child asked.

---

*by Andrea Piescik, age 7, in her third year at Sacred Heart Church Atrium, Southbury, CT.*

Where the shepherd watches over us

Where the sky is blue and where the grass is green.

Where the rivers flow

Where the sheep drink

Where it is nice. O I love it.

It is so beautiful.

# "O TASTE AND SEE

*Translated from Italian by Nikki Gleasure & Joan Parasine*

My Dearest Friends,

As we all know, the occasion of First Communion presents us with an opportunity every year to prepare for the Eucharist in a special way. It is a great privilege to be able to do this with the children. It seems to me that the full wealth of doing the catechesis with the children is found condensed in the preparation that immediately precedes First Communion.

We all know how focusing on a topic helps us see it gradually enlarging before us. Ever wider horizons and deeper depths are opened which appeal to us with ever greater force.

In this preparation the children are a precious help; they compel us, somehow, to share their needs for simplicity and essentiality. Wordlessly, they impose upon us an exacting and healthy discipline aimed at establishing within us an inner order, as well as a growing power to contemplate the Mystery in awe, and to allow ourselves to be drawn by it.

The Eucharist is the focal point of the Christian life, and so we could say, with confidence, that the whole catechesis is a preparation for Eucharist. But, there is a moment when this preparation is intensified.

## Here are some of the main phases as we "live" them (in the Atrium) at Via degli Orsini:

- The announcement by the priest begins the immediate preparation; the child, who thinks that the right moment has come for him/her, may write his/her name on the appropriate card.

- Personal interviews by the catechists and priest conducted with each child; of course, there is a discussion between the child and his/her parents.

- When the decision is clear, the priest reads out the name of each candidate during the celebration of the Mass, and solemnly presents each child with a copy of the New Testament.

- There are five or six special meetings for the children involved in this preparation, devoted to the True Vine, Reconciliation, presented within the framework of the Parables of Mercy, and of the Eucharist (peace, "blessed are those who are called…"). These meetings are special; they are meditations, with no work done with the materials. They last slightly longer than an hour. They may be held in a place different from the Atrium. At the same time as the children's meetings, similar topics are being presented to the parents.

- Finally, there is the four-day retreat. These days are occasions of great expectation and joy; they provide some of their best memories when these children become adults.

It is advisable to have extended sessions; presently we operate from 9:00 a.m. to 6:30 p.m. However, things worked better when the schedule was extended to 8:00 p.m., so that the evening meal could be shared with the children. I have my doubts whether the children should stay overnight; there is too much novelty and it may cause overexcitement. We go to a beautiful convent (or monastery) with a room available for setting up a few materials. The room should be close to the chapel to permit the children to go there on their own, to pray

*Elizabeth, age 7, Christian Family Montessori School, Mt. Rainier, Maryland, drew this picture of "The Holy Spirit coming down on the bread and wine." The lines coming down from heaven were covered with yellow, representing light. The form behind the cross represents the earth and yellow rays surround the cross. The cross inside the chalice was also yellow.*
**(Note:** *Yellow does not reproduce well, so not all of the yellow from Elizabeth's drawing can be seen in the replication shown above.)*

# THAT THE LORD IS GOOD"

silently or to read their Gospels. It is desirable to have a garden close by so that anyone who feels tired can go there for a little walk, if necessary.

I believe it is very important not to give new presentations during the retreat days. Even if there might be some gaps in the children's preparation, this is not the right time to fill those gaps. Rather, this is a time to enjoy fully, in the perfect calm, what has been achieved and to focus on the grandeur of the gift which is about to be received.

In general, we bring along the following materials:

- the Gospel
- the Synthesis of the Mass
- Baptism
- Reconciliation
- the Maxims
- the list of baptismal promises

**It is of utmost importance to celebrate the Mass daily.**
Every morning, the first thing we do upon arrival is to prepare for it. Then we celebrate the mass in peace and quiet. In this way, most of the morning is taken up with this celebration.

I realize that some may encounter difficulty upon this point, because obviously the children do not receive communion. However, the liturgical decree of the Council (*Sacrosanctum Concilium*, No. 55), makes provision for participation without reception of communion.

Daily mass is certainly a very effective way of initiating children to the Eucharist in a gradual manner. *These are highly emotional moments for adults and children alike.* If you would allow me a personal reminiscence, I can say that some especially deep, rich periods of silence are among the most beautiful memories of my life as a catechist. I remember one time, when everyone had been meditating very nicely, and then, right at the end, after the adults had received communion, a child started chattering. After the Mass, I complained about it, saying that, during that moment of intense prayer, I had been disturbed by a child. The child told me, "If you had really wanted to pray, I would not have been able to disturb you."

During the preparation, the children indicate the texts they wish to hear during the celebration. Sometimes, as a start, we seek out a facet of the Eucharistic liturgy we wish to focus upon, and taking off from this point, we choose a gospel text which illustrates it. For instance, from the gestures of peace we go back to the Last Supper; from the gesture of epiclesis, and therefore, from the gift of the Spirit and the presence of Christ, we go to the Good Shepherd who gives up his own life; from the gesture of offering we are led to the parables of the Good Samaritan and the Lost Sheep who was found again. This is a very effective way to live the Bible-Liturgy union which can be expressed through different texts.

The remaining portion of the first two days goes by without a scheduled program. The children work with the materials we brought along and engage in simple activities such as decorating candles, preparing small cards with the names of their family members to be placed on the pews during the celebrations. They draw some pictures and might even do some collages. They read the Gospel a great deal. During these days it is a good idea to stop all activities at least once a day and help the children gradually achieve a deep silence. Let them have all the time they need so that they can enjoy the silence fully.

> I believe it is very important not to give new presentations during the (retreat) days. Even if there might be some gaps in the children's preparation, this is not the right time to fill those gaps. Rather, this is a time to enjoy fully, in the perfect calm, what has been achieved, and to focus on the grandeur of the gift which is about to be received.

Dr. Montessori used to have rosaries made during days such as these. We did something similar for many years, too. Nowadays, though, the rosary is not very widespread and a retreat is not a suitable occasion to introduce it to the children. Nevertheless, it was an excellent activity which linked "handiwork" to doctrinal content.

On Saturday morning, the Mass is celebrated once again. The afternoon is devoted to the solemn celebration of the Sacrament of Reconciliation. First of all, we make an examination of conscience together, starting with the consideration of the gifts we have received and helping one another with a reading of the Maxims.

Then we go to the church together and individual confessions take place. The children often select one or two maxims to read together with the priest upon which to base their confession. While those in attendance, children and adults alike, one after the other, go to the priest (to make their private confessions), the others sing. However, there is a pause at the moment of the imposition of the priest's hands over each individual, for everyone, in great silence, to call for the coming of the Holy Spirit

*continued on next page*

## "O Taste and See that the Lord is Good, *continued from previous page*

upon the person who is making his/her confession. The priest hands out a cross to each child.

Then there is a need for an extended interval prior to continuing the celebration. Together with the parents, the Baptismal promises are renewed, the robe is presented and the child puts it on at the foot of the altar with the help of a person chosen by each child; then the Liturgy of the Light is celebrated. There is no set structure for this celebration, and we see no need to create one. What matters is that the presentation of the robe and the light to each child, and the words of the Baptismal ritual are not hurried. Everyone should be able to feel united to each child receiving the signs of baptism again. It is also essential to leave room for silence once the presentation of the robe and the light is completed. If the children feel sufficiently free, they should be given the opportunity to express their individual prayers.

**Next, having been made beautiful inside and out, everyone goes home to await the following morning.**

Parents are asked, on an earlier occasion, not to mar the day with photos and gifts. I remember a girl who wanted a bicycle very much and had not yet received one. When she returned home on Sunday night and saw the bicycle, she burst into tears; that was not the right moment.

Once the Mass is over, the children stay with us until the afternoon. After spending some time with their parents in the garden, the children, without being asked, spontaneously return to the room and, one after the other, gradually return to their work, and, most importantly, to the silent and peaceful atmosphere of the previous days. In the afternoon, we prepare a final celebration which is attended by the parents. The children help with these preparations. It can assume different structures. Sometimes, if the group is not too large, each child chooses to read a short passage from the Gospel as his/her own personal gift to the family. In any case, on this occasion, too, we do not want to set up a fixed program.

When everything is concluded, it is not easy to send the children home. Though some object to this extended Sunday program, there are several good reasons for it. The children have experienced a high level of intensity during these days. It is essential that they are not taken away from it suddenly. Instead, we must help them to relish these experiences slowly. If they were removed to a different environment from that of the retreat, the intense experience they have had might somehow be spoiled, or even cancelled out.

To those who argue that, by doing this, we exclude family participation, we respond that the family is repeatedly called upon to participate, on an exclusively religious level, beginning with the special meetings to which parents are invited at the same time as their children's meetings, but in another location. It is suggested that parents organize a family celebration the following Sunday.

The main reason, however, is that we see how happy the children are to extend their retreat time. The moment of leaving always comes too soon. Kathy Dahl-Bredine of Silver City, New Mexico, wrote in *Gathered Grain*, No. 12, "All the children were very eager to stay for the rest of the day after their` First Communion, and that was something I was apprehensive about."

To those who are in doubt about this point, I just want to say, "Try it."

—*Sofia*

*Erika Kuehn, age 6, St. Frances Cabrini Atrium, Minneapolis, Minnesota. Erika drew this picture of herself and her mother at the Eucharistic Table after the presentation of the Eucharistic Presence and the international figures. There are several chalices and patens because "so many people will come." Over the altar, she drew bursts of yellow, telling me, "This is the light of Jesus." She also said, "Each of these flowers is the love of Jesus." (Note: Notice the similarity in the drawing of light over the bread and wine in this picture and in "The Last Supper" which is shown on page 4 of this issue.)*

## First Communion Dates

It is our custom to list the dates of First Communion so that all of us, as a community, will keep the children and catechists in our prayers during their retreats and celebrations of Eucharist.

| | |
|---|---|
| April 15/16 | Communion Retreat<br>St. Barnabas Episcopal Church<br>Chicago, IL |
| May 1 | Via degli Orsini, Rome, Italy |
| | St. Frances Cabrini<br>Minneapolis, MN |
| | St. Giles Catholic Community<br>Oak Park, IL |
| | St. Charles Church, Arlington, VA |
| May 22 | Holy Family Catechetical Center<br>Phoenix, AZ |

*We ask you to send us dates for First Communion, as well as relevant artwork, pictures and articles.*

## In Everything Give Thanks

*by Ruth Scheef*

**Editor's Note:** *The following article was originally printed in Ruth Scheef's parent newsletter, for St. Edward's Episcopal Church in Plymouth, MN.*

As I was waiting to go up for communion, I looked over and saw Sarah Swacker (6 yrs. old) and Russell Kirby (4 yrs. old) going up the aisle to receive communion. What caught my eye, my heart, and my God was the complete comfortableness and joyfulness that seemed to radiate over Sarah as she first held out her hand to shoeless Russell, and then they proceeded to skip up to the Altar. What a delight to witness!

---

That cloudy, cool, second Sunday of Easter, we had just celebrated the "Liturgy of the Light". This is where we prepared the Paschal Candle by tracing over the cross, the Alpha, the Omega, the current year and placed the five incense nails for the wounds of Jesus. Then we lit the candle, knowing that this new light represented the Light of our Risen Lord, who has passed over from death to life. With Molly Freese as our candle bearer, we entered the area outside of the elementary atrium, turned off the lights and stopped three times to sing, "The Light Of Christ Has Come Into The World". Concluding in the preschool atrium, each person lit their own votive from the Paschal Candle. With all the candles lit, there was a prayerful silence, filled with the light of our candles; and the unspoken presence of Jesus.

After this moment, during the prayer time, Sarah Swacker said, "When I was holding my candle I felt Jesus in my heart."

**Alleluia. The Lord Is Risen.**

**The Lord Is Risen, Indeed.**

**Alleluia.**

A listener, too!

*Rachel Voller, age 10, St. Frances Cabrini Atrium, Minneapolis, MN.*
*This is how Rachel decorated the folder in which she keeps her work.*

# The White Garment worn for Eucharist, also

*"See in this white garment the outward sign of your Christian dignity."*

—From the Rite of Baptism

*Editor's Note: Children receiving First Communion still wear white dresses and suits, but these are individual choices. In celebrating First Communion in the Catechesis, the children are asked to wear a similar white garment, boys and girls. Following is Tina Lillig's communication with parents in an effort to change the usual dress for First Communion to the white garments. We thought it would be helpful for you to see her process. We have also included her notes on patterns and the sewing of the garments.*

Dear parents,

I am very excited to write this letter to you, the parents whose children are anticipating First Communion. In less than two months, your children will begin the direct preparation for First Communion. But we all know that a great deal of indirect preparation has already taken place—in your home, in the atrium, and in the community. It is really a whole process that begins at baptism. Baptism, one of the three sacraments of initiation, is followed by Confirmation and then Eucharist (though for centuries the church has switched the order of the latter two).

On the day of baptism, your child received the light, the life of the risen Christ. Prayer and a life lived in love has kept that light bright. A relationship with Jesus has been developing toward a new moment of radiance and splendor.

So much has happened in the atrium: the first presentations of the altar; the Good Shepherd calling the children by name to green pastures and fresh water; Jesus at the Cenacle, around the table, saying, "This is my body...." We can understand why a child at 7 or 8 (or sometimes 6) will express a desire for First Communion. What we have seen in the atrium is that the child enjoys a relationship. First Communion is a celebration of that relationship—a moment of fullness.

Many of you know that for the past 10 summers I've attended Catechesis of the Good Shepherd training somewhere in the United States or Canada. Much of the training, and also much of our whole catechesis focuses on the child's First Communion. Our First Communion preparation and the liturgy of First Communion in St. Giles Community has been shaped by the Catechesis of the Good Shepherd approach to religious formation. One part of First Communion that I've learned about in training but we haven't yet incorporated in the community is the wearing of the white garment. It is a long white garment, the garment of baptism/initiation, worn by both boys and girls, and made to the size of the child. Every summer I enjoy seeing pictures of the First Communions in other parishes—many with children in their white garments (enclosed).

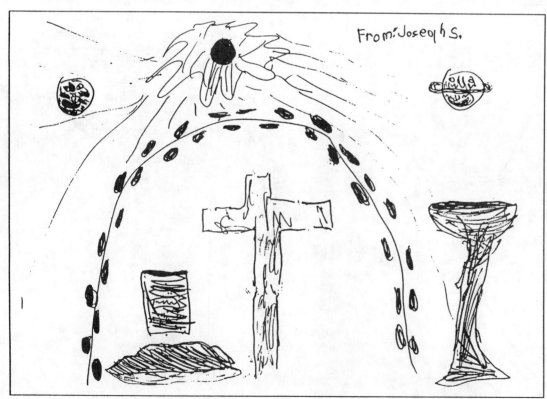

*Joseph Schweigert, age 6 ½, St. Frances Cabrini Atrium, Minneapolis, Minnesota. Over the bread is the book, representing The Bible. The rainbow is "the grape vine." In the corners are planets (with faces). The cross was surrounded with yellow.*

In the summer of 1991, five SGC catechists took the 6-8 year old training in Notre Dame. Together we came to a very deep appreciation of the beauty and meaning of this garment and its link with baptism. We wondered if we could ask the parents to change from suits and ties and white dresses and stoles to the wearing of the white garment. This year Alyssa Hagen, one of the first communicants, could wear the white garment of her initiation for her April 25th baptism. Perhaps all the communicants could put on the white garment of initiation with her one week later for First Communion.

The purpose of this letter is to ask you to think about it between now and our parent meeting in February. You can decide together at that time.

Even if you decide not to choose the white garment, I'm hoping we can set aside the stole. At one time the stole was a rich tradition in our community with most adults and children wearing stoles on many occasions. But a renewed understanding that has permeated the church more recently is that baptism—not priesthood—is the root of all our ministry. Please think about this, too. Hope to see you all in February,

Love, Tina Lillig

**Pattern notes:**
*McCalls' 5569*—round neck, trumpet sleeves, comes in four sizes. Medium is for sizes 8-10, or

*Simplicity 8153*—straight neck, very much like the *McCalls'* with less 'trumpet' to the sleeves, one size for sizes 2-12.

Both patterns are available at *JoAnn Fabrics*. The *McCalls'* was available at *Minnesota Fabrics*.

**Fabric:**
1. Lynette Solid, $4.49/yd., a linen-look, 50/50 polyester/rayon
2. Bingham, $7.99/yd., also linen-look, 50/50 polyester/rayon
3. At Minnesota Fabrics, a sportswear solids fabric was found on sale for $1.97/yd. This was 50/50 polyester/cotton. It worked well.

**Some tips from Marihelen:**
1. Buy four yards of fabric, unless it is 60-inch width (in which case you may only need 3 and one half yards).
2. Those who are sewing should measure each child well. Garments should be ankle-length. Parents can call the persons who are sewing to arrange to have the child measured very soon. After mass is a possibility.
3. The person sewing should prepare the fabric—wash, dry and press before cutting out.

I have told the people who are sewing that parents will cover all expenses, including if the person needs to charge for her time.

**To prepare white garments for the children**, make sure each one is marked well with the child's name. *Kinko's* has a parchment type paper that is appropriate for making name cards to pin on each garment.

Roll them and tie them with a cord or ribbon, and put them in a basket lined with cloth or something nice.

Presentation of the garments to the children should begin with the words:

> On the day of your baptism, you were filled with the light of Christ. A white garment was put on you so everyone could see that you were filled with light.
>
> On the day of your First Communion, you will put on a new white garment because you will be filled with the light and life of Christ.

*Susan Schweigert, age 8, from St. Frances Cabrini Church, Minneapolis, MN. Susan explained that her drawing is of "the true vine that grew from the mustard seed, and this is all our community."*

*This drawing shows the roots that grow underneath the soil from the seed, as well as the vine that grows above the soil for all to see.*

Catechesis of the Good Shepherd

# The Story of Bread for ages 9 to 12

*by Sofia Cavalletti*
*Translated from Italian by Nikki Gleasure & Joan Parasine*

This topic has taken an extended prehistory. Many attempts were made but they always turned up to be unsatisfactory. We were unable to achieve the necessary essentiality and the presentation was jerky and complicated.

Finally, the format developed in the presentation of last December–the last time we did it. It seems to have achieved the linear, yet rich qualities we were seeking. At least this format is better than what we have obtained up to now.

The essential point is the Eucharist as the Sacrament of the Covenant. The Covenant we celebrate in the Eucharist has cosmic dimensions. Heaven and earth are co-involved.

In this presentation, the focus is on the presence in the Mass of the earthly elements from the sap of the earth to the work of humankind, as well as on the obvious love of God, expressed in the gift Jesus offers of himself.

Most of the children were about 9-12 years old, a few were 8 years old. We gathered around a circular table on which a tablecloth and a loaf of bread were arranged.

I think that the figure of the Good Shepherd was there as well. It was the same table which, in previous meetings, was used for the presentation of the mystery of faith. Therefore, this recalling of the Mass was very explicit.

I told the story contained in the booklet I am sending you *(see next page)*. It brings back many memories of my holidays at Gianna's house in the country.

The children listened very attentively. The atmosphere was one of absorbed listening. Their involvement was rather noiseless, quiet yet conducive to meditation.

Then, the material was shown to some of the children: the booklet, then the same story written on 13 loose, unnumbered pages.

The work consists of arranging the loose material in a sequence, and later, in copying and illustrating it. At first nobody started to work with it but in the following sessions it appears that the material is sought out, and presently a small group is working with great interest.

Perhaps the aim of this presentation is too ambitious, as if we were to begin the celebration at the point of convergency of the universe. I believe that this is the meaning of the "Sacrament of the Covenant."

What is a celebration? It seems to me that it is an action upon which time and space are concentrated.

There is the previous history made concrete by the liturgy, that is realized by liturgy. Read again the Fourth Eucharistic Prayer. It begins with a mention of the creation and then enumerates some essential points of the history of salvation. These are not mentioned (in the prayer) as an expression of a beautiful poem; instead, we live them again in their totality in the celebration.

Within this little piece of bread, there is then the whole universe from the deepest layers of the earth to the presence of God. We cannot imagine anything more cosmic or more omnicomprehensive.

We agree, the aim is ambitious but it is a mistake to state it as too ambitious. We are aware that when dealing with essential realities—as in this case undoubtedly, it is our obligation to transmit them to the children because children are gratified by essentials.

We are not saying that we are able to do so with this presentation. This is why I am sending you the material so that you also can try and then let me know about the reactions you receive. Good Work!

—*Sofia*

---

### THE STORY OF BREAD

**Ages:** 9-12

**Material Description:** An orange folder with two pockets. In one pocket is kept the booklet, *The Story of Bread*, measuring 8 ½" by 5 ½" with an orange cover. There is no picture on the front of the booklet. The pages of the booklet are white. (There are no illustrations in the booklet.) This is the control. In the second pocket is another copy of the booklet kept as loose, unnumbered pages.

**Presentation:** Prepare a table with a white cloth, the statue of the Good Shepherd, and a plate with leavened bread. Meditate with the children on the Story of Bread, using the text from the booklet. Also, refer to the article which accompanies this album page.

#### Children's work:

1. To take the loose pages and put them in order, then they can check their work with the booklet.

2. Copy text and illustrate with their own drawings.

*Note:* *Text for The Story of Bread booklet is shown on the next page.*

# Text for *The Story of Bread* booklet

*Page 1*

If we want to know the story of the bread which is in front of us, we must go down deeply into the earth where once there was placed a seed.

*Page 2*

It was in the autumn - and a worker walked through the fields that were stripped barren, bare and unadorned. They were waiting only. The worker scattered the seed and the seed made its way into the earth. It too seemed to be scanty and meager, so much that it died.

*Page 3*

But since that moment in the earth's womb, there began slowly a work of pulling back to the seed all the juices that crisscross the deep veins of the earth. The rain was called towards the seed, as well as the sun with its heat, and caused the seed to grow.

*Page 4*

The work of the earth, rain, and sun is very slow and mysteriously lasts the whole winter. Only in spring time, the field which was bare and barren earlier is transformed into a green carpet. But the seed has not yet ripened.

*Page 5*

Summer must come so that the seed is ripened. Then the field changes color: it is gold all over – the seed has become a stalk of wheat with many ears of grain. This is the result of the work by the earth, the sun, the rain, and the air. This activity is carried out with no human intervention.

*Page 6*

At this stage, men and women return to work the field. The ears of wheat are gathered; the grains of the ears are separated from the chaff. Then they are ground into flour. Huge combines help the human beings throughout this working process, to harvest, thresh, and mill the grain.

*Page 7*

When the flour is ready, it is sent out to other environments and to other hands. Other elements are called to contribute to the transformation of the wheat seed; water, yeast and fire. Thus it becomes bread. Baked in the heat of the oven, the bread is ready to be brought to our table.

*Page 8*

Women, men and children gather around the table. The bread is broken to satisfy their hunger and make their meal more pleasant. The bread of our tables is a gift we receive from God; it is the fruit of the earth and the work of many people.

*Page 9*

At this stage, both the earth and humankind have fulfilled their task. The hands of the human being have taken the seed to the highest level of efficiency. Yet, at this moment, the process comes to a halt. It cannot go any farther.

*Page 10*

Human beings cannot go any farther, but God can. Indeed, there is a gesture that the human being can perform so that the seed reaches its highest level. This time it is a gesture of prayer.

*Page 11*

We can ask God to transform the bread into a sign of the presence of the Risen Christ, with these words:

"Send your Spirit to transform this bread and this wine so that they become for us the Body and the Blood of our Lord, Jesus Christ."

*Page 12*

We obey the will of Jesus Christ when we ask God for this gift.

Jesus, our Lord, who once said over the bread: "This is my Body." The bread has become the Bread.

*Page 13*

These elements converge in the Bread: the sap of the earth, the action of the rain and sun, the zestful work of the human beings, and the immense love of God, so that Jesus Christ, who died and is risen, is made visible in a particular way in our world.

# Enjoying the Gift:
## The Communion Retreat in the Episcopal Church

*by Carol Nyberg*

On a Monday evening in March, seven children and two adults gather in a living room. On a small table in the center of the chair there is a Bible, a candle and an ivy vine. On each chair there is a Bible. Together the children and adults read and meditate on Jesus' words, *"I am the true vine and my Father is the vine grower."* In a few moments the air is filled with words of peace and joy, a sense of deep contentment spreads. The candle burns as we read aloud the words of Jesus. Together we have begun to reflect on the wonder of relationship; with Jesus, with the Father, with each other, through the Spirit. A relationship that has been nourished by the bread and the wine of communion. All of the children sitting in this circle have received communion for as long as they can remember from the time they received a drop of wine from their parents finger, until today when they lift their own hands to receive the gift. We have found over the last five years that this special time of coming apart to reflect on and to enjoy the gift of communion is very rich for these children who have received communion from a young age. We call it simply the Communion Retreat.

We follow the same format as those who are preparing for First Communion. The difference is not so much in kind as in emphasis. With these children we are meditating on a gift they have experienced all their lives. A gift they know intimately and one they value greatly. Much of what we contemplate affirms what they already know. They truly "know" that each Sunday they are receiving Christ, Himself.

The church community is involved in this time of reflection and enjoyment. The parents are given some of the same meditations as the children. Each child chooses someone to be their prayer partner to pray for them during this time of refreshment. The congregation celebrates with them at three moments in this process. First, when they decide to be part of the communion retreat. They sign their name in the communion retreat book in front of the congregation and from that moment they are prayed for at every service. The Sunday before they go on the retreat the children are marked with the sign of the cross by the celebrant and their parents and sent out by the community. On the Sunday of the retreat they are welcomed back and play significant roles in the celebration of the Eucharist. A simple reception follows. The church community also serves them by preparing their white garments, preparing their food for the retreat and assisting in the many details and logistics that make the retreat possible.

So far we only have a two-day retreat, although this may change over time. On Friday they are excused from school. Friday's focus is on the Sacrament of Reconciliation; Saturday's focus is on the renewal of their baptismal vows.

## Outline for the Retreat

1. Introduce the Communion Retreat. Children decide if they will go in consultation with parents.

2. Enrollment: Celebrated with the parish community at Sunday liturgy. Children sign names in a special book. They are then prayed for during the **Prayers for the People** beginning that Sunday and continuing through the Sunday of the retreat.

3. The five meditations begin, once a week on an evening for one hour.

4. Children choose a prayer partner to pray with them during this time. This person may be a Godparent, a catechist or an older friend. They are also given a workbook they may do at home with their families. We use *Life in the Eucharist: A Communion Program for Children* from the Anglican Book Centre in Toronto, Ontario. This is completely optional and was used to meet the parents' needs to have something to do at home.

5. The Sunday before they go on retreat there is a **Rite of Sending** for the children at the Sunday Liturgy.

6. Our retreat is two days. Children take Friday off from school. We meet Friday from 9:15 a.m. to 7:30 p.m. This year we will celebrate First Reconciliation on Friday afternoon.

    Saturday, we meet from 9:15 a.m. to 5:30 p.m. The focus on Saturday is the renewal of Baptismal vows. Parents and prayer partners are invited to the Eucharist for the renewal and the children receive their white garments.

7. Sunday they return to the community and have particular roles in the liturgy. They process in their white garments, carrying their candles. They lead the **Prayers of the People** that they have written on the retreat. They assist the priest at the altar. They bring forward the oblations including the communion bread they have prepared. They also choose one of the communion hymns. They receive communion first and following the service there is a reception for them.

Spring 1994 Newsletter

# First Eucharist Liturgy Planning Forms

## Planning the Liturgy

We sit down with the children and choose the readings and songs together.

1. Opening Song: _____
2. First Reading: _____
3. Psalm: _____
4. Gospel: _____
5. Prayers: _____
   _____
   _____

*We choose two to three children to compose prayers of thanksgiving/petition or whatever the celebration calls for. These children then lead the reading of the prayers.*

6. Offertory Song: _____
7. Communion Song: _____
8. Closing Song: _____
9. As needed:

   Prayer read together: _____

   *Note: this again would depend on the liturgy. If you were having a Reconciliation Service, all could read the Confession/Confiteor. Thanksgiving: all could read a Psalm of praise. Our Father, etc.*

10. Gesture/
    Response from group: _____

*Note on music: When choosing music, we always try to choose at least one song that has open verse, e.g. "Oh Lord, Shout for Joy." The children compose verses appropriate to the celebration (see example on next page).*

Music:

    write/compose verses _____
    _____

## Selecting the Children's roles during the Liturgy

*Before the Liturgy*
Light Candles:

_____

Prepare the Environment:

2-3 children prepare the atrium or place where Eucharist will be celebrated, e.g. gathering the articles (chalice, paten, cruets), decorating - flowers, arranging chairs, and so on.)

_____
_____
_____

*During the Liturgy*
Readers:

    First reading _____
    _____

    Psalm _____

    Gospel _____

Prayers of the People:

_____
_____

Offertory Procession:

    Corporal: _____
    Chalice: _____
    Purificator: _____
    Pall _____
    Bread: _____
    Wine: _____
    Water: _____

Wash priest's Hands:

_____
_____

Place Altar Book Stand on Altar: _____

Place Altar Book on Stand: _____

*After the Liturgy*
Snuff Candles: _____

# Songs for First Eucharist

## Song of the True Vine

Copyright © Words and music by Pauline Smith, Minneapolis, MN, March 1990 for the First Communion Children of St. Frances Cabrini, Minneapolis, MN

Vs. 1 Sweet green leaves grow-ing on the bran-ches, grow-ing on the bran-ches; sweet green leaves.
Vs. 2 Je-sus said you are the bran-ches, you are the bran-ches, I am the vine.

Chorus: Sweet is Je-sus' love for us; sweet is the vine, the bread and the wine, the

vine is the life blood of Je-sus in us.

## O Lord! Shout for Joy

**Traditional Verses** (repeat each 2 times)

2. Feel like shouting, Shout for joy!

3. Feel like praying, Shout …

4. Now I'm getting happy, Shout …

*Words and music: Traditional Negro Spiritual*

**Verses** by children of St. Frances Cabrini

> For Susan and Eric, Shout for joy! *(Naming of children continued until all of the children receiving First Communion were named).*
>
> For Jesus and Mary, Shout for joy!
>
> For the Angels, Shout for joy!
>
> For the Lamb, Shout for joy!
>
> For the Good Shepherd, Shout …
>
> For Creation, Shout for joy!
>
> For the whole earth, Shout for joy!
>
> For the Bread, Shout for joy!
>
> For the Wine, Shout for joy!

# The Mystery of Faith Booklet

We realize that the presentation of "The Mystery of Faith" always goes well, yet our the children do not work with the material on their own. In fact, it misses a guide to the personal work.

I present you with such a guide here and request that you try it with your children. I look forward to hearing from you about how the use of this material goes with your children, and I send my hope that it will all be filled with joy!  *Sofia*

**Ages: 6-8**

This is a booklet for the child's personal work. It should have an orange cover, and be sized 8 ½ by 5 ½ inches.

On the cover is to read "The Mystery of Faith."

*Page 1*

(*Prepare the table, placing:
the table cloth, the Good Shepherd,
the paten, the chalice.*)

The Good Shepherd calls us to his table and we encounter his presence in the Bread and the Wine.

*Page 2*

How is our encounter with him?

For example, how did the people who lived at the time of Jesus know him before the resurrection?

Would their encounter be more beautiful; or is ours more beautiful?

*Page 3*

What is it that they knew about the person of Jesus?

(*Place on the table the picture of
the Crucifixion of Jesus.*)

Those people knew that Jesus suffered death the same as each person dies. Yet, they did not know…

*Page 4*

A Great thing that we know:

(*Place on the table the picture
of the resurrection.*)

Jesus has conquered death.

Our encounter is with the Risen Christ!

Then which encounter is more beautiful, theirs or ours?

*Page 5*

Still, they saw him, listened to his voice.
On the contrary, our eyes cannot see him; we are unable to sustain the splendor of the resurrection.

Yet, will it always be like this?

*Page 6*

No; it will not always be like this. We look forward to the day when our bodies will be transformed, and our eyes will see Jesus in all the splendor of his resurrection. We look forward to the day of his coming; the day of the Parousia.

(*Place on the table the picture of the Parousia
and place the labels under the pictures.*)

*Page 7*

The "Mystery of our Faith" is

Jesus,

who died and is risen,

who is present now

in the Bread and in the Wine

and who is coming again in glory.

(*Place on the table the label,
"The Mystery of Faith."*)

# Reconciliation for the older children

*by Francesca Cocchini*

For quite a few years, during Lent, we have initiated a series of meetings to assist the children who have already received their First Communion, to experience the Sacrament of Reconciliation with greater awareness.

It is really more a question of investigating, on a deeper level and in a particular way, elements which for the most part are already known, but with a different focus, namely, the examination of conscience.

In a book entitled *The Duties of the Heart*, by Bahja ibn Paquada, a Jewish mystic writer of the 12th Century, Sofia has found some interesting characteristics of the so-called "examination of conscience." In order to make an examination of conscience, one must know and reflect on the mystery of God (Deut. 4:39). One must "taste and see how good the Lord is" (Psalm 34:8), "To know and worship the God of our fathers (I Chronicles 28:9), since "only the person who has known his beneficence can observe his precepts." (Deut 11: 2-8).

Therefore, the person who is examining him/herself tends to focus on God primarily, and then on one's deficiencies or defects only in a second moment. This, and only this, is what St. Augustine calls the "religious confession."

I wish to share with you the experience we have had with the children along these guidelines.

We begin by giving two messages: the first is a passage from the Letter to the Ephesians, 5:8: "Once you were in darkness, but now you are light in the Lord. Live like children of the light." The second text is from the Letter to the Romans, 13: 11-12. "You know the time has come; you must wake up now; our salvation is even nearer than it was when we were converted. The night is almost over, it will be daylight soon - let us arm ourselves and appear in the light."

We spend some time discussing the first text. It is the announcement of a gift we have received; we point out how important the phrase " in the Lord" is because it permits us to be "light." We stress that this is a reality which we do not have to strive to obtain because it is already ours. This represents the pleasurable moment of our relationship with God, which must never be lacking and which is essential in order to go on to the so-called "examination of conscience." We must never take this for granted and think it unnecessary. There should always be sufficient time spent repeating this, in remembering and being amazed at it.

As to the second text, we focus on the image of the "weapons." The light, which we are, must be defended and increased. There is still some darkness in us against which we must fight, some obstacles which impede or slow down the diffusion of the light. If the children are already acquainted with the material entitled "The Plan of God," one can make reference to the obstacles which are present there and help the children understand that they are also caused by the darkness within us.

We examine the image of "weapons of light" in 3 or 4 meetings. First of all we try to identify these "weapons." Most of the time the children choose the maxims. They are "weapons" to be worn, made use of and not to be left in the corner. At

*William McKinley-Ward, age 7, drawn on the day of his First Communion. Christian Family Montessori School, Mt. Rainier, Maryland.*

every meeting, therefore, we invite the children to choose one or two "weapons" to be used during the coming week. At the next meeting we ask ourselves about the use we made of them. It may be that some child has forgotten completely; another child may have been able to make some use of them, but with difficulty. Usually, at every meeting, we introduce a new maxim (Matt. 7:1-5, 6: 19-21), the parable of the foolish rich man, (Luke 12:16-21) and recall the text we know.

After the first two meetings, we begin to ask ourselves how we feel when we realize that we are not always able to make use of the "weapons of light." We spend some time on this aspect; we must help the children to become aware of their own limitations and deficiencies in a positive way. Limitations and deficiencies do exist but we have been assured that we *are* already "light" and that the Good Shepherd does not feel disappointed by our deficiencies; on the contrary, he loves us even more and he comes looking for us to give us greater strength. The awareness of one's own limitations urges us to feel the need for the Sacrament. Then we speculate on whether we would prefer not to be aware of our inabilities. Which is better? To be conscious of one's weaknesses or ignorant of them? How did we come to discover them? It was possible because of the increase of light within us. Was this a useful activity or not? We recall the parables of mercy, and the Sacrament of Reconciliation as a special expression of God's love.

In the last meeting preceding the Penitential Liturgy, we take another look at the cards on the Sacrament of Reconciliation (like the ones for Baptism, picturing different moments of the rite.) Together we try to verbally make a definition for each card. This activity sums up the experience lived while using the "weapons" and which is preparatory to asking for help, one of the specific conditions of this sacrament.

As I have already said, we have experimented with this way of deepening our knowledge of Reconciliation for many years. It is apparent to us that we are confronted with one of the "constants" we often encounter in our work. First of all, the image of the "weapons of light" is incarnated by the children; that is, it becomes part of the psyche, it sums up and evokes the entire process of conversation - which is what this is all about, after all. It is full of content and therefore we can link it to things already known to the children. In turn it can stimulate and be a source for further connections. Lastly, it is an experience which is deeply in tune with the spirit which animates our catechesis. This is the reason I felt it useful to share it with you so that you in turn may present it to your children.

## More on Reconciliation

*This is a continuation of Francesca's presentation, providing some more details about what we do during Lent as a preparation for the Sacrament of Reconciliation.*

In giving up the entire six weeks of Lent for this purpose, the development of the themes we present during the year certainly comes to a halt. On the other hand, it seems to me to be very important to return to this topic every year, thus further developing the discussion begun at the time of the child's First Communion. After all, it is a well-established tradition in the Church to devote Lent to reflections in the area of reconciliation. Naturally, the main points mentioned here are only broad guidelines which should not influence your work. Please observe the children's reactions and keep us informed.

In our presentations, proven over many years, there are some elements which are repeated every year, and others which are alternated so that the children won't feel that its just a "rehash" of the "same old thing."

*continued on page 18*

*First Communion cross by Keely Young-Dixon, age 7, St. Frances Cabrini, Minneapolis, MN.*

## Reconciliation for the older children

*continued from page 17*

**The "fixed" elements are:**

- the message: "you are light." (Ephesians 5:8), and the invitation to use the "weapons of light" (Romans 13:11-12).

- the link with history, particularly the "Plan of God" (time-line), a unitarian plan in which divisions, separations and wars are found; the question is asked: "What is the source of this discord?"

- reflection on the maxims

- card materials on the details of the Rite of Reconciliation

**The alternating elements are:**

- the miracle of the paralytic at Capharnum (Matt 9:1-8) which sheds a good deal of light on the effects of sin and the sacrament, comparing it to the physical condition.

- the parable of the foolish rich man (Luke 12:16-21)

- the parable of the two sons (Matt 21:28-31)

- a detailed examination of the parable of the father and the son (Luke 15: 11-24) which is usually presented for First Communion in a very general way. It is interesting to contrast the verbs which illustrate the father's actions, which are all actions of love, and those which describe the actions of the son.

- a comparison between the parable of the father and son and the various moments of Reconciliation (for instance, writing the actions of the father and those of the son on small cards and then matching these cards with the card material on the Rite of Reconciliation)

- some new maxims/texts:

    "It is not the one who says Lord, Lord ..."
    (Matt 7:21)

    "He who puts his hand to the plow..."
    (Luke 9: 62).

    "Enter by the narrow gate ..."
    (Matt 7:14)
    *[Note: I would omit the words: "and only a few find it." ]*

    "It is not the healthy who need a doctor..."
    (Matt: 9:12).

## Resource Materials

The following materials are available from the Montessori Training Center in St. Paul.

**Presentations:**

**Renilde Montessori** (*granddaughter of Maria Montessori*) *speaking on*

### The Child's Quest for Discipline
*(a one-day workshop presented in March 1992 in St. Paul)*

| | |
|---|---|
| **Set of 4 tapes** | $40.00 + $3.00 Shipping/Handling |
| **Transcript** | $15.00 + $2.00 Shipping/Handling |

**Books:**

### The Discovery of the Child
by Maria Montessori     $16.50

### The Absorbent Mind
by Maria Montessori     $16.50

### The Secret of Childhood
by Maria Montessori     $9.75

### Understanding the Human Being
(*The Child from Birth to Three*)
by Dr. Silvana Montanaro     $14.75

### Maria Montessori: Her Life and Work
by E.M. Standing     $9.70

Handling and Shipping charges:

(**Note:** These charges are based on Book Rate. First Class or overseas shipping would require additional charges).

| | |
|---|---|
| For 1 book | add $1.50 |
| For 2 books | add $2.00 |
| For 3 books | add $2.50 |
| For 4 books | add $3.00 |

To order, send your request, along with a check for the correct amount for the items and the shipping/handling charges to:

**Montessori Training Center of Minnesota, Inc.**
P.O, Box 16272,
St. Paul, MN 55116.

# The Child's Spiritual Life: Another Perspective

*by Nancy Wood*

**Vision and Character, A Christian Educator's Alternative to Kohlberg** by Craig Dykstra. Paulist Press, 1981.

Reading the title of this book, one might easily pass it by, thinking it some kind of textbook. And indeed the only way I discovered it was because it was assigned reading for a course, "The Development of Religious Identity." To my surprise and delight it was an extremely readable and valuable book, containing much insight for those of us who work in the Catechesis of the Good Shepherd. I want to highlight some of the key points which intersect with the Catechesis.

The book is ostensibly a critique of the theories of psychologist Lawrence Kohlberg who described the development of moral reasoning based on Piaget's understanding of cognitive learning. However, one can easily read it without being familiar with Kohlberg or Piaget. For Dykstra, moral development and the spiritual life are inextricably connected and it is to the spiritual life that he gives most of his attention.

According to Dykstra, sin is a natural and anxious concern for ourselves which distorts our relationships with others and our perceptions of reality. We don't see reality as God sees it. Dykstra calls this "moral egocentrism." We live our lives behind a "falsifying veil," all our psychic energy going into preserving our distortions. Conversion takes place through the "transformation of the imagination," i.e. developing a new way of seeing (hence his title, *Vision and Character*).

While Dykstra sees the primary source of this transformation to be revelation, something that *God does* through the work of Christ and the Spirit, we can help the process through three interrelated disciplines: 1) repentance, 2) prayer, and 3) service.

Dykstra addresses how this spiritual life is lived out during various stages. His description of the young child resonates deeply with our experience in the Catechesis: the child's capacity to relate to the concrete and the immediate while possessing an amazing ability to apprehend mystery, and the child's need for security and love which provides the foundation for later moral development.

Though we usually think of the disciplines of repentance, prayer, and services as confined to adulthood, in their own way children can also experience these rudiments of discipleship (albeit more "sporadically and spontaneously" than the adult). Their ability to recognize at times that they are not the center of the universe is a kind of repentance. We have all observed children absorbed in or "paying deep attention" to realities beyond themselves, a form of prayer. And their capacity for compassionate presence to another person, animal, or things in nature displays Dykstra's understanding of true service which is free of manipulation and need to be "effective," (traits commonly found in adults).

I also found inspiration in Dykstra's description of a teacher's role. (Though the Catechesis tries to get away from the word "teacher," these insights apply, as they would also to a spiritual director, counselor, etc.). As we learn in the Catechesis, the catechist's role is inextricably intertwined with *oneself*. Dykstra claims that teachers must be persons who are themselves actively engaged in the disciplines of repentance, prayer, and service and have "pierced the veil of the distortions brought on by moral egocentricity." A humbling and tall order!

Leaving our "arsenal of techniques" behind, we come before the child as "an inexhaustible mystery." We must be fully attentive and receptive to the wider reality of God's truth and value to which we direct the attention of the learner. Dykstra goes on to claim:

> As much as it is the teacher's responsibility to guide the explorations of the learners, the teacher does not and cannot pretend to do the exploration for the learners. What the teacher sees is important. But it is not so important as that the learners see, and see in their own terms. The revelation of the mystery of a particular reality is not the teacher's to give.... Teachers do not provide new ways of seeing ...rather, they provide occasions for the learners' own new visions.

Thus, for Dykstra, the essence of the spiritual life is this encountering of mystery. He refers to Fredrich Buechner who compares the gospel to fairy tale (the crucial difference being our claim that the gospel is true). Like the gospel, the fairy tale enters a world of "magic and mystery, of deep darkness and flickering starlight, a world where terrible things happen and wonderful things too." In describing the relation of the fairy-tale world with the ordinary world, Beuchner says, "It is as if the world of the fairy tale impinges on the ordinary world the way the dimension of depth impinges on the two-dimensional surface of a plane, so that there is no point on the plane ... that can't become an entrance to it." (*Telling the Truth, The Gospel as Tragedy, Comedy and Fairy*). This image provides a beautiful vision of the atrium. Each point of encounter in the concrete world of the atrium is an entrance for the children into a deeper reality. In the Catechesis we speak about the coming together of two mysteries: the mystery of God and the mystery of the child. Dykstra's description of mystery contributes significantly to our vision:

> We are exposed to a wondrous world, which we are drawn to explore. And the more we explore, the more we find being unfolded to us; we never exhaust it. Through revelatory images, a world of inexhaustible particularity, richness, and depth is illuminated. In this experience, we become conscious of having encountered both the mystery of the world and the mystery of the Power in which that world is held and by which our seeing has been made possible.

# 1994 Catechist formation courses

## Part I of 3 - 6 Level:
*Offered in four 1-week sessions*

Location/Dates:  Grand Rapids, MI
  Week 1  June 10-15, 1994
Staff:  Linda Kaiel, Portland, OR
  Week 2  Fall 1994
  Week 3  Spring 1995
  Week 4  June 1995
  Additional Staff to be announced

For details, contact:
  Mary Wernet
  730 Hillside Ct.
  Lowell, MI 49331
  (616) 897-6485

## Part I and II of 3 - 6 Level
*Offered in four 1-week sessions*

Location/Dates:  Phoenix, AZ,
  Week 1 begins June 27, 1994 &
  Week 2 begins July 25, 1994

**Staff** and **contact person:**
  Marty O'Bryan
  721 W. Wilshire Dr.,
  Phoenix, AZ 85007
  (602) 258-9623

## Part I of 9 - 12 Level
*Offered in two 2-week sessions*
*Part II to be offered in June 1995*

Location/Dates:  Jackson, MS June 13 - 24. 1994

Staff:  Carol Dittberner, St. Paul, MN
  Catherine Maresca, Washington, D.C.

For details, contact:
  Laurie Cummings
  3388 Eden Midway Rd.
  Yazoo City, MS 39124
  (601) 746-0912

## Part II of 3 - 6, 6 - 8 and 9 - 12 Levels

Location/Dates:  Houston, TX, July 10 - 22, 1994
Staff:  Betty Hissong, Cleveland, OH
  Maria Christlieb, Mexico City, Mexico
  Judy Schmidt, Chicago, IL
  Francesca Cocchini, Rome, Italy

*(See note about Francesca below)*

For details, contact:
  Sherry Mock
  3831 Riley St.
  Houston, TX 77005
  (713) 661-9148

---

We are pleased to announce the presence of
FRANCESCA COCCHINI
at the 1994 summer
formation experience in Houston.

**Francesca** will offer one week of on-going formation for those catechists who are working with children and have completed the three levels of training. She will present the timeline of the History of Israel, as well as the changes in the Peoples and Plan of God timeline. Her lectures will expand on the themes of the 9-12 level, Old Testament typology, and moral formation.

Francesca grew up in the Catechesis. Her mother, Clotilde Cocchini, was a catechist for children in the 6-12 atrium. Francesca was a child in Sofia's and Gianna's atrium. Presently, Francesca is a catechist for children in the 6-12 atrium. She assists in the formation of adult catechists, teaches church history at the university level, and has published books and numerous articles on the Fathers of the Church. Her presence in Houston this summer is a unique and exciting opportunity for experienced catechists to further their 9-12 level training.

*For details, write to the address listed above.*

## Part II of 3 - 6 Level

**Location/Dates:** Denver, CO, July 25 - August 5, 1994

**Staff:** Carol Dittberner, St. Paul, MN
Rose Paul, Bloomington, MN

**For details, contact:**
Linda Roberts
St. John's Episcopal Cathedral
1313 Clarkson St., Denver, CO 80218
(303) 831-7115

---

## Part I: 3 - 6 Level

**Location/Dates:** Amarillo, TX, July, 18-29, 1994

**Staff:** Catherine Maresca, Washington, D.C.

**For details, contact:**
Laura Higgins
St. Andrews Episcopal Church
1601 So. Georgia, Amarillo, TX 79102
(806) 379-9738

---

## Part I: 3 - 6 Level

**Location/Dates:** Tulsa, OK, July 5-15, 1994

**Staff:** Catherine Maresca, Washington, D.C.

**For details, contact:**
Bert Bibbons
Office of Trinity Episcopal Church
(918) 582-4128

---

## Part II of 3 - 6 Level *(offered in two 1-week sessions)*

**Location/Dates:** Pasadena, CA,

**Staff:** Marty O'Bryan

**Contact Person:**
Tracy Gaestel
1275 Church St.
Pasadena, CA 91105
(213) 258-6370

*Joseph Kosowski, age 6, St. Frances Cabrini, Minneapolis, MN*

# Next Newsletter to be Published: Spring 1995
# Next Issue to Feature: Rome Visit

## *A letter from Sofia to Carol Dittberner*

**Thank you, Carol.** Many thanks, too, to all the staff of the Newsletter, and to all the catechists of Minnesota.

With my most heartfelt thanks for the last 10 years of work. You have rendered a priceless service to all who work, or even have an interest, in the *Catechesis of the Good Shepherd*.

You have helped further communication between us; you have made possible the exchange of experiences among us, of giving a deeper understanding of important points, of preserving both the memories of people who have worked with us, and of important moments in our history.

These reasons alone ought to be sufficient enough to deserve thanks, but there is even one more. You have helped us all to know the child better.

The child is revealed in the pages of the *Newsletter* as a living and speaking person. The "metaphysical child" is present here with all the deep spirituality, seriousness and spontaneity of his bearing. One could say that the "metaphysical child" holds a "professorship" (so to speak) and in a manner most congenial to him, that is, with a subdued and prayerful voice, without even knowing it, without putting on any "airs" about it. He involves us in his prayer life; he allows us a glimpse of his mystical rapport with God and sometimes admonishes us to hold fast, to continue on, to recommit ourselves, because, as Andria says, "God will still do things on earth if we still have hope."

—*Sofia*

## Your stories make our newsletter

Articles about your atrium, training, book reviews make this newsletter an important communication vehicle for Catechists worldwide. Tell us how we can help you by writing us about the newsletter or with your questions about our work with children.

## Notes about children's artwork, photographs

To obtain the best possible newsletter image, we ask for original artworks whenever possible. We will return all work as soon as possible. Since this is a black and white newsletter, black and white photographs are ideal; however, color photographs are also acceptable. Include the artist's name, age and tell us a little about the child, and the work. This information should be written on a piece of paper attached to the artwork with a paper clip or carefully printed on the back. Also tell us the name of your atrium, and in what city and state.

With any materials that you would like returned, please be sure to include the address. Thank you.

---

Please send all Newsletter materials directly to:

**Barbara Disch**
**P.O. Box 1084, Oak Park, IL 60304**

**1994 Staff in U.S.A.**
   Carol Dittberner
   Carol Stenborg
   Italian Translators:
       Joan Parasine, Nicolina Gleasure

**Staff in Chihuahua:**
   Maria Ines Gonzalez
   Bertha Sofia Quiroz de Marquez
   Emilia G. de Sandoval
   Noemi F. de Lopez
   Maria de Los Angeles Christlieb

## *Membership*

**The Catechesis of the Good Shepherd,** An Association of Children and Adults, welcomes members throughout the year. Members receive the annual newsletter, all mailings and a directory of catechists and friends of the Association.

Mail requests for membership and other information to:
   The Catechesis of the Good Shepherd, P.O. Box 1084, Oak Park, IL 60304

© Copyright 1994: The Catechesis of the Good Shepherd, P.O. Box 1084, Oak Park, IL 60304

# The Catechesis of the Good Shepherd

Number 11, English                                                                                           Fall 1995

*Lois Trego from the United States visited Sofia in her home before the International Conference got underway.*

A short walk from St. Peter's Square and over a ponte. Down several busy streets congested with small cars, noisy motorbikes, buses and taxis. It is a warm fall evening. Eventually we turn down a cobbled alley, once upon a time a fitting passageway for chariots and then, another turn and we find ourselves in a quiet courtyard having finally arrived at Via degli Orsini! A large fountain covered in green ivy greets us with the peaceful sound of flowing water. We proceed up an esplanade of stone steps with vaulted archways and marble landings, ancient grillwork and iron balustrades. One hundred steps to be exact and one wonders if there is not something essentially "Roman" in that! We pause to catch our breath in front of the vast, well-varnished wooden doors with brass fixtures and the simple bell plate bearing the name "Cavalletti." A push of the finger brings Augusta throwing wide the heavy door. Freshly dressed in a white uniform and obviously having benefited from her own good cooking, her greeting to us is as large and as warm as the open door. We are each embraced in her big arms and broad smile. She loves to laugh. Sofia stands to the side, so stately, gracious and gentle. Perhaps even aristocratic.

A huge arrangement of sunflowers in a large urn has been beautifully placed in the foyer. Sofia inquires about each of us and thanks us for coming and making this occasion so special for her! She invites us in to her sitting room, passing a chapel and pausing briefly in her library. Twelve foot ceilings with heavy beams separate it into two parts, each divided further into small squares that have been delicately painted in blues and golds. Large double windows with wide sills and wooden shutters stand open to the evening air. Lots of activity in the alley below. Sofia would like to sit and serve tea while we visit but all attention is focused on yes – the delight and labor of her life, the atriums! The expectation we feel is enormous. The environment

*continued on page 2*

# Contents

- Let Us Pray with the Children ..............3
- Letters from Sofia and Gianna ..............4-5
- Religious Experience with the 3-6 Child ..............6-10
- New Board Members ..............11
- Cosmic Character of the Mass ..............12
- Mystery of Our Faith:
  - Album Page ..............13-15
- Conference Details ..............16-19
- International Reports ..............20-23
- The Eucharist with the Children:
  - Additions to the Last Newsletter ..............24
- Life of the Catechist ..............25
- About Our Association ..............26

*Continued from cover*

almost defies description, the work a joy to behold! Everything has been so carefully arranged. Small tables and chairs with rush bottom seats. Tiny antique kneelers. Very fine tapestries. What a holy place, this space set aside and given over for a specific purpose, a place for God's presence to be made known to children. The materials, now forty years old, are original. Each one is so simple, so beautiful, so essential. The materials bear a beautiful patina, a richness obtainable only through love and respect as shown by children over time as they have used and taken care of the materials. Sofia shows us a wooden box, a beautiful "treasure box." She opens the lid and we see hundreds and hundreds of small strips of paper, each bearing a child's name which had been written in demonstration of their desire to receive First Communion. Each child had beautifully signed and decorated their piece of paper. Sofia tells us that whenever she has a reunion for the children, they come and one of the first things they do is to eagerly search through the box for their own name. Some of these "children" are now 45 years old!

*-Lois*

---

Dear Friends,

It is with great joy (and some relief) that we publish the 11th annual newsletter, this year from Chicago. The topic is the International Conference held in Rome, October 18-23, 1993. Many of the participants during that exciting week have shared their reflections, summaries of lectures, and country reports.

Throughout you will find prayers and artwork from the children. Please note the follow-up to The Eucharist and the Children from the last newletter on First Communion (page 24).

We wish to thank all contributors to this newsletter and especially Carol Dittberner and Carol Stenborg for sharing their expertise to get us started.

May this newsletter serve to connect us all.

Peace,

Joan & Toby

*Jessica, age 7, Little Community, St. Charles, Illinois. The cover of a booklet which contains tracings of the Infancy Narratives.*

# Let us pray with the children . . .

*by Ryan, age 8, St. Charles, IL*

Dear God and Jesus,
Your definition of us and you together was great!

*by Katy, age 10, St. Charles, IL*

God is so good to me,
God is good to you and me.
Thank you God
for all the life
we have and for
all good and bad people.
Thank you so much!
Oh what am I most
thankful for God.
It's you, oh yes it's you.
God I love you so much.
You give me everything I need you with me.
Oh, thank you God
 for everything you give me!

*by Rebecca, age 10*

*by Bill, age 6, Fremont, MI*
*after hearing the presentation of the History of the Gifts.*

Thank you for all the animals
Thank you for all the trees that we can make with houses and cabinets

It's a good thing that Mary had you.
Thank you for all the metals we could use for pennies and steel.
Thank you for all the sea animals and the shells.

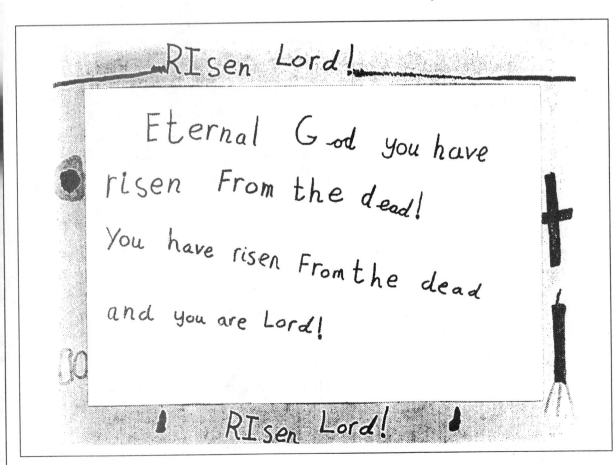

*This Easter prayer card was drawn by Josh Frens-String, age 7, St. John's Episcopal Church in Fremont, MI. The prayer is surrounded by colored cross, tomb (closed and open), Paschal candle and fire.*

# LETTERS FROM ROME

*The International Conference was held in Rome in October, 1993. Here, Sofia Cavalletti and Gianna Gobbi reflect on their time together with the catechists.*

## Aftermath of the Conference

How many persons were there at our conference? So many adults and so many children! Did you notice them? How did the apartment at Via degli Orsini hold all of them? They had come not only from the six representative countries, but also, as a crowd, from many places, from Africa, east Europe and the Middle East as well. It was so nice to welcome them in person, to share with them the joy of meeting again, of listening to each other.

Never as in those days was it obvious to me that our work has a choral dimension! We exchanged experiences, we listened to a voice telling us of the work carried out here and there and then, immediately, behind those experiences, behind that voice, there appeared images of many adults, of many children. we imagined them in their atria: some were rich, others very poor, but, in spite of their poverty, they were still rich; some even were gathered under a tree. Everyone was as busy as a bee with his/her work in preparing the materials and practicing with them. All of them were engrossed and absorbed in listening to the message together and, above all, they were very joyful.

Indeed, in our work, it is not possible to say that I made that piece of apparatus and you made this one. In each of our meetings we find the contributions of many persons were already refined, as in the process of distillation. How many are the children who are our guides in focusing on the essential themes of the Christian message, in helping these themes to be embodied in the materials in a special way, in answering to the children's need for meditation. How many are the catechists, who, because of their particular abilities, their experiences, their loving observation of the children, help us to continue the work and to examine it more thoroughly?

Any possible personal satisfaction vanishes in this sea, in this choir, singing only one note, which belongs to no one, because it belongs to God, and, for this reason, it forms the joy of everyone.

What we lived, in the distilled condition throughout the meeting, we then found again concentrated at the liturgical moment. That Saturday morning we all truly were listening to the Word, the resonances of which were inside each of us. That Word came from above and in it we found the echo of many voices simultaneously. That Word, slowly, naturally, and spontaneously, was our guide to the heart of the Mystery. The room appeared to be "full" in a particular way on that Saturday morning.

Beside the choral aspect, it became so obvious to me that the characteristics of our work are not speculative. We had prepared some plans of work, as it is usual to do in meetings of this kind. We almost did not look at them! Presently, we are examining them. At that time, they were not put aside on purpose; it was as if we were guided unintentionally by a kind of "instinct." I asked myself, "What kind of instinct?" The answer I was able to formulate is that the catechesis, above all, is a gift and, just like any other gift, it must, first of all, be received, enjoyed, relished, scanned, compared, and examined thoroughly. During our meeting, we lived the first moment, now the second one has come.

In the beginning of those days I was looking over them as if they were the retreat for First Communion, when nothing new is given, yet we relish things already known to us. Thus we lived those days. Presently the time commences when they have to be translated slowly, yet set in an operative mode.

I began the presentation of this meeting animated by a considerable feeling of gratitude towards God, first of all, and towards all the persons who made it possible. I now relive this same sentiment, more profoundly, in my memory.

While calling back to our memory the various stages which preceded this experience of ours, one could almost cry out, "Dayenu". This is the answer given by every Jew, anytime he recalls the many

*continued on next page*

*Continues from page 4*

works the Lord has done to him. The expression is not easily translated. Maybe the phrase which is nearest to its spirit could be "Already enough for us!" Each gift of God would already be enough for our limited horizon, since it could satisfy our inadequate ability to love. Nevertheless, this does not satisfy God's ability to love. God's horizon is much vaster than any expectations of ours. Thus our life is filled with inexhaustible hope.

*Sofia*
*Rome, December 10, 1993*

## Gianna's Reflections

What can I say of our week-long conference in Rome? Our daily concerns and work have resumed their usual rhythm, yet they cannot erase the memory of those days. There has not been sufficient time for our heart to relax and let out the feelings it holds inside.

What else can I say and remember? I remember the joy at again meeting so many dear people with whom for years we have shared our work, have exchanged experiences and have reciprocated affectionate sentiments. I remember the joy when talking to one another, although not so long as we would have wished. Above all I remember the joy of being together with God to Whom belongs all that we have and that we give to our children.

What else remains in our mind? Many things, so many questions and proposals; so many open windows in front of which we stand watching a foggy view. But we know there is a beautiful panorama below.

It is a fact well known that few proposals reach a conclusion at these conferences. However the foundations for our future work were laid.

With God's help, the children's guidance and the cooperation of each of us, we will succeed in overcoming those unavoidable difficulties in our work. We want this work to be the best. As catechists and educators, we know how to face it sustained by the spiritual values of justice and humility. I stress justice because our successes do not belong to us but are due to God. I stress humility because we are conscious of being "small" in front of the Mystery of God and the Child.

Meanwhile, each of us has her own space. There she brings forward her own work of catechesis, strengthens and improves upon the groups already in operation and helps the new ones with the moral power and confidence given by the Child. As Maria Montessori taught us, this same Child will reveal himself to us in his work.

*Gianna*

*US catechists gathered at Via degli Orsini. From left: Sofia Cavalletti, Rebekah Rojcewicz, Betty Hissong, Carol Nyberg, Catherine Maresca, Tina Lillig, Randall Trego, Linda Kaiel and Anna Guida.*

# The Religious Experience with the Child Three to Six

*Presented by Gianna Gobbi on Thursday, October 22. Summarized by Betty Hissong.*

*For years I had heard her name, spoken by many with real love. She was the Montessori teacher with whom Sofia worked for years to develop the Good Shepherd Catechesis. When I first heard how Sofia got started, when asked to prepare a child for first Communion, I remember being told that Sofia's reaction was, "But, I don't know anything about children." After all Sofia was a Hebrew and Scripture scholar in a university setting. "That's O.K.," she was told, "you know a lot about God, and we'll get you acquainted with someone who knows a lot about children." This someone was Gianna Gobbi. Gianna was a teenager when she began working in a Montessori environment. She has spent her life serving children.*

*It wasn't until 1986 that I met Gianna in Toronto. Immediately I knew she was a good Montessorian. Her childlikeness, her simplicity, her directness, her warmth, but mostly her sparkling smiley eyes made me realize she did know children. I felt drawn to her just like I'm sure the children are drawn to her, and even though she spoke no English I felt like we were friends immediately.*

Gianna began by saying that the word "initiation" may not be an accurate description of what she has to say since the word itself indicates an action on the part of the adult outside of the child. Inasmuch as it is an adult activity, it does not really express the true position needed by the adult in our work. Instead the attitude and posture needed by the adult in our work should rather be one of humble observer. In the child there exists a hidden, but profoundly religious nature, which the child desires to live out. For a child to reveal this true nature the adult needs to be prepared for the task of helping this revelation to occur. We need to recognize that our primary call is to be a humble and attentive observer of life. Probably a better title for this talk would be "How to Help a Child's Religious Experience."

Maria Montessori took as a model for Montessori teachers that of the image of a scientist. The scientist is one who probes and observes nature in a kind of self-forgetfulness, for the love of what is being observed. How much more important this is in the religious field! We know how deeply the children respond to religious experiences. How do we know? Mostly through the joy and wonder at hearing the parables. We see the enchantment they experience with the mustard seed and leaven. Over and over again they respond so positively to the essential themes given to them.

Even before age three, one can observe their religiousness. It shows itself in a special form. The young child will express and communicate his experience with his face and his whole body. Gianna gave us a concrete example from a time she observed a very young child really contemplating. After this particular child finished dinner, he was accustomed to a particular ritual each evening—taking a walk in the field. Imagine Gianna and the young child as they stroll together. They spoke only a few words. Gianna would say "sunset" or "birds," etc. The child and she would contemplate the landscape. They would stop and listen to the church bells. There was much silence. There was much joy. Above all there was peace. Gianna watched all this and wondered: "What can all this mean?" The child was so at peace, and this peace lasted until bedtime where he went in great peace.

Gianna concluded from this kind of experience that a child has a real capacity for contemplation and that this contemplation always generates peace. It is, however, expressed by the child in a modality different from adults. The child is really what Sofia calls "the metaphysical child." The child seems to move at ease with the transcendent and actually savors contact with God. This "discovery of the religious child" was parallel to that of Maria Montessori's discovery of the child's true nature and potential. We all know what happened in the first Casa dei Bambini when the chil-

*continued on next page*

dren were placed in a prepared environment where they were allowed to be themselves and show their true nature. They displayed concentration, self-discipline, love of order, love for culture and learning—behavior that was considered impossible for children. This San Lorenzo experience in 1907 helped Montessori discover the real nature of a child. This discovery gave new direction to education and ended up as the Montessori Method. Today we speak of Montessori philosophy, which is understood as the search for the real child, the real nature of human beings. This philosophy is a science, because it probes, observes,, experiments and discovers the universal laws which are in each human being. Montessori did this. Hers was a life lived with love and lived with children in many different cultures.

With the discovery of the new child, and subsequent discovery of the religious child, the role of the teacher, and even more importantly the role of the catechist, had to change. The "new child" called for a "new teacher" and a new kind of catechist. The call of the catechist was no longer simple. For the catechist it means, first of all, the careful preparation of the environment with all the beautiful materials, which will aid the child in his contemplation of God. But most importantly, the catechist must realize that our primary job is to help the child make contact with God so that a real relationship can develop between God and the child. To do this the adult needs to have a real respect for the growing life, especially the religious life, ensuring freedom for the child and thus allowing the authentic being to show itself. The preparation of the adult for this work involves a real respect for the mystery of the child and the mystery of God. This realization and respect does not allow us to "ascend the throne" and assume a position above the children. We need to come before the children as humble observers and servants.

There are certain basic characteristics and attitudes we are called to embrace in order to be ready for this difficult task of helping the child in his religious life. In describing the preparation of a teacher Maria Montessori suggested the need for several things:

- **1.** Learn **SILENCE.**
- **2.** Rather that teach, **OBSERVE.**
- **3.** Instead of assuming self-pride that makes oneself important, one must put on the mantle of **HUMILITY.**

If these attitudes are needed for a Montessori teacher, how much more important are they for the catechist. Development of these attitudes is essential. Nothing is ours; the child does not belong to us and the message is also not ours. It is given to us by God. *(Betty: I might also add that the actual work done is not done by us. We merely prepare the conditions whereby a loving relationship can develop between God and the child. And who does the actual relating? God and the child, not us.)*

Up to this point Gianna spoke mostly about the role of the adult in the religious life of the child. She then went into what we might call the role of the child in society. She quoted Montessori as saying, "The child and the adult are two distinct poles of humanity. They must come together."

*Nakeeta Charles, age 8, Our Saviour Atrium, Chicago. This colorful picture has a red house, blue sky, green grass and two brown figures, one orange and one black.*

*continued on next page*

# RELIGIOUS EXPERIENCE . . .

*continued from page 7*

Montessori continues by saying that the child is a real part of reality, but that pole of humanity has its own laws of nature that are different from the adult's. The qualities and natural laws of children can and should be of real service to humanity in general.

Gianna gave as an example of what happens among animals. It seems to be a natural law that in the animal kingdom we see different instincts in animals that are young and animals who are adults. It is especially apparent when animals have babies. Their whole way of behaving changes. Two examples will suffice. Among the most ferocious of species, the adult animals seem to lose their violence when having young. Among birds who have no fixed home or eating habits, a change occurs with the arrival of little birds. The adult birds set up a home and a definite eating pattern emerges.

What meaning does Maria Montessori see in this? It seems that God gives little things the sublime task of saving and preserving what He has created. Creation is a sign of God's love, and the appearance of the new, young and little is a sign of His desire to save and continue all of creation.

> **Creation is a sign of God's love, and the appearance of the new, young and little is a sign of His desire to save and continue all of creation.**

Civilization, however, has developed as if there were only adults—no children. It seems to be based only on adult qualities and therefore is often based on violent conquest, war, and conquest of victims. What is still lacking in the development of civilization is a peaceful world. Maybe the child will change this. And adults need to be prepared for their task as educators and catechists, allowing children the freedom to show their true nature, showing us the adults that our society can become better.

If we take time to reflect on the role of the child in society we might realize that children are also a key for ecumenical dialogue. Some indication of this was apparent in Montessori teacher training courses. There were no conflicts among students even though they were a heterogeneous group. There were many people, all from different places and different cultures. There were Catholics, Hindus, socialists, etc., all coming because of one common cause—the interest of the child. It was the child that brought unity among diverse peoples. Mr. Joosten, a Montessori teacher trainer, was giving a course in India. In the beginning of the course all the people who were from India sat on one side while all the others were on the other side of the room. At the end of the course, the people of India were on both sides amidst others of the different countries.

We here are Episcopalians and Catholics. (Some things are also already happening among other faiths, like the Lutherans.) Perhaps we should reflect on this phenomenon. If the child creates harmony as it has here, does the child have a role for unity among all people? Is there in the child a capacity to open the doors of a new world?

## Prayer

In speaking about prayer and children it is important to realize that this calls from us the greatest respect for the child. One of the greatest challenges is to maintain a balance between spontaneous prayer and formal prayer. Prayer can be considered as "listening to God." It is a key that opens the door between God and man, a key that God gives to all of us. Yet all pray in different ways, according to culture, country, different traditions. In the atrium we can organize moments of communal prayer. Then it is necessary that we consider our different cultures. Consequently we must choose prayers that create bonds—both vertical between God and the community, but also horizontal, bonds among the community. Jesus already taught us one such prayer: the Our Father.

Gianna told the story of a child who said to a priest, "Jesus does miracles." The priest asked the child, "What miracles?" to which the child responded, "Jesus taught me to pray." Adults cannot teach children or others how to pray. Obviously that child knew better than we that it is Jesus who teaches us to pray. Prayer is a personal response to God. The Good Shepherd calls each by his own name and each person, adult or child, must respond to that call. What we are called to do, if we can't claim to teach the children how to pray, is to reflect on a few simple items that help prepare the conditions for prayer.

The first is the necessity to prepare the environment to be an atmosphere for prayer, a place for silence and

*continued on next page*

*continued from page 8*

recollection. The environment should facilitate concentration and should facilitate "Listening" with a capital "L." In the atrium a special area should be set aside for prayer. It might include a table with a statue of the Good Shepherd, a candle, flowers, etc.

Gianna then described how we would go about a communal prayer. First one should gather the children and invite them to silence. Make silence and then light the candle. A very brief song could then be sung. It's O.K. to have silence in between. The catechist should always stay behind the children especially if we have a guitar. If one is in front of the children the children will tend naturally to look at us and be drawn to us rather than to God and prayer. The length of time of this prayer is really entrusted to the children's needs. Often the prayer is interspersed with silence, which can also be an authentic prayer.

> **The environment should facilitate concentration and should facilitate "Listening" with a capital "L."**

To invite the children to give verbal responses requires a long time of preparations. Don't be surprised if it takes a long time to move into this. Different times and themes will also affect the children's responses. It seems that spontaneous prayer is usually evident especially at the time of the presentations on Baptism. When the infancy narratives are shared with the children this is not always so. In baptism the children clearly see this as gift, and therefore want to say "thanks." Once during the baptism presentation one child spontaneously said, "My body is happy." In the infancy narratives one could say something like, "Let's praise God as the angels did."

It is important that we not be overburdened by a sense of formality. There is a need, especially in the beginning, to have some external form and structure since spontaneity does not occur immediately. Even in a regular Montessori class we won't find spontaneous things happening right away. Montessori herself said that in the initial phases a teacher can approach tasks as she wishes. She should "draw" the children to a variety of activities. The actual activities are not that important. And one does not have to worry much about intervening. The children's psychic processes haven't kicked in yet, and we need an external atmosphere or ritual for getting to the children. But as one sees the children becoming concentrated we adults need to change our behavior and allow for spontaneity which will be forth coming as they become "normalized." *(Normalization is a Montessori term for a child who is acting according to his true nature.)*

Ritual is a profound need of the children. It is especially important to establish this for prayer. Once when speaking to a catechist, Gianna was asked, "Is all this ritual really necessary? Doesn't this exclude spontaneous prayer?" Gianna's reply was, "Rituals are very important. Silence and gestures are essential." The importance of preparing the children for prayer accurately will be the thing that will lead to the peace and joy one can see the children experiencing after they've had a chance to pray.

Before direct prayer one should consider certain activities which help bring the children to a point of being able to pray. There are primarily three elements that can help the children:

- **1. Silence**
- **2. Control of bodily movements**
- **3. Language**

The whole Montessori approach to education prepares the soil for prayer, because all activities which lead to concentration will be of help. One activity especially, however, is a direct help, and that is the silence game. Incidentally, the silence game is a very attractive activity for the children. In traditional schools silence is imposed when the adult needs order. This is not true in the silence game. In Montessori we help the children bit by bit to bring their body to a point of immobility. It is not an imposed silence, but a matter of the child's own self-control. And it is something that goes beyond their body. A child becomes aware of his inner self and, as Montessori says, "The silence activities show a child's desire to elevate himself." What we're hoping to achieve in helping the children achieve silence is to help the children enjoy the experience of silence. A child needs an awareness of his physical body, and the ability to control it by making it immobile, is an individual achievement. Gradually the child becomes more conscious of how to be really still in a group. Thus it becomes a collective kind of silence.

The silence game can also lead to mastery of one's will. The exercise is really an indirect preparation for

*continued on next page*

# RELIGIOUS EXPERIENCE . . .

*continued from page 9*

self-discipline. Most importantly when we help a child to be able to achieve silence we are taking the child to a deeper level. Gradually we help a child not to listen to silence, but rather to listen to SOMEONE. That's why the silence game prepares a child for prayer.

Another very important preparation for prayer are the practical life exercises. These activities make the child more aware of his bodily movements. The practical life exercises are of great interest to the child and help him refine his movements. He performs these activities with fun while at the same time he is using his body to perform actions that are under the direction of his mind. The practical life activities are an indirect preparation for prayer, especially the gestures of prayer. There are some activities which are a more direct preparation for prayer like the genuflection and the sign of the cross. These can be called prayers of the body. Prayer involves not only the heart and mind but the body as well. When a child understands the different positions his body can take, he becomes gradually more conscious that these positions can and do have meaning.

All of these exercises and activities are really creating a condition for an encounter with God, which is what prayer is. When the body is ready through the silence game and practical life activities, then we can help children with the language of prayer. We can introduce a psalm of praise, which in itself is enriching language. It helps us and the children when we don't have words of our own to express what we wish to say, when we want to respond to God who has called us by name.

## Betty's Response

*As I sat listening and trying to absorb all of Gianna's words of wisdom I was struck by a thought that still haunts me. All that Gianna said about the children—their ability to contemplate, their hunger for God, the ease with which they can converse about God and know Him, the need they have for silence and prayer—aren't all these things that we as catechists need? Maybe that's one reason why it's important for us to observe the children so that we can learn from them how to develop and grow in our relationship with God instead of risking becoming as "sounding brass." How much we need silence! How much we need to contemplate God and converse with Him! It is the child and THE CHILD who will lead us to prayer that can bring us peace and joy.*

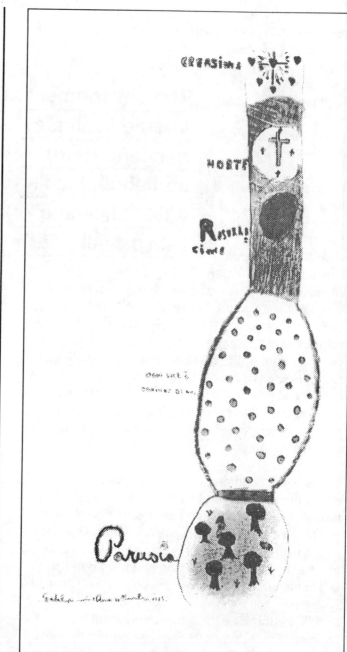

*Laura, 8 years old, Rome 1975. A drawing of the synthesis of the History of Salvation. The writing on the right side says: "Creation, Death, Resurrection, Each light is one of us, Parousia." This picture is brightly colored with oranges, yellows and reds. The writing on the side is blue except for multi-colors used in the words "Resurrection" and "Parousia."*

# NEW BOARD MEMBERS

**Julanne B. (Judy) Schmidt** read Religious Potential of the Child early in 1984, was "hooked," and has been engaged in the Catechesis of the Good Shepherd in one capacity or another ever since.

A primary/elementary teacher for many years, wife, mother of five, grandmother of 23, active in Christian Education in the Episcopal Church, Judy came simultaneously to the Catechesis of the Good Shepherd and to ordination to the diaconate as "later day" vocations.

After working briefly in the atrium she and Ruth Scheef had established at St. Edward the Confessor Episcopal church, Plymouth, Minnesota, Judy returned to her "hometown" of Glen Ellyn, Illinois, where she worked at St. Barnabas Church until her ordination in 1989. She lived and studied in the Centro di Catechesi, Rome, in 1990-1991, returning to Glen Ellyn to the atrium at St. Barnabas, where she continues the work of the Catechesis of the Good Shepherd with children and adults. She has helped in the formation of catechists in local, regional, and national formation events.

Judy's primary concern as a member of the board of the Association of the Catechesis of the Good Shepherd is to maintain a high degree of integrity in training and materials—a direct reflection of the precious gift God has given children and adults alike, through the work of Sofia Cavalletti and her colleagues in Rome.

**Kathy Dahl-Bredine** is administrator and founder of Guadalupe Montessori School in the small mountain town of Silver City, New Mexico. Kathy and her husband, Phil, became Catholics three years after their marriage, then formed a community of Catholic Worker families and Franciscans in Chicago. An outgrowth of that community led them to a farm community life at a Franciscan monastery in Burlington, Wisconsin for 8 years, and finally to New Mexico to do outreach work across the border. They have seven children: Erica, who spent 4 years as a volunteer in the Archdiocese of San Salvador, is now finishing a double MA in Latin American studies; Peter is music director in a San Antonio parish; Chris is a wilderness guide; Maria and Teresa are students at Loyola-New Orleans and Yale Universities respectively; Andrew is in high school and Dominic is in an Erdkinder, an outgrowth of G.M.S.

Guadalupe Montessori School serves a bicultural mix of 92 children, many low income, in a majority Hispanic area. The school has atria for ages 3-12 and serves a total of 130 children, including Montessori and after-school children from public schools. The Montessori children are from various faiths and some from no church background.

**Laura Bastulli-Parran** *has recently finished her Montessori training. Her catechesis training includes South Bend and Houston. Laura also has a BS in nursing and a MBA. She presently is a full-time mom to Teddy 8 3/4, Krista 5 3/4, and Tommy 3 months. Laura is also teaching the Catechesis of the Good Shepherd to 6-9 year olds.*

I was first exposed to the Catechesis of the Good Shepherd work in The Montessori School of University Heights. The school is under the direction of Betty Hissong. Our oldest child was a first-year student at the time and Betty gives a 12-hour introduction course in the Catechesis of the Good Shepherd and also in the basics of Montessori to familiarize the parents. I attended both courses and was very happily surprised by the fact that I, being a person with some rather scruffy edges, had a desire to do this work of God. I had received spiritual direction for four years previous to this time so when the catechesis kept coming up in my prayer I decided that I needed to listen. I began taking catechesis training in South Bend in 1991. I also began Montessori training in 1992 to earn a 3-6 certifcate. I would like to contribute to the building of God's kingdom in the hearts of people and on the earth. I am willing to help this work in whatever ways I can giving both my time and effort.

# THE COSMIC CHARACTER OF THE MASS

*by Sofia Cavalletti*
*Summarized by Catherine Maresca*

In this lecture, Sofia explored two aspects of the cosmic character of the Mass: its inclusion of the material world, and its inclusion of all people of all places and all times. She began by quoting a Benedictine monk, Cyprian Vagaggini, who wrote that the "elevation and transfiguration of the created world into the Divine life... is the most wonderful example of the importance of the role played by the material world in the Divine plan."

Sofia then offered two quotes by de Chardin. One, like Vagaggini's, was a reflection of the importance of the material world in the Eucharist. The other was about the presence at Eucharist of those people God has given us, those with whom we share an affinity of hearts, and the "anonymous crowd" who help to sustain us.

How can we offer these beautiful insights to children? Sofia and those who work with her are still searching. They offered us two new presentations, both for 9-12 year old children, that are the fruit of their ongoing search.

Before the presentation, Sofia recalled with us Ricoeur's understanding of the first and second "moments" of an encounter. The first step is to receive and surrender ourselves to the presence of the known. This is a unitive moment, in which there is no distance between the knower and the known. The second step is reflective, a search for meaning, in which there is distance between the object and the subject of knowing.

In the 9-12 work, copying the Missal is an important work, but one which is a "second moment" endeavor. The two presentations Sofia offered are ones she hopes will be encounters of the "first moment."

*Rebecca, age 9, Our Saviour, Chicago, Illinois*

The first presentation builds on the Eucharistic Presence in the 3-6 work and the Mystery of Faith in the 6-9 work, moving onto the Prayers of Intercession which follow the proclamation of our faith in the Eucharistic prayer. These intercessory prayers should not be confused with the prayers of the faithful. With the prayers of the faithful we pray FOR those in need. With the intercessory prayers we pray WITH the local church, the universal church, the whole world, the dead, and the saints.

In the presentation, pictures of these groups with whom we pray are placed on the table with a paten, chalice, Good Shepherd statue, and pictures representing the Mystery of Faith. Together we imagine and enjoy the fullness of the Eucharistic community, called by the Good Shepherd, and united in the broken bread and shared wine.

A discussion of the doctrinal points followed the presentation. With about thirty catechists involved the list was long, but here are a few of them:
- We are one in Christ.
- Liturgy is a means of unity.
- Liturgy is a sign and a way to be with all people.
- Liturgy is an experience of the True Vine.
- Liturgy is ecumenical.

The second presentation, titled "History of a Bread" focused on the role of the material world in Eucharist. We gathered around a table covered with a white cloth, and placed on it the statue of the Good Shepherd and a paten with a piece of bread on it.

The presentation was a reflection on the history of that piece of bread from its beginning as seeds sown in the earth. Aided by the earth, rain, and sun the seeds grew until their harvest was ready. Then people worked to transform the grain into the bread before us. At this point our work ends, but God's can continue. The bread is transformed again (here we recall the gesture of Epiclesis) into the Bread, Jesus Christ. So in this Bread converge the seed, the earth, the sun, the rain, the leaven, the fire (which baked the bread), the work of people, and God's immense love.

Our morning ended with Silvana Montanaro noting that these presentations, which are intimate encounters, are moments of **formation**, rather than **information**.

# Mystery Of Faith and Prayers Of Intercession

*An outline for presenting the Mystery of Our Faith and the Prayers of Intercession:*

## Description of the Material

- **Box** which contains:
  - **3 pictures** representing the Mystery of Faith, 5" X 6"
  - **Small wooden statue** of the Good Shepherd, 2 1/2" diameter paten with matching chalice
  - **5 pictures** representing the Prayers of Intercession, and 5 matching prayer cards, 5" X 6"
  - **Five prayer cards** as follows:

    *(Catholic tradition)*
    1. Welcome into your kingdom our departed brothers and sisters, and all who have left this world in your friendship.
    2. May he make us an everlasting gift to you and enable us to share in the inheritance of your saints, with Mary, the Virgin mother of God, with the apostles, the martyrs, and all the saints, on whose constant intercession we rely for help.
    3. Lord, may this sacrifice, which has made our peace with you, advance the peace and salvation of all the world.
    4. Strengthen in faith and love your pilgrim church on earth; your servant, pope John Paul, our bishop _____, and all the bishops, with the clergy and the entire people your Son has gained for you.
    5. Grant that we, who are nourished by his body and blood, may be filled with his Holy Spirit, and become one body, one spirit in Christ.

    *(Episcopal tradition)*
    1. Grant that all who share this bread and cup may become one in body and spirit, a living sacrifice in Christ, to the praise of your name.
    2. Remember, Lord, your one holy catholic and apostolic Church, redeemed by the blood of your Christ. Reveal its unity, guard its faith, and preserve it in peace. Remember (NN. and) all who minister in your Church.
    3. Remember all your people, and those who seek your truth.
    4. Remember all who have died in the peace of Christ, and those whose faith is known to you alone; bring them into the place of eternal joy and light.
    5. And grant that we may find our inheritance with the Blessed Virgin Mary, with patriarchs, prophets, apostles, and martyrs, and all the saints who have found favor with you in ages past. We praise you in union with them and give you glory through your Son, Jesus Christ our Lord.

- Three **5" X 1" paper strips** with the words of the Mystery of Faith on them and one longer (14") title card "The Mystery of Our Faith"
- **White cloth** for presentation table large enough to lay out the materials on.
- **Booklet** for the personal work. The booklet is 8 1/2" X 6" white pages and orange cover. The title of the booklet is "The Mystery of Our Faith and the Prayers of Intercession." There is no picture on the cover.

---

*Page 1*

In black at the top of the page:

**In our celebration of the Eucharist the risen Christ is present among us in the Bread and in the Wine.**

In red at the bottom:

**(Place the figure of the Good Shepherd, the Bread and the Wine on the table.)**

---

*Page 2*

In black at the top of the page:

**Then we confess our faith saying:**

**"Christ has died.**

**Christ is risen.**

**Christ will come again."**

In red at the bottom:

**(Lay out the pictures of the death, resurrection and parousia, and the corresponding words. This is the Mystery of our Faith.)**

---

*continues on next page*

# An Album Page For Ages 9-12

*continued from page 13*

*Page 3*

In black at the top of the page:

**This presence among us of the risen Christ at the Eucharist is such a great event it is difficult to understand its importance.**

**The first ones involved is the small group gathered around the altar.**

In red at the bottom:

**(Find the picture of the local church and read the words of the invocation over the faithful.)**

---

*Page 4*

In black at the top of the page:

**But the presence of the risen Christ goes beyond our little group, and reaches all the Christians of the world: The Catholics, the Episcopalians, the Lutherans, etc.**

In red at the bottom:

**(Find the picture of the universal church, and read the corresponding prayer.)**

---

*Page 5*

In black at the top of the page:

**And even all the men, women, and children, believers and non-believers, of the entire world, are in some way involved in this event of the presence of the risen Christ.**

In red at the bottom:

**(Find the picture of the world, and read the corresponding prayer).**

---

page 6:

In black at the top of the page:

**The presence of the Christ finally goes out of the limits of our world, and reaches each of those who have preceded us to the fullness of the world of God.**

In red at the bottom:

**(Find the picture of the cemetery, and read the corresponding prayer.)**

---

*Page 7*

In black at the top of the page:

**When we participate in the Eucharist, we participate in an event that involves**

**all men,**

**all women,**

**and all children.**

**We participate in an event bigger than all of our world.**

---

*Page 8*

In black at the top of the page:

**The celebration of the Eucharist continues in this way to unite**

**all men,**

**all women,**

**and all children**

**until all people,**

**together with the Mother of God,**

**the apostles,**

**and all the saints in eternity**

**sing to the glory of God.**

In red at the bottom:

**(Find the picture of the heavenly church, and read the words of the corresponding prayer.)**

Fall 1995 Newsletter

# Wooden Storage Box
## 1/4" birch plywood
## 15 1/2" x 8" x 3"
## Divided into 4 Compartments

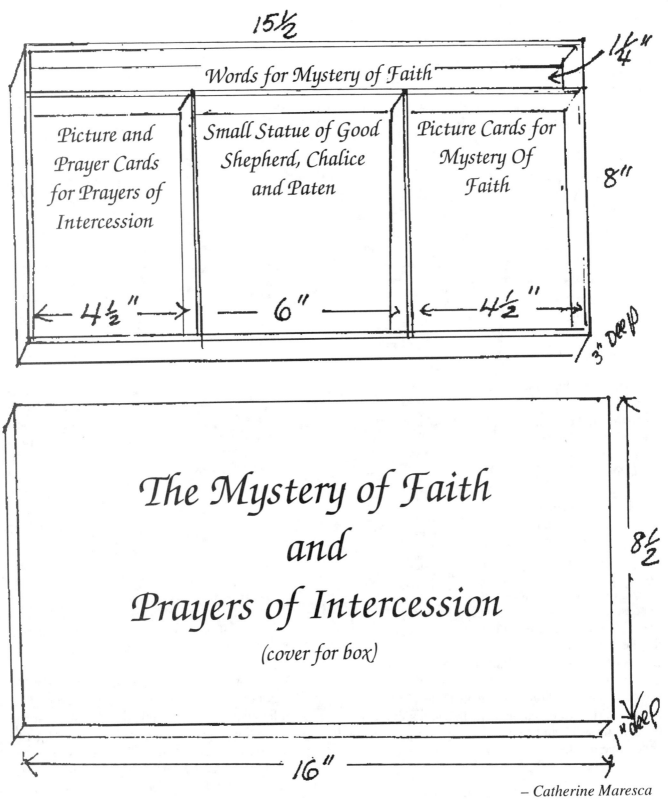

15½

Words for Mystery of Faith — 1¼"

Picture and Prayer Cards for Prayers of Intercession

Small Statue of Good Shepherd, Chalice and Paten

Picture Cards for Mystery Of Faith

8"

←— 4½" —→  — 6" —  ←— 4½" —→

3" deep

## The Mystery of Faith and Prayers of Intercession
(cover for box)

8½

←——— 16" ———→  1" deep

— Catherine Maresca

# SUMMARY OF THE CONFERENCE...

## Welcoming
*Sunday, October 17, 1993, early evening*

Seeing Sofia again was wonderful. All the hugs were strong and joyful. We were in a room in Silvana Montanaro's apartment building for a reception to welcome the participants. When we entered we were handed a True Vine name tag on which was written our name, city, and country. Gianna also greeted each of us warmly, speaking slowly in Italian so we could understand. At one end of the room was a table filled with refreshments which were graciously offered again and again. As we moved around the room, meeting and introducing each other, we could hear excited voices speaking the different languages of the "convegno."

We were very impressed to meet Luigi Capogrossi, the president of the Italian association. He was very kind, sincere, and completely unpretentious. As a child he had been one of the bambini in Sofia's atrium. Luigi was the only one who addressed the group that evening in a speech of welcome, translated into English by Patricia Coulter. One thing that he said was that in Europe it seems there has not yet been a "response worthy of the work." Whereas in the countries represented at the reception there seems to be a great response. He expressed the hope for our enjoyment of the coming week and also that the meeting would be generative for the work.

## Monday, October 18, 1993, 9:00 a.m., Via degli Orsini

Forty-six of us sat close together in a room near the atria. Sofia reminded us that when we gather for a course, we always begin with a song of the Good Shepherd. We do this "even though we may sing very badly." She asked that we sing in the three languages that were predominant at our meeting: Italian, Spanish, and English.

Vieni qui, Gesu.
Vieni, Buon Pastor.
(Come here, Jesus.
Come Good
Shepherd.)

Jesus, me pastorea.
Yo voy con el hasta
el fin.
(Jesus, shepherd
me. I go with you
to the end.)

Like a shepherd
he feeds his flock
and gathers the
lambs in his
arms, holding
them carefully
close to his
heart, leading
them home.

The songs had the simple melodies that children sing, and it seemed we were hearing their echo in over a thousand atria around the world.

After a prayerful silence, Sofia welcomed us, speaking in the three languages of those present. (The rest of the meeting was in Italian with other catechists translating.) She first spoke about the unique friendship we have as catechists. She said when we come together, we feel we have already met, and even that we have been friends forever. She continued by say-

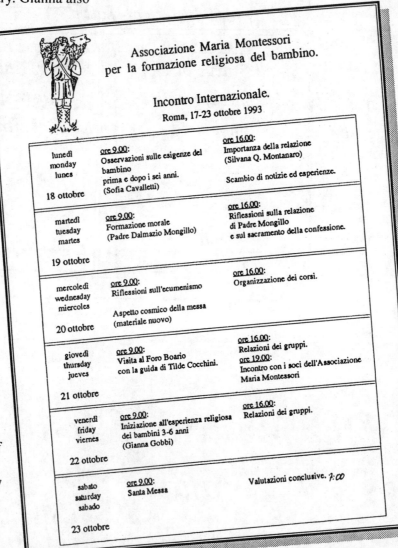

ing that this deep friendship applies not only to those of us who were in the room. It includes those who are far from us with whom we are very deeply linked. To be far doesn't have importance in this friendship.

In Sofia's welcome, she also spoke about our relationship with the children and how it has changed over the years. "As adults, in the beginning, we always place ourselves as a teacher (willingly or unwillingly). It was a long process to see that the real teachers were the children."

Sofia then named the things that were on the table in front of us: the Bible, a statue of the Good Shepherd, made by the hands of Bert O'Bryan, The Roman Missal, The Book of Common Prayer, the document of Lima, "Baptism, Eucharist, and Ministry" (a document of the World Council of Churches, the result of 50 years of work), and another document, "We Confess One Faith, We Believe in One God." In this simple way we were drawn together—those present and absent, children and adults, with our different languages and traditions.

*– Tina Lillig*

### Thursday, Oct. 21, 1994

Thursday evening was set aside for the international delegates to meet the Italian association and to share with them the story of the growth of this work. I imagined that we would be having a very quiet evening and I anticipated a slower pace than we experienced in the daytime sessions. The evening turned out to be another high impact moment celebrating the life, the work and the people in what I fondly cherish as a glimpse of the Parousia ahead.

That evening the city of Rome was hit and washed by a torrential thunderstorm. We wondered if we should even venture out into the night; it seemed so risky! Then, covered in plastic bags from head to toe, we left the convent and in ankle deep water ran to catch a bus. After waiting for what seemed to be an eternity, we managed to get a taxi with the help of Betty Hissong's gallant son, John. We arrived at the reception held in a hall of the Chiesa Nuova, just around the corner from Sofia's home. Leaving the dark, wet night behind us we peeled off our wet layers of plastic and entered a great white hall. For a moment I stopped to question myself, "perhaps I had been hit by lightening, died and now I was at some kind of reception area in heaven! There were so many joyous faces, long tables of food, an abundance of wine and we were being served by men in white coats and gloves. The ceilings in this room were so high that it looked as if a host of angels was about to make their appearance. As my body slowly warmed up, reality sunk in and I realized that it was impossible that all of us had been hit by lightning. In many ways it seemed very much like a homecoming and I wondered, "Who had called us here?"

The hall was filled with the chatter of the three main languages; Italian, English and Spanish. everyone was mingling and conversing with the others. Help with translation was not necessary at this point. The international language of love and laughter communicated all. (The wine helped too!)

On that evening, Sofia, Gianna, the catechists, friends and family members moved around as if

*continues on next page*

### A Walking Art Tour With Tilde

Tilde Cocchini (right), who is a catechist for 6-9 year olds with Sofia, is also an artist and art teacher. She conducted a wonderful tour of some of Rome's most beautiful and ancient and not so ancient sites. Aided by a map and a translator (Joe Tanel from Canada, in glasses) we walked for about two and a half hours, stopping to listen to Tilde's explanations of the art and architecture around us. Our tour included the Basilica of St. Mark, the ruins of an ancient Roman house, the Roman forum, the Temple of Apollo, and much more. Tilde was a tireless and enthusiastic guide, whose love of Rome and its art gave us an intimate taste of this fascinating city.

*– Catherine Maresca*

# Summary of the Conference...

each person was part of a golden thread being woven into a tapestry. Meeting so many of the people in the Italian association, who helped make our stay so comfortable, made me feel a great sense of gratitude and profound appreciation for the many years that they have worked to develop the Catechesis of the Good Shepherd. It was also wonderful for me to spend time with the Mexican delegates. I thought of them as true sisters sharing the same fortunate experience of being trained by Maria Christlieb! It was also another great moment to be with the American catechists. We have shared many formal opportunities for training and thoroughly enjoy our few opportunities for social gatherings. I was very grateful that they were there in number and they spoke English! A real thrill for me was to see "my Sister Evelyn O'Boyle" from Arizona. She dropped in that evening to meet the people in Rome and was planning to spend a few months studying with Sofia.

Earlier in the day, we had been given the format for the events of the evening and nowhere was it discussed that we would be singing. The Mexicans began it. As soon as it started Sofia marched right over and she joined in too! Thank heaven they sang in Spanish and we were not expected to join in. This was great entertainment! At first it seemed that they were singing hymns but it soon became clear that their repertoire contained many songs with a wide variety of topics. The Italians joined in and sang with them and added a few songs of their own. The Americans and the Canadians slowly drew together and started to mumble, "What are we going to sing; what are we going to sing?" It's not as if we don't know any songs or as if we are too shy but the more the Italians and the Mexicans sang the more our minds became blank. We just knew that they would eventually run out of songs to sing and that we soon would be expected to represent our countries in song. We stood frozen in panic. The moment arrived and out of one of our mouths came the great old standby, "I've been working on the Railroad." Yes, we knew that, and all English speaking people sang with joyful gratitude making this our musical contribution of the evening!

Sofia gathered the leaders from each country on stage. They all spoke of the work being done in their countries. They shared their journey, their joy, their growth and their love for this work, Their words were more than just ideas shared with us; they took on a quality of prayer in the presence of the Good Shepherd. We knew that we were coming to the end of the evening and close to the end of our week in Rome. I knew that I would remember this moment and that every time I would see such a large white ceiling again, I would relive this night and wonder, "Where are all these good people?"

**Members of the newly formed Consiglio**

Front row from left: Nora Bonilla-Paris (Colombia), Gianna Gobbi (Italy), Maria Christlieb (Mexico), Lupita Palafox (Mexico); Back Row from left: Herminia Wasserzug (Argentina), Patricia Coulter (Canada), Deborah Presser-Velder (Germany), Sofia Cavalletti (Italy). Not present: Rebekah Rojcewicz (USA).

And as if this was not enough, more surprises; the night was not over! More food, a hot and cold buffet, sweet pastries, more wine, conversation and laughter. As the evening ended I felt a great sense of peace and love and that yes, this was a glimpse of Parousia and that the Kingdom was amongst us. Thanks be to God!

P.S. Going back to the convent that night, I couldn't help but think that if we should ever be invited to another one of these international gatherings, that we should start now to plan what the Canadians will sing!

– *Susan Furlan*

## Our Last Night at Sofia's

Allora! We were all invited to Sofia's for a banquet. A banquet had indeed been prepared for us. The warmth and hospitality continued. The wonderful dishes included different kinds of pasta, meats, vegetables and lots of wine. It was wonderful! Then this stupendous dessert comes out. The joy, the spirit of love and celebration is difficult to describe. The whole week was beyond our expectations, but this evening was the icing on the cake.

After feasting we moved to another room where we all shared our favorite songs. The singing went on and on. I was singing Spanish songs I never heard before. There was so much love and joy. One wanted to "remain" forever, but we had to say our good-byes. These were moments of deep love. To try to put in words the experience of Saturday night is difficult. For me it was a home-coming and kind of Parousia with Christ in the center through faith and love. It was a wonderful sheepfold. I am grateful Sofia called me by name and opened the door for me to go in. I had to go out again, but a changed "sheep" both physically and spiritually. I think one day when all is well again the banquet will never end....E vero!

– *Paula Mugan*

# REFLECTIONS ON THE CONFERENCE . . .

Having the privilege of working with children, the best part of humanity, we are in a situation of feeling and touching the greatness of the human being's mind and soul while, at the same time, we witness that acceptance is needed, at the different levels, in order to offer the environment for the growth of the many talents each child brings into life.

– *Silvana Quattrocchi Montanaro*

Gianna Gobbi, Sofia Cavalletti and Rebekah Rojcewicz.

I'm back! It always seems a miracle to be here. Always it is an experience of coming home, but this time it's different. This time it's a true homecoming, a family reunion, for my siblings are here with me. My sisters and brothers from the far corners of the earth, some that I have met before, others that I have only known in my heart and anticipated meeting in person. . . .

– *Rebekah Rojcewicz*

Today, during the course for the catechists, I spoke about typology: each event of history is not closed in itself but opens to future, awaits completion? It is a mystery that, with time, becomes clearer and acquires sense. I am now thinking of our gathering: it was prepared, in the thoughts of God, from the moment that Gianna and Sofia started their first tries to work with children to help them meet with God; it was celebrated with so many present and those absent, it will go on growing where none of us is, until Parousia.

– *Francesca Cocchini*

A luminous moment in the History of Peoples was recently added to the "Fettuccia" in the History of the Gifts. This moment is the week of our meetings.

– *Tilde Cocchini*

Somehow the small winding streets that are around and include Via degli Orsini keep reminding me of the common man and the cobblestones which mark the Eternal City, worn smooth by so much coming and going.

– *Linda Kaiel*

The difference of language, culture and religious formation disappeared when we gathered around the Good Shepherd. We began our daily work with the meditation of the Word, prayers, silence and songs.

– *Giuliana Genovese*

We had interchange of opinions, we became acquainted with people from far away places that live with the same ideals. We prayed together, we were bestowed upon with great riches as the fruit of the Lord endures—we brought back with us a sharp and permanent communication—permitting us to grow with total experience.

– *Herminia Wasserzug*

# INTERNATIONAL CATECHISTS' REPORTS

*Sofia asked that each visiting country at the International Conference in Rome present a brief history of the progression of their work. The following is a synopsis of each presentation.*

## A Report from Argentina
### by Herminia Wasserzug

We have had the Catechesis of the Good Shepherd for eight years. Actually, there are three atriums in the diocese, in the majority of the boarding schools. Two in the Diocese of Santa Fe, Provence of Santa Fe, one is in San Martin and three in San Isidro where they also have an atrium in the Cathedral, These last two diocese are in the Provence of Buenos Aires. There are children in the first and second levels.

The major effort at this time is changing the formation of the Catechesis of the Good Shepherd and organization of the courses. If we can obtain (for each atrium) a good number of catechists necessary to attend the growing number of children—also be able to give priority time to the periodical meeting with the parents.

If we wish to synthesize the Catechesis of the Good Shepherd in Argentina—we know that it will progress very slowly but it will be continuous—until it appears as a seed springing forth (or it takes hold) into a profound life of prayer, conversion for the adults and children rejoicing.

## The Canadian Experience
### by Joe Tanel

Our presentation took the form of a time line. The work of the Catechesis of the Good Shepherd had its origins many, many years ago and its history extends back perhaps as far as when the History of the Kingdom of God began—it began as a seed but when full grown is the largest of plants. We are all part of the History of the Kingdom—our tradition is a part of this growing bush.

We are aware that the work that we do to help our branch grow is not our work, but rather, it is truly the work of the Spirit—the Spirit that has been working through time.

As catechists we have come to realize the importance of signs in the work of God. Signs not only help us to know God's love and presence, they also show us God's way. Two very important signs that continue to work among us, come to us in the form of two persons—Sofia Cavalletti and Gianna Gobbi. The work that they began in the 1950's has become a new branch on the bush. We Canadian catechists have become part of this branch.

In 1975 Patricia Coulter found out about the work that Sofia and Gianna had been doing in Rome. She met Sofia in St. Paul, Minnesota, and subsequently went to Rome to study. In the years that followed, work was done with children at various parishes in the Toronto area. Several people have helped this branch to grow in Canada. Alicia de Arocha helped with a graduate course directed by Sofia at the University of St. Michael's. Rebekah Rojcewicz, Maria Christlieb, Tina Lillig, Betty Hissong, Anna Mae Guida, and Lupita Palafox are a few of the people outside of Canada that have helped to nurture the work. Many Canadians have also taken advantage of the courses offered in the U.S.

Perhaps the highlight of the Canadian experience occurred in 1986 and 1987. After much planning and several meetings with Bishops Marcel Gervais and Aloysius Ambrosic, Sofia and Gianna assisted by Canadians, Americans and Mexicans offered a course dedicated to the young child. The course acted as a catalyst for the continuation and opening of several atriums.

Presently there is much interest in the work and the following locations have working atriums: St. Benedict's Parish, Holy Name Parish, Paula Mugan's home atrium in London, St. Norbert's Parish, Blessed Trinity Parish, Our Lady of Sorrow's Parish.

Along with the work done with children there has also been a great deal of work done with adults. In 1990 the University of St. Michael's Continuing Education Programme included a five-part series titled "The Spirituality of Young Children." In subsequent years the archdiocese and the university joined together to co-sponsor an adult formation programme for catechists. Presently, the University of St. Michael's offers a certificate program on the Catechesis of the Good Shepherd. Two groups of participants have completed the Part One Level of this programme.

During one of our talks in Rome, Father Mongillo reminded us that everything initiates from God, but also that God works through people. It has been from God's initiative through Sofia and Gianna that we began our work in Canada. In Canada our part of the branch has grown slowly and mysteriously and with the help of the Holy Spirit.

## Colombia
– Nora Maia Bonilla Paris

The Catechesis of the Good Shepherd began in Bogota, Colombia, in 1976 with Nora Maia Bonilla Paris taking the first course of Catechesis in Mexico City with Sofia Cavalletti.

Since that time about 13 courses have been given in Colombia with over 311 participants. In Bogota there are 6 atriums which support the work of 1400 children.

Our goals include training more people as Montessori guides and to continue the preparation of a team of people who will lead the formation of catechists. We also propose to establish a Colombian Association for Religious Formation and to form an Institute for Research and Catechetical formation.

## Development in Germany
– Deborah Presser-Velder

Hermann Hesse, once wrote: "In jedem Anfang wohnt ein Zauber inne..." (Every beginning is filled with enchantment.) This enchantment is the more wonderful, when it comes and is accompanied by God's grace. Truly the development of our work in Germany is a sign that the parables of the kingdom can become a palpable reality.

Sofia's work has been known in Germany for many years, but up to 1988 no concrete development was palpable. In that year, Prof. Hellbrugge, a renowned pediatrician, who has done great pioneer work in developmental rehabilitation for handicapped children in Germany and in many other parts of the world, and who has passionately fought for the right to integrate normal and handicapped children in schools using the Montessori Method, learned of Sofia's work through Silvana Montanaro. He then approached Sofia through Claudia Schmitt, asking her to introduce her work in Munich at a symposium on religious education. At the same time he offered Claudia a three-year (in the meantime four-year) scholarship, so that she could study the catechesis in Rome and bring it to Germany and the German-speaking world.

Without knowing about Prof. Hellbrugge and Claudia, I had become very interested in the Catechesis of the Good Shepherd since 1986, when I met Betty Hissong by coincidence at a Montessori Convention in Chicago. She had "The Religious Potential" in her hand, gave it to me and said "You have to read this book." I did and realized that I had found what I had been searching for in the past years. I went to Rome in 1988, met Sofia and Gianna and took an intensive course in Rome one year later after preparing myself through the Toronto-course cassettes and other visits to Rome. In October 1989 I opened the first atrium in my parish in Feldafing.

Claudia and I met three months later. We prepared the first symposium with Sofia, which took place in Easter 1989. A second symposium followed at the end of November, sponsored by both the German catechetical association and the Lutheran School office. A third symposium followed in May 1992 and a fourth in Easter 1993. This one was particularily intense and beautiful. By now a small but dedicated group of catechists has been formed and it is through and with them that this work is beginning to expand. Sofia will return to Germany and will offer an intensive course for this nucleus of catechists. We will concentrate on reviewing the essential themes and going deeply into them. The course is titled "Ad Fontes: The Child—Bible and Liturgy." The course will take place on April 15th to 17th in Munich (1994).

After the second symposium we saw the necessity of keeping the interested people together and to maintain contact in order to deepen the experiences. So we formed an "Arbeitskreis," a study group, as an informal but visible instrument. The work has not been easy, but its most important function, to keep the organization going, has been fulfilling itself. Another important aim was to translate "The Religious Potential" into German. This book was translated by Gabriele Neuroth, whom I met at a theology seminar. The translation was finished at the end of 1993. It is being revised by Prof. Schulz Benesch, who has edited and revised all Montessori's work in German. The book will be published hopefully by April 1994 in the Herder Publishing House.

As the group of dedicated catechists is growing, we see the necessity of forming an association in order to ensure the continuity and quality of our work. It is encouraging to learn so much from the associations in the different countries. The exchange of ideas at the convegno in Rome made it clear to us that this is the next step for our young group.

Claudia has invested much energy in the training courses.

*Continued on page 22*

# INTERNATIONAL REPORTS...

*Continued from page 21*

## Update from the United States
– Linda Kaiel, Rome, October 18, 1993

Today we gave Sofia the gift from the U.S. catechists, a blue binder bulging with information about some of the U.S. atria. Tina Lillig was editor for this work, compiling all the information sent to her prior to departure for Rome. I had made divider pages for each of the states, so that at a glance Sofia could see where "South Dakota" was in relation to the U. S. map, coloring the borders of the state highlighted. Each information sheet mailed by an atrium, was slipped inside a plastic page protector, along with children's work or photos or anecdotes that were included. An example, Sr. Kathryn Madden was in the Toronto course. She is a guide in a Montessori class in the Red Cloud Indian School, located in Pine Ridge, South Dakota. Within the parameters of her classroom, are included materials from the Catechesis of the Good Shepherd. In one photo can be seen a Indian tepee (large enough for a child to enter). Not far from it is located the prayer corner table, decked in the appropriate liturgical color. Also included are photos of celebrations which take place in the nearby mission church. My favorite was a photo of a dark-eyed girl in pigtails, holding up with her hands the loaf she had produced in their preparation of "The Kingdom of Heaven and the Leaven" with her friends. Each listing gave the name and location of an atrium, the denomination, the number of children, the number of catechists and their respective formation, and the levels 3-6, 6-8, 9-12 as appropriate. Also was listed the starting date of the atrium, and sometimes a thumbnail sketch of the children who attend and how often they meet.

Thursday evening we are scheduled to meet in the evening with the Montessori community in Rome, a celebration of Gianna and Sofia's contribution to the work of children. Our respective groups are asked to bring timelines, banners, etc. which highlight the work of the catechesis in our geographic area. There will also be the sharing of stories, and a chance to savor the international flavor of this work. Our blue binder is well over three inches in diameter, on the cover is a drawing of the True Vine which was sketched in Houston last summer from a photo Maria Christlieb had brought. The frontispiece of the binder included the commemoration cards which were a gift of the U.S. delegates, in four languages, English, German, Spanish and Italian. Centered among the cards was the icon print of the Good Shepherd which Anna Mae Guida had brought to share with all the delegates. On the next page was the dedication, done in Rebekah's calligraphy, thanking Sofia, Gianna, Luigi and the Italian association for sharing the Catechesis of the Good shepherd and for hosting the first international convention, *con molto affetto* (with much affection). Several of the next pages were photo pages of the formation experiences in Washington D.C., Notre Dame, and Houston, which Sofia did not "experience" with us (though she was in on all the planning of the contents!). Then came the listings of the atriums by states.

Just as in the personal album of each catechist, this binder was also meant to be a "living account" of the work, and so I took a blank blue binder and left it with Sofia for the additional information that would arrive after the international gathering.

Perhaps the most poignant message leafing through the album brings, is the delight in the faces, the delight in the stories shared, the delight in the dining together in the presence of the mystery. And of the many catechists whom I've met these many years in the work in the U.S.....I think of each of us, worn like the cobblestones of Rome, somehow in God's time and design, coming together to build "the new Jerusalem."

## Growth in Mexico
– Maria Christlieb

**"Out of the mouth of babes and sucklings you have fashioned praise."**
—Psalm 8:3

Our thanksgiving history is a song to the wondrous deeds of the Lord, rejoicing in Him, just as children asserting their strength which shines and glistens.

Sofia Cavalletti was invited to Mexico in 1976, which resulted in a course of 30 participants. Two atriums, in Mexico City and Chihuahua, were created that fall. Today more than 20,000 children between the ages of three and fourteen have participated in an atrium setting. We also have almost 2000 catechists working in atriums or with albums (personal workbooks).

A relationship with bishops exists in every city where we work. Some provide us their support with great interest, knowledge and love. Others simply respect us and let us

*Continued from page 22*

do our job. In several dioceses, the Good Shepherd Catechesis is one of the evangelization designs officially recommended by the bishop.

Besides working with children some atriums have grown to work with individuals with special needs, such as: children with autism, mental retardation, deafness, blindness and cerebral palsy; people from low income areas, street children and children in jail; as well as married couples.

Since 1982, the Mexican Association for Religious Formation of Children was created primarily to further catechist formation. This goal is accomplished through catechist training, translation of catechesis books into Spanish and support of individual atriums and catechists.

---

As this newsletter goes to print, we would like to share a global update of the growth of the catechesis since the October 1993 *Convegno*.

Through the work of Claudia Schmitt in German-speaking Europe, both Austria and Germany are preparing many catechists and Germany held its first association meeting. Poland has begun formation work and Croatia is sending a third catechist to Rome to study.

In August an atrium opened in Panama through the work of Herminia Wasserzug, with much local enthusiasm. Mid-September saw a formation gathering in Brisbane, Queensland, Australia, to begin work there.

Germinal plans are underway to gather the *consiglio* in Rome, with Francesca Russo, who was a child in the Rome atrium, volunteering to serve as secretary.

—*Linda Kaiel*

---

## CONFERENCE PARTICIPANTS

**Italy**
Sofia Cavalletti
Gianna Gobbi
Francesca Alessandri
Adelaide Balmas
Luigi Capogrossi
Mirella Cassano
Lidia Celi
Clotilde Cocchini
Francesca Cocchini
Fabian Gallico
Giuliana Genovese
Maria Rosa Russo Jervolino
Manuel Jimenez
Giulia Marcelli
Silvana Montanaro
Giancarlo Pani
Margherita Pendenza
Antonietta Piredda
Alessandra Pollastri
Antonietta Romano
Bernardetta Ruggeri
Onda Siniscalchi

**Argentina**
Herminia Wasserzug

**Canada**
Patricia Coulter
Susan Furlan
Paula Mugan
Joe Tanel

**Colombia**
Nora Bonilla Paris

**Germany**
Deborah Presser-Velder
Claudia Schmitt

**Mexico**
Sara Auxilio Parra Hernandez
Maria Christlieb
Alicia De Arocha
Mirella Del Valle
Cristina Garcia Triana
Cristina Alicia Lozano de Touchez
Teresa Ortiz de Argona
Lupita Palafox

**USA**
Anna Mae Guida
Betty Hissong
Linda Kaiel
Tina Lillig
Catherine Maresca
Carol Nyberg
Rebekah Rojcewicz
Randall Trego

# The Eucharist with the Children

### Addition to the Article:
## The Eucharist with the Children

Among the various elements with which we emphasize the most important moments of the preparation for First Communion, we have thought of adding a "consignment" (Latin "tradition," meaning "handing over") of the "Our Father." It is an old custom of the Roman Church, which in turn received it from the African Church. Saint Augustine practiced it at Carthage and the Pope at Rome. We have no particulars of the rite which accompanied the "consignment;" in a Roman text of the sixth century it appears that the Pope referred to the text, "When you want to pray, enter into your own room, etc." Nothing is known of how the "restoration" or "return" (Latin "redditio," meaning "return") might have taken place, but it took place the week after the solemn presentation.

It seems a very opportune time to point out or to focus ("to put in evidence," so to speak) a prayer which most of the children know from memory since they were little, but which they may know only rather mechanically.

We write it by hand on a small beautiful sheet of paper, of a size and shape that may fit into their own copy of the New Testament. The first day of the retreat the priest, at the moment of the Lord's Prayer in the Mass, entrusts one to each child, introducing it with some words of explanation.

For the "restoration" (or "return") not having any indication in the sources, we had to be a bit inventive about it. Last year, on the Saturday morning, at the moment of the Lord's Prayer, the children gathered closely around the altar and we asked them to sing it, with little or no support from the adults.

I would also like to add some advice with respect to Confession. The children, as you know, in general, copy the Maxims during the retreat so as to have a copy to carry with them later to the priest at the moment of the sacrament. It is not, however, advisable for them to carry all of them. I believe it would be better to tell them to select two or three (or even just one) which seem to them the most beautiful, which they would most like to be able to put into practice, copy them (or it) on a sheet of paper, and center the sacramental encounter on these. To carry them all might be to scatter one's attention instead of concentrating on a few specific points.

—*Sofia*

*Stacey, age 8, Little Community, St. Charles, Illinois. Drawn on her first communion retreat.*

## Life of the Catechist
## A Way for Continued Growth

From time to time as catechists we should be aware that we have need for spiritual renewal. We need to watch for our own spiritual growth. Sometimes this growth needs to be guided by the Holy Spirit through the gifts of a Spiritual Director.

This Spiritual Director could be anyone, a priest, a religious or a lay person who is well-traveled in this journey of faith. This person becomes a companion who helps us to see ourselves more clearly in the light of Christ.

This year, I was graced with a very special person who guided me in the 19th annotated Exercises of St. Ignatius. These exercises have many parallels to the Catechesis of the Good Shepherd. Like the Catechesis, the Exercise of St. Ignatius, is not for the weak of heart. While the exercises did not include the physical work of building materials, it is a continual delving deeper into the greatness of God.

The Complete Exercises of Ignatius can be done on a thirty-day retreat. Parts of it can be done on a shorter retreat, or this experience can be spread out over many months. For most of us with families, aging parents and atria this is the only way we could ever hope to do the exercises. Bit by bit as children we enter into this special time.

To begin the exercises, my companion had me begin with the 23rd Psalm. Like a child, I was instructed to take one line from the psalm to pray over each day. This forced me to slow down. To once again reflect intensely on the words of sacred scripture, to allow the Holy Spirit to write these words deeply into my heart.

After completing the exercises, I found a book on the subject to help me understand more fully what I had experienced. St. Ignatius said, "The director of the exercises should permit the Creator to deal directly with the creature, and the creature directly with his Creator and Lord." Isn't this exactly what we do with the children? The Inner Teacher works with the child at his or her own pace?

From time to time during the exercises, I was asked to meditate again on a familiar topic. Only this time I was invited to apply the five senses to the contemplation. Once again this forced me to slow down. How often do I take these gifts of seeing, hearing, tasting, feeling and smelling for granted? The children are not so separated from these faculties. This Creator God has given so much in these gifts. How could I not be filled with gratitude.

The three kinds of humility that Ignatius talks about have a direct relationship to the role of the catechists. He says, "I desire to be accounted as worthless and a fool for Christ, rather than to be esteemed as wise and prudent in this world."

Sofia Cavalletti talks about this same humility when she talks about the adult as the "unworthy servant." Maria Montessori also talked about how every meeting with the children should be preceded by an examination of conscience, In particular with regard to pride and anger. This is nothing more than the Examen which Ignatius tells us to practice throughout the day. This practice will help us to grow in humility.

Jesus humbled himself to share in our humanity. He was the obedient Son. If I am willing to share in His resurrection, so I must also be willing to share in the Passion. This gift of the Catechesis of the Good Shepherd is invitational. I must be willing to invite in — time and again. I must rejoice when I'm not understood or when I'm rebuked or even when I'm attacked as being weird or "off beat", knowing all along that I am doing the will of the Creator who has called me to this work. I TOO must wait patiently for parousia when these divisions will be healed. I TOO must lay aside my own agenda.

What does this mean for us as catechists? I believe that we must ask ourselves many questions, reflecting on our response to God's benevolent friendship. The questions we ask the children are also for us, only we are required to go deeper. Is this catechesis the precious pearl that we hold on to and at times horde for our own enjoyment or is the gift ours to carry but for a time (like a mother who carries new life within her body)? Has our patience been a reflection of a Creator God who prepared the universe for us so carefully? If we have been created to praise and reverence our God have we meditated with joy today on the wonder of this gift?

There are many questions that we need to think about. You may ask yourself if all this self-scrutiny is good. Socrates said that the unexamined life is not worth living. We must know ourselves. St. John of the Cross said that self knowledge was absolutely necessary for all growth in prayer. We must ask ourselves these questions in order to walk more faithfully with Jesus. We must continue our formation and transformation — as Catechists of the Good Shepherd and as lambs of God.

— *Marilyn Krause, July 1992*

# 1996 Newsletter to feature Material Making

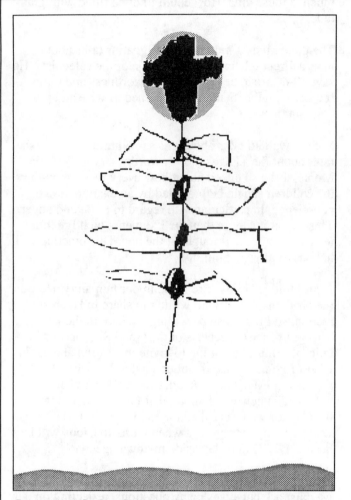

*Stacey, age 5, Our Saviour, Chicago. The kite is yellow, the cross is black and the tails and string are blue. It flies above a field of green grass.*

### Your stories make our newsletter
Articles about your atrium, training, book reviews make this newsletter an important communication vehicle for catechists worldwide. Tell us how we can help you by writing us about the newsletter or with your questions about our work with children.

### Please share your children's artwork and your photographs
To obtain the best possible newsletter image, we ask for original artworks whenever possible. We will return all work as soon as possible.. Include the artist's name, age and tell us a little about the child, and the work. This information should be written on a piece of paper attached to the artwork with a paper clip or carefully printed on the back. Also tell us the name of your atrium, and in what city and state. Since this is a black and white newsletter, black and white photographs are ideal; however, color photographs are also acceptable. All artwork that we receive must have permission by the artist and their parents to be used in print now or at some time in the future.

With any materials that you would like returned, please be sure to include the address. Thank you.

---

Please send all Newsletter materials directly to:

**Tina Lillig**
P. O. Box 1084
Oak Park, IL 60304

**1995 Staff in U.S.A.**
Joan and Toby Roberts • Tina Lillig
Kathy Van Duser • Rebekah Rojcewicz
Linda Kaiel • Barb Fleming Disch
• Randall Trego

**Italian Translators:**
Joan Parasine • Nicolina Gleasure

---

# *Membership*

**The Catechesis of the Good Shepherd**, An Association of Children and Adults, welcomes members throughout the year. Members receive the annual newsletter, all mailings and a directory of catechists and friends of the association.

Mail requests for membership and other information to:
**The Catechesis of the Good Shepherd, P.O. Box 1084, Oak Park, IL 60304**

© Copyright 1995: The Catechesis of the Good Shepherd, P.O. Box 1084, Oak Park, IL 60304

# The Catechesis of the Good Shepherd

## Psalm 100

Make a joyful noise to the Lord,
all the earth.
Worship the Lord with gladness;
come into his presence with singing.

Know that the Lord is God.
It is he that made us, and we are his;
we are his people, and the sheep
of his pasture.

Enter his gates with thanksgiving,
and his courts with praise.
Give thanks to him, bless his name.

For the Lord is good;
his steadfast love endures forever,
and his faithfulness to all generations.

*–NRSV*

## CONTENTS

- LET US PRAY WITH THE CHILDREN ............ 29
- LETTERS FROM SOFIA AND GIANNA ......... 30-31
- THE ESSENTIALS OF MATERIAL MAKING ........ 32
- ON MATERIALS AND MEANING ................ 33-34
- MATERIAL MAKING: STIMULUS FOR ADULTS ... 34
- MAKE OUR OWN MATERIALS? ................... 35
- HOW DO I MAKE AN ALBUM PAGE? ........ 36-37
- THE CARE OF THE ATRIUM ..................... 38
- ST. ANDREW'S FIRE ............................. 39
- LETTERS TO SOFIA ............................. 40-41
- CONSIGLIO REPORT ............................. 42-43
- LIFE OF THE CATECHIST ....................... 44-45
- ABOUT OUR ASSOCIATION ...................... 46

Dear Friends,

It is with great joy that we publish the 12th annual journal. This journal is about material making. Thank you for your patience. We have tried to combine the theory ("Why Do We Make Our Own Materials?" by Sofia Cavalletti) with the practical (Material Tips). If you have been shy in producing your own materials, you will receive encouragement and support within these pages.

Please note that the pages are numbered sequentially since the 11th edition. This publication will now be referred to as a journal rather than a newsletter.

We would like to dedicate this issue of the journal to Sister Sheila Sentiff who produced the first 3-6 material making manual. Although that manual required updating as the work grew, she bravely pioneered the first edition which proved helpful to so many. Thank you!

We also gratefully thank all who have contributed to these pages and hope for its readers great joy in their work.

Joan and Toby Roberts

## 1996 BOARD ELECTIONS

This past October, the national meeting of the Catechesis of the Good Shepherd Association was held in Michigan City, Indiana. There both Carol Nyberg and Kathy Dahl-Bredine were reelected to the national board. Carol is from Houston, Texas, and Kathy is from Silver City, New Mexico. Board positions are held for three years. Thank you to both Kathy and Carol for their hard work and faithful hearts as they continue the work of the national board.

*Carey, age 7, The House of the Good Shepherd, Ottawa, Ontario, Canada.*

*Carey described the tiny baby Jesus as great. In her words, "kind of like a mustard seed."*

# LET US PRAY WITH THE CHILDREN

God's Gifts
God you have gave us so many Gifts. You gave us Jesus Christ to take away our sins. Now comes Christmas. What can we give you?

–Josh, age 7, Fremont, Michigan
(Written as a Christmas prayer.)

God made the oceans and the fish, the mountains, the rivers. God made animals and ivy and the fruit trees. Too God made me and you!

–Stacey, age 7, Chicago, Illinois

"It's nice to come to this quiet place when you have had a day like I had."

–Adele, age 7, Chicago, Illinois
(Said to catechist after setting up altar work.)

Love leads to Peace,
Peace leads to Hope,
Hope leads to JOY.

Rebecca, age 9,
Chicago, Illinois

Thank you Lord for my family and friends, for the food we eat, and the good times we share. Thank you for making me and your sheep. Thank you Good Shepherd. Love Amber

–Amber, age 8, Oak Park, Illinois

The New King grew up as a shepherd.

–child, age 6,
St. Charles, Illinois
(Written after nativity presentation.)

The Father, the Son and the Holy Support.

–Fritz, age 7,
St. Charles, Illinois

I just read a story called The Birth of Jesus And The Adoration of the shepherds. It is one book I wish I had. It made me fell worm inside my heart. That is all I can say about my fellings.

Richard, age 7,
Gesu Parish,
Detroit, Michigan
Christmas, 1992

Dear God, I pray for the church. I pray for the homeless people. I pray for my family. I pray for the world. I pray for my dog and all other animals. I pray for love around the world. I pray for peace

Austin,
Christ
Episcopal
Church,
Waukegan,
Illinois

# LETTERS FROM SOFIA AND GIANNA

## Let's make the material with our own hands

First of all, we wish to explain that making the materials with our own hands is not linked to the difficulty of finding ready-made materials, or of having people who will make them according to our requirements. I believe that making the materials with our hands, like an artisan, corresponds to the spirit of our work. Even if there were a manufacturer who made them in a superlative manner, and even if we were able to purchase them from him, something—and not an insignificant something—would be lost in our work.

Let us try to understand why this is so.

Making the materials is, first of all, a very particular mode of meditation and prayer. Saint Benedict used to teach, "Ora et labora," "prayer and work," not to divide the day into two separate activities, but so that the two might permeate each other.

It is a method which, by its very nature, binds or links us to the concrete, leads us to the essentials of the theme or topic to be presented, compels us to focus on the message, dare I say, to contemplate it, without sinking into a morass of psychological and moralistic explanations.

The contrast between the simple and poor media we handle and the powerful message which is transmitted through them is so great that it fills our spirit with awe. This contrast fills us with reverent awe when confronted with a reality which, though so great, needs so little to communicate itself. Discovering the "great" in the "small" is always a great joy.

Making the materials with our own hands is a stabilizing factor with regard to the intensity of the studies our work entails. It prevents us from taking refuge in the abstract and from achieving the self-satisfaction of intellectualism.

To be sure, the result of the work with our hands is achieved at a much slower pace than if we were to purchase what we need. But herein lies its value. Manual labor prevents us from haste, the ready-made product, the efficiency of "go out and buy it." It disposes us to a rhythm which is more in harmony with matters of the spirit.

The result is often less brilliant or perfect than what we could achieve by buying a material made by a specialist. It is odd, yet I believe that there is value even in this. I do not mean to say that the materials should not be made with care and love, or that they ought not to be beautiful. Instead, the difficulties we may encounter, our limited capabilities, help us maintain a simple and sober style, while staying away from commercialism.

In making our own materials, we may discover a very powerful educational tool or instrument for our catechists. This instrument is also demanding because it asks us to adopt certain values which are not the usually accepted ones of our times. It suggests a plan of an artisan-like character in an industrial, almost post-industrial, world.

Are we behind the times? I would be pleased to know what you catechists think about this topic. As far as I am concerned, I believe that the values connected to this view of the world are attuned to the spiritual needs of the children, to their mode of living the relationship with God. It is a mode based (or founded) on the concrete; it proceeds at a slow rhythm; it refuses complexities or embellishments.

> **It is useful to remind those who are just beginning, that it has taken us 43 years to assemble all the materials we now have. One is not expected to have everything immediately.**

Genelda Woggon, in her account of her formative experience in the summer of 1991 at Notre Dame, Indiana, said, "Material making is itself an act of both discipline and devotion."

I think that if we do not remain faithful to the discipline and spiritual attitude imposed upon us by the making of materials, we run the risk of not being faithful to the children, either.

Some practical advice:

It is useful to remind those who are just beginning that it has taken us 43 years to assemble all the materials we now have. One is not expected to have everything immediately.

Profit from everything which is available and could be useful. In Mexico, I saw candleholders made from metal bottle caps. These caps, with the addition of a nail, once varnished, fulfilled their function quite well. Thus, it was possible to keep expenses down and not give the impression, which we sometimes unfortunately give, that the Catechesis of the Good Shepherd is costly and, therefore, suitable only for the rich.

When there is something to be done which is too difficult for us, we ask our family and friends (for help), explaining fully what is needed and why. This could be an excellent method of catechesis for adults.

In conclusion, at the risk of repeating oneself, let us

*continued on next page*

review some of the characteristics of good materials.

First of all, a good material must be objective, that is, it must be reflective of the theme to be presented, without distractions. An example is provided by the materials for "baptism," which take into consideration only the baptismal theology in its totality.

The materials which are produced with our "gimmicks" are not "good" materials. Materials which lead us to say "How clever I was to think of it" are worthless. A good material is one which compels us to say, "How great is the message contained in it." Materials ought to be simple and essential, without arbitrary additions, centered on a theological point.

The material ought to be "poor." A material that is too "rich" risks the danger of attracting attention to itself, distracting from the message it is supposed to convey. I believe that the great impact that the material often has on adults depends exactly on its "poverty."

And so, I would like to know your views of a "good" material.
*Sofia Cavalletti*

## The experience of making one's own material

Whenever work is discussed, many of its aspects come to mind. Psychology and the social sciences have produced a vast body of writing on the subject. In the field of education, many authors extol the indispensability of work as an important component in the formation of the human personality.

In this regard, Maria Montessori in her book, "The Secret of Childhood," Chapter 43, developed a very interesting philosophy. I invite you to read these pages because the meaning and desirability of work, together with its importance in the formation of the human personality, are examined there.

The close relationship which was established, from the very beginnings of the human species, between humans and their environment, entailed work as a natural consequence. Truly, it is only through work, that human beings are able, by means of their intelligence and their hands, the only tool in their possession, to master and transform the environment while adapting themselves to it, and in turn, adapting it to themselves. The many-fold applications of work, its significance, its role in society, have changed with the passing of the ages, yet work has always remained one of the principal manifestations of human behavior, as well as a characteristic of the human species. One could develop the theme (of work) starting from its fundamental aspects, such as a means of subsistence, of satisfying basic needs and as embodiment of social ties. However, this is not the purpose of this letter. Sofia, my dear friend and workmate—we taught in the same middle school and have always worked together in the catechesis—asked me this question: "What meaning did the manual work have for you, since it always permeated your whole educational experience?" I want to thank her for providing me with the opportunity of making some reflections about a very special facet of my experience with the children, that is, preparing the materials for the catechesis. The work of our hands has accompanied our catechetical experience from its inception. One can appropriately state that the catechesis would not have developed into the present format without the support of our manual work. This has indirectly contributed to clarifying and distilling the essential content of the Christian message.

Preparing a few materials with our own hands may seem useless, almost a waste of time to the modern mentality of the technological and information age. Nevertheless, upon more careful reflection, one can discern in it an educational value, even for us adults. Linking one's thoughts to the work of one's hands, organizing and assembling the materials or personally recopying the Biblical passages are useful, often essential, moments for elucidating and absorbing the message, so that it can later be conveyed to the children in an effective and striking manner.

**Therefore, the work of our hands is not superfluous; actually it can be of great value in our stressful, frantic society. It can provide us with periods, although of short duration, for quiet and silence.**

The meditation, which is fundamental in the preparation of the catechist and which is especially advisable prior to meeting with the children, will be enriched by this work. Father Beno, a Somasco priest (an Italian order), related to Sofia what enjoyment he had in making the material of "The Sacraments." This work became a real and fitting meditation for him.

Furthermore, manual work, in contrast to work done by machine, compels us to maintain a rhythm patterned upon human beings. It accustoms us to respect the rhythm of the children's work, which differs greatly from that of adults. It also helps us to restrain our impatience.

Therefore, the work of our hands is not superfluous; actually it can be of great value in our stressful, frantic society. It can provide us with periods, although of short duration, for quiet and silence. It is useful and beneficial for adults, as well.

*Gianna Gobbi*

# The Essentials of Material Making

*By Linda Kaiel*

"Teach us to number our days aright, that we may gain wisdom of heart....prosper the work of our hands" (Psalm 90, vs. 12,17). We continue the conversation which has gone on with God for centuries, as we pray these words of the psalmist. "Prosper the work of our hands"... these materials which we so lovingly put together for the children's meditation. Whether we are carefully scanning catalogs for just the right size simple glass containers for cruet preparation, or seeking the wood scrap in the shop that can be cut into the backdrop for Elizabeth's house, or shaping clay into a miniature chalice and paten for the Last Supper work...each is a work which passes through our hands and is also a ripe space for our own meditation during the production process.

What is essential to a work and what is superfluous? Each material is designed to help the child to interiorize the content of the Scripture which was shared. The material then must be faithful to the Word and must help the creative meditation of the child. The dioramas of the infancy narratives may be sparse, with perhaps the distinction of Mary's home in Nazareth, and Elizabeth's home in the hill country of Judea being the scene observed from the open window looking out on the neighboring village (which you have painted or sketched on the back of the box). In the small child the materials assume the function of making the Scripture text "visible." Be careful that your work remains plain and simple.

The colors in the atrium also speak a language to the children. The covers of the Scripture booklets (white for infancy narratives, blue for parables, red for the passion texts, green for miracles) will be a silent aid when the children begin to synthesize and put together on their work mat what links particular texts and events in salvation history. The colors of each of the gesture booklets (Epiclesis, Offering, and Gesture of Peace) will be a silent language the children recognize when they begin to work with the Structure of the Mass and the colored base materials in the 9-12 atrium. The continuity of the use of a particular color helps to identify which part of the Mass we are pondering in this work.

The drawings used in the tracing packets should also be large enough so the child can cover them with a tracing paper and successfully make a copy. The drawings should be simple. The Maxims are carefully lettered, so that they are easily read and then copied. Any Florentine borders or ornamentation would be frivolous. As the child copies the work it is then his/her work to create a border or drawing of choice. Children who have just begun to write and are proud of their skill, have copied the prayer card "Amen" and then lovingly written on the border of their paper their other words, mom, dad, cat, dog... This is their response, gift shared, prayer made visible and flows from their interior. Lovely parchment paper can be used for the prophecy texts and also examples of illumination with children in the 6-12 atriums. That is also an age to share Giotto's work and other fine art which reflects the themes of the infancy narratives. These can be a springboard for the children's own art and meditation on an art piece. Spend some time reflecting before you prepare the backdrop of your Cenacle. What will the last supper backdrop be? What will the early church building backdrop be? Will they distract from the central theme of this work, Jesus present through history in the bread and in the wine, through the transforming action of the Holy Spirit? In all liturgical work, we should visually reflect the best our church has to offer.

Esther de Waal says that "the God who chose to be revealed in human flesh was using one of the commonest materials, albeit one of the most sacred. Unless we also give ourselves time to handle the common and ordinary we may easily lose touch with this most vital truth." We let the material itself be poor and simple, with the simpleness of God. The elements of the parables....yeast hidden in dough, a seed holding the potential of life, a shepherd caring for the flock, young women preparing lamps to meet the bridegroom....take the raw stuff of life and become a doorway to a Kairos moment where we step into God's time. Each atrium material in the simplest way possible, also needs to perform that same function. We reverence the intimacy of each child's response to a loving God by stepping back from the encounter. We set the scene for nurturing such encounters by the sparse simplicity in which we prepare the atrium for the children's use. The creator of snowflakes and frost crystals, did not house his own child in a "one star" inn in Bethlehem....taking this simple birth scene as a cue, can help us reflect on the accessibility of a God whose invitation is magnanimous. Our materials spread that invitation....

## Material Tip

Here is a fairly effective method for removing candle wax from linens:
1. Scrape off as much wax as you can with a dinner knife.
2. Cover the wax stain with a few pieces of facial tissue and iron with a warm iron.
3. Put the cloth in a sink and pour boiling water over the stain.
4. Wash and iron as usual.

*—Tina Lillig*

Some tools that prove essential early in material making include:
- paper cutter for booklets and tracing cards;
- scroll saw for parable figures; and
- radial arm saw for backdrops and boxes.

*—Marilyn Krause*

# ON MATERIALS AND MEANING

*By Alice M. Renton*

A girl, just under three, stands at a shelf holding a starfish. She turns it over and over in her hand, completely absorbed in looking first at the top part, then at the bottom. As she turns it, she begins to sing very softly to herself, "Inside...and outside...inside...and outside."

A toddler is walking with a group of children by a stream lined with big cottonwood trees. He stops at one of them. The rough bark has peeled away from one part of the trunk and left exposed an oval section of wood, beautifully grained in a vertical pattern. Over and over, as his hand traces the design in the smooth, silky wood, he says to himself, "Tree...tree...tree."

Another toddler on a playground is carrying some sand in a round, blue tray. He walks slowly, tilting the tray, watching the sand move from one side to the other. He stands still, intent, tilting more and more slowly. As the sand moves back and forth, he says to himself at exactly the same tempo, "s..l..i..d..i..n..g.....s..l..i..d..i..n..g.....s..l..i..d..i..n..g."

These were some of my initial experiences of children under three years of age in prepared environments. As I thought about them, I realized that they had some common elements. In all of them, the children were relating to organic objects. There was intense concentration. There was calm, repetitive movement, appearing to respond to the natural form of the object itself. There was deep silence, with the child totally focused on some essential aspect of that form. Then, at a certain moment, language arose, seemingly called forth from the child by some profound exchange of energy. And in each instance the word was repeated, simultaneously with the movement, as though to crystallize that exchange in a kind of meditative chant.

In infant and toddler environments, I have observed many similar instances of very young children deeply engaged. Each time I am reminded of these words of Maria Montessori's in <u>Education for a New World</u>: "The world is acquired psychically by means of the imagination. Reality is studied in detail, then the whole is imagined. The detail is able to grow in the imagination, and so total knowledge is attained. The act of studying things is, in a way, meditation on detail. That is to say that the qualities of a fragment of nature are deeply impressed upon an individual." (p. 35)

I believe that the youngest children are teaching us to look again at the prepared environment and the materials we provide. Because they do not speak much, we are compelled to observe and learn from what they do. Like natural contemplatives, they truly become one with what they see, touch, hear, taste, and smell. It is the inherent quality of a material that engages their attention and perhaps determines the quality of their response. Consider what was so deeply absorbing to these three children: The contrast between the patterned top of the starfish and the delicate underside with its tiny opening; the shape and texture of the polished wood standing out from the surrounding bark; the minute clinging together and separating of the grains of sand rolling across the smooth surface of the tray. Perhaps it is the simplest of objects—especially "fragments of nature"—that most truly serve children's spirit, awakening the senses rather than bombarding them.

And bombarded they are—we all are—by a steady stream of "things" and messages about them, urging us to get, buy, and have: more! better! different! Children are targeted as con-

*continued on next page*

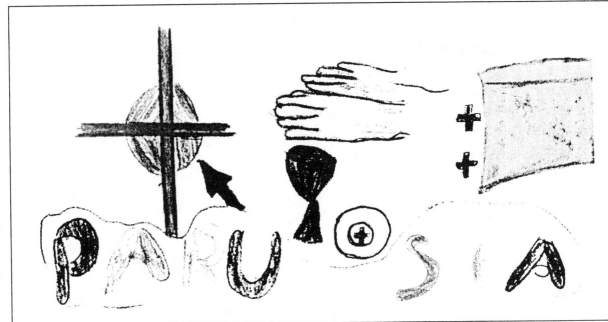

*Juan, age 9, Scuola Villa Bosch, Argentina. Sofia finds the link between the Eucharist and parousia interesting.*

## ON MATERIALS AND MEANING (CONTINUED)

sumers—of toys, clothes, food, furniture, educational materials. Things made "especially for children" assault them with speed, noise, loud colors, synthetic materials and smells. Children are thought to "need" a pre-fabricated, mass-produced "entertainment," complete with remote controls so that it can be "zapped" instead of entered into. Can interacting with these things result in calm of movement, tone, or language that arises from a inner exchange with the energy of an organism? Do they focus children's energy or diffuse it?

The wordless experience of the minute differences that make up a harmonious whole—the beginner's mind or the absorbent mind that Maria Montessori described so eloquently—is steadily being replaced by mediated experience. Those who are studying children and television tell us that children are losing their capacity to develop imagery—the imagination that she saw as crucial to an understanding of the whole.

Children's need for real activity is as acute now as it was when Montessori observed the children picking up the bread from the floor to work with it. In the modern technological environment that surrounds us there seem to be fewer and fewer places where children are allowed the time, space, and freedom to experience simple things. We worry that they won't learn enough soon enough, and that they won't be able to "keep up." We may be forgetting that they will be unable to "keep up" if they never develop the capacity to be in touch with their own experience—be it caressing a tree trunk or discovering the inside of a starfish.

Often it is in the simplest environments that children can focus best. If there is beauty, reality, and order in the materials, children pay attention. We can see them becoming deeply absorbed with an assortment of shining pebbles, a gourd full of multicolored beans, the transparency of water contained in a cleanly curved glass pitcher. A few years ago in Chile, a Montessorian I visited was apologetic about her environment: "We don't have very many materials; we're so far away from everything and they're so hard to get." The materials were indeed very simple, but carefully selected and organized. In contrast to the richness and sophistication of American early childhood consumerism, there was not much in the classroom—but the children were calm, absorbed, and purposeful. In a set of slides from a school in Oaxaca, Mexico, the teacher points out small pottery jugs full of red, yellow, and blue flowers: "We don't have color tablets, so we pick flowers every day to learn the colors."

Thirty years ago, starting out in Montessori education, many of us spent untold hours making our own materials. A few years ago, I stood in the middle of an exhibit of Montessori materials—two floors of venders—and remembered those times. Our work is much easier because of this availability, but we must continue to think deeply about the essential purpose of any material: will it set in motion the child's own experience, will it "allow the soul to function from its own powers"? To concentrate means "to be with one's center." Perhaps now more than ever, a prepared environment needs to be a nest for the child's mind, a place where, in Montessori's words, everyone can "learn to control himself and how to engage in calm and silent activity, for no other purpose than that of keeping alive that inner flame on which life depends." (Discovery of the Child, p. 305)

### Material Tip
Sand and prime your wood before you trace and cut out your parable figures. That way you don't have to trace the figures twice.
–Marilyn Krause

## MATERIAL MAKING AS A STIMULUS FOR ADULTS

*By Bernadetta*
*(Bernadetta is a catechist of the Roman group, who began an atrium in the parish church of "Jesus of Nazareth.")*

I believe that the love and devoted care, which admittedly cannot be dispensed with in material making, are very closely linked to the loving attention given to the proclamation we are preparing to convey, as well as to our anxious expectation about the spiritual growth of our children. While we are making the materials with our hands, we gradually move from the concrete plane of wood, nails, cardboard, etc. to that of the content of the message. The message manifests itself and takes shape, form, and life in the tools we handle.

In their most concrete aspect, the materials teach us to be patient and careful, working the same way artisans and farmers do.

From a certain viewpoint, it seems to me that, for the adults, the preparation of the material is somewhat like the work of the children with the same materials. I received confirmation of this when a mixed group of children and adults helped me to set up the atrium. This work provided the opportunity to go more deeply and thoroughly into the topic and was sometimes an occasion of true meditation.

Moreover, I find that this experience, though undoubtably very burdensome, leads us to develop great inventiveness in finding constructive solutions, and, at times, in discovering capable help in unexpected people and places.

# Why Should We Make Our Own Materials?

*By Claudia Schmitt*

As per Montessori philosophy, the materials are pedagogical instruments which help the child develop his physical and spiritual potential.

The pedagogical materials should also be for us, but in reality, unfortunately we separate ourselves. Why should the materials be a meditative instrument for the child and not for us? How can I give to the child something which isn't also mine? Do we possess that spiritual order that we need in order to work with the children? The material directs us to that spiritual order. True. But only if we make them. By doing this we can hope to unite our knowledge and our meditative feelings with the material. Make it unified! Make it integrated!

Our senses are the contact points to our surroundings and our understanding is realized. As we work with our senses, the message is engrained in us, until we reach a point where inside and outside are one. Once we've reached this place can we say that we are ready to work with the child.

Everytime I teach a class there is always one person who doesn't want to make their own material. They see it as a waste of time. It would be more practical to buy it. True. This is the capitalistic consumer mentality of our day.

Once when a person who thought like this worked with making materials, their whole expression changed. She was happy, moved and with tears in her eyes, said now she understood the why.

What happened? The meaning came with the hands on work with the material and became one with her. It was beautiful to see this process.

When I visited a Montessori school in Dar es Salaam (Tanzania), I saw future Montessori directresses—ones in training—each making their own materials. How wonderful! What a treasure!

Material making is a gift to the catechist.

---

Dear Catechists,

I want to share with you the personal experience I have had in making materials for all three levels of the Catechesis of the Good Shepherd. Over the years I have felt inferior, hurried, harried and just plain inadequate but I have continued. I have always found a peace and quiet working with the wood. My time working on materials has also been a time alone for me. The time I have spent with the wood became my time with God. Several times while carving a disciple, cutting out a box, or just putting together a wooden environment, I would find myself in deep concentration. I know that not everyone can work with wood, maybe not carve; but I do think that everyone can work a scroll saw. The scroll saw is so much like a sewing machine really! If you just can't seem to master any kind of saw then go ahead and order your wooden materials but do the painting yourself. Oh, I know that old excuse, "I can't paint!" Well, I couldn't either. I must say that I think I have gotten better over the years. I may even get pretty good if I keep it up for ten more years. The point I am trying to make is this: I don't think it is how wonderful these pieces look when we finish painting them; but more what we have put into them, how much of ourselves is invested in each piece. If the materials mean something to us I think this carries over to the children.

As you can tell, making materials has meant a lot to me over the years. When I think of atriums being filled with materials that I have made, I think of these atriums being filled with a part of me. Please give material making a try, on whatever scale you feel called. Certainly from the diversity of materials we have in the atriums there is something each one of you can do and enjoy doing it.

— Laurie Cummings

---

There is a little girl named Hannah who is very sweet but often not attentive especially during presentations. Earlier in the year I had presented the Epiclesis and the Offering. This particular week I was doing the Good Shepherd. I was very busy on the opposite side of the room while the children were working. Hannah had taken the Good Shepherd and I happened to see her working with it. To my amazement she had the sheep and the shepherd in the fold and was doing the Epiclesis over the fold. This was not quickly done. When she finished that she picked up a sheep and the Good Shepherd and held it up in offering. I might add all the while she was conversing with the shepherd and the sheep. This speaks to me of the profound effect this work has on the children and how intuitive they are concerning the things of God.

–Sister Sheila Sentiff

# How Do I Make an Album Page?

*By Betty Hissong*

Recently I was speaking to several people in a formation course who were a bit confused about album pages. After some moments of conversation one of them said to me, "Would you say it's sort of like a lesson plan?" When I replied in the affirmative somehow the mystery of what the album page is seemed to vanish. However, I reluctantly say it's like a lesson plan. Lesson plans are associated with teaching facts and helping develop intellectual concepts within a school setting. That's not what we are about in the Good Shepherd Catechesis. Our job has to do with introducing the children to God by announcing the kerygma, and then allowing God to work within the child to develop a relationship. How often I have heard Sofia say, "We need to de-school catechesis." Consequently one can say the album pages are a little like a lesson plan, but its purpose is NOT to help us teach something. It's a guide for us in announcing God's love to the children.

Before tackling the job of writing album pages it's a great help if you start with prayer about the mystery you are going to share with the children. This puts the proper focus on it. You'll probably be surprised at how much guidance you actually receive from the Holy Spirit. When God chooses us to do this work, divine help is always present. The album pages are a form of help to the catechist to be God's announcers. Prayer is essential. As you prepare for a session with the children, go over your album pages and pray again. One needs to be in contact with the Lord in order to be his instrument.

We have found that many of you who take the formation course are somewhat intimidated by the album pages unless you have Montessori training. Consequently, the following remarks are meant as a guideline to help you tackle the job of making album pages. I will take each part of the album page and attempt to summarize what each part should contain. The following parts are the ones I use, though I realize some formation courses have presented a slightly different form.

**TITLE:** This is the name given to the specific presentation. For example: Annunciation, Pearl of Great Price, Altar I, etc.

**CATEGORY:** Most of the 3-6 presentations we give to the children will fall into one of the following categories: Eucharist, Baptism, Parables of the Kingdom, and Life of Christ, which is further sub-divided into Infancy Narratives, Prophecy, Geography, and Pascal Narratives. I'm all for writing album pages in Practical Life also. Being clear about what category the presentations fall in helps to know which presentations to give and how to give them.

**AGE:** Ask yourself what particular age of child seems most appropriate for this presentation. Often there is a range of ages and not one specific age. However some things are more appropriate for a three year old considering the needs of the child and others would be best left for an older child. For example, a three year old will really enter into the Good Shepherd parable even though it might be a year or two before the child realizes he or she is a sheep. They really enjoy this parable and enter into it wholly. On the other hand, presenting the wolf and the hired hand is best left for children five and older.

**SOURCES:** Specific scriptural references used or the liturgical rites involved in the presentation should be listed under sources. It should also contain a list of any suitable background reading such as specific references in The Religious Potential of the Child; The Good Shepherd and the Child, A Joyful Journey; and the *Materials Manual*. Be sure to include page numbers. It could include course notes and background theology readings that would help the catechist prepare for the presentation. If the presentation is sacramental, for example Baptism, you might also include pages from the Sacramentary or the Book of Common Prayer.

**LITURGICAL TIME:** This is the time of the liturgical year that would be most appropriate for the particular presentation. For example, Annunciation would be most appropriate during Advent. Some other presentations, however, do not have a specific liturgical time.

**DOCTRINAL POINTS:** This is perhaps one of the most important parts of the album page and needs to be prayerfully considered. One needs to see clearly the doctrinal content of the mystery to be presented to the children, not that one gives these to the children directly, but knowing what the doctrinal content is helps one to see how to make the presentation. Often there are many related doctrinal points, some more important than others. I have often heard Rebekah Rojcewicz speak about "eking this out." Only with "eking these out" can we get a clear idea of what is the most important part of the message we share with the children.

**DIRECT AIM:** Catechists need to be extremely focused on what the specific and primary aim of each presentation is. This will always flow from the doctrinal points and is one reason to spend enough thought and prayer on the doctrinal points. There is usually one primary point to be considered even though there may be many other items that could be considered. For instance, in the Infancy Narratives the direct aim is to help the children become conscious of the incarnation—God becoming man. One also needs to keep in mind that we do not merely cover "material" with the children. Each presentation has some major and specific goal which we hope the children discover. For example, in the presentation of the Pearl of Great Price, like most parables, there are many layers of truths to realize and often many facets of the parable to enjoy and relish. However, the central theme or purpose is helping

*continued on next page*

young children appreciate and enjoy the tremendous value of the kingdom. This is paramount and should be the focus of our presentation and any wondering or meditative questions we use. On the other hand, some presentations like Altar I will have a simple focus: nomenclature.

**INDIRECT AIM:** This gives us an opportunity to recognize and list any other fruits that might result from the meditations. For instance in Altar I, the primary purpose is really getting to know the names of the articles used at mass. However, we also make the announcement of Christ's death and resurrection even though that is not the direct aim of the presentation. Often presentations will be long-range preparations for participation in the Mass, or prayer, or recognition of our role in the kingdom. All of these can be part of the indirect aims.

**MATERIAL DESCRIPTION:** This consists of a description of the specific material used in the presentation that will later be used by the children when they are working and meditating with the material individually. Keep in mind that these materials are not teacher's visual aids, but are meant to aid the children in meditation. You could say they are a concrete sign of a transcendental reality. It is wise to include the approximate sizes and kinds of materials needed. Sometimes drawings and photos are helpful. Specific references to the manual should be included. Be sure to include any Scripture booklets or prayer booklets required.

**PRESENTATION:** Every Scripture presentation should have the following points:

1. Introduction. This consists of a few introductory remarks that somehow link to what the children have already experienced.

2. Oral presentation. This is the telling of the incident in one's own simple words trying to stay as close to the Scripture passage as possible. Write out simple major points.

3. Solemn reading of Scripture. Use lighted candle, solemn voice.

4. Presentation with materials. Show children the material naming the items and move the materials following the Scripture passage.

5. Meditative or wondering questions. These should be really a part of all of the above, but be sure to include these in your album page so as to be aware of helping the children respond. There can be a special section after the presentation with materials for this kind of response.

6. Closing. This could be song, prayer, silence. It should also include putting material away and inviting the children to use it.

I have seen many different forms in this section of the album pages. Some people write out every word and use it as a script. Others find it most useful to just list major parts. My own experience is that having a script makes one a kind of slave to the script. I think the script has advantages when one is preparing for the presentation, but has real disadvantages when used with the children. One is present to the script instead of to the children and to the Word. At any rate the album page should really have only the major points of the presentation. On the other hand they should not be so sketchy that one misses important aspects of the meditation.

**CHILDREN'S WORK:** The first thing to be listed here is always the use of the materials by the children themselves. Incidentally this is by far the most important part of any lesson. It's easy to think the most important part is the catechist's presentation. The Holy Spirit, of course, can work in any time or place, but most often is working alone within the child as he meditates on the materials. Other things that could also be included here would be things like art work, copying texts, tracing, etc.

**OBSERVATIONS & REFLECTIONS:** These are observations and reflections of the catechist. Included could be things that children might say as a response, things you've observed them doing, thoughts on how to make the presentation better, etc. These are often things that could be shared with Sofia as she tries to gather data on this great way of helping children get to know and enjoy God.

---

### ALBUM PAGE

Title:                    Category:

Age:

Sources:

Liturgical Time:

Doctrinal Points:

Direct Aim:

Indirect Aim:

Material Description:

Presentation:

Children's Work:

Observations and Reflections:

# The Care of the Atrium

*By Tina Lillig*

"Isn't it beautiful?" said one 4-year-old as she stood with her mother at the threshold of the atrium. Another child, age 3, confided to his mother, "I could live here."

In our church community, in Oak Park, Illinois, we have the gift of many children, and so several groups of children use the same atrium. The atrium for the 3- to 6-year-olds may welcome up to four different groups, scheduled at various times. The same is true for the 6-9 and 9-12 atriums. So the care of the environment and materials has become very important for us, especially when we observe how much this means to the children.

Over the past 23 years, the "rooms" that are the atrium have changed from time to time. I have worked in at least five different ones. The size of the atrium and the style of its furnishings can vary greatly. What seems to matter more is that the materials are simple and clean, pencils are sharpened, vases are ready for new flowers, different-size papers of the needed measurements are in place, and tables are clean and unsticky. Silence and work somehow depend on these things.

I have noticed that a well-cared-for environment is a real help for the children. Their work is more peaceful and without the need for frequent assistance from the catechists to find what is missing. They also begin to take ownership of the atrium. They restore materials that a younger child put in the wrong place. They set aside a broken pencil and get more paper when they use the last piece.

For the catechists, too, it is better when everyone works to keep the atrium beautiful. We grow to appreciate how each material should be made, be revealed, be used, be returned, and be maintained.

What are some things we can do to prepare the atrium, especially when many groups of children share it?

Most of us have a little routine we follow immediately before the children arrive. For the 3-6 children, we might:
- prepare the materials we hope to present
- wet the sponges
- put out fresh flowers and fill water pitcher
- set out wine and water
- make sure there is enough flour, yeast, and warm water
- check paper and pencils
- fill a small container with warm water to hold used glue brushes
- prepare attendance chart
- pray and center ourselves

Each catechist's routine will be particular to the atrium and to the age group of the children.

Over the years I have also enjoyed cleaning the atrium a little more thoroughly on a regular basis during the year. How often this is done depends on the need and on how many children use the atrium. This cleaning usually involves:
- sweeping or vacuuming the floor
- emptying wastepaper baskets
- cutting new paper
- sharpening pencils
- cleaning the polishing work
- washing tables
- dusting shelves
- checking the materials
- laundering linens, polishing cloths, and dust rags

For the older children the list would be different. But it is the same idea. At the end of the year, linens are washed and ironed and each material is cleaned and covered for the summer. Then in the fall we can simply uncover the materials, polish the brass things, and we are ready to greet the children.

It is helpful to have a place to keep cleaning supplies near the atrium. A bucket, liquid soap, soft cloths, and a scrubbing sponge are used often. My best discovery was to keep an old toothbrush for washing cruets or vases that have a narrow neck.

The Catechesis of the Good Shepherd here in St. Giles Community has been blessed over the years with catechists who enjoy cleaning the atrium. Some like to work in silence, and others talk together or listen to music while they work. It can also be a time of prayer:

> O God, may the small hands that will hold
>   these pencils express
> what you have written on their hearts.
>
> Thank you, God, for Sarah, who loves to prepare
>   this vase with flowers.
> May she always be filled with your praise.
>
> May the child who will pour from these cruets
>   help to draw us all into your mystery.

## Material Tip

Two products that have been wonderful to work with are: **BIN Primer** by Zinsser which covers well and dries quickly but cleans up with ammonia, and **Muralo Waterborne Polyurethane** which goes on beautifully, dries clear, and requires only soap and water clean-up.

—*Joan Roberts*

# St. Andrew's Fire

What can catechists do when everything is lost as it was when our church was destroyed by fire?

Watching the firefighters pour hundreds of gallons of water for hours onto the flames on that frigid February morning, we prayed that somehow the materials in our four basement atria and the storage rooms would be spared.

But when we were allowed to look into the rooms, we knew that everything had been lost, not burned, but ruined by heat and water and soot. It was a dark, desolate scene, sooty mud everywhere; a jumble of waterlogged wall plaster and burned wood; children's artwork charred and curling on the walls; cabinets fallen over, with their contents carried off by the four-foot flood of water that had filled the basement.

We cried. And we brought out everything we could recognize, mostly metal and glass and cloth articles that we thought we could clean. And we lamented over what we had to leave behind—our albums, the handmade wooden materials and furniture, paper materials too damaged to restore, and so many more materials in the workroom and storage closets that we could not even enter.

And foremost in all our minds was the thought: where do we begin to start over again?

First, we had to find new space. The gift of space came to us from our church youth program and the day school whose students had been coming weekly to our atria. We were mobilized into action by Laurie Higgins who almost singlehandedly furnished both atria. She was resolved that the children would not miss even one catechesis session!

In three days, her third graders were sitting at a prayer table in a sparsely furnished 6-8 atrium. When the preschool building opened the next week, children were able to work longer in a new 3-6 atrium that was larger and closer to their classrooms.

Some of the catechists were relieved to see the "new" atrium with a prayer table, sheepfold, altar and cruets, Cenacle and some art and practical life. Some grieved because they saw what was not there, the sacristy, parables, infancy narratives, city of Jerusalem, baptism work.

Within ten days we met with catechists, parishioners, parents, and friends to tell them what materials we needed and how to make them, and we handed out assignments. Although we had decided what we needed first and were prepared with drawings and pictures and manual pages, we learned that it is not a simple thing to describe how to make something you cannot show.

The most difficult things to replace have been the wooden materials. Laurie is now determined to learn woodworking so we can make our own sheepfolds, figures and boxes.

Was it good that we had put together the space and materials immediately to keep going? Or should we have stopped for a while for respite and to comfort each other?

I don't know. We all felt God's gift of healing as the children blessed us when they came to work quietly with the materials that were there, happy to be in their atrium.

There was richness of response in the 3-6 atrium. Kindergarteners who had only seen presentations now had time to work, and their classroom teachers were all amazed at their capacity to move quietly, meditate, and respond.

Yet, having to work in a new environment that had problems while still mourning was difficult to do, and emotions were high.

So many decisions had to be made: Is it better to have an almost complete material than no material at all? What can we give to the children now until more materials can be added? How will six catechists from two atria work together in one? How will we continue the Level I training begun last month?

At times, there were angry words, suppressed feelings. Some catechists felt decisions were being made without their input. Some felt unfulfilled because they had not been invited to put the new atrium together.

After several angry confrontations, we decided things were moving too fast. SLOW DOWN! was the message we had gotten from the national office and from Sofia, and we began to understand what that really meant.

Perhaps we should have sat together in a empty space for a while, envisioning together the new atrium.

So we stopped to listen to each other and learned that, for some of us, working and being busy was necessary, while others found solace in moments of rest and withdrawal. We supported each other simply by acknowledging our differences.

And we have slowed down (somewhat), accepted our loss, and know there will continue to be problems. But we rejoice in our different gifts which strengthen us as a community and unite us in our work in God's kingdom.

–Karen Nikaido
*St. Andrew's Episcopal Church*
*Amarillo, Texas*
*July 28, 1996*

# LETTERS TO SOFIA

5 Hale Grove Gardens
Mill Hill London NW7 3LR
28th February 1994

Dear Sofia,

Ever since arriving home from Rome I have been thinking of the evenings that I spent with you at your centre. Once again I was so impressed and touched. It is such a wonderful work that you are doing.

One of the things that impressed me was the fundamental nature of each piece of the material. It is all so truly Montessori. Each piece in its depth and simplicity is a wonderful key, opening the exact door for which it has been designed thus guiding the user to new and wonderful fields of exploration on all levels sensorial, intellectual and spiritual. It is truly magnificent.

It would be possible to discuss all the levels of the material but on this occasion it was its simplicity that really spoke to me. This is probably because my mind was focused on Africa. I am always looking for possible ways of furthering the work there and whatever we do there must be simple, but also because we need to help the adults everywhere to appreciate the true "raison d'etre" of the prepared environment and to help them to realize the beauty and role of each piece of Montessori apparatus within the environment.

The fact that it is so obviously possible to make many of these catechetical materials by hand, with simple tools and raw materials, also gives each piece a freshness that is very inspiring and refreshing in today's sophisticated world. I am sure it touches something special within each child that uses it.

Making materials, or for that matter anything else by hand, immediately creates a relationship between the object and the maker which is completely different from that which usually exists when an object has been bought. There comes a feeling of respect and of achievement. Each piece takes on a quite different value from anything that is manufactured. Especially if it has been made with love, one presents it to the children from a completely different stance, because in a way one is sharing part of oneself. As we all know, in Montessori, each piece of apparatus is a key and for that reason the number of pieces is limited. Usually it is only necessary to have one or sometimes two keys to open any door—many just complicate the situation. It is the same in any field of exploration, at any level, but more particularly in the early years of life.

One only has to watch the children working and to listen to their discussions and conversations, to understand the beauty and fundamental nature of the work of the centre, much of which is sparked by a simple, handmade piece of material.

Thank you, Sofia, for allowing me to share with you all once again.

–Muriel Dweyr

*This is a letter Barbara Fleming Disch sent Sofia of a childhood experience. Barbara has given permission for its use here.*

Dear Sofia,

Between the age of 4-6 I remember trying to share with my parents the remarkable experience I had.

I felt as if I was one with all; like knowing the experience of the baby bird swallowing the worm, or understanding the man down the street who spoke only Italian. These were complete and joyous days.

I went in the house one summer night and decided to announce, with great delight, my understanding of the world to my family at dinner. I said: "It is when the light meets the light

*continued on next page*

## Material Tip

In order to avoid the black drops on clean altar cloths from the candle snuffer....before the children come (and never in their sight) hold the snuffer over a candle in a simple stand (like the one used for each Scripture reading) to heat the snuffer and then wipe it with a tissue until the inside of the snuffer is clean. You can also show a clean snuffer to the children and some will begin to wipe it clean after they complete the altar work or use brass polishing to clean it. This could be done when an altar cloth has been soiled with black residue, so the children know we are striving to avoid this by keeping the snuffer clean, and extinguishing the candles each time putting the snuffer down until we see white smoke (which eliminates the carbon wax buildup). —Linda Kaiel

Take a camera with you during your Catechesis training. Not only do the pictures jog your memory several months later when you are making the material but it proves invaluable when you are unsure of the appropriate color for each item. I place the pictures in plastic sheets especially made to hold them in a notebook and sort them in my albums to correspond with my notes and album pages.

—Joan Roberts

that everything happens."

My adult understanding indicates that I was speaking of kairos time. I meant it is when light within meets the light of anything in the world, knowledge happens through communion. I have learned many things this way, but these were the only words I could say at this age.

No one responded to me so I said it louder: "It is when the light meets the light that everything happens." My mother said: "It is time to say grace, please, be quiet."

My adult question is: How I could feel in union with all and have other people not feel that, too? As a child I had no framework with which to think about all this; I just felt all the energy of joy jam up in my body and it burst out with a yell: "It is when the light meets the light that everything happens."

This outburst took everyone by surprise and I was sent to my room. All the energy turned into a tantrum. They had to hold the door closed to keep me in the room. I remember the dark, dark door I was kicking and the bright, bright light coming through the window. I fell asleep on the floor and when I woke everything was quiet in the family again.

I came to think this light must be a wonderful secret I had discovered, and so I did not talk about it too much. I loved liturgy and nature and felt complete there.

—Barbara Fleming Disch

*Mustard Tree*
*Lance, age 7,*
*Good Shepherd Atrium,*
*Gesu Parish,*
*Detroit, Michigan*

*Katie, age 6,*
*The House of the*
*Good Shepherd,*
*Ottawa,*
*Ontario,*
*Canada.*

*Each star is colored yellow and there are yellow rays emanating from them. Katie said about her artwork, "This picture is from God. Jesus is born, says Mary."*

# Consiglio Report

*The consiglio is a council. The Catechesis of the Good Shepherd is an international council made up of representatives from each country.*

*By Linda Kaiel, Rebekah Rojcewicz, and Judy Schmidt*

A chorus of voices crescendo, revealing excited Italian comments, equally lively Spanish remarks, with an occasional English phrase undulating in the background...the scene is the 9-12 atrium space in Rome where the Consiglio is holding the first international meeting, October 20-26, 1996. Twenty-one representatives encircle the room, where the main conversation is taking place in Italian. This gathering of catechists from around the globe has come together to develop a structure for the international committee, to review the characteristics of the Catechesis of the Good Shepherd, to share from their wealth of experience in this work with children and in their local formation of catechists, and to voice concerns and challenges to the work. Most of the English-speaking catechists are gathered at a central table, clustered near Rebekah Rojcewicz as she attempts to aid their understanding of the Italian proceedings.

"Our catechesis is one of covenant. We celebrate our past. We await in hope our future. The parable of the mustard seed contains our work. Our structure is imperfect, but not primary. We live the rhythm of the child." These opening remarks of Sofia's follow prayer and song. And we begin in earnest to review the written characteristics of the work, first shared in 1993. Careful phrasing is attended to as well as the nuance of meaning and experience. There is a real struggle to clarify and modify some of the points. Does each point reflect what we have lived with the children? There was a discernible difference among the nationalities as to their approach to problem solving: the Italians are almost tortuous in their attempt to untangle the ball of string of an idea or point. The Germans go right to the heart of an idea and hammer out the points of it, da dum da dum da dum. The Spanish and English speaking are more relaxed—give a little here and there, figuring it will all come right in the end. These differences were fascinating to observe as the document slowly came together. And so the days took on a rhythm and were more than full. Some of us began to dream in Italian, and whether our mother tongue was Spanish, Italian or English, Silvana Montanaro or Maria Christlieb graciously acted as our translators when we tried to find a language for our thoughts and spontaneous comments during the proceedings. As we complete the characteristics, we adopt a draft of statutes/guidelines for the consiglio/council. The seat will be in Rome at Via degli Orsini 34. The executive committee is named: Sofia Cavalletti (president), Gianna Gobbi (vice-president), Silvana Montanaro (secretary) and Adelaide Balmas (treasurer). Each country will choose their own representatives and meetings will ordinarily take place every three years, usually one week in duration. Various aims of the committee are: to aid in communication, exchange experiences and mutually support one another; to further research on the themes of the work, both doctrinal and methodological; to review new themes and materials.

*Cutting the cake at the Consiglio farewell gathering. From left to right: Silvana Montanaro, Sofia Cavalletti, Gianna Gobbi, Adelaide Balmas and Tilde Cocchini. (Photograph by Patricia Stenton)*

*continued on next page*

Representatives will be those who have experience with children, know the three levels of the work, work with the formation of adult catechists, and have a global vision of the work. It has been recommended that one of the two representatives selected be a returning member (was present at the last Consiglio meeting) to foster continuity in the work of the council.

Thursday morning Tilde Cocchini, who had faithfully been taping the proceedings, took us to visit the necropolis beneath St. Peter's Basilica. Rome, the Eternal City, blessed us with clear autumn days and moonlit nights as we crossed the Tiber on our walk home to Villa Lante, the convent where we were housed near the Trastevere region of the city. It was a joy to spend time with the delegates, to continue or begin new friendships. Especially of interest has been the reports shared by each of the countries, reflecting on the challenges, growth and work. This has initiated some lively conversations. We also heard reports on the birth of the work in Panama and Australia. How the work of formation is done in each country and how the children and catechists are nurtured is a space for each of us to reflect on our own pastoral work and learn from other's ventures.

Saturday, our final day, began with a lecture from Father Dalmazio Mongillo on the theme of justice. "We live in a specific moment in time, but are part of a whole. We awaken to our solidarity in humanity, we learn to live this reality. The work of God...the realization of a humanity coming to fullness..." We are all given gifts, many gifts, differing gifts, and the justice of God has to do with God's plan that while we enjoy these gifts, we also share them in order that all people might receive the fullness of God. With these reflections, we begin a day that will also include an evening Eucharist where Father Mongillo placed a copy of the signed constitution of the Consiglio under the chalice and the paten, offering them as a "priestly work." This is followed by a farewell party and repast in Sofia's dining room, with a cake to celebrate the birth of the Consiglio.

Thank goodness it was the evening the clocks changed, so we had an extra hour to pack and pace our farewells as we left at various times on Sunday for the airport or further travel in Italy. Now comes the work of reflection and the translation of the proceedings from Italian to English to share with the catechists at home. Francesca Cocchini sends greetings as "big as Texas" to all whom she met at Camp Allen. Tucked in our suitcases was an Italian copy of Sofia's book, <u>The Religious Potential of the Child, 6-12,</u> which was published in Italian in fall, 1996. Portions of the text are currently being translated to English and reviewed for publication. We all agreed we look forward to greeting one another again soon. Arrivederci Roma!

### Representatives:

**Argentina**
Anna Maria Macchieraldo
Herminia Wasserzug

**Austria**
Claudia Schmitt

**Canada**
Susan Furlan
(Patricia Coulter)
Patricia Stenton
(Joe Tanel)

**Colombia**
Tere Lopez
Nora Bonilla Paris

**Germany**
Deborah Presser-Velder

**Italy**
Adelaide Balmas
Sofia Cavalletti
Francesca Cocchini
Tilde Cocchini
Gianna Gobbi
Silvana Q. Montanaro
Alessandra Pollastri

**Mexico**
Lupita Palafox
Maria Christlieb Robles
Concepcion G. de Valladolid

**USA**
Linda Kaiel
Rebekah Rojcewicz
Julanne Schmidt

---

### Material Tip

Whenever possible, print prayer cards and booklets by hand. Our experience has been that the children more readily copy and trace handwritten cards as opposed to computer generated material.

*–Judy Schmidt*

# Life of the Catechist: Healthy Priorities

*By Kathy Van Duser*

Have you ever felt overwhelmed by material making? Have your kitchen table, dining room table, or any and all workable surfaces in your home been covered with materials in progress? When you begin making a material, has the process taken you three times longer than you first estimated? I believe this experience has been common to many catechists. It has been my experience too, and I would like to share my story.

About nine years ago, a friend from my church approached me asking for my help starting the Catechesis of the Good Shepherd. She told me a bit about this catechesis and it did sound wonderful. At the time, I was beginning a new community group for women, so I told this friend of mine, "No, I don't have the time to do both of these activities right now." However my husband and I did enroll both of our children in the Catechesis of the Good Shepherd at church. A parent meeting was offered to those parents who had children in the program. When I went to this parent meeting, the presentation of the Parable of the Good Shepherd was given. Hearing this parable, I felt like James and John in Matthew 4:21 who, when asked by Jesus, "Come, follow me," at once left their nets, the boat, and their father, and followed him.

In my case, it was more like leaving the dirty dishes, the supper, the dusting, the cleaning, and sometimes my children and my husband to follow.

This call I felt from the Good Shepherd was personal, strong, and spoke directly to my heart. I knew I had to do this work of the Catechesis of the Good Shepherd.

So it was with enthusiasm and love I began to attend catechist training meetings and to make materials.

The very next year, I was making more materials for a group of 6- to 9-year-olds. My own children were in this age range now, and I really wanted them to be able to grow closer to the Good Shepherd through this catechesis.

In my zeal to answer this call of Jesus, often my house had stacks of album pages and handouts. (Who has time to file when making materials, doing presentations, and raising a family!!?) My home also had various materials in progress and various household chores undone.

Toward the end of my second year involved in the catechesis my husband Paul said to me, "I wonder, for our own children, how much having the Catechesis of the Good Shepherd balances out living in chaos during the week?"

Paul's comment stopped me in my tracks. I began to think about that question and to focus on the first call I received from God to be a wife and mother and then to my call as catechist. I knew God had called me to each of these works, but in my passion to do the work of the catechesis, my focus on my family was not clear. After all, my husband and children are my favorite people to be with. Was I taking away from their Good Shepherd experience by being so zealous about my own work in it? Was my family feeling like the catechesis meant more to me than they did?

All of these questions prompted me to pray about and evaluate my life choices. Some of the following ideas helped me prioritize and find a balance in responding to my call from God.

Most helpful to me was slowing down. In slowing down, I
*continued on next page*

Charles, age 5, Our Lady's Montessori School, Kansas City, Missouri. "At the bottom is my name and my sister's name. This is a picture of me, and this (the crosses) is Jesus." Charles and Bobbie came to the school in March. Their first two experiences in the atrium were the Seder meal and the Liturgy of the Light. Two months later he drew this picture.

allowed more time for prayer in my life, asking God to help me prioritize. God has helped me keep the people in my life first. I have also been shown how my elaborate, complex ideas can be pared down to simple, essential ideas that are still beautiful.

My great concern that my own children be presented with this catechesis now before they grew too old has dissipated. Our marvelous God finds all kinds of ways to bring us to him within and without the catechesis.

"Who will do this work? I physically can't do all of it." In praying and asking for workers, I've learned to let go and simply believe workers will be sent.

Instead of having a new presentation every time the children met, time was planned for just working in the atrium. This has been a great joy for the children, and it has allowed me rest time before a new material needs to be made and a presentation given.

When making the schedule for the following year, I reduced the number of meeting times, but lengthened to two hours each time the children met. This helped limit the number of materials the adults needed to make and it gave the children time to experience deeply the work they chose to do.

Find the most convenient time to make materials. For me this turned out to be mid-May through early June. The Catechesis of the Good Shepherd meetings were finished until the following September, and my own children were still in school. It was a quieter time of the year for me. A majority of the materials I make are done during this time. Having this one month period for material making helps because it means materials are spread out and worked on for a short, limited time. Sometimes I have found working early in the morning before children are awake or at night after they are in bed can be managed if I'm not too tired.

What would be the least stressful time of the year or day for you? Other people have found group meetings of catechists working together a few times a year are a good way to make materials. Often churches divide material making among many people, that way no one person has too much. Good directions/plans are important so people know exactly what needs to be made.

Materials need to be essential, but they don't need to be perfect. If something isn't centered exactly, or there's a smudge or a word accidentally gets left out, it doesn't mean the material isn't usable or has to be remade. Maybe the smudge can be covered or lived with, perhaps the word can be added, and just maybe the off-centered material doesn't matter to the children. God uses each of us and we're not perfect. Sometimes we are also a little off center. We can use a material that's not what we would consider perfect.

Being selective about other activities I commit to beyond my family and being selective about the work I focus on in relation to the catechesis, helps me avoid burning out. If I keep as central in my life my relationship with God and my commitment to my family, it is then that my work in the Catechesis finds its place. For me working with the Catechesis of the Good Shepherd has deepened my relationship with God and with my family. It has filled a creative need. It has required daily prayer, thought, and humor to keep a balance. I still have things to file and materials to make, but my family knows they are my priority.

*Matthew, age 6, Church of Our Saviour, Chicago, Illinois. Matthew described his picture as "Jesus rising from the cross." When the catechist commented that Jesus looks happy, Matthew replied "Yes, he's going to God."*

# NEXT JOURNAL TO FEATURE THE CONSIGLIO

Amy, age 7, Church of Our Saviour, Chicago, Illinois. In this color drawing, the candlesticks and chalice are yellow. Both the crosses are multicolored and the hearts are red. Carol, Amy's mother and a catechist, describes this drawing as a vision of the epiclesis.

## Your stories make our journal.

Articles about your atrium, training, book reviews make this journal an important communication vehicle for catechists worldwide. Tell us how we can help you by writing us about the journal or with your questions about your work with children.

## Please share your children's artwork and your photographs.

To obtain the best possible journal image, we ask for original art work or color copies whenever possible. We will return original work as soon as possible. Include the artist's name, age, and tell us a little about the child and the work. This information should be written on a piece of paper attached to the art work with a paper clip or carefully printed on the back. Also tell us the name of your atrium, and in what city and state. Since this is a black and white journal, black and white photographs are ideal; however, color photographs are also acceptable. All art work that we receive must have permission by the artist and their parents to be used in print now or at some time in the future.

Please be sure to include your address with any materials you would like returned. Thank you.

---

Please send all journal materials directly to:

**Attn: Tina Lillig**
**The Catechesis of the Good Shepherd**
**P. O. Box 1084**
**Oak Park, IL 60304**

**1997 Staff in U.S.A.**
Joan and Toby Roberts • Tina Lillig
Linda Kaiel • Kathy Van Duser

**Translators:**
Joan Parasine • Nicolina Gleasure
Janet Griffing

---

# *Membership*

**The Catechesis of the Good Shepherd**, an association of children and adults, welcomes members throughout the year. Members receive the annual journal, all mailings, and a directory of catechists and friends of the association.

Mail requests for membership and other information to:
**The Catechesis of the Good Shepherd, P.O. Box 1084, Oak Park, IL 60304**

© Copyright 1997: The Catechesis of the Good Shepherd, P.O. Box 1084, Oak Park, IL 60304

# INDEX OF ARTICLES, FEATURES AND CONTRIBUTORS

*Contributors who are not identified by surname in the text do not appear in this index.*

"And a Little Child Shall Lead Them"
    (Cavalletti), 167–69
Anderson, Becca, 210
Anderson, Michael, 37
"Angelina and the Good Shepherd"
    (Maresca), 112–14
"Anointings at Baptism, The" (Maresca), 41–43
Arnold, Robert, 197
Bardy-Gagner, Cecilia, 221, 233
Bettendorf, Erin, 220, 232
"Bible in the Prayer Corner, The"
    (Bonilla-Paris), 194
Billoro, Monica, 225
Bonilla-Paris, Nora Maria, 158, 194, 273
"Book Reviews," 121–22, 136, 221, 227, 249
Briosso, Laura, 225
Brown, Matthew, 193, 205
Brownlee, Sara Jo, 233
"Building Up an Atrium" (Stenborg), 137
Caballero, Santa, 233
Cain, Caitlin, 213
Calderon Quiroz, Claudia, 129
"Care of the Atrium, The" (Lillig), 290
"Catechesis as Celebration" (Coulter), 73
"Catechesis in Munich, The"
    (Presser-Velder), 198–99
"Catechesis of the Good Shepherd in Argentina"
    (Wasserzug), 137
"Catechesis of the Good Shepherd in
    Chihuahua, Northern Mexico, The"
    (Christlieb), 9–10

"Catechesis of the Little Ones, The" (Gobbi), 154
"Catechesis Shared in Colombia, The"
    (Bonilla), 158
"Catechesis with Adults" (Quiroz), 200–2
Cavalletti, Sofia, 4–8, 25–30, 34–35, 38–40,
    60–61, 66–68, 73, 97–99, 132–33, 136,
    150–51, 161–62, 167–69, 183–85, 195,
    196, 205, 213–17, 221, 226–27, 234–36,
    240–41, 256–57, 264, 276, 282–83
"Celebrating Ten Years of an Atrium"
    (Hernandez de Sanchez), 155
"Celebration of First Eucharist," 62–64, 104–5
"Celebration of Light, A" (Christlieb), 129
Celi, Lidia, 110–11
"Characteristics of Catechists of the Good
    Shepherd, The" (Cavalletti), 60–61
"Characteristics of the Good Shepherd
    Catchesis" (Cavalletti), 25–30
Charles, Nakeeta, 259
"Children Are Not Angels, The"
    (F. Cocchini), 135
"Children in Front of the Mystery of Death"
    (Cavalletti et al.), 38–40
"Children's Center in Houston, Texas, The,"
    51–52
"Children Show Us How to Pray Joyfully, The"
    (C. Dittberner), 202–3
"Children, the Eucharist, and Their Happiness,
    The" (Sandoval), 106–7
Christlieb, Maria, 9–10, 69–72, 77–79,
    88–89, 129, 140, 274–75

## Index of Articles, Features and Contributors

Cocchini, Francesca, 24, 135, 246–48, 271
Cocchini, Tilde, 131, 271
"Communal Prayer" (Cavalletti), 195
Conale, Maria Sara, 225
Conale, Virginia, 225
Conaughton, Sr. Marie, 53
"Consiglio Report" (Kaiel et al.), 294–95
"Cosmic Character of the Mass, The"
    (Cavalletti), 264
"Cosmic Vision of the Mass, The," 141
Coulter, Patricia, 4–8, 25–30, 73,
    210–12, 213–17
Cremona, Lucia, 100–2, 134
Cullen, Sr. Patricia, 54
Cummings, Laurie, 287
Dahl-Bredine, Kathy, 165
"Development of the Catechesis in a Lay School"
    (Celi), 110–11
"Development of the Catechist, The"
    (Dosh), 171–72
Diáz, Fernanda, 225
Diáz Pumora, Celina, 225
Disch, Barbara Fleming, 292–93
Dittberner, Carol, 65, 105, 115–16, 121–22,
    130, 156–57, 202–3, 217–18, 227
Dittberner, John, 76
"Does God Have a Sense of Humor?"
    (Searle), 222–23
Dosh, Millicent, 171–72
"Dream, A" (Christlieb), 88–89
Dweyr, Muriel, 292
"Enjoying the Gift: The Communion Retreat in
    the Episcopal Church" (Nyberg), 242–43
Ericson, Susie E., 59
Eskro, Mark, 225
"Essentials of Material Making, The" (Kaiel), 284
"Eucharist with the Children, The"
    (Cavalletti), 276

"Experience of Lent, An"
    (Quiroz de Harquez), 135
"Experience of Making One's Own Material"
    (Gobbi), 283
"Experiences in the Atrium," 69–72, 74
"First Catechesis Course Given" (Schmitt), 224
"First Communion Journal, A" (Christlieb), 140
Fisher, Martha, 136
"Food for Thought," 16
"Formation Experiences Reviewed"
    (Huisken), 220
Fortune, Alissa, 201
Fox, Michael, 128
Frens-String, Josh, 255
Fruzzetti, Juliana, 165
Furlan, Susan, 145, 269–70
Gannon, Andria, 193
Gardeas, Vanessa, 114
Genovese, Giuliana, 271
Giannone, Silvia, 209
Gleasure, Nicolina, 183–85, 194, 195, 196,
    221, 226–27, 234–36, 240–41
Gobbi, Gianna, 152–53, 154, 170,
    257, 258–62, 283
Goodwin, Katherine, 89
Griffing, Janet, 198–99, 224, 225
Haches, Stella Mara, 225
Halbach, Katrine, 76
Hanson, Matthew, 208
Hernandez, Ruben, 106–7
Hernandez de Sanchez, Conception, 155
Hissong, Betty, 39–40, 258–62, 288–89
"History, The," 179–81
"History of the Research on the Mass"
    (Cavalletti), 183–85
"How Do I Make an Album Page?"
    (Hissong), 288–89
Huisken, Holly, 220

# Index of Articles, Features and Contributors

"In Everything Give Thanks" (Scheef), 237
"International Catechists' Reports," 272–75
Kahn, Barbara, 11–14
Kaiel, Linda, 271, 274, 284, 292, 294–95
Kosowski, Joseph, 132, 181, 214, 251
Krause, Marilyn, 277, 284, 286
Kuehn, Erika, 236
"Let's Make the Material with Our Own Hands" (Cavalletti), 282–83
"Letter from a Catechist, Houston, Texas" (Pechacek), 174–76
"Letter of Love from a Catechist, A" (F. Cocchini), 24
"Letters from Rome" (Cavalletti and Gobbi), 256–57
"Let Us Pray with the Children," 36–37, 58–59, 94–95, 128, 148–49, 165, 192–93, 209, 233, 255, 281
"Life of the Catechist," 277, 296–97
Lillig, Tina, 117, 144, 238–39, 268–69, 290
"Liturgy of the Hours, The," 197
Maresca, Catherine, 41–43, 105, 112–14, 145, 160, 173, 264
"Maria Montessori and the Religious Education of the Child" (Montanaro), 177–78
"Material, The" (Cremona), 134
McKinley-Ward, William, 246
Meyer, Jacob, 165
Miller, J. W., 84
Mohn, Martina, 199
Mohn, Mary Lou, 166
Mongillo, Fr. P. Dalmazio, 17–20
Montanaro, Silvana Quattrocchi, 31–33, 177–78, 271
Montessori, Maria, 2, 231
"Montessori Cosmic Vision and the Bible, The" (Cavalletti), 213–17
Mugan, Paula, 271

Mullin, Elizabeth, 33
"Mustard Seed Is Planted in Japan, The" (Coulter), 210–12
"Mystery of Faith and Prayers of Intercession," 265–67
"*Mystery of Faith* Booklet," 245
Nelson, Andy, 75
Nelson, Jessica, 3
"News from the Minnesota Catechists," 199
Nikaido, Karen, 291
"1989 Course for 9–12 in Washington" (C. Dittberner), 156–57
Nyberg, Carol, 242–43
O'Brien, Briana, 166, 226
O'Bryan, Bert, 53, 144
O'Bryan, Marty, 53, 144
"On Materials and Meaning" (Renton), 285–86
"On Moral Formation" (Cavalletti), 132–33, 150–51
"On Taking of Photographs" (Cavalletti), 205
Orrben, Patti, 74
"O Taste and See" (Cavalletti), 234–36
"Our Association and the True Vine" (Furlan), 145
"Our Association Takes Birth" (Rojcewicz), 44–46
"Our Visit to Chihuahua, Mexico" (Fisher), 136
"Outline for Communal Prayer," 196
"Out of the Mouths of Babes" (Maresca), 160
Parasine, Joan Marie, 97–99, 100–2, 132–33, 134, 183–85, 194, 195, 196, 221, 226–27, 234–36, 240–41
Pate, Charlie, 219
Paul, Nicole, 170
Paul, Rose Marie, 55, 186–88
Pechacek, Anne, 174–76
"People Walked in Darkness, The" (Rainville), 182

## Index of Articles, Features and Contributors

Perry, Colleen, 233
Piescik, Andrea, 233
"Pili and the Sacrament of the Sick"
    (Sandoval), 154
Pollastri, Sandra, 142–43
Polta, Mary, 50
"Power of God's Love, The" (Maresca), 145
"Prayer for the Association," 85
"Prayer to God" (Rice), 40
Presser-Velder, Deborah, 198–99, 273
Quiroz, Eva Elesa, 200–2
Quiroz de Harquez, Berta Sofia, 135
"Rainbow, The" (Maresca), 173
Rainville, Joel, 182
"Reconciliation for the Older Children"
    (F. Cocchini), 246–48
Reed, Maria, 53
"Reflections from a Course, 1990"
    (R. Paul), 186–88
"Reflections on the Conference," 271
Reichardt, Mary, 54
"Religious Experience with the Child Three to
    Six, The" (Gobbi), 258–62
"Religious Formation and Later Childhood"
    (Cavalletti), 4–8
*Religious Potential of the Child, The*, preface to
    (Mongillo), 17–20
"Remembering . . . And I Was There" (Roufs), 15
Renton, Alice M., 285–86
"Report from Rome, A" (Polta), 50
Rice, Joel, 40
"Richness of Early Religious Experience, The"
    (Cavalletti), 66–68
Riordan, Claudia, 34–35, 54, 66–68, 110–11
Roberts, Joan, 290, 292
Rojcewicz, Rebekah, 44–46, 55, 80–84,
    271, 294–95
Roufs, Fr. Cecil G., 15

Sandoval, Emilia, 38–39, 64, 105,
    106–7, 138–39, 154
Scheef, Ruth, 237
Schmid, Kate, 14
Schmidt, Judy, 294–95
Schmitt, Claudia, 224, 287
Schweigert, Joseph, 238
Schweigert, Susan, 192, 203, 239
Searle, Mark, 222–23
"Seed Grows, The," 20–21, 53–55
Sentiff, Sr. Sheila, 287
Smith, Amy, 209
Smith, Pauline, 244
"Social Justice: A Question of Relationships"
    (Cavalletti), 97–99
"Songs for First Eucharist," 244
Spaulding, Joshua, 76
"St. Andrew's Fire" (Nikaido), 291
Stenborg, Carol, 106–7, 137
"Story of Bread for Ages 9 to 12, The"
    (Cavalletti), 240–41
"Story of Hope — The Story of Israel, The"
    (Cavalletti), 226–27
"Summary of the Conference"
    (Lillig et al.), 268–71
"Take This, All of You, and Drink from It"
    (C. Dittberner), 65
Tanel, Joe, 272
"Tent of Meeting, The" (C. Dittberner), 115–16
"Ten Years of the Catechesis in Rome"
    (Pollastri), 142–43
"Ten Years of the Catechesis of the Good
    Shepherd" (Cremona), 100–2
"Thanks for the Catechesis"
    (M. Conale et al.), 225
"Thy Kingdom Come" (Sandoval), 138–39
Trego, Lois, 253–54
Trujillo, Trevor, 148

# Index of Articles, Features and Contributors

"Twenty Years of an Atrium at Our Lady of
 Lourdes" (T. Cocchini), 131
"Two Visions of Education" (Gobbi), 152–53
Van Duser, Kathy, 296–97
"Visit with Sofia and Jerome, A"
 (C. Dittberner), 218–19
Voller, Rachel, 237
Wagner, Michael, 72
"Washington Experience, The" (Kahn), 11–14
Wasserzug, Herminia, 137, 271, 272
"Water and the Wine of the Eucharist, The"
 (Cavalletti), 34–35

"When to Start Religious Education"
 (Montanaro), 31–33
"White Garment Worn for Eucharist, Also, The"
 (Lillig), 238–39
"Why Should We Make Our Own Materials?"
 (Schmitt), 287
Wilkinson, Margaret, 54
Wood, Nancy, 249
Woodfill-Hanson, Anders, 30
"Working with Adults" (Christlieb), 77–79
Yonikus, Sandi, 130
Young-Dixon, Keely, 247

# INDEX OF SUBJECTS AND PERSONS

*Absorbent Mind, The* (M. Montessori), 170
Aguilera, Msgr. Francisco Maria, 155
Alman, Kathleen, 156–57, 189
Ambrosic, Bishop Aloysius, 272
Anointing of the Sick, sacrament of, 154
Argentina, catechesis in, 137, 158, 180, 225, 272, 285
Arlington (Virginia), catechesis in, 237
Arocha, Alicia de, 86, 272
Atrium, concept of, 11–12, 28
Augustine, Saint, 18–19, 28, 276
Australia, catechesis in, 275
Badger, Sr. Mary, 53
Balmas, Adelaide, 294
Baptism, sacrament of, 41–43, 100–102, 134, 187
Bastulli-Parran, Laura, 263
Benedict, Saint, 282
Benesch, Schulz, 273
Ben-Gurion, David, 89
Bergren, Gayla, 156–57
Berryman, Jerome, 51–52, 218–19, 221
Berryman, Thea, 51
*Bhagavad Gita*, 223
Biagi, Alberto, 142
Bonilla-Paris, Nora Maria, 137, 155, 158, 270, 273
Bouyer, Louis, 202
Brazil, catechesis in, 161
Buechner, Fredrich, 249
Bunge, Fr. Alejandro, 225
Canada, catechesis in, 272, 280, 293

Capogrossi, Luigi, 268
Casper (Wyoming), catechesis in, 148
Cassano, Mirella, 3, 131
Casulleras, Fr., 177
Catechesis
    of adults, 77–79, 200–202, 286
    characteristics of, 17–20, 25–30, 152–53, 154
    in a lay school, 110–11
    role of catechist in, 18–20, 27–29, 60–61, 171–72, 277, 296–97
Cavalletti, Sofia, 9–10, 11–14, 15, 18–20, 33, 46, 47, 50, 51, 61, 72, 77–78, 86, 88, 112, 131, 137, 155, 156, 174, 178–79, 187, 199, 210, 218–19, 227, 253–54, 257, 268–71, 272, 273, 274, 277, 294
Celi, Lidia, 110
Cereceres, Fr. José, 77, 140, 154
Chad, catechesis in, 100–102, 134
Chardin, Pierre Teilhard de, 264
Chicago, catechesis in, 20, 62, 104, 180, 217, 237, 254, 255, 259, 264, 276, 278, 281, 297, 298
Chihuahua, catechesis in, 9–10, 13, 14, 24, 38–39, 62, 63, 64, 77–79, 104, 105, 106–7, 129, 135, 136, 142, 180, 181
*Children Living in the Church, The* (M. Montessori), 178
Christlieb, Maria, 24, 46, 47, 85, 136, 156–57, 187, 270, 272
Ciudad Juarez (Mexico), catechesis in, 62, 104

# Index of Subjects and Persons

Cleveland, catechesis in, 20, 21, 39–40, 62, 180, 193, 215
Cocchini, Francesca, 184, 225, 295
Cocchini, Tilde, 3, 137, 269, 294, 295
College Station (Texas), catechesis in, 141
Colombia, catechesis in, 158, 180, 181, 273
Conale, Maria Sara, 225
Conaughton, Sr. Marie, 53
Confession. *See* Reconciliation, sacrament of
Confirmation, sacrament of, 100–102
Coulter, Patricia, 50, 167, 268, 270, 272
Cullen, Sr. Patricia, 54
Cyprian, Saint, 34
Dahl-Bredine, Kathy, 157, 189, 236, 263
De Angelis, Fr. Angelo, 161–62
Death, reaction of children to, 38–40
Detroit, catechesis in, 281, 293
Developmental phases of childhood, 4–8, 31–33, 66–68, 152–53, 167–69, 249, 258–62
Dittberner, Carol, 21, 46, 55, 86, 157
Dittberner, John, 87
Dittberner, Sopana, 87
Dosh, Millicent, 137, 157
Dosh, Terry, 137
Dowdy, Laurie, 156–57, 189
Dykstra, Craig, 249
*Education and Peace* (M. Montessori), 27–28
*Education for a New World* (M. Montessori), 285
El Paso, catechesis in, 62
Eucharist, character of, 5–6, 19, 34–35, 60–61, 65, 183–85, 202–3, 205, 264. *See also* First Communion
*Eucharist* (Bouyer), 202
Farhat, Marjorie, 156–57
Felix, Claudia, 154
Felix, Pili, 154
Fernando, Chulanganee, 86

Fierro, Fr., 64
First Communion
    celebrations of, 62–64, 104–5, 106–7, 217, 237
    preparation for, 10, 59, 61, 135, 140, 142–43, 192–93, 201, 232, 234–39, 242–44, 276
Fisher, Joshua, 156–57
Fisher, Martha, 136, 156–57
Fisher, Red, 136, 156–57
*Formation of Man, The* (M. Montessori), 213
Fourzan, Gloria, 87
Freese, Molly, 237
Fremont (Michigan), catechesis in, 255, 281
Furlan, Susan, 128
Gallo, Fr., 106
Gargano, Sr. Angela, 53
Germany, catechesis in, 198–99, 273, 275
Gervais, Bishop Marcel, 272
Gilbert, Joan, 156–57
Giuntella, Christina, 142
Gleasure, Nicolina, 157
Gobbi, Gianna, 50, 155, 157, 178–79, 199, 218, 258–62, 269–70, 271, 272, 274, 294
God, children's relationship with, 4–8, 16, 18–19, 27, 67–68, 112–14, 167–69, 171–72
*Godly Play* (J. Berryman), 221
Good Shepherd, parable of, 5, 29, 79, 96, 99, 112–13, 183, 296
Griffing, Janet, 199
Guida, Anna Mae, 50, 86, 257, 272, 274
*Guiding God's Children* (McCarroll), 121
Hagen, Alyssa, 238
Halpin, Sr. Marlene, 122
Heille, Fr. Gregory, 20
Heschel, Abraham, 216
Higgins, Laurie, 291
Hissong, Betty, 20, 60, 157, 198, 257, 269, 272, 273
Hissong, John, 269

# Index of Subjects and Persons

History, nature of, 4–8, 98–99, 151, 213–17
*History of Salvation, The* (Cavalletti), 186–88
Holloway, Paige, 53
*Holy Mass Explained to the Children, The* (M. Montessori), 178
Hopton, Pam, 157
Houston, catechesis in, 11, 13, 51–52, 77–78, 174–76, 221, 274
Huisken, Holly, 219
*Human Being, A* (Montanaro), 136
Iowa City, catechesis in, 54
Irenaeus, Saint, 35
Islamic tradition, 115–16
Israel, trip to, 88–89
Jablonski, Helen, 157
Jackson (Mississippi), catechesis in, 181, 199, 208
James the Great, Saint, 222–23
Japan, catechesis in, 210–12
Jewish tradition, 30, 88–89, 115–16, 218, 226–27, 246
John Paul II, 3, 131, 135, 143
Joosten, A. M., 50
Kahn, Barbara, 21, 46
Kaiel, Linda, 157, 189, 257
Kansas City (Missouri), catechesis in, 296
Kendrick, Jo, 55, 156–57
Kerbawy, Greg, 156–57
Kerygma, concept of, 6–7, 150, 288
Keshner, Annie, 156–57
Keshner, Mary Ann, 156–57
Kirby, Russell, 237
Klier, Sr. Mary Elizabeth, 55, 156
Koenigsberger, Mary, 55
Kohlberg, Lawrence, 249
Kral, Janice, 157
Krause, Marilyn, 156–57
Lambertville (New Jersey), catechesis in, 53
Lanciana, Nicoletta, 142

Lanternier, Michael, 183, 196
Lewis, Lillian, 86
*Life in Christ, The* (M. Montessori), 178
Lillig, Tina, 20, 87, 156–57, 257, 272, 274
Lopez, Noemi F. de, 87
Lounder, Leonard H., 103
Lugli, Massimo, 184
Macklin, Donna, 156–57, 189
Madden, Sr. Kathryn, 274
Maresca, Angelina, 112–14
Maresca, Catherine, 46, 55, 87, 156–57, 189, 257
Maresca, Kevin, 113–14
Maria, Fr. Flor, 200–202
Martinez, Fr. Jose, 155
Materials, making of, 134, 186–89, 219, 239, 240–41, 245, 265–67, 282–92, 295
Matsumoto, Maria, 210–12
McCarroll, Tolbert, 121
McCarthy, Dan, 137
Mérida (Mexico), catechesis in, 181
*Messengers of God* (Wiesel), 227
Mexico City, catechesis in, 9, 62, 69–72, 104, 129, 139, 140, 149, 151, 154, 155, 156, 157, 162, 180, 209, 217, 274–75
Miller, Joan, 47, 157
Minneapolis–St. Paul, catechesis in, 11, 13, 21, 46, 55, 62, 74–76, 78–79, 85–87, 88, 103, 104, 105, 115–16, 164, 166, 180, 137, 181, 182, 192, 193, 197, 199, 201, 203, 205, 213, 214, 217, 220, 221, 225, 226, 232, 233, 236, 237, 238, 239, 247, 251
Mongillo, Fr. P. Dalmazio, 272, 295
Montanaro, Silvana Quattrocchi, 136, 155, 264, 268, 273, 294
Montessori, Maria, 2, 131, 185, 218, 235
  career of, 177–79
  on childhood development, 4–8, 67, 112, 150, 170, 171, 231, 258–62, 283, 286

## Index of Subjects and Persons

on nature of education, 11–12, 27–28, 98, 110, 152–53, 154, 213–17, 285
Montessori, Renilde, 212
Moran, Msgr. Bernard, 54
Morelia (Mexico), catechesis in, 63
Mt. Rainer (Maryland), catechesis in, 233, 234, 246
Napa (California), catechesis in, 54
Nash, Kathie, 20
Nashville, catechesis in, 219
Nelson, Getrud Mueller, 122
Neuroth, Gabriele, 273
New Zealand, catechesis in, 209
Nobiloni, Massimo, 161
North Carolina, catechesis in, 173
Notre Dame (Indiana), catechesis in, 274, 282
Nyberg, Carol, 157, 257
Oakland, catechesis in, 54
O'Boyle, Sr. Evelyn, 270
O'Bryan, Bert, 87, 130, 156–57, 189, 269
O'Bryan, Marty, 87, 156–57, 161, 189
Padilla, Fr., 39, 64
Palafox, Guadalupe, 155, 200, 270, 272
Panama, catechesis in, 275
Parables, importance of, 5, 27, 72, 79, 187, 218, 234
Parenesis, concept of, 6–7, 150
Parousia, concept of, 5, 188, 270
Paul, Saint, 29, 222–23
Paul, Jodie, 188
Paul, Rose Marie, 21, 55, 157
Pechacek, Rebekah, 175
Phoenix, catechesis in, 53, 181, 237
Pius X, 177
Plotti, Fr. Sandro, 142–43
Poland, catechesis in, 275
Pollastri, Sandra, 142
Polta, Mary, 21, 86, 88

Prayer, by children, 26, 36–37, 40, 58–59, 94–95, 128, 148–49, 165–66, 172, 192–93, 195, 196, 197, 202, 209, 233, 255, 260–62, 281
Presser-Velder, Deborah, 270
Prichard, Mary Nell, 156–57
*Puddles of Knowing* (Halpin), 122
Ragonesi, Msgr., 143
Reconciliation, sacrament of, 7, 73, 201, 246–48, 276
Reed, Maria, 47
*Religious Potential of the Child, The* (Cavalletti), 13, 17–20, 72, 131, 161, 178, 196, 198, 222, 273, 288, 295
Ricoeur, Paul, 8, 264
Riordan, Claudia, 54
Rochester (New York), catechesis in, 176
Rojcewicz, Rebekah, 21, 46, 55, 156–57, 186–87, 257, 271, 272, 274, 294
Rome, catechesis in, 3, 13, 14, 24, 34, 39, 50, 62, 64, 78, 104, 110–11, 131, 135, 137, 142–43, 173, 180, 182, 188, 209, 217, 224, 237, 253–54, 256–57, 262, 268–71, 275, 294–95
Roufs, Fr. Cecil G., 21, 87
Ryan, Fr., 130
Sandoval, Emilia, 64, 87, 136
Schaffer, Diane, 157
Scheef, Ruth, 157
Scheuermann, Jane, 156–57
Schmidt, Judy, 157, 263
Schmitt, Claudia, 199, 273, 275
Schoekel, Fr. Alonso, 26
Searle, Mark, 222
Sears, Teresa, 189
*Secret of Childhood, The* (M. Montessori), 283
Sentiff, Sr. Sheila, 21, 50, 86
Shields, Vicky, 199
Silver City (New Mexico), catechesis in, 210, 216

# Index of Subjects and Persons

Social justice, 97–99, 132–33, 138–39, 150–51
Soley, Rob, 55
Southbury (Connecticut), catechesis in, 233
Stenborg, Carol, 137
Stenborg, Fred, 137
St. Paul, catechesis in. *See* Minneapolis–St. Paul
Swacker, Sarah, 237
Sweeney, Kathleen, 156–57
Takanohashi, Esther, 211
Tanel, Joe, 269
Tanzania, catechesis in, 224, 287
*Teaching Doctrine and Liturgy* (Cavalletti and Gobbi), 178
Tent of Meeting, 115–16
Thomas Aquinas, Saint, 18–19, 35
*To Dance with God* (Nelson), 122
Toronto, catechesis in, 21, 128, 133, 141, 180, 181
Torreon (Mexico), catechesis in, 62, 104, 165, 192–93
Tosco, Holly, 173
Trego, Randall, 189, 257

Vagaggini, Cyprian, 264
Vanier, Jean, 12–13
Vatican II, 34
Via degli Orsini, center at, 24, 34, 62, 64, 78, 104, 110–11, 131, 137, 182, 188, 217, 224, 237, 253–54, 256–57, 268–71. *See also* Rome
Villalobos, Lupita, 106
*Vision and Character* (Dykstra), 249
Waal, Esther de, 284
Walsh-Mellett, Judy, 55
Washington, D.C., catechesis in, 11–14, 15, 21, 55, 63, 104, 105, 145, 156–57, 174, 175, 180, 186–89, 274
Wasserzug, Herminia, 270, 275
Wiesel, Elie, 227
Wilkinson, Margaret, 54
Williams, Jo Ann, 156–57, 189
Woggon, Genelda, 282
Yonikus, Sandi, 46, 130, 161
Zackheim, Michele, 115–16